Eva

PUBLICATIONS
OF THE
ARMY RECORDS SOCIETY
VOL. 3

THE NAPOLEONIC WAR JOURNAL OF
CAPTAIN THOMAS HENRY BROWNE
1807–1816

Portrait Miniature of Thomas Henry Browne (c. 1805).

THE NAPOLEONIC WAR JOURNAL OF CAPTAIN THOMAS HENRY BROWNE 1807–1816

Edited by
ROGER NORMAN BUCKLEY

Published by
THE BODLEY HEAD
for the
ARMY RECORDS SOCIETY
1987

British Library Cataloguing in Publication Data

Browne, Thomas Henry
The Napoleonic War Journal of Captain
Thomas Henry Browne, 1807–1816.
1. Great Britain. *Army*. *Royal Welch
Fusiliers* 2. Napoleonic Wars, 1800–1814
——Personal narratives, British
I. Title II. Buckley, Roger Norman
III. Army Records Society
940.2'7'0924 DC226.5

ISBN 0–370–31121–3

Printed in Great Britain for
The Bodley Head Ltd
32 Bedford Square, London WC1B 3EL
by The Bath Press, Avon
Set in Linotron Ehrhardt
by Wyvern Typesetting Ltd, Bristol
First published 1987

TO
THE MEMORY OF MY BELOVED
PARENTS
ELAINE COGGINS BUCKLEY
AND
RALPH C. BUCKLEY

From the trophies of war, from the spear and the shield,
From scenes of destruction, from perils unblest;
Oh! welcome again, to the grove and the field,
To the vale of retirement and rest.

Felicia Hemans,
To My Younger Brother

Contents

List of Illustrations

Grateful acknowledgements are due to the following for permission to reproduce illustrations: To a descendant of Sir Thomas Henry Browne for the Frontispiece and plates 1, 2 and 14; to The National Army Museum, London, for plates 3, 6, 10 and 15; to the Bibliothèque Nationale, Paris, for plate 4; to The British Library for plates 5 and 7; to the Print Collection, Lewis Walpole Library, Yale University, Farmington, Connecticut, for plate 8; to the Anne S. K. Brown Military Collection, Brown University Library, Providence, Rhode Island, for plates 11, 12, 13 and 16. Plate 9 is in the Editor's collection.

The sketch map of Fort Royal, Martinique is reproduced from Crown-copyright records in the Public Record Office and appears by permission of the Controller of H.M. Stationery Office; the map of the Peninsula campaign is drawn by Ken Yoder; the last three sketch maps are from the Journal of Captain Thomas Henry Browne.

Preface

Thomas Henry Browne (1787–1855), the author of the Journal, was a member of a regenerated British army, whose spirit had been revived by internal reform and improvements and by successful strategic employment. In 1805 Browne obtained an ensign's commission in the 23rd Royal Welch Fusiliers, a distinguished marching regiment. Some twenty-one months after his entry into military life, Browne began a long service overseas for virtually all of the period from 1807 to 1816, which is the time covered by the Journal. This lengthy span of service coincided with that landmark era in the Napoleonic Wars, which saw France tumble from the pinnacle of power to defeat and foreign occupation. During this time Browne participated in the controversial seizure of the Danish fleet at Copenhagen in 1807, the speedy but difficult capture of Martinique in 1809, and the great and hard-fought victory in the Peninsular War, 1810–1814. Two brief tours of duty in the forested wastes of Nova Scotia, one just before and the other immediately after the expedition to Martinique, were the only times Browne escaped the carnage of Napoleonic warfare.

The Journal that Thomas Henry Browne modestly described as being based on a "little memoranda I made in a rough book of notes" is an important contribution to the literature of the Napoleonic Wars. As we have already seen, Browne's service in such vastly different theatres of operation as Europe, North America and the West Indies, in so short a time-span, informs the reader of the varied and spasmodic nature of British military service. It was, no doubt, this feature of the service that prompted that affable Scot Sir Ralph Abercromby to pen: "There are risks attached to the British service unknown to any other." Many of the published diaries of British veterans of the 1793–1815 war describe one or two campaigns only, as in the case of the *Wheatley Diary* (edited by Christopher Hibbert) which describes the experiences of the author, Edmund Wheatley, during the final stages of the Peninsular War, 1813–1814, and the Waterloo Campaign, 1815. To Browne's varied experiences in dramatically different parts of the world are added his duties in the army. From the time he joined the 23rd Foot, in 1805, until 1811, Browne experienced war with the troops in the field. Consequently, his Journal opens the world of the regiment and the battlefield to the reader. It was in this capacity that he received his first serious wound, in Martinique in 1809. During the years 1812 to 1814, however, he served as a Deputy Assistant Adjutant-General on the staff of the Duke of Wellington in Spain and Portugal. Hence, his Journal also depicts the workings of the Adjutant-General's department which, along with Wellington's personal staff, the civil departments and the Quartermaster-General's office, managed the army daily. As a staff officer, Browne also had the unusual good fortune to have regular meetings with the Duke, who clearly thought very highly of his young staff officer. These initimate portraits of that great soldier are unique, for, as S. G. P. Ward has indicated in his *Wellington's Headquarters*, many of the approximately 850 officers who comprised the staff saw Wellington but once or twice during their entire service, while some never saw him at all. Although he served in a department which functioned separately from Wellington's personal staff, Browne was apparently one of a select few outside the inner circle of officers who regularly associated with the commander. This combined experience as a field and staff officer thus gives the reader of the Journal an unusual wide-angle view of wartime soldiering.

If there was wartime soldiering, there was also peacetime soldiering, which actually filled up most of the soldier's time. Unlike the snippets of information contained in, for example, the well-known *Recollections of Rifleman Harris* (reprinted in 1970 by the Military Book Society), Browne's Journal gives a number of detailed and wonderfully evocative episodes of the "waiting about" time in the army. Given Browne's dual employment with the army, plus the fact that he was an interesting and perceptive observer, the range of incidents is predictably broad. Thus, the reader is introduced to, for example, tough and proud soldiers' wives, a North American Indian named (by Browne) "Whisker Tom", and villainous Spanish guerrilla leaders.

The Journal of Thomas Henry Browne makes yet another important contribution. Browne was a member of a successful and talented family, which included among several brothers and sisters the poetess, Felicia Hemans (née Felicia Dorothea Browne, 1793–1835), who was much celebrated during her own lifetime and whose popularity rivalled that of such contemporaries (and friends) as William Wordsworth, Lord

Byron, Lord Jeffrey and a youthful Shelley. As one who lived during the war in the Peninsula, Felicia Hemans, despite her youth, was deeply inspired by that stirring event, as is indicated in her poetry. It was, however, the service of her two older brothers, Thomas Henry and George Baxter, in that cause which fired her lively imagination and extraordinary intellect. Felicia Hemans was particularly attached to Thomas Henry, who, no doubt, communicated his war experiences, particularly those of the fighting in the Peninsula, to his eagerly receptive sister. Thus, in 1808, when she was still only fourteen, warlike themes ardently enter her poetry. The Journal of Thomas Henry Browne hence serves as yet another window, this one affording valuable insights into the rich variety of Felicia Hemans' verse, which, now largely forgotten, deserves rediscovery.

In 1828 Browne enlarged the original Journal which he apparently compiled during his active military service. In addition to the "little memoranda", the revision was based on official army papers and correspondence, which are in the possession of Browne's descendants, who made them available to the editor during the summer of 1985. Publication was not the object of this revision, although he regretted that he had not kept a more detailed account, which, as he put it, "might have been worth offering to the public." Rather, it was the pleasure he derived in retracing the scenes of his exciting military career that encouraged him to expand his original Journal. His work, then, was to be its own reward. That effort was considerable, nonetheless, and fills 419 pages in a clear and even cursive in a single brown leather-bound volume with distinctive marbled endpapers and gold-leaf edging to the pages. The volume measures 21×26×4.5 cm.

It is quite likely that Browne was moved to revise the Journal by an event that occurred in 1827. In that year a small book was published with the title *The Vicissitudes of a Soldier's Life*. The author was John Green, a servant of an officer attached to the staff, who waited frequently upon Browne at the latter's mess in the Peninsula, where the two men became acquainted. A private in the old 68th Durham Light Infantry Regiment, Green acknowledged this association and the conviviality of Browne's mess in his book in this way: "After our dinner was over I had to wait at Lieutenant Broun's, of the adjutant generals' department, where my master used to dine. We passed the evening there very comfortably."* Browne cited Green's book which he found interesting and which

---

* (Louth, U.K.: 1827; reprint ed., East Ardsley, U.K.: E.P. Pub., Ltd, 1973), 133.

probably moved him to revise his Journal. The extent to which he expanded his memoirs is regrettably unknown since, apparently, no trace of the original remains. This is unfortunate because the original may have contained a description of Browne's activities, from October 1805, the date he joined the 23rd Foot, to July 1807, the start of the expedition to Copenhagen, all of which is omitted from the revised Journal. A possible explanation for this omission is that Browne considered only his overseas experience worthy of recording for posterity. There is also the possibility that the original Journal itself commenced in 1807 only, as in the case of the revised copy.

What does the Journal tell us of the personality of the author? While not infrequently providing the reader with humorous and evocative cameo portraits of soldiers and soldiering, the Journal also reveals Browne to be an intensely serious young officer who apparently sublimated all else in favour of his military career. (This helps to explain why he served continuously, from 1805 to 1815, without a single leave of absence.) There is, for instance, virtually no mention of his family in Wales. Nor is there any reference to his beloved sister, Felicia. Moreover, Browne appears curiously detached from the events he himself experienced. At first glance this may appear odd. However, upon close examination of the system of leadership in the army at the time, this *modus operandi* was in keeping with the ideal army officer, who was expected to exhibit calm self-possession and patience in the face of toil, fatigue, danger, fear, even death, almost without seeming to feel them. Here is a glimpse of the sangfroid of an officer, in Wellington's day.

Authors of journals and diaries frequently make the unintentional mistake of assuming that the reader knows more about the events described than they actually do. Browne could afford to make this assumption, for English society at the time was well acquainted with the Napoleonic Wars. William Thackeray's *Vanity Fair* and Jane Austen's *Pride and Prejudice*, for example, confirm this. But that was then. Few today know much about the nature of Napoleonic soldiering. Hence, a full essay introduces the Journal, the purpose of which is to reconstruct the world of the British army officer. To accomplish this, I have attempted, for example, to fashion the missing period in the Journal, 1805 to 1807. In order to do this, I have relied to some degree on literature and invention. Additionally, the Introduction serves to shed light on the British army drill, the history of and regimental life in the

23rd Royal Welch Fusiliers, the pattern of Browne's military career, and the nature of Napoleonic warfare. Other aids include explanatory notes, a bibliography, biographical notes on persons mentioned in the Journal, an appendix section containing pertinent manuscript records, and illustrations which, when appropriate, were used as historical documents. Finally, each section of the Journal is preceded by a brief summary statement.

There are a few in academe who have committed the unpardonable sin of tampering with historical documents. In one such case, a well-known scholar had the effrontery to inform his readers that he "reworded" certain documents "in a great many places for stylistic reasons and to reflect my own understanding of the particularities". Not so this editor, who believes that historical records should remain in their pristine state. Except for a few minor changes in punctuation, there has been no departure from the text of the Journal, which has been faithfully reproduced in its original form.

Roger N. Buckley

Avon, Connecticut
February 1986

Acknowledgements

I can never thank enough the great-granddaughter of Sir Thomas Henry Browne, whose gracious permission has made this publication possible. Her warm hospitality and patient help of all kinds have left me in her debt.

I am also grateful to the staffs of the following institutions for allowing me to consult and use manuscripts and illustrations under their care: the National Army Museum, Public Record Office and the British Library, London; the Anne S. K. Brown Military Collection, Brown University, Providence, Rhode Island; the Bibliothèque Nationale, Paris; the Public Archives of Canada, Ottawa; the Scottish Record Office, Edinburgh; and the Lewis Walpole Library, Farmington, Connecticut. The opportunity to examine these records was made possible by financial assistance from the National Endowment for the Humanities, Washington, D.C.

For a variety of rich suggestions, leads and aids I am deeply indebted to Susan Joy Debevec, graduate student, Department of History, University of Connecticut; W. D. Cribbs, Head of Common Services, Ministry of Defence; and Field Marshal The Lord Carver, G.C.B., C.B.E., D.S.O., M.C.

I also owe much to the assistance and co-operation of P. B. Boyden, Department of Archives, National Army Museum; Carol M. Whitfield, Operations Manager, Halifax Citadel, Nova Scotia; and Timothy Dubé, Archivist, Public Archives, Canada.

My final debt is owed to my secretary, Dorothy Belli, who, with great skill and patience, typed and retyped major portions of the manuscript.

Abbreviations

A.G.	Adjutant-General
A.Q.M.G.	Assistant Quarter-Master-General
C.O.	Colonial Office (Papers, Public Record Office)
D.A.A.G.	Deputy Assistant Adjutant-General
D.A.G.	Deputy Adjutant-General
D.A.Q.M.G.	Deputy Assistant Quarter-Master-General
K.C.H.	Knight Commander of the Royal Hanoverian Guelphic Order or Knight Commander of Hanover
K.G.L.	King's German Legion
K.H.	Knight of the Royal Hanoverian Guelphic Order or Knight of Hanover
M.P.H.	Miscellaneous Maps and Plans (Public Record Office, London and Kew Gardens)
P.R.O.	Public Record Office (London and Kew Gardens)
R.M.C.	Royal Military College
R.W.F.	Royal Welch Fusiliers
W.O.	War Office (Papers, Public Record Office)

Introduction

The censorious dispatches of the Duke of Wellington tend to obscure the fact that the long war against France, which began in 1793 and which was waged almost continuously until 1815, bred a vastly improved regimental officer for the British army.[1] If, however, Wellington's officer was an improvement over his predecessor who obtained a commission in 1793, he was not yet a modern professional, that is a practising expert who shares a sense of organic unity and consciousness with others in the group and who demonstrates his special skill when required to do so by society.[2] Except for the Royal Artillery and Royal Engineers, the technical services of the army, the British officer cadre[3] at the time still largely subordinated the military values of skill, discipline and responsibility to the pre-professional aristocratic ideals of bravery, individualism and luxury. The eighteenth-century or pre-professional officer was typically an amateur at officership. He considered himself a participant in an enterprise that lacked ends and standards of its own, one which was largely incidental to his real or imaginary position in society. Along with fishing, hunting, exploring, leisure and comfortable living, military service was but a part of his ideal. The aristocratic military ideal thus triumphed over military professionalism in England, and remained ascendant until the dual executive and legislative control of the army came to an end during the nineteenth century, with the supremacy of Parliament over the prerogative of the monarchy.[4]

Thanks, however, to the effective reform of the army, begun when the Duke of York became Commander-in-Chief in February 1795, many of these amateurs became competent soldiers. By 1809, the year Britain resumed a strategic offensive against France in Portugal and Spain, with Wellington's army once again as the instrument,[5] the prodigals and peacocks had disappeared from the officer cadre. Those who remained were hardy and serious soldiers. These qualities were essential in one who routinely endured a spartan existence with few amenities of life;

1

exhaustion from exposure and countless marches; surgery without anaesthetics; the nasty and lonely work of the rear guard; dead and abandoned women and children; shattering volleys delivered at forty paces, and less; and, of course, the gripping terror of the suicidal dash into the breach—the bone and marrow of warfare in the Peninsula. If not professional, as in the case of their Prussian contemporaries who set the standard of the military profession in the West in 1808,[6] British officers were serious, diligent and habitually brave. They were also careerists: they entered the army usually for life and advanced by competent service.

Thomas Henry Browne was a member of this brotherhood. He was born in Liverpool on 8 September 1787, the first of seven children, three brothers and four sisters. Although his first name was Thomas, to his family and friends he was known as Henry. The Brownes came from County Cork, Ireland. Thomas' father, George Browne, emigrated to Liverpool where he established himself as a merchant of considerable importance. It was in bustling Liverpool that George Browne met and married Felicity Wagner, the daughter of the Imperial and Tuscan Consul at Liverpool. She was a highly cultured woman who became the centre of a close and warm family life. Serious financial setbacks around 1800 led to the move of the family to North Wales, where Thomas spent much of his youth. For the next nine years the family resided at Gwrych, near Abergele, Denbighshire, a large old mansion close to the sea. In 1809, when Thomas was twenty-two, the Brownes moved again, this time to Bronwylfa, near St Asaph in Flintshire. Some years afterwards, Thomas Browne purchased this handsome three-storey house, near the River Clwyd, and made it his home.[7]

Browne's military career began on 28 October 1805, the date of his non-purchase or free commission as an ensign in a distinguished marching regiment, the 23rd Royal Welch Fusiliers.[8] At first glance it would seem unlikely that Thomas, as the eldest son, would seek a career in the army, a prospect reserved for younger sons. Customarily, he would have followed his father into commerce. As we have seen, however, his father suffered commercial reverses, the losses from which were apparently significant and explained George Browne's decision to abandon the bustle of Liverpool for the distant tranquillity and peace of the Welsh countryside.[9] We can easily concur with Thomas Browne's appropriate silence regarding the evident collapse of his father's Liverpool establishment. This would be too delicate a matter to discuss in the pages of his Journal, which was certain to be read by others. Nevertheless, one can conclude with some justification that the event would tend to discourage Thomas and his brothers from going into commerce. All, in fact, decided on a military career.[10]

In 1805, when Browne resolved to enlist, there were those in England who still believed in the incompetence of the British army, that is, the army's inability, since the war began in 1793, to defeat France decisively in Europe. None, perhaps, regarded the soldier with such utter contempt as the sailor. According to Southey, the seamen expressed their scorn with characteristic crudeness in the following scale of comparison: "Mess-mate before ship-mate, ship-mate before a stranger, a stranger before a dog, and a dog before a soldier."[11] Nonetheless, there were several reasons why a young gentleman should choose soldiering as a career.

Under the demands of a large wartime army virtually any young man who desired to serve and was literate would experience little difficulty in obtaining a commission. (Literacy, not land or wealth, restricted the selection of officers.) In 1792, the last year of peace in Europe, there were 3,107 officers. By 1814, the last year of the war in the Peninsula, the number had more than tripled to 10,590 on full pay, exclusive of foreign regiments and veteran battalions. During the same period the number of officers serving in Ordnance units also sharply increased, from 361 to 912. At the same time there was a heavy attrition. The average annual requirement of the army during the Peninsular War, for instance, was about 1,000 men.[12] The traditional sources of officer material, namely the landed gentry and nobility, the lesser gentry, army families and old Huguenot families, could no longer supply the need. The ease with which one could obtain a commission in the army is evident in the simple application process. The candidate just applied for a commission on a form issued, through an army agent, from the Adjutant-General's office. It listed the formal qualifications which were few and simple:

> No person is considered eligible for a commission until he has attained the age of sixteen years. All recommendations shall certify the eligibility of the person recommended in respect of character, education and bodily health, and that he is prepared immediately to join any regiment to which he may be appointed. His Christian names and place of address must also be particularly stated.[13]

He signed the form and then submitted it through an agent. The letter of recommendation had to be signed by an officer of not less than field rank. A suggested model for it was:

> I beg leave to recommend .... as a gentleman fully qualified to hold a cornetcy/ensigncy in his Majesty's .... regiment of Dragoons/Foot.[14]

If the young man intended to purchase his commission, he then had to deposit with the agent through whom he obtained the form, a sum of money to buy his position of ensign, which was £450 in the Royal Welch Fusiliers. Whether he planned to purchase or obtain a free commission, the candidate would now have to wait until a vacancy occurred.[15] The availability of commissions did not result in a flood of men with little genuine enthusiasm for serious soldiering. (A similar need for officers during the first years of the war did indeed attract numerous candidates totally unsuitable for military leadership, which prompted an exasperated Major-General John Moore to complain in 1796 of "blockheads at the head of Regiments".[16]) As we have seen, the reforms of the Duke of York and the harsh conditions in the Peninsula extirpated the wastrels and the dandies from the officer cadre.

A stunning uniform awaited those who made the decision to take the King's pay as a soldier. As his detailed pattern book attests, the military tailor spared no effort to make the wearer as attractive as possible to the opposite sex. Striving for gorgeousness and display, the crafty tailor designed a decorative uniform which heightened masculine characteristics with a mélange of bright fabric, mainly red and blue, and pretty fluff: lace, cord, piping, embroidery and metallic thread. The uniform thus created made it extremely difficult for the wearer to function as a soldier should; discomfort, however, was a small price to pay for a proven aid to seduction.[17] Looks, figure and manner, according to Jane Austen, were simply not enough for a gentleman. He required "only regimentals to make him completely charming".[18] And once a female was smitten by military fashion she was not likely to forget the experience. Jane Austen's Mrs Bennet recollects with nostalgic sentimentality "I . . . the time when I liked a redcoat myself very well—indeed so I do still at my heart. . . ."[19]

Opportunity and ostentation were great inducements to serious young men, like Thomas Browne, to seek a career as an army officer. To these was added an intensely patriotic mood which reigned supreme in

England following the resumption of the war against France in 1803.[20] On 17 May the government of Henry Addington declared war on France. Though England opened hostilities, it was not to be an all-out war. Largely because the regular army was then deficient in numbers, Addington planned a war of home defence, which placed greater reliance on the militia, volunteers and Royal Navy. The latter would dominate the seas, particularly the Channel, the likely invasion route of Napoleon.

A war of national defence predictably ignited the martial spirit which swept through all ranks of society. Some were prepared to make boasts and wear fancy warlike dress only. Many others took the threat of a French invasion seriously. Addington set the tone by appearing in Parliament in uniform. Martial music was to be heard everywhere. Every district raised a corps of volunteer soldiers. The boys of Shrewsbury School drilled earnestly with wooden muskets which they implored their startled parents to exchange for real, but light-weight weapons. Fashion-conscious women paraded in so-called "rifle" dresses of dark green velvet with matching "rifle" hats. Less fashionable women of Neath petitioned Addington, requesting permission

> to defend ourselves as well as the weaker women and children among us. There are in this town about two hundred women who have been used to hard labour all the days of their lifes, such as working in coalpits, on the high roads, tilling the ground, etc. If you would grant us arms, that is *light pikes* . . . we do assure you that we could in a short time learn our exercise . . . I assure you we are not trifling with you, but serious in our proposal.

Guards of old men and young boys watched on the coasts at night, ready at a moment's notice to fire warning beacons if the French were sighted.

> In Britain is one breath;
> We all are with you now from shore to shore;—
> Ye men of Kent, 'tis victory or death!

wrote William Wordsworth, as he summoned the men of Kent in the simple language of the common man to prepare for a patriotic death.[21] Sprawling military camps were also constructed. One of these, at Meryton, which contained the headquarters of a militia regiment, greatly delighted Catherine and Lydia Bennet, daughters of Jane Austen's irrepressible Mrs Bennet.[22] This show of impassioned patriotism, along with the riveting fear of invasion, would largely continue until just after 21 October 1805, the day Admiral Nelson destroyed the French fleet off Cape Trafalgar.[23]

We must assume that Browne was touched by these stirring events; after all, he was sixteen in 1803 — an impressionable age. Wales, his home, was not denied what one newspaper described as the "spirit of unanimity and patriotism, unexampled even in the annals of this favoured country".[24] For instance, a gentleman travelling through the region in September 1803 was almost arrested in Radnor by locals who incredibly mistook him for Napoleon.[25] (Before a formal arrest was made, someone, apparently, had the good sense to note the singular unlikelihood of the First Consul travelling alone through wild Wales.) The patriotic current, perhaps the strongest of all, joined with the others to persuade Browne to enter military service in the fall of 1805.

If Browne was affected by the patriotic exuberance of the times, his decision, as well as those of his brothers George and Claude, to enter the army, had a deep influence on the writings of his younger sister, Felicia Hemans, a renowned poet in her day, now remembered less for her writings than for her friendships with the literati of her time. *England and Spain; or, Valor and Patriotism*, written when she was fourteen, was inspired by her elder brothers, Thomas and George, being called away on active service, the former as member of the expedition against Copenhagen in 1807, the latter as a participant in Sir John Moore's expedition of 1808 to the Peninsula.

According to the muster roll of the 23rd Royal Welch Fusiliers, Thomas Browne joined the 2nd Battalion at Chester on 28 October 1805, the same date of his commission as ensign. Before reporting to the 2nd Battalion, however, which was then a recruiting and depot unit feeding troops to the 1st Battalion, we can imagine him hurriedly engaged in making his final preparations before joining his regiment.

Once the decision had been reached to serve with the Royal Welch Fusiliers, he must make the acquaintance of the regimental agents, Messrs Greenwood and Cox of Craig's Court, London. This was a necessary meeting since the agency's responsibilities were considerable. It was, for example, the sole accountant for all regimental expenditures. This meant that it was through the medium of the regimental agent that Browne was to receive his pay.[26] The agency of Messrs Greenwood and Cox had been enlarged on several occasions to meet the expansion of the business. For example, the 3rd Foot Guards and seven regiments of the line were transferred to Greenwood and Cox when the agency of Ross and Ogilvie failed in April 1804. In 1806, the artillery, the engineers, the waggon train, nineteen regiments of cavalry, twenty-one regiments of militia, and 163 battalions of infantry were represented by Greenwood and Cox. The establishment of clerks was enlarged to meet this increase in business. By 1810 seventy-seven clerks were employed. This number steadily increased to exactly one hundred by the time of the battle of Waterloo in June 1815.

The prosperity enjoyed by the firm was due to the great wealth as well as to the right connections of the senior partner, Charles Greenwood. A bachelor, Greenwood entertained in his rooms overlooking Craig's Court. For many years he served as the financial adviser of the Duke of York, whom he counted among his close friends. His portrait was painted by Sir Thomas Lawrence. (It was rumoured that Greenwood died while playing whist with King William IV, in 1832.) Charles Greenwood also held numerous public offices. He was, for instance, treasurer of the Royal Military College, from 1799 to 1805, and of the Royal Military Asylum, from 1800 to 1819. The meeting with Mr Greenwood was not, therefore, a perfunctory visit to an obscure regimental paymaster. The young ensign wished to make a good impression on one so wealthy and influential.[27]

Going in the direction of Westminster from Trafalgar Square, Browne would have found Craig's Court on the left-hand side of Whitehall. He entered the premises and passed through a swarm of busy clerks, one of whom directed him to the office of Charles Greenwood. He surprised the eminent banker when he enquired as to when he should report to the regimental depot of the 23rd Foot. The busy agent solemnly advised the young ensign-to-be that the 1st Battalion was about to embark from Ramsgate on an expedition to northern Germany to drive the French from Hanover. (The 1st Battn./23rd Foot actually sailed from Ramsgate on 29 October 1805 for the Elbe River.) Then, peering over his desk which contained a sheaf of war office correspondence, the agent advised Browne to report to his regimental depot immediately upon receipt of orders from the Adjutant-General's office. The Duke of York periodically requested information, through regimental agents, showing the number of officers absent.[28] Unlawful absence, he added, could be detrimental to his career. Messrs Greenwood and Cox expected their patrons to behave as gentlemen ought to, that is they should comply immediately with all regulations. Grasping the point of this forceful lesson, Browne took quick leave of his carping agent and hurried off to more pleasant matters—to Leadenhall Street in the City, to fetch the uniform he had ordered soon after applying for a commission.

The ante-room of the military tailor was filled with gentlemen, some waiting to collect uniforms, others flipping through the decorative pages of the pattern books. Once again, we can picture Browne as he made his way through the room, the walls of which were covered with the portraits of famous soldiers who, one suspects, were clients of the tailor. Upon leaving the main room Browne entered the hushed and unhurried world of the military tailor: of obsequious apprentices and massive bolts of rich, heavy red fabric; of pencil sketches and worn copies of clothing regulations; of swatches; and, of course, dramatic final fittings. To this was added the soft reassuring voices of the tailor and his assist-ants whose conversation was studded with a bewildering and exotic nomenclature: laceless regiments, "bastion" loops, plaided cords, "Russia Braid", "Gilt Chain Wings" and "waterfall" and "cartwheel" ornaments.[29]

The resplendent figure in the tailor's full-length mirror could easily have been the inspiration for William Thackeray's "military Adonis"[30]. Atop his head he carefully placed an enormous black, crescent-shaped cocked hat with a large white plume attached to a black cockade with gold loop with button. On a nearby side table was a second hat worn in full dress, a cap similar in shape to the large bearskins worn by the Guard regiments, but slightly smaller and made of seal or racoon. Browne's full dress coatee was scarlet with dark blue facings with gold horizontal loops and buttons arranged in pairs. A single gold loop adorned the high collar which surroundeed the black silk stock. A white frill protruded delicately from the front of the opened collar beneath which came a gorget of gilt metal suspended by ribbons of the facing colour. His breeches were white. A straight sword hung at his left side from a white leather cross-belt worn over the right shoulder. Wound snugly around his waist, and tied on the left as befitting infantry officers, was a beautiful red web silk sash trimmed with bullion tassels. Towards the close of the seventeenth century, an officer's sash was very large and was designed to form a hammock-stretcher by inserting a pole or pikestaff through a hole at each end, to remove the officer from the battlefield if he became a casualty. In 1805 the sash retained this function. It was strong enough to haul a man up a precipice, and in action it could be used to support a damaged limb or arrest bleeding.[31]

But something was missing in his appearance, as he carefully surveyed his profile in the tailor's mirror. It was his hair! The rather free style in which he now kept his blond wavy locks did not conform to army regulations. He immediately formed a mental picture of the remarkable manner fusilier officers then dressed their hair. It was formed into a long braid or plait, which was then turned up to the top of the head where it was fastened with a small comb. The locks at the sides of the face, the prescribed length of which was one inch, were "frizzed" by rubbing with the palm of the hand. The whole was then dusted with powder. What a capital addition this would make to his already fine soldierly appearance, he mused.[32]

Browne subsequently posed in uniform for a miniature portrait, the first of two painted studies of him in his regimentals. The extensive collection of miniatures at the National Army Museum, London, attest to the popularity of this art among British army officers. Indeed, it is reported that Lord Richard Wellesley, when Governor-General of India, from 1798 to 1805, regarded the commissioning of portraits as a significant and even necessary activity.[33] The commonness with which officers posed for portrait miniatures may be seen in the hectic schedule of Frederick Buck, a native of Cork, Ireland, born in 1771. Working in Cork, a busy Irish port during the Peninsular War, Buck was given so many orders for portrait miniatures by soldiers leaving for war that he developed a system of mass producing them. He accumulated a number of ivory painting grounds with the body of a soldier painted in, but which wanted a face and head and the specific accoutrements of the sitter's particular regiment or department. A soldier going off to war could then have his own features rapidly filled in so that he could leave a likeness behind with loved ones.[34] Thus, portrait miniatures were always commissioned and not simply painted as art for the sake of art.

A miniature could be executed in any medium, such as watercolour, oils or plumbago; and it could be rendered upon virtually any material, ivory being the most frequently used painting ground at the end of the eighteenth century. It had to measure not more than seven by five inches. In addition to being in the miniature style, the head in the portrait had to be not more than two inches long. The portrait of Browne, painted in oils on a thin oval-shaped slab of ivory, measures a mere two and a half inches in height.

The officer's portmanteau was conspicuous by its presence in the centre of the Browne drawing-room in Gwrych. For several weeks the family had watched with mounting anguish as the large leather packing case slowly filled with the war paraphernalia of a gentleman officer: several neat wooden boxes of preserved meats and "portable soup"; bedding and linen; glass and cutlery; jars of pickle and a tin of tea; a few dark green bottles of porter; a favourite fishing reel and a brass spy glass; spare clothes and several new note books; and the brilliant uniform, including greatcoat. Browne also managed to tuck in a few useful military works. Included in this modest portable library was General William Roy's *Military Antiquities of the Romans in North Britain* (1793). Also included was a well-thumbed copy of the 1762 revised edition of Captain Samuel Bever's *The Cadet. A Military Treatise*. A brief but popular guidebook for young officers when first published in 1756, it was primarily a collection of the thoughts and maxims gleaned from the writings of such great military leaders and theoreticians as Vauban, Turenne, Saxe and Puységur.

Once Browne went on active service he would quickly learn how spartan an officer's life was and how few amenities he could actually carry with him. He may have been moved to cram his suitcase as he did by the incredible tales that drifted back to England from India of British officers campaigning in luxurious comfort. If so, he acted unwisely, as did others before him. Except for what he could carry on his person, most of his personal effects would be consigned to the officers' baggage from which he would be frequently separated when on active service. Such an eventuality never occurred to Browne as he fastidiously recorded the contents of the portmanteau on a large sheet of paper which was carefully pinned to the inside of the opened lid.

The portmanteau was more conspicuous, even ominous, now that it was closed and locked. Large black lettering just beneath the padlock identified the owner as "THOMAS HENRY BROWNE GENT".[35] There it remained until that dreadful day of departure, in October 1805. All was cheerful until the four-wheeled post chaise arrived at the door, when the weeping began. Browne's departure was particularly difficult for twelve-year-old Felicia, whose creative and sensitive spirit was irrevocably touched by the sorrow of the occasion. And none of those gathered could possibly know that it would be some ten years before any of them would clap their eyes on their son and brother.[36]

Britain's desire to recover Hanover, which had been seized by France in 1803, and a wish to limit French expansionism, led to the creation of the Third Coalition[37] of European states against Napoleon in April 1805. Forged by William Pitt, who succeeded Addington as prime minister in April 1804, the Coalition included among its members Great Britain, Austria, Russia, Sweden and several German principalities. The central part of the grand strategic design of the alliance was to strike at France through north Germany. This meant a major campaign to free Hanover and an allied invasion of France itself through the Batavian Republic, as Belgium and the Netherlands were then known. In August 1805, when the Coalition became effective, there were about 30,000 Russian and Swedish troops at Stralsund (in east Germany) who could co-operate with a British force. Before the end of 1805, Pitt dispatched a considerable force of 60,000 British troops to the Elbe River in a bold but doomed attempt to establish a front in northern Europe.[38] The largest unit in the British expeditionary force was the 5,000 men of the King's German Legion, an élite corps built on the foundations of the Hanoverian army in 1803.

The 1st Battalion/23rd Royal Welch Fusiliers was part of the British contingent. The unit had sailed from Ramsgate, 726 strong, at the end of October and arrived at Cuxhaven, at the mouth of the Elbe, only on 17 November, owing to contrary winds. After a gruelling march the battalion went into cantonment on the Lower Weser River.[39] Any thoughts the men of the 23rd entertained of a successful expedition were quickly dashed. On 20 October, nine days before the 23rd left Ramsgate, an Austrian army of 27,000 men surrendered to Napoleon at Ulm. This blow to the alliance was rapidly followed by the French occupation of Vienna on 14 November and Napoleon's decisive victory over a combined Austrian-Russian army at the battle of Austerlitz on 2 December 1805. The Third Coalition was smashed. Russian troops were retreating to their own territory, while Emperor Francis of Austria anxiously appealed to Napoleon for a truce, the negotiations for which turned into the Treaty of Pressburg, on 26 December 1805.[40] The British expeditionary force, which was to have been commanded by the Duke of York, aided by a staff composed of all the notables at the Horse Guards (the headquarters of the Commander-in-Chief at Whitehall), was now in an untenable position in Germany. In January 1806 British troops were in possession of Bremen, the port of entry on the River Weser, and Verden, some twenty miles to the south-east of Bremen on the Aller River. The cataclysm of Austerlitz, however, led to the ignominious re-embarkation of the army on 15 February from Cuxhaven, now a familiar place to British troops. The 23rd received orders to re-embark on 13 February. An embarkation return put the total strength of the battalion at 746.[41] The regiment stepped ashore at Harwich at the end of February, and was stationed at Woodbridge from March to May. In June 1806 it was removed to Colchester, where, it is thought, Browne joined.

While the 1st Battalion campaigned in Germany, Browne received his basic training. The system of officer training then current, devised by the Duke of York, which can be best described as on-the-job training, was both simple and practical. Officers commanding regiments were responsible for the instruction and advancement of the officers under their command just as they were for the drill of the rank-and-file. Every officer, for instance, was expected within two years of his entering military service to be able to lead and exercise an infantry company or a troop of cavalry under any conditions, as well as being fully knowledgeable about its provisioning and discipline. Officers were also expected to be proficient in the duties of the field officer, to be familiar with those regulations that governed the activities of the other ranks, and to conduct themselves as confident and intelligent leaders of men. Incapacity or inattention to these instructions would normally prevent promotion to a higher rank. Continued negligence or incompetence might result in dismissal from the service.

It follows that if the standard war training of the new army officer was elementary, formal instruction must also be inadequate, which it was. It limited the new officer's education to regimental routine and field manoeuvres, and made virtually no provision to teach the officer more. Formal or professional army officer training was similarly inadequate. (There were, of course, a few small private institutions in Britain, which were attended by a small number of young officer cadets.) This mode of officer training was provided by the establishment of the Royal Military College by the warrant of 24 June 1801. (The College should not be confused with the Royal Military Academy, which was founded by Royal Warrant in 1741, and which trained officers for service in the artillery and engineers.) Although the R.M.C. was of considerable value to the service, only a portion of those enrolled were trained as future regular officers, the rest being prepared for staff positions. Moreover, only in 1810 did the College become an exclusively army institution, when the technical services, which had been using the College, transferred all cadets to the Royal Military

Academy at Woolwich. It is therefore understandable that some parents bent on forging a successful army career for their sons sent them to the Continent (as well as to private British academies) for instruction. The Duke of York had been sent by his father, George III, to Germany to receive his military education. The parents of the future Duke of Wellington sent their son to the Military Academy at Angers, France. Likewise, but on a more modest scale, Dr John Moore personally accompanied his son, the future Sir John Moore, to Brunswick, Germany, where the boy was daily instructed in the Prussian exercise by a hired sergeant.[42]

As already noted, Browne received whatever military training his regiment provided soon after joining the colours. Success-orientated, as his career indicates, and doubtlessly awed by the fame and high standards of the Royal Welch Fusiliers, he would readily have devoted himself to studying the current drill regulations, while attending the mounting of parades, guards and, particularly, drills. Probably under the command of a senior non-commissioned officer,[43] Browne learned how to execute the manual and platoon exercise of the musket, as well as the numerous variety of movements, commands and posts it was the raw ensign's duty to master. During his training, Browne also discovered that the basic training curriculum for British infantry had two phases. Introduction to and command of certain skills associated with the drill—which during the eighteenth century comprised five main components known as the manual exercise, the platoon exercise, the evolutions, the firings, and the manoeuvres—constituted the first phase. Briefly, the manual exercise was the protracted, slow and elaborate sequence of movements constantly drilled into the recruit whereby he learned, for instance, how to load and fire his musket and to execute the bayonet drill. The platoon exercise was the core of the manual, volley firing. Unlike the manual, however, it was carried out rapidly and to only a few words of command. The evolutions were the quick, precise motions, such as right-turns and about-turns. The firings constituted the rather complex systems and sequences according to which musket fire was given and controlled by sections told off into varying numbers of fire-divisions and units of fire-divisions. Lastly, the manoeuvres were the intricate and extensive range of close-order linear movements.[44] The second phase, begun upon the completion of the first, consisted of ceaseless drilling. William Bell, a new ensign in the famous 88th Connaught Rangers, and a contemporary of Browne, refers to this universal and mechanical character of basic training in the British army, when he wrote:

> I have been out at six o'clock in the morning for some time past—since I joined the regiment. We are drilled with the men exactly the same as the private soldiers. We began with the facings and went through all the different steps and evolutions of the marching squads. We were then exercised with the firelock.[45]

Why was it considered necessary, however, by the trainers of the British army of the time to subject the soldier (and officer as well) unrelentingly to what Houlding calls the repetition of a series of mechanical skills? To a great many officers the British soldier could be made to perform his exercise properly in the field only by disciplining his perceived natural clownish temperament and blunting his British tendency toward impatience. It was hoped that this type of training would, thus, diminish what conventional wisdom held to be his innate liveliness, particularly if he happened to be Irish, and encourage the robot. As Houlding put it in his brilliant analysis of the training of the army for the period 1715 to 1795, the findings of which were also largely true of the army when Browne joined, a total and docile compliance and robot-like reflex responses to commands were the yardstick of the rank-and-file; endless repetition of a few rudimentary skills, combined with inflexible discipline held in place by a brutal, unnecessarily violent and, ultimately, inhuman system of military punishment, appeared to guarantee both requirements. The tactics of the eighteenth-century army sought to eliminate chance in favour of control; initiative, one of the many attributes of the modern soldier, was still largely anathema in the British army when Browne received his commission. Moreover, the official attachment to a mechanical approach to basic training, that is, an endless, punishing drill which would produce (it was hoped) a uniformed automaton, remained the hallmark of basic training in the army throughout the nineteenth century. The long string of somewhat dubious military victories over restless native peoples throughout the sprawling empire during the century following the battle of Waterloo in 1815 doubtless reaffirmed official belief in the system of training. (Apparently, the luminaries at the Horse Guards overlooked the fact that colonial warfare against courageous but poorly equipped native soldiery did not provide a valid test of the system of basic training. Britain's war against the truculent Boers, from 1899 to 1902, did fully test the system and found it wanting. But this lesson, too, was disregarded with pernicious consequences.) As in that future holocaust, World War One, British soldiers continued to be trained and drilled as blockishly as in the day when Browne served, and with horrifying results.[46]

What effect did this severity have on the ordinary soldier Ensign Browne expected to lead? As in World War One, the system appears to have defeated him. Except in those rare cases when the human spirit had been pushed to its absolute limit of endurance, as in, for instance, the bloody aftermath to Wellington's pyrrhic victory in the breach at Badajoz in 1812, the evidence indicates passive acceptance of the system. Confronted with the impossibility of changing a system which degraded them and which threatened them with summary corporal punishment, the vast majority accepted the situation and compensated with a boisterous and ribald humour which many officers judged to be innately characteristic of the common soldier. All this notwithstanding, the ordinary ranker was obedient as he was loyal and brave. If the stress of his military condition led to mutiny, it was only in his heart. A few reacted quite differently, and would not countenance any opposition to military discipline. To these men success meant identification with the system. They were the prototypes of Denis Winter's "brisk and bustling men" of World War One. Some became non-commissioned officers, while others rose through the ranks to become officers. During the Peninsular War one officer in every twenty had risen from the ranks. The majority of these promotions were for long and steady service with the colours.[47]

In an army where the soldier was driven from his bed at five o'clock in the morning each day in order to prepare for a vigorous drill period, which consumed three full hours,[48] the importance of the non-commissioned officer was naturally considerable. We can imagine the smartly accoutred, fierce-looking non-commissioned officer in drill order as he menacingly viewed his inexperienced charges. His mission was simple: to teach them the rudiments of soldiering and to preserve them from the bane of all soldiers—idleness. Thus, the manner in which he energetically put his wards through the many prescribed manoeuvres evokes the historian Josephus' description of the spirited drill of the Roman army during the first century A.D. "Each soldier", he exclaimed, "daily throws all his energy into his drill, as though he were in action."[49] Drilling was arduous, and could indeed be a violent business, witness the following incident described in 1796 by George Pinckard, a British army physician, of the drilling of African recruits for the South American Rangers, a colonial corps subsequently taken on the British Establishment in 1798 as the 11th West India Regiment. Pinckard begins by describing the rather pathetic human material the NCOs were given to transform into soldiers.

> The activity and exertion which are required, to bring such recruits into habits of method and order, are almost beyond belief. Where the whole, from being bred up in ignorance and constant toil, are very much upon a parallel with oxen taken from the plough, you will imagine what the most stupid of them must be, who form that select body termed the "awkward squad". Upon beholding them when they first assemble, it might seem nearly as practicable to train a party of mules to carry arms. Tenfold the patience of the all-submissive patriarch must be necessary to teach them the air and carriage of soldiers, and to bring them into any thing like military discipline.

The flagrant blunders of the hapless recruits, combined with the "despotic" disposition of a swarm of rough and impatient sergeants and corporals, resulted in the inevitable violence. Pinckard continues:

> Frequently the "awkward squad" is led out to drill, with a proportion of non-commissioned officers nearly equal in number to the privates, each giving the word of command in the most authoritative manner, holding a short pipe in his mouth, scarcely extending to the point of his nose; and each busily marching his party to the right and left, backwards and forwards, and in every variety of direction, pushing, pulling, and cuffing them about, as if they were machines, totally devoid of sensibility. Often when stepping forward to the words "left, right, left, right," a stout black serjeant suddenly seizes the leg of someone who does not put it forth to his mind, and jerks it on with a force that endangers the dislocation of his hip; when the poor fellow, forgetting that his body must maintain the military square, whatever becomes of his limbs, looks down to see that he steps out better next time; but another serjeant instantly lodges his coarse fist under his chin, and throws back his head with such violence as almost to break his neck. Again fixed erect, he unfortunately looks to the left, instead of

the right, when his angry commander grasping with both hands, twists round his neck, with a force nearly sufficient to wring off his head.

And when fists failed to bludgeon the recruit into the desired "habit and method of order", the more sadistic trainers resorted to other devices.

Still some unfortunate member forgets itself, and strays out of place: an arm perhaps falls an inch before the line in which it should hang; when one of the attending sergeants, or corporals, forces it back with a thrust that might put out the shoulder. Next a knee is off its guard, and, bending itself into ease, meets with a severe rap from a huge grenadier with a shingle, or any other rough weapon which happens to be in his hand. Then, by some mistake, the right leg advances instead of the left, or the left instead of the right, the remedy for which is a hard kick or a rough blow upon the shin. Perhaps when resting under the word "attention" the heels are placed at an angle a little more acute than is desired, upon which a broken board, or some other rough piece of wood is thrust between the naked ancles, to wrench them asunder; and not unfrequently, at the expense of a painful excoriation: thus the poor black is beset on all quarters and at all points, and, whether standing or moving, feels the weight of the cane, the fist, or some other weapon, upon either his head or his shoulders, his back, knees, shins, or naked toes.[50]

Some may wish to argue that the above gruesomely detailed description distorts the actual conditions of basic training and drill in the British army at the time, since white soldiers, who were, after all, the majority group in the King's service, were not victimized in the way their black counterparts were in the West Indies. They might contend that West Indian society, unlike Britain's, was a slave society in which all blacks, slave and free, were systematically wronged, particularly the slave. Thus, although they enjoyed an elite status as armed soldiers vis-à-vis the common field slave, the Rangers were, nonetheless, black and consequently mistreated. Those who might argue in this manner need be reminded of three conditions which suggests the underclass status of the white soldier, a standing which is comparable to that of the black soldier and one which invites the claim that whites were treated in much the same manner as blacks. First, the basic training of the army mirrored the attitudes of contemporary British society. The complete sublimation of the individual through punitive discipline, which was the indispensable prerequisite for harmonious action on the battlefield, was also the pillar upon which the entire social fabric rested. And the political and military convulsions of the French Revolution animated the ruling classes to conserve the old order. Second, there was the universal contempt for the soldier, which even found expression in the leadership of the army. The Duke of Wellington's vicious and flagrantly biased pronouncement that the ranks of the British army were crammed with "the very scum of the earth"[51] is the best known. Why, one may ask, should worthless men be treated differently to blacks in the West Indies? Are not both equally undeserving of humane consideration and treatment? There were other officers who went so far as to suggest publicly that the soldier be governed by that system of punishment reserved for the slave. The anonymous author of *The Military Adventures of Johnny Newcome*, who identified himself only as "An Officer", was one. He shamelessly sentenced the common soldier thus:

> The way I estimate a British Soldier—
> He's stouter than a Frenchman, as is bolder;
> But such a set of wanton idle Knaves!
> You're forced, by G-d! to treat them all like Slaves.

The following explanation, intended by the author as a justification for his condemnation of the soldier, was added as a footnote: "This is a melancholy truth. The immorality of the British Soldier is disgusting, and it is only by strict attention and severe discipline it is at all kept within bounds."[52] This leads us to the third condition, the equally well known savage discipline of the soldier. The army's court-martial records for the 1793–1815 period, for example, confirm the sad truth that the maxim at the time was that the cat-o'-nine tails (so named, according to one source, because it leaves marks like the scratches of a cat) made the soldier. In 1805, the year Browne joined the Royal Welch Fusiliers, the average number of lashes awarded was 916![53] The view that the white and black recruit were treated similarly in basic training needs further research before it can be well established. Nevertheless, all who survived the calculated severity of basic training undoubtedly became the hoped-for armed and insensate automaton.

There were occasions when groups of recruits were not subjected to the customary abuse and violence of the drill ground. What spared these men was the presence in the group of new officers, like Ensigns William Bell and Thomas Browne. It was obviously unthinkable that gentlemen be exposed to this outrage, particularly at the hands of social and professional inferiors. An ordinary ranker could consider himself lucky if his band of military novices included an ensign or two.

In accordance with their importance in the basic training of the army, NCOs were carefully selected by officers commanding regiments from among the most experienced and reliable men, who were initially recommended by the captains. NCOs were also the subject of special attention in the semi-annual Inspection and Confidential Reports, which were assessments usually compiled in early May and October to acquaint the commander-in-chief of the army with the actual state of each regiment. The non-commissioned officers of, for example, the 3rd West India Regiment in October 1812 were described as "Active, intelligent, and ... their duties in Quarters and in the Field are performed with Energy and promptness, and they promote the Discipline of the Regiment to the best of their abilities."[54] And, as already mentioned, non-commissioned officers, usually old sergeants, were not infrequently charged with drilling fresh-faced ensigns. Major-General Sir George Bell recorded that when he reported to the depot of the old 34th Cumberland Regiment in 1811 as an ensign, he "went to drill under the command of an old Sergeant, who used to say that he was preparing me for a great General some day, if I didn't fall on the bed of honour before my time."[55]

There was yet another reason for this drill, dull, repetitive and harsh though it was. Consider thousands of brightly clad men formed into opposing ranks only a few score yards apart and firing muskets and cannons at one another, while comrades are falling wounded and dead all about. The soldier could at times distinctly see the enemy taking deliberate aim at him while he might be in a defenceless state, such as when he was in the complicated act of loading his musket. Reason and instinct alike would recoil from this method of warfare, this standing still in the open and dying on one's feet. Yet European soldiers of the period did it as a matter of course. Only endless drilling, which rendered the soldier robot-like, combined, of course with brutal discipline, made this remarkable mode of warfare possible. Put differently, drill prepared the common soldier to die at the command of a sergeant.

Proficiency in drill was not limited to the smart movements of the parade ground. The well-prepared infantry officer of Browne's time was expected to know the official literature which governed the drill of the British army. To achieve this officers were required to have in their possession various regulations published by authority. At first, it seems, officers were to be issued copies of these publications. In 1795 the Duke of York as Commander-in-Chief ordered that every infantry officer "be provided" with a copy of the *1792 Regulations*, which served as the foundation of the British infantry drill to the Crimean War, 1853–1856. (In 1804 *General Orders and Observations on the Movements and Field-Exercise of the Infantry* was issued to elucidate the *1792 Regulations*.) By August 1811, perhaps even earlier, infantry officers were required by General Regulations to purchase *General Orders*. They were also instructed to purchase *Regulations for the Formation, Field Exercise, and Movements of the Forces*, the *Manual and Platoon Exercises*, *Regulations for the Exercise of Riflemen and Light Infantry*, and even a copy of *Regulations for Establishing and Conducting Regimental Schools*. And to prepare officers for that day when they would be called upon to sit on and preside over courts-martial, officers were similarly required to purchase copies of the Mutiny Act and the Articles of War.[56]

If he wished to, the officer could supplement this imposing list of required reading with private publications. These made up a large and important body of literature. Since Roman warfare impressed the British military as much as it did Josephus, Caesar's *Gallic War* and *Civil War* appeared in numerous editions during the eighteenth century. Thucydides' *Peloponnesian War* was similarly popular.[57]

As important as the drill evidently was, it did not occupy all the time an officer devoted to learning his craft. Military administration, or the interior economy and management of a regiment, demanded much of his attention and the patience of Job. In this respect Browne was quickly acquainted with the twice yearly Inspection and Confidential Reports, preparation for which was a constant and demanding administrative function. Inspections were undertaken by general officers commanding brigades, and the resulting reports were forwarded to London to the Adjutant-General, the principal staff officer at Horse Guards. This key officer in the army's central administration dealt with all matters relating to military regulations as well as applications for leave of absence, discipline, and the arming and clothing of the troops. As mentioned previously, the reports were not considered merely assessments of a regiment at a particular time, but rather, the result of a continuous process of inspection. Some of the many headings of examination were officers, staff, non-commissioned officers, drummers, buglers, musicians, privates, men to be discharged, recruits, drilling, words of command, state of the barracks, hospitals, storehouses, arms and ammunition, colours, clothing, mess, books and accounts, complaints and courts-martial, religious service, and the hospital fund. The most dramatic part of the periodic inspection required the regiment to be formed up and instructed to carry out the several elements of the drill, all under the critical gaze of the inspecting officer and his staff. This was a time of considerable excitement as well as stress for the regiment under review, but particularly for new officers like Ensign Browne.

The inspection headings, though numerous, belie the detailed nature of periodic regimental examinations. Few things, if any, in the complicated life of a regiment escaped the attention of the inspector. Regulations saw to that. Regimental hospitals, for example, were examined to determine if they were constructed and managed in conformity to regulations laid down by the Medical Department. In the West Indies, at least, hospitals were checked for their location (high ground being preferred to low terrain) and the height of the ceilings in the wards. The diet of sick soldiers was also carefully studied for volume and quality of provisions, as was the number of sick, deaths and the length of time each soldier remained hospitalized.[58]

A regiment like any other complex human organization produces information, the preservation of and access to which is usually considered crucial to continuing successful operation. The management information generated by an infantry regiment during Browne's day was vast and important and thus required by regulation to be preserved in volumes specifically designed for that purpose. And because the activities of a regiment were so varied, these volumes were numerous, numbering thirty-two by 1812. The books varied in size and were grouped by major regimental operation, of which there were five. The number of books varied within each category, yet each dealt with a specific activity. Where there were more than one book in a group they were usually numbered consecutively. These records constitute a priceless and as yet a still largely unexploited source of information for army life, the internal administration of a regiment, and the identity of the otherwise anonymous ranker. The books of an infantry regiment for the period 1811–1812 were as follows:

REGIMENTAL BOOKS

No. 1. General Order Book
No. 2. Regimental Order Book
No. 3. Description and Succession of Officers
No. 4. Description of Soldiers
No. 5. Letter Book
No. 6. Monthly Return Book
No. 7. Miscellaneous Return Book
No. 8. Effective and Daily States
No. 9. Registry of Furloughs
No. 10. Description of Deserters
No. 11. Account of Defaulters
No. 12. Court-Martial Book
No. 13. Registry of Deceased Soldiers
No. 14. Record Book
No. 15. Registry of Marriages and Baptisms

QUARTERMASTER'S BOOKS

No. 1. Account of Clothing
No. 2. Account of Accoutrements
No. 3. Account of Arms
No. 4. Account of Ammunition
No. 5. Account of Fuel, Forage and Provisions
No. 6. Letter Book
No. 7. Account of Grenadiers' Caps, Colours and Pioneers' Appointments

INFANTRY COMPANY BOOKS

No. 1 Memorandum or Day Book
No. 2. Ledgers
No. 3. Order Books
No. 4 Description or Size Roll Book
No. 5. Clothing and Accoutrement Book
No. 6. Weekly Mess Book

REGIMENTAL SURGEON'S BOOKS

Medical Diary
Medical Register
Hospital Accounts

PAYMASTER'S BOOK

Estimate and Bill Book

Regulations described in endless detail what information was to be recorded and where it was to be entered in each book. Rules even set the paper size for each volume. As with most rules, they were at times apparently ignored by those for whom they were intended. As an officer, Browne would be responsible for maintaining several of the books, particularly the company books. How successful he was at these largely clerical tasks is not now known. Once he became aware, however, of this responsibility of gathering and recording vital regimental statistics, we can assume he diligently studied the appropriate regulations during quiet moments in quarters. If they had been available to him, it is virtually certain that he would have leaped at the opportunity to peruse previous inspection reports (which, as we have seen, were forwarded to the Adjutant-General for the eventual attention of the Commander-in-Chief). A reading of these records would have acquainted Browne with the fastidious care given to the completion of the examinations. He would also discover the errors others had made in the incorrect performance of their administrative duties. These ranged from the omission of information to books "Not in possession of the Regiment", a most serious charge. A common fault was, in the words of another report, "Book not of the Demy Paper as required."[59] The candour expressed in the periodic inspection reports makes it evident that regimental management was a complicated business, minutely governed by detailed regulations, hence the wisdom of the order requiring officers to purchase what was in effect their own personal military reference library.

When not parading for inspection, seeing to administrative duties, and cultivating in his men what has been described as the commendable but cold "canine virtues" of obedience, fidelity and courage,[60] Browne was busy being steeped in the history and tradition of the 23rd Royal Welch Fusiliers. The regiment was originally named after its first Colonel, Charles Herbert, a relative of Lord Henry Herbert, who raised the corps in Wales and adjacent counties in March 1689. Headquarters were then at Ludlow in Shropshire. The numerical designation, a device adopted throughout the army in the eighteenth century, indicated the order of seniority for line regiments and was based usually on the date when the unit was raised. At the time Browne joined the 23rd in 1805, the Regiment was "Welch" in name only. A return for 5 December 1806 shows the 2nd Battalion with a total effective strength of exactly 400 sergeants, corporals, drummers and privates. Of these only 74 were identified as "Welch". The largest ethnic contingent was English (221), followed by Irish (97). Scots, numbering only eight, comprised the smallest "nationality". Since the 2nd Battalion served as a reinforcement unit for the 1st Battalion, the latter presented a similar demographic picture. This is confirmed by an inspection return of the 1st Battalion at the Colchester Barracks on 26 March 1807 (almost four months to the day before the unit embarked at Harwich for Copenhagen, Browne's first active service). It shows the senior battalion with a total effective strength of 991. Only 146—two sergeants, two corporals and 142 privates—were recognized as "Welch".[61]

Recruiting outside Wales helped to limit the number of men in the ranks from that ancient principality. Owing to the paucity of recruits in the north-Wales men-catching grounds of Wrexham, Beaumaris, Caernarvon, Llanwrst, Holywell, Bala and Mold, recruiting parties of the 2nd Battalion were "beating up" for elusive volunteers across the border in the English Midlands, at Birmingham and Stourbridge, and to the north-west in Lancashire, at Wigan and Stockport, in 1805. Two years later, in 1807, recruiting teams went even further afield in their constant harvest of men. They were reported not only in Liverpool, but also in York, Manchester and Darlington. At the same time parties were also beating up for the 23rd in northern Ireland, at Magherafelt, and in southern Ireland, at the busy port of Cork.[62] Browne was employed in this recruiting effort. After the mandatory training period, from about October 1805 to early March 1806, he was sent on recruiting duties in Ireland, from 25 March to 24 June 1806, after which he returned to Wales. On 25 December he was detached to recruit in Manchester, where he remained until about May 1807, when he joined the 1st Battalion at Colchester.

The practice of drafting men, when applied to the 23rd, likewise kept the number of Welchmen in the Regiment small. Under this common-place system men were routinely taken from one regiment not likely to see action immediately and transferred into another regiment already on active service or under embarkation orders.[63] It is very doubtful if the county titles of the various regiments in use at the time, which were generally adopted throughout the army from about the 1780s, accurately reflected the regional origins of most of the men serving in them. As we have seen, it was not the case with the 23rd Foot.

If the county title of the 23rd was misleading, there was no confusion concerning the service record of the Regiment, which was as long as it was distinguished. In 1690 the Regiment took part in the Battle of the Boyne River (in Ireland) where William III defeated an army led by the deposed James II. The Regiment also served at the siege of Namur in 1695, one of the principal engagements of the War of the League of Augsburg, 1688–1697. During this war, in 1694, the colonelcy of the Regiment passed to Lord Ingoldsby. The unit was thus referred to as Ingoldsby's Regiment until 1714, when it received the title of the Prince of Wales' Own Royal Welch Fusiliers. This new designation contained two regimental distinctions. First, the Regiment was officially recognized as being armed with the fusil, an improved type of musket which was used only by elite units. (It is likely that the 23rd had been armed with fusils at an earlier date, as in the case of the old 20th Regiment of Foot which had been given the fusil in the seventeenth century but did not become a Fusilier regiment until 1881.[64]) Second, was the designation "Royal". This award entitled the Regiment to a distinctive uniform. In the middle of the eighteenth century "Royal" regiments were permitted blue facings and blue breeches. (Line regiments, typically, wore red breeches.) Moreover, the Clothing Warrant of 1751 ordered drummers of "Royal" regiments to wear the royal livery: a red coat with blue lining and facings, adorned with royal lace. (Drummers of line regiments wore coats of their regimental facing colour, trimmed with regimental lace.[65]) These apparently small regimental distinctions were not trifles. They were, on the contrary, proven aids in the development of *esprit de corps* and thus were jealously guarded by officers and rankers even into the present century when challenged by clothing standardization. The reasons for these honours were no doubt attributed to the Regiment's illustrious service under the Duke of Marlborough, at Blenheim (1704), Ramillies (1706), Oudenarde (1708), and Malplaquet (1709) during the War of the Spanish Succession, 1702–1713.

The 23rd also saw heavy fighting at Minden (1759), which is regarded as one of the greatest victories in the annals of the British army. The Regiment, along with the other "Minden Regiments", which share in this great victory, annually celebrate the event. On 1 August 1806, the forty-seventh anniversary of Minden, Browne stuck a rose in his Racoon-skin cap as did his regimental comrades. This act was in memory of those who, in the advance through rose gardens to the battlefield on 1 August 1759, decorated their grenadier caps and tricorne hats with the emblem of England.[66]

The American War of Independence, 1775–1783, ended in a major defeat for British arms. However, the 23rd once again served with honour, this time at Bunker (actually Breed's) Hill (1775) and Brandywine (1777). During the war against Revolutionary and Napoleonic France the Regiment gained additional laurels. In the Egyptian campaign of 1801, for instance, the 23rd, ferried from the troopships in naval rowing boats, were the first troops to land at Aboukir Bay, near Alexandria. This feat was achieved before a strong and determined French army fully prepared in entrenched positions at the water's edge.

Browne eventually came to know the splendid history of the 23rd. Evidence of stupendous soldiering crowded him at every turn and aided his transition into military life. Captured enemy equipment, adorning the officers' mess, formed tangible links with distant victories, as did the many battle honours blazoned on the approximately six foot square regimental colour of richly embroidered silk, which he doubtlessly carried during his days as an ensign. This process of indoctrination was deliberately designed to instil courage, resolution and steadfastness in the new warriors of the Regiment.

We can conclude from the above that the proven ability of the 23rd on the field of battle gave Browne a sense of regimental *esprit de corps*. The British regimental system was especially effective at building such strong unit pride. The extraordinary extent of this phenomenon fills a vast literature. There are countless examples where individual soldiers and entire units have attained the highest possible standard and have not broken even in the face of total annihilation.[67] Ability, however, is not the only source of *esprit de corps*. It can also come from regimental customs, those time-honoured practices which to the outsider appear to be nothing more than entertaining foibles but which to the soldier represent the very soul of the regiment. The object of intense regimental pride, these customs took several forms, such as the annual commemoration of great victories, periodic rituals, and certain so-called "peculiarities": regimental mascots and unusual uniform distinctions, for example. The Royal Welch Fusiliers adhered to a number of these which diminished, somewhat, the structured monotony of military life by enhancing the regiment's identity.

On 1 March, the anniversary of their patron Saint, David, all ranks of the 23rd wore leeks in their headgear. Officers celebrated the event with a ceremony known as "eating the leek." No matter where the Regiment was on that appointed day, be it in barracks or on a rolling troopship in mid-ocean, each officer was required to eat an entire plant-bulb and dark green leaves. Saint David's Day, 1 March 1808, found the Regiment at sea, en route to Halifax, Nova Scotia. With the officers and men scattered among several troopships, amid the cramped conditions of life between decks, festivities associated with the anniversary were kept to a minimum. This inability to celebrate the day in style disappointed Browne and reminded him of past celebrations, an evocative account of which he recorded in his Journal (see p. 73).

An earlier description of this custom refers to the playing of the old tune "The Noble Race of Shenkin" by the regimental band. At this time, according to the same account, a little drummer boy made his dramatic appearance, elegantly dressed, mounted on a goat richly caparisoned, and led three times round the officers' mess table in procession by the drum major. No one could guarantee, of course, that the goat would behave according to script. And it happened, in 1775 in Boston, that the animal, perhaps unnerved by the crescendo of noisy voices, sprang on to the mess table where he undecorously dumped his little rider, bounded over the heads of the startled guests, and dashed in all his fluttering accoutrements for the sanctity of his pen, to the unrestrained amusement of all (excluding, surely, the drummer boy).[68]

The goat in the ceremony was not just the ordinary horned, bearded ruminant rented or, perhaps, even commandeered for the occasion. Rather, as Browne suggested, the animal was the unit mascot, already a regimental institution by 1808. The Regiment's pet was not then unique to the British army; other regiments retained pets as mascots, usually unofficially. Mascots were apparently trained to listen to martial music at close quarters without showing fear, or worse, resentment, particularly if the animal had horns. Some regiments even took their mascots with them on active service, among them the Royal Welsh Fusiliers, whose goat died during the bitter Mons retreat of 1914. The animal was given a funeral with full military honours and buried in a Belgian cemetery, to the amazement of the local inhabitants. According to one expert, the earliest recorded regimental mascot was the goat belonging to the Royal Welch Fusiliers. It was reported with the Regiment at Bunker Hill, in 1775. At a review two years later, the 23rd was preceded by a goat with gilded horns and adorned with ringlets of flowers, which is probably how the animal was dressed when Browne served with the Regiment. Towards the end of the eighteenth century the presence of the goat with the 23rd was acknowledged then as an old practice. It was not, however, until around 1834 that the regimental goat of the 23rd was officially recognized. This tradition has continued to the present period. The goat, with horns encased in polished brass and wearing on his forehead a silver shield inscribed with the name of the sovereign who presented him, takes his position on special ceremonial occasions. The mascot is at this time under the immediate supervision of the "Goat-Major", as his Fusilier attendant is termed.[69]

The "flash", a set of five black ribbons, sewn together, one above the other, to the back of the collar, is yet another traditional distinguishing mark of the 23rd.[70] Originally, this was a bow of broad ribbon tied to the pigtail ("queue") or club. Its function was to keep the grease, with which the hair was thickly coated, off the collar of the coat. The custom of thus dressing the hair was discontinued in 1808, as we have seen, but not the fancy bow. The bow at some point evolved into the flash which the Royal Welch Fusiliers continued to wear, long after 1808 and in obvious breach of army regulations. This practice was apparently not noticed officially until 1834 when the Regiment returned to Britain from service overseas. At its first inspection the 23rd was summarily ordered to end the practice. Colonel Harrison successfully appealed through the army's central administration to William IV to be permitted to retain the flash permanently. (At the same time he made a similarly successful appeal to keep the regimental goat.) The request was granted in November 1834 amid, no doubt, numerous toasts to the King. Until 1902 only officers, warrant officers and staff sergeants wore the flash, after which the custom was extended to all ranks of the Regiment.[71]

It was customary in the British army to bestow endearing nicknames on regiments of foot. The origin of the practice is in question but not the suitability of the appellations accorded the 23rd. The Regiment was variously called "The Nanny Goats", "The Royal Goats" and "The Flash", which pleased the Fusiliers.

All of these practices, and others not mentioned here, generated a common spirit of comradeship, devotion and enthusiasm to a cause among all ranks of the Regiment. The elements of inter-unit rivalry and pride in the long history and accomplishments of the 23rd pervaded the thoughts of each Fusilier and presented him with an ideal to live up to and a record to keep untarnished. Regimental customs were to ensure that each new Fusilier would make the declaration: "We are not just a regiment. We are the 23rd Royal Welch Fusiliers, who were at Blen-

Bronwylfa (c. 1860s-1870s).

William Edward West, *Felicia Hemans* (1827).

C. Hamilton Smith, *Privates, 23rd Royal Welch Fusiliers and 6th (1st Warwickshire) Regiment* (1815).

Eugène Delacroix, *Troupes Anglaises – Le Bagage de Campagne*
(1813).

heim, Minden, Brandywine and _____."[72] It remained only to insert a new unit honour.

It is difficult to exaggerate the critical importance of *esprit de corps* in the British army of the period. The soldier was then unjustly regarded as a pariah of the nation and predictably condemned by a society which generally agreed with Wellington's vicious accusation. To metaphrase Rudyard Kipling's "Tommy", the British soldier remained a brute even when the guns began to shoot during the hard fought wars against France. The rejection of the value of the soldier's effort by British society could breed dissatisfaction, even open defiance. The soldier, however, generally avoided this condition since he saw his efforts appreciated by his military unit.

The *esprit de corps* of the Royal Welch Fusiliers was a condition Browne could experience only after he had joined the unit. The Regiment's fame, however, certainly preceded this and was to a large degree publicized by recruiting parties which regularly "beat up" in north Wales where Browne lived. We can picture the men of a recruiting party, an officer, one or two non-commissioned officers, and a drummer (to "beat"), in their resplendent regimentals. As the drummer entertained those who were too young to serve, the officer and NCOs captivated their listeners (Browne among them, perhaps) with stirring accounts of the feats of the 23rd over tankards of beer which served to stretch the imaginative powers of storytellers and audience alike. The 23rd's outstanding reputation as an elite, hard fighting regiment undoubtedly influenced Browne's decision to join. This action speaks highly of Browne since he was not intimidated by the repute of the 23rd, as some might have been. It is a fact that mediocre and frightened men are embarrassed by the presence of an elite.

The highest expression of *esprit de corps* is less a desire to fight than the willingness to fight well. Browne learned this as a member of the Royal Welch Fusiliers. It was well that he did, for the battles of the period, which were essentially severe trials of strength lasting several hours and fought on a narrow terrain, were fearsome and bloody. Even when compared to the horrific conduct of warfare of the present century, Napoleonic battles were large-scale pounding matches to the death. Consequently, opposing armies suffered appalling casualties, so much so that Stendhal's Julien Sorel, a Napoleonic veteran, could exclaim: "In those days a man like me was either killed or became a general by the age of thiry-six."[73] Artillery and infantry fire rapidly shrouded the battlefield in an acrid smoke, blinding and confusing the combatants downwind. Cannon fire also produced a deafening and terrifying roar, while soldiers marched, manoeuvred, ran, stumbled, fired shoulder to shoulder, literally collided with their foe, and attacked them with bayonets in a simple and direct effort to push the enemy off the disputed ground. The soldiers had to obey their officers' and sergeants' shouted commands to close ranks and fill the gaps left by comrades struck down by metal projectiles of various calibre, for at the least sign of disorder squadrons of horsemen were waiting to swoop down, trampling, hacking and spearing those in disarray.[74] The only way to prepare for this terror was to envelop oneself in a unit with other chosen men who were willing to train assiduously for war.

In our efforts to plot the career of Thomas Henry Browne, we have explored those reasons which led him, most certainly, to seek a career in the army and service with the Royal Welch Fusiliers. With the aid of imagination, we have watched Browne prepare for war in the manner of his contemporaries in the military. This was followed with a brief discussion of the nature of military exercise and the responsibilities of military leadership and regimental management. What we now need to chart is Browne's service record, which began in 1805 as a humble ensign and peaked in 1854 when he became a lieutenant-general. To do this, however, we must first construct the larger picture of career patterns established by army officers, against which we can compare Browne's record. This will enable us to determine if Browne's career conformed to the norm for army officers, or if it had exceptional characteristics, and if so, why.

Michael Glover's important analysis of all army promotions and first appointments (excluding brevet promotions) listed in *The London Gazette* during two sample periods, September 1810 to August 1811 and March 1812 to February 1813, provides us with a clear picture of purchase and promotion patterns during the Peninsular War.[75] The study excludes the Artillery and Engineers who reported to the Master-General of the Ordnance. It similarly leaves out Britain's separate armies (the militia, volunteers and fencibles) as it does the numerous foreign corps in British service. Thus, Glover's analysis takes into account only that portion of the regular army administered directly by the Duke of York as Commander-in-Chief. What precisely does this study tell us about career patterns in Wellington's army?

During the twenty-four months covered in the sample periods there were, for instance, 3,941 appointments, infantry and cavalry combined. These were commissions to the several regimental ranks, from ensign (in the infantry and cornet in the horse regiments) up to and including lieutenant-colonel. Of these 1,790 were first commissions as ensigns/ cornets, second lieutenants, or as lieutenants in the 7th Royal Fusiliers. Only 349 of these commissions, or 19.5 per cent, were by purchase, however. The rest were free commissions. (In the infantry of the line, there were 1,368 first commissions of which 232 were by purchase.) Approximately two-thirds of those who obtained first commissions, whether by purchase or free commission, were without prior military experience with the regular army. (A soldier could have acquired military training in one of Britain's separate armies before becoming a regular.) These men were designated "Gent" in the *Gazette* and were expected to spend the first months of their service diligently learning the rudiments of soldiering.

The small number of purchased commissions reflect a general pattern for the army as a whole during the sample periods. Glover's study shows that in virtually 80 per cent of all commissions and subsequent promotions, purchase played no role. In the vast majority of cases it was seniority within the regiment that determined promotion. Glover's work should put to rest the stubborn myth that rank in the British army of the period was largely bought. The fact that purchase was not the normal method of appointment and promotion during the Peninsular War stems in part from the reforms of the Duke of York. Soon after he took overall command of the army on 10 February 1795, the Duke quickly moved to abolish the system whereby an officer of means could move immediately to high rank simply by purchase. He also ordered that an individual could not become a captain until he had served two years as a subaltern, which was increased to three years after 1809. The Duke further decreed that six (after 1809, seven) years of commissioned service were required before anyone could be promoted to the field rank of major. These reforms ended the most repugnant features of the system of purchase.

A successful army officer's career, one that began as an ensign and continued to a general's rank, fell into three distinct phases, according to Glover. The initial stage was the eventual acquisition of a captaincy. The step from ensign/cornet to lieutenant took ordinarily less than three years and, as a result, few officers, only 17 per cent of those eligible, found it worth purchasing. The next step, to captain, was crucial, and looking at the army as a whole, that is, the infantry and cavalry only, the time it took to attain a captaincy was approximately seven and a half years. As a result the rate of purchase increased to 28 per cent. The second stage, the progression from captain to lieutenant-colonel, usually involved a considerable waiting period. The longest wait entailed the first move to regimental major. An officer might have to wait as few as six or as many as seventeen years, before he could succeed to a free majority. Predictably, the proportion of purchasing officers rose to its highest for any rank in the army, reaching 30 per cent. The following step, from major to lieutenant colonel, was actually easier, in consequence of which the proportion of purchase decreased sharply to under 14 per cent.[76]

Before going on to the final stage of an officer's career, it is necessary to pay closer attention to the rank of captain. Regimental seniority largely determined promotion to captain in the vast majority of cases. That changed once an officer became a captain, for he was eligible for any army rank which actually bore little relation to his regimental rank. Captains, as well as majors, were eligible for brevet promotion up to lieutenant colonel on grounds of long service or merit. The significance of brevet promotions was that it permitted an officer to jump over officers senior to him who had purchased their promotion.

In the third stage, from lieutenant colonel to general, only seniority decided promotion. To balance what was actually an automatic promotion, neither full colonels nor generals of any grade were paid as such unless they held some definite appointment. And because there was a shortage of appointments, more than 25 per cent of senior officers customarily kept their regimental rank, with the result that it was not unusual for unemployed major generals to be drawing pay as lower-grade regimental officers.

What were the patterns of promotion of Browne's career? Typically for the army of the period, Browne was a so-called "non-purchase" officer since he obtained a free commission in the newly created 2nd Battalion/23rd Royal Welch Fusiliers, an augmentation unit.[77] Numerous 2nd battalions were created in existing regiments as a result of the enormous wartime expansion of the army. As in the case of the majority of men then entering the army as officers, he was without prior military experience. Browne's rise through the regimental ranks was untypically rapid for the period. As we have seen, the move from ensign to lieutenant usually took just under three years. Browne, however, was promoted in about ten and a half months, the time between the date of his commission as ensign, 28 October 1805, to his promotion as first lieutenant, on 18 September 1806.

It took Browne seven and a half years, 18 September 1806 to 15 April 1813, to progress from lieutenant to captain, which was the average for the army. His subsequent promotions were rapid. He obtained a majority by brevet promotion in just over four years, on 21 June 1817, and an army lieutenant colonelcy, again by brevet promotion, only eighteen months after that, on 21 January 1819. This was very rapid promotion especially since Browne went on English half-pay, or semi-military retirement, on 25 December 1814 with the regimental rank of captain in the 23rd.

One is tempted to attribute Browne's rapid promotion solely to his connections, for which there is both circumstantial and direct evidence. For example, he informs us in his Journal that when his regiment was ordered to do service in Nova Scotia in 1808, he carried with him letters of introduction from his mother to Sir John Wentworth, then outgoing governor of the colony. It seems that Felicity Wagner Browne had known Sir John in England and was on intimate terms with his wife, Lady Frances Wentworth, who convalesced for some time at the Browne family home in Wales. As a direct consequence of this bit of familial influence, Browne was "commissioned" (as he termed it in his Journal) to wait on Lady Wentworth for a short time.[78] If this affiliation did not further Browne's career, the cushy nature of this duty certainly made it a pleasant undertaking.

Consider, however, his subsequent appointment to Wellington's staff in the Peninsula, a nomination Browne imputed solely to his command of the Spanish language in which he gained proficiency soon after arriving in Portugal. Some time in 1812 Browne was appointed to the staff of the Adjutant-General as a Deputy Assistant Adjutant-General.[79] The rule nominally governing staff appointments to the Adjutant-General's Department, according to S. G. P. Ward, the authority on the central administration of Wellington's army in the Peninsula, was that nominations were first made by the King on the advice of the Horse Guards. In practice, however, particularly as it concerned the military staff, an army preparing for foreign service was provided with a staff selected by the Adjutant-General at the Horse Guards. Once his recommendations had been made, some authority was then delegated to the Adjutant-General of the expeditionary force to nominate additional officers in his department, subject ultimately to the commander of that force. Therefore, in the case of the British expeditionary army in the Peninsula, the Adjutant-General at the Horse Guards prepared the original list and nominated others as the war continued. Major-General Charles Stewart, the A.G. with the army from 1809 to 1813, then selected others from among those (Browne being one of them) already serving in Portugal and Spain, who were then confirmed in this service by Wellington.[80]

During his period as D.A.A.G. to Charles Stewart, Viscount Castlereagh's half-brother,[81] Browne made a favourable impression on Wellington. When his request for Browne to be assigned to his new staff, formed in April 1815 to meet the threat caused by Napoleon's escape from Elba, had been refused by the Horse Guards, Wellington, according to Browne, was "much annoyed". As if to demonstrate that he had indeed nominated Browne for a staff position, Wellington, in the company of Browne, ordered his Military Secretary, Lieutenant-Colonel Lord FitzRoy Somerset, to produce a copy of the list of recommendations for staff appointments sent to the Horse Guards. Next to Browne's name was recorded "indispensably necessary at Head Quarters". Browne noted in his Journal that when he saw his nomination, he "was quite cast down when I saw how the Horse Guards had served me." Angered and evidently embarrassed by his glaring failure to secure a staff post for Browne, Wellington shook Browne's hand and consoled him with the words: "I see how it is [at the Horse Guards], & as far as I can be of use to you hereafter you shall not be a sufferer. . . ."[82]

This snub by the British army command underscored Wellington's main complaint regarding the officer cadre, which was that the power of reward, accorded hitherto to every British commander-in-chief on active service, was denied him. Lacking, therefore, the power of patronage in the field, Wellington was hampered in his efforts to stimulate the fervour and energy of his officers. The inability of the Duke to place Browne, whose nomination was after all a minor one, causes one to question the claim of Sir John W. Fortescue, the historian of the British army, that this evil was remediable and subsequently remedied.[83]

Despite this setback, Browne found employment once more on the staff of Charles Stewart. He served as Stewart's aide de camp at the headquarters of the Austrian, Russian and Prussian armies during the

Waterloo campaign, March to June 1815. After Waterloo, Browne accompanied Stewart first to Paris and then to Vienna, where he served briefly as private secretary at the British embassy.

To suggest that Browne's rapid rise through the regimental ranks was due to influence only would be unkind as well as inaccurate. Browne's rise through the grades to the rank of general was due less to connections than it was to his bravery and dedication to the service. He campaigned with the 23rd at the siege of Copenhagen. In addition to serving twice with the Nova Scotia Command, he participated in the capture of Martinique (February 1809), where he was seriously wounded in the arm. Landing in Portugal in November 1810, he saw considerable field service before his appointment to Wellington's staff. In that capacity he was present at every major action from Salamanca (22 July 1812) to Toulouse (10 April 1814). Staff service had its obvious rewards, but it was not without its dangers. During the French debacle at Vitoria (21 June 1813), Browne was wounded in the head with a sabre cut, taken prisoner but rescued the same day by units of the 15th Hussars. Among his decorations for field service is the war medal with eight clasps.[84]

In the third and final stage of Browne's military service, from lieutenant-colonel to general, only seniority mattered, as Glover has shown. Consequently, it took some eighteen years for Browne's next step to full colonel (10 January 1837) and another seventeen years before he became lieutenant-general (20 June 1854).

Recognition of his long and continuous service followed quickly. On 28 September 1814, a little more than five months after Napoleon's first abdication (6 April 1814), the leading citizens of the county of Flint proposed to give a public dinner in commemoration of Browne's distinguished service with the army in the field. This decision, according to the invitation requesting his presence, represented the "unequivocal testimony of the high sense entertained by your neighbours and countrymen of your services abroad".[85] The banquet was to be held, appropriately enough, in Mold, one of the principal recruiting areas of the Royal Welch Fusiliers.

In 1818 Browne was made a Knight of the Royal Hanoverian Guelphic Order, or, simply, Knight of Hanover (K.H.). This was a British as well as a foreign military order instituted by George IV, when Prince Regent, on 12 August 1815 — his birthday — to commemorate the establishment of Hanover as a kingdom.[86] "NEC ASPERA TERRENT"

(Nor do difficulties deter), the motto of the Order, was later worked into a device with the family motto "SPECTEMUR AGENDO" (By our deeds we are known) and was used by Browne as his bookplate. This award entitled Browne to the half-pay of a major. (The 1818 portrait of Browne presumably shows him wearing the badge of the Order as well as the uniform of a member of the staff of the Prince Regent, yet another honour.[87]) In 1821 Browne was elevated in the Order to Knight Commander of Hanover (K.C.H.), which permitted him to collect the half-pay of a lieutenant-colonel. Five years later the first entirely British honour came when he was made a Knight Bachelor. The monetary entitlement for this honour was the same as for the K.C.H.[88] In addition to these distinctions, Browne was given the colonelcy of the old 80th Staffordshire Volunteers' Regiment.[89] Finally, on several occasions Browne was offered commands as a general officer, all of which, curiously, he declined.[90]

Now that we have formed a picture of Browne's career, we need to go back in time to 1807. In July of that year Browne, now a lieutenant, participated in his first expedition—the siege of Copenhagen. Because of the evident significance of this event in his career, he commenced his Journal in July 1807. What determined the expedition was the British government's belief, reached in 1807, that the regenerated army—in concert with Continental allies—was then capable of protracted operations against Napoleon in Europe. Heretofore, the army had been twice driven in ignominious defeat from the Continent, in 1795 and again in 1799. What military success there was was essentially confined to secondary theatres of operation, as in the West Indies. Thanks to his reforms, the Duke of York must be given much of the credit for the vastly improved state of the army. An equal share of this honour goes to Robert Stewart, Lord Castlereagh. As War Minister from July 1805 to February 1806, and again from July 1807 to September 1809, Castlereagh provided sound strategical direction and the manpower the army required. One of his first acts in the war ministry was to develop plans for a "disposable" or expeditionary force to menace Napoleon along the maritime frontier of that portion of Europe under French hegemony.[91] Immediately upon his return to the ministry in July 1807, a disposable force was quickly and carefully organized and dispatched to the Continent. Thus, on 25 July 1807, Browne and several thousand of his comrades in arms marched from Colchester to waiting troopships at

Harwich, a distance of twenty-one miles. These ships would ferry the British expeditionary force to Copenhagen, to capture the Danish fleet which Napoleon planned to use in conjunction with other naval units against the Royal Navy.

For Browne, the expedition to Copenhagen marked the end of the "waiting about" time that, as Reginald Hargreaves has written, filled up much more of the soldier's life than the actual business of killing on the battlefield. During quiet, pensive moments along the road to Harwich Browne's thoughts fixed upon those concerns all soldiers necessarily ponder before they test themselves and the capriciousness of life in battle. For Browne, as well as every other soldier, the essential condition of soldiering was danger and the fear it begets. "How would I deal with fear?" he must have mused—fear of pain, fatigue and death, the concomitants of battle.

It is also likely that, being new to war and a member of an elite regiment with a high *esprit de corps*, Browne was exhilarated by the thought of battle and martial glory. Unfortunately, we have no evidence of what Browne actually thought regarding this matter, as he did not record his first impressions of battle. Another British officer, a high spirited Peninsula soldier, did. He was pleased with the opportunity to observe his first battle, *at a safe distance*, and he has left us this candid and poignant testimony, which may provide a window into Browne's thoughts. "This was the first battle I saw," wrote Ensign Edmund Wheatley of the 5th Line Battalion of the King's German Legion,

> and I was delighted at first, but when crowds of groaning, wounded Spaniards and French prisoners filled Irun [a village in north-west Spain], my look of satisfaction was soon clouded, and a violent reaching and giddiness was the punishment for enjoying the horrid spectacle of human butchery with indifference.[92]

If Browne was enthralled with war at first, it was just as well since it gave him the confidence he would need, for looking beyond the impending struggle with the Danes loomed the inevitable Armageddon with the French who were then at the pinnacle of military success. The bitterness of that future contest was due in large measure to the *élan* and *esprit de corps* in the French army. The intensity of that warlike spirit may be judged from the way the ghost of Napoleon animated Stendhal's Julien Sorel, the would-be hero. "Ah! Napoleon was really sent by God for the young men of France!"[93]

There are many things the soldier can do to prepare for war. Soldiering, however, is so unpredictable that it necessarily subjects the soldier to many events for which there is frequently no warning and thus no preparation. One of the most disconcerting of these was the immediacy of general orders to proceed to a new station or on an expedition. Once these orders were read to the troops, they were usually allotted only a few hours in which to take leave of a familiar barrack room, their friends and loved ones. (During the evening hours of 16 January 1808, the 23rd received orders to march in three divisions to Portsmouth for embarkation for foreign service in Nova Scotia. The first division was instructed to begin its march on the morning of 17 January, followed by the second division on the 18th and the third on 19 January.[94]) Orders of this type ordinarily involved wrenching separations from wives and children, most of whom were not permitted by regulations to accompany the troops overseas. The anonymous author of *The Military Adventures of Johnny Newcome* has memorialized this spasmodic nature of military service in amusing verse.

> An Order now arriv'd at the Depôt,
> "That Ensign *Newcome* should to Hilsea go."
> Altho' John relish'd not these hasty ways,
> He bolted off to Hilsea in a chaise;
> And then a Note was handed to our Spark,
> "That without loss of time he should embark."
> "Upon my soul," says John, "this is no jest,"
> "They won't allow a man a little rest."
> Boxes and trunks were cramm'd into a Boat,
> And Johnny *Newcome* found himself afloat.[95]

The need to defend an ethnically diverse colonial empire, coupled with a tradition of intervention into Continental politics when British interests were threatened, exposed the soldier to a bewildering kaleidoscope of different peoples, customs, languages, climates, flora and fauna, odours, foods, strange and deadly diseases, and terrain. Overseas service, particularly duty in the tropics and sub-tropics, also revealed to the unsuspecting soldier new and strange effects of light and colour and atmospheric phenomena.[96] With the army (including the Royal Navy) given the task of defending the empire and Continental interests, the question was not *if* the army would be dispatched overseas, but rather, the frequency and length of this service. For Browne, service outside

Britain meant living among Danes, who delighted him with their inventiveness, and Canadian colonists and native peoples towards whom he was somewhat indifferent. It also involved a brief but dramatic sojourn in the West Indies, among transplanted Europeans and black African slaves, whose dark skin and different features troubled him. Most of Browne's overseas service, however, was a slow passage among Portuguese, Spaniards and French. And his Journal confirms what students of the Peninsular War know: the British preferred the Portuguese to the Spaniards and the French over both. The French, as Fortescue has stated, returned the compliment. They viewed the British as friends compared to their loathing of Spaniards and Portuguese alike,[97] a situation which arose from the efforts of these proud peoples to end Napoleon's brutal occupation of the Peninsula.

Perhaps the most startling surprise of all to the newcomer to British military service was the presence of women and children. The ideal military society was by definition one of adult single males. However, as official regulations and contemporary illustrations of British military life indicate, women were conspicuous. On any given day they could be seen washing, breast-feeding and rearing their children in barracks as best they could under deplorable conditions. In the field they could be found cooking, nursing, doing laundry, "recreating" with soldiers, and doing a host of other regimental duties. Although non-combatants, they were not spared the ravages of war. After battles pathetic female figures could be seen moving apprehensively among the dead in search of missing husbands. And in the wake of British retreats in Flanders and the Peninsula, particularly during bitter winter months, their dead bodies littered camp sites and roadsides. Their presence was universally welcome to the rank-and-file (if not at the Horse Guards) since they softened military life and turned the army into something resembling a normal society.

The life of the British army woman was miserable and tenuous. This well documented fact is curiously missing in Rowlandson's happy scenes of military life in which women appear well-fed, contented and serene. Eugene Delacroix's gripping "Troupes Anglaises—LE BAGAGE DE CAMPAGNE" (1813), albeit an exaggeration, is the more accurate depiction of the army woman. A primipara nearly twice removed, she is care-worn with that hollow facial expression of abject resignation. The title of the caricature accurately denotes the condition and status of women in the British army. A marriage allowance, for example, was paid to a militiaman's wife, but not to the wife of a regular soldier. Married quarters in barracks, contrary to Rowlandson's idyllic "ENGLISH BARRACKS" (1788), were simple to the point of indecency. The utter wretchedness of women and their children was most evident in the army's policy regulating the number of soldiers' wives permitted to accompany their husbands on overseas service. In 1800, for instance, six women per hundred men in each regiment were permitted to embark with their husbands. Only "lawfull" wives and children under ten years of age, "born in lawfull Wedlock", could embark. It is not clear how the army determined legitimate births and legally contracted marriages. Nor is it clear how the selection process worked, whereby a limited number of women, out of a much larger group, were permitted to leave Britain with their soldier-husbands. Yet official evidence indicates that it was not unusual for women, some with children of various ages, to be refused permission *at dockside* to embark with their husbands on foreign service. It also appears from official sources that women, again, some with children, habitually journeyed from various — even distant — parts of Britain to embarkation ports with the intention of sailing with their men. Women and children thus exposed did receive some assistance. In 1800 it was ordered that each distressed woman from England be paid one guinea for herself and five shillings for each child. Women and children similarly exposed from Scotland and Ireland, and able, apparently, to demonstrate a lawful relationship with a soldier, were likewise compensated. They were also provided, if necessary, with a free sea passage to the port nearest their homes. Nevertheless, it is not difficult to imagine a scene, repeated frequently in British ports, in which clumps of abandoned women and children mournfully watched as their husbands/fathers sailed away to distant garrisons for an indefinite time. Common-law wives and illegitimate children shared the same grief with no compensation.[98]

Given the hardship of this service, the purpose of which was to discourage marriage, the number of women and children in the army was relatively small. Compare this to the Prussian army which recognized the importance of women in military life and marriage as the best means to limit prostitution. By 1802 there were approximately 59,000 wives and 78,000 children in the army for every 100,000 men from Prussia in military service.[99]

In view of the omnipresence of women in eighteenth-century armies, we should not be surprised that Browne frequently observed them and carefully recorded their diverse activities. He provides, for instance, a wonderfully evocative scene of proud soldiers' wives of his own regiment refusing to permit their husbands' heads being shorn of the pigtail which they took evident pride in preparing. He also recounts women stripping the dead of their clothes and a solitary English woman frantically searching among the freshly killed for her husband, who also lay dead on some undiscovered part of the battlefield. On a very different note, Browne describes a small contingent of boisterous Spanish prostitutes, who, colourfully dressed and sitting astride mules, vigorously shouted "Viva Wellington" as the Duke passed by, much to his reluctant amusement.[100]

Browne recorded only the unusual incidents involving women. This is, perhaps, understandable since scenes of mutinous behaviour, plundering, despair and moral indiscipline are more likely to be remembered than those activities which are commonplace. Yet it was the cooking, washing, cleaning, hauling, nursing, marching, childbearing and dying that comprised the essence of women's bitterly hard and inestimable service in the army.

It was (and remains) the duty of the soldier to serve wherever his country required. In doing so, in a service of great imminent danger, Thomas Henry Browne's life was full of adventure and experiences. What wisdom he extracted from these events is not fully known, although his almost daily confrontation with calamity and death gave his life as a soldier an intensity, variety and richness beyond the experiences of most men. Such is the nature as well as the promise of soldiering. As a country squire in Wales soon after his return from overseas in 1816, Browne undoubtedly lived in the memories of his army days, as did all soldiers. His past was unavoidable since he served at a time of unusual national danger and during an age of great historical significance. The satisfaction of having forged a distinguished military career may have lessened the pain associated with his three marriages. His first wife, Louisa Anne, daughter of Robert Gray, Lord Bishop of Bristol, died in childbirth in July 1823. His second wife, Elizabeth Anne Burdon, of Castle Eden, county Durham, also died during childbirth, in February 1826. Two years later, in March 1828, he married Elizabeth Brandling of Gosforth House near Newcastle-on-Tyne. This union produced two sons. The first, Henry Ralph, was born at Gosforth on 29 December 1828. Like his father, Henry Ralph entered the army and eventually attained the rank of general.[101] A second son, Ralph Charles, was born on 18 February 1830 and became a clergyman. Unfortunately, the marriage to Elizabeth Brandling ended in a penitential separation for Browne, followed by his subsequent move to 19 Camden Terrace, Camden New Town (now London), where on 11 March 1855 he died of pneumonic complications in his sixty-eighth year.[102] A memorial tablet to Sir Thomas was later erected in St Asaph Cathedral by his elder son, Henry Ralph Browne.

By his descriptive and perceptive gifts, Browne gives the reader of his Journal a vivid picture of soldiering in the Napoleonic era. His Journal shows us the condition of that service, as seen from the field with the troops and from the headquarters of Wellington's army.

The Journal of
Captain Thomas Henry Browne

I
Copenhagen 1807

The need to counter the formation in 1800 of the Second Armed Neutrality of the North,[103] the purpose of which was the destruction of British trade with Germany and the Baltic States, led to the first battle of Copenhagen. On 2 April 1801, Vice-Admiral Horatio Nelson, the second-in-command of the British fleet, sank, burnt or captured all seventeen of the Danish first-line ships caught in the harbour of Copenhagen. In 1807 a second major threat developed in the Baltic. Learning that Napoleon planned by a secret clause of the Treaty of Tilsit (7 July 1807, between France and Russia) to seize the Danish fleet at Copenhagen, the British government of the Duke of Portland quickly despatched Admiral Lord James Gambier with twenty-five ships-of-the-line and 25,000 troops under General Charles Murray, Lord Cathcart, to forestall this possibility. As Denmark rejected Britain's demand to surrender its fleet until a general peace had been secured, British troops began landing at Webek, a little village about eight miles north of Copenhagen, on 16 August 1807. The principal action of the expedition was the siege of the Danish capital. The position of the 23rd Royal Welch Fusiliers during the siege was due north of and some 2,500 yards from the massive outer walls of the city. A regular siege was not contemplated, as it was already late in the season. Nonetheless, a savage bombardment commenced on 2 September and continued until 5 September. Two days later, Crown Prince Frederick agreed to turn over the Danish fleet which was subsequently sailed to Britain. Between 22 September and 5 October a working party of the Royal Welch Fusiliers was employed in the naval arsenal. On 18 October the 23rd embarked for Britain. One section of the regiment sailed in the *Heir-Apparent Frederick*, a Danish prize ship. According to the regimental history of the 23rd, a Danish lad was so taken with the smartness of the fusiliers that he managed to smuggle himself on board the prize ship; he was somehow taken on the strength of the regiment but subsequently discharged when his identity was discovered. The last British troops were withdrawn in October.

Although of short duration, the bombardment destroyed a considerable part of the city and was the subject of a number of popular drawings. Major-General Thomas Grosvenor, who commanded a brigade that included the 23rd, recorded in his journal that fires resulting from the bombardment destroyed about 1,800 houses and killed or wounded 600. British losses were put at forty killed and 150 wounded. Total losses for the 23rd: three killed and two wounded.[104]

The siege of Copenhagen, a brilliant military stroke, was not without its costs. The attack, which profoundly shocked European opinion, probably prompted Russia to declare war on Britain sooner than she had planned. In Britain, too, the expedition incurred some severe criticism. The great damage and suffering caused by the bombardment moved Wordsworth to doubt that Britain was indeed a "bulwark to the cause of Man".[105] The expedition also attracted the mockery of the caricaturists. One unsigned print, which was published in November 1807 when the expedition returned to Britain, depicts a weeping Britannia. It also shows John Bull as a soldier astride a once proud lion turned ass on the boulder-strewn road to Denmark.[106]

JOURNAL OF THE EXPEDITION TO COPENHAGEN JULY 1807

THE British Government having received authentic information, that a secret Treaty had been concluded between France and Denmark,[107] by which the powerful fleet of the latter, was to act in conjunction with the navies of France, a demand was made by the English Ministry, on the King of Denmark,[108] that this Treaty should not be carried into execution. The existence of the Treaty was in the first place denied by Denmark, and secondly she would not admit the right of the British Government to interfere with her arrangements with other Powers.

Upon this, the correctness of the information in the possession of the British Cabinet was proved to that of Denmark, and the demand repeated, that the Treaty with France should be annulled, and in addition, that the Danish fleet, should be sent to England to remain in British Ports, as the only security against forcible possession being taken of it by the French, who were at that time in considerable strength on the southern Frontier of Danish Holstein. Great Britain offered at the same time to guarantee to Denmark the preservation of the Danish Ships, in the best possible repair, and the faithful delivery of them, to that Government, on the conclusion of Peace between France and England.

To add force to this demand a powerful expedition was prepared, the military command of which was given to Lord Cathcart, and the naval force was placed under the orders of Lord Gambier. The number of the Troops was about 25,000; and that of the Ships of war very considerable. The division to which I belonged, embarked at Harwich, on the 25th of July, having marched that day from Colchester, a distance of twenty one miles, and consisted of three Brigades; the 28th 92nd and 95th Regiments, under General Ward, the 4th and 23rd Regiments, under General Grosvenor, and the 50th and 79th Regiments under General Spencer; the Division itself was commanded by Sir David Baird. This body of Troops, was to be joined by about 10,000 men who were to embark at Yarmouth.

We remained at anchor, until the first of August, when ammunition was served out to the men, and the usual arrangements made, and orders issued preparatory to landing in the face of an enemy, boats were hoisted in, anchors weighed and the Fleet got under sail, convoyed by the Comus Frigate, Captain Heywood.

The wind being foul and scanty, we did not make land till the 6th, which proved to be the Skaw, the northern point of Jutland. The Breeze was light and we fished for Macharel, of which we caught abundance, baiting the hook in the first instance, with a drilled shilling, and a small bit of scarlet cloth; after a fish was caught, this bait was changed for pieces of the fish itself. During the 7th we beat about in the Categat, and were joined by many more Transports and Ships of War, with Troops on board. On the evening of the 8th the Breeze freshened a good deal accompanied with thunder and lightning, and very dark clouds; these were succeeded by a beautiful moon and light Breeze, and we sailed past Kronenberg Castle from which the Danish Flag was flying, the bands of our Regiments playing national airs as we glided by. This entrance into Elsinore roads is narrow, and appeared by the moon-light of that evening, to be one moving mass of Ships. We cast anchor about ten o'clock. Watches were set on board the different Ships, and shortly afterwards all was still, except the occasional splashing of the oars, of the guard-boats, sent from the Men of War to keep watch on the water, during the night. An hour before day-break, Bugles were heard in all directions sounding the Reveillèe. The Troops mustered in arms, on the decks of their different Ships, and shortly afterwards a Gun from Kronenberg Castle, announcing sun-rise and day-light shewing that all was quiet, the Soldiers went between decks again, and cooking began. Woe to the Cook, who had not been sufficiently careful in this provision for a day-break stomach; the talents and genius of hungry hundreds, were most actively roused, in pouring forth invectives, worthy of so serious a disappointment. The greatest misfortune which can happen to the soldiers early meal on board ship, is that of its being smoaked; he makes no sort of allowance, for the different currents of wind, occasioned, when at anchor, by the flapping of sails let loose to dry, or when at Sea, by sailing close hauled upon a wind, but proceeds instantly to try the Cook by what is called a company Court-Martial. The Cook as invariably (knowing that he himself has tried and condemned many a preceding Cook for a similar crime) throws himself on the mercy of the Court. feelings of mercy are out of the question, and shew themselves only in sentencing the Cook to be cobbed. This ceremony is performed by the Soldiers forming two ranks, facing inwards, making the Cook pass between them, and cobbing him well about the head with their foraging caps; he is not allowed to run through them, but to march in slow time, and if he attempts to hurry his pace he is made to begin again. The infliction of this sentence, it may perhaps be supposed would prove a satisfactory penance for the crime which occasioned it; nothing however is farther from the fact, for every accident and untoward event of that day, is attributed to the Cook's having smoaked the broth in the morning.[109]

August 8th. Ships of war and Transports continued to arrive during this day, and a fresh attempt at negociation with the Danish Government was begun. Many reports were in circulation on this subject, having no better foundation, than the private feelings or opinions of those who chose to circulate them. Several Officers went on shore to Elsinore, and did not meet with any insult.[110]

August 9th. I went with a brother Officer to Helsinborg on the Swedish side of the Straits. This place is the Brighton of Sweden, and the summer resort of the King. We went to the theatre, and saw a play performed which appeared to excite great laughter and applause in the audience. The decorations and dresses were however miserable. My brother Officer and myself were dressed in our English uniforms, and [we] were treated with the greatest possible kindness and civility. Room was made for us, to pass to the front seats, and explanations given us in French, by those next us of what was passing on the stage. My companion who understood French no more than he did Swedish, acknowledged the attention by repeated bows to his obliging interpreter, looking at me whenever he had an opportunity, for my approbation of his very great tact in thus concealing his ignorance of the language without permitting his neighbour, as he thought, to make the discovery himself. I was myself a little better circumstanced, but was too much occupied in looking around me, to benefit much from my Swedish friend's explanations. After the play was over, a very well dressed Swedish Gentleman came to us, and begged we would accompany him to his house to supper, which we were obliged reluctantly to decline, as we had not leave to remain on shore much longer than the time we had already taken. In the boxes of the Theatre I remarked several Swedish Officers, having white handkerchiefs bound round their left arms, which was a distinction given by Gustavus the third to those Corps, which assisted him in 1772 to free the regal dignity from the degraded state in which he found it. This was the Monarch who was afterwards assassinated in a public ball room, by Ankarstrom, a Captain of the Guards.[111] The night was very dark when we returned from Helsinborg to our Ship, and we were rowing about till two in the morning before we reached her.

From the 9th to the 16th of August we remained at Anchor, waiting the issue of the pending negociations. Troops and heavy Artillery arriving daily from England. On the 15th at night Lord Cathcart and the German Legion arrived from Stralsund.[112] At day-break on the 16th we weighed Anchor, and about three o'clock in the afternoon of that day moored about six miles from Copenhagen.

August 17th. Preparations were made for landing, it was a beautiful morning. The boats filled with troops, assembled alongside the respective Ships, and on a gun being fired from the Admiral and a flag hoisted at the Main, the whole pushed off at once for the shore. They kept in line as they rowed, in every tenth or twelfth boat, the colours of a regiment uncased and blowing open with the breeze. In different parts of the line were boats having field pieces in their bows. The men were ordered to sit down and keep silence. There was some surf on the beach, but not sufficient to obstruct the landing seriously, and few accidents happened. When the boats touched the shore the men leaped out, and immediately formed themselves into companies, and regiments, loaded their fire-locks, and fixed bayonets. They then moved forwards, and occupied strong ground, on the right and left of the landing place.

Two Danish Cavalry videttes, were seen, observing our landing, but not a shot was fired to oppose it. The colours of the 23rd regiment were carried by Lieutenant Blankley and myself, the two senior second Lieutenants of the corps, and I must acknowledge when we planted them on the Danish shore, we had by no means an indifferent opinion of ourselves. We moved on unmolested on the high road to Copenhagen, about two miles; the night was very dark, and as we proceeded, some horses from a neighbouring pasture broke through the leading ranks of the column, and occasioned some confusion in the line of march. General Grosvenor's brigade, the 4th and 23rd regiments, halted that night in the large open area of the Palace, called Charlottenland. We lay on the sand of an inclosure in which the horses of the King of Denmark were usually exercised, and was full of Askers[113] which tormented us very much. Charlottenland seems an old uncomfortable Palace, about two miles from the Sea-shore, & four from Copenhagen; no injury whatever was done by the troops, to the interior of the building, but the gardens in which there was a good deal of fruit, as well as plenty of grapes in hot and green houses, were pretty well ransacked. I relieved a Danish gardener of a bunch of the latter, which he was bearing as a tribute of gratitude for the visit paid him by the English, to General Grosvenor. The negociation for them was carried on in dumb show between the gardener & myself, who seemed greatly chagrined at the change, which the subtraction of my portion made in the dish. I remember this gardener well, he was a little man with long fair locks, hanging over both his shoulders, and an immensely broad brimmed hat on his head.

August 18th. The Brigade was under arms at day-light. The men in fact rose at once into their places, as they had lain down the preceding night in their proper ranks, their arms alongside of them and their knapsacks for pillows. We proceeded to take up our first allignement about two miles from the Capital. Some Danish videttes made their appearance, but as our picquets advanced they rode off. A Danish gun-boat attacked and took in our sight, a Transport having horses of the German Legion on board, and burned her. We were bivouacked in the fields, and made ourselves huts of boughs of trees, sheaves of corn, doors &c. My own den was of the most comfortable description, as I had discovered that the coach-house doors of a Danish Admiral, (who at such a moment had no doubt, full employment for his carriage and horses elsewhere) could be borrowed by taking them off their hinges, which two or three Soldiers of my company had no difficulty in doing, and by placing them together, as children do the two first cards when building what they call houses, I had almost the best mansion in the whole camp, & whenever I was out on picquet, or at the advanced posts, this luxurious tenement was an object of much Competition with my brother Officers. Several of the natives, came near us this day, but as they talked no language but Danish, it was not possible to have any communication with them. They appeared to gaze at our operations, with vacant countenances, & perfect unconcern. The dress of the men from the shoulders upwards, was the same as that of the Danish gardener before described. We gave them the general name of Bosses, which appellation they retained, to the day of our departure from Denmark.

August 19th. The 32nd and 50th regiments, took up their ground this day, their left resting on the Sea, and their right on our brigade, and thus became the left flank of the whole line which was from its position a good deal exposed to the fire of the enemy's gun-boats. The Danes made a reconnoissance this Evening with about 1000 men, and our advanced Posts were sharply engaged with them. We barricadoed the high-road, leaving open embrasures for two guns, which raked the road.

August 20th. Several deserters came in from the enemy, & reported that they suffered a good deal in the skirmishes of yesterday evening. Picquets again engaged but with trifling loss. As the weather was hot, we began to feel that a change of Linen would be rather refreshing, but as no part of the baggage had landed, it was a refreshment to which we could only look forwards with hope, as we could not enjoy it. We discovered this day one of the large reservoirs of water from which pipes were laid to supply Copenhagen, and we kindly cut them all off.[114] A battery was this evening marked out in an old salt-petre work on the right of the 32nd regiment.

August 21st. Mortars and heavy cannon were this day landing from the fleet, and we were told that some baggage would be sent us in a few days. The enemy discovered our salt-petre battery, and began a heavy fire on our working parties, but they had already thrown up a sufficient quantity of earth to be pretty well covered, & we did not suffer much. Several other batteries were marked out in different parts of the line, of which the Guards were the right, their right flank resting on the Sea, near Friderichsberg, which completed the investment of the place. During this time the morning & evening parades of such parts of regiments as were not on duty in the batteries, or at the advanced posts, took place regularly as in England, & we constantly observed crowds of Danish genlemen & ladies looking on from the Steeples of the Churches in Copenhagen. A shell was occasionally thrown at us, but seldom with any effect.

August 22nd. The enemy began a heavy cannonade against our salt-petre battery, & two officers & three privates of the Artillery, & two men of the 82nd regiment were killed. Some horses also fell, which were bringing guns into the work. A flag of truce came out to ask permission, as we understood, for the free passage of one or two Danish Princesses to the shore, to embark for Holstein where the King & the rest of the Royal family had gone during the time that we were at anchor in Elsinore roads. Permission was given, & a string of some dozen carriages filled with Princesses, maids of honour, & band boxes in most ridiculous array passed thro' our lines. Whether they enclosed any beauty or not, this journal cannot declare, as the blinds of the carriages were down. When they passed thro' the lines, our troops presented arms, & they were furnished with an escort to the sea-shore, & a passport, to prevent their being detained by our ships of war, which were cruizing all round the island.[115] After their departure, the palace of Friderichsberg became the head quarters of the Guards.

August 23rd. Our picquets were surprised this morning in a wood behind the house of a Mr. Tutin. They were driven in, and fell back on their reserve. The enemy was in considerable strength, commanded by the Danish General Pyman, whose force consisted of two regiments of the line and a corps of students of the University. It was intended for a strong reconnoissance. The reserve of the picquets formed line and moved on to repel the attack. A sharp skirmish took place, which ended in the repulse of the enemy. General Pyman was shot through the left thigh, & when our picquets reoccupied the post from which they had been driven, they found on the ground about 80, of the Danes, who had fallen. Amongst the dead, there was a considerable proportion of the young Danish students, some of whom did not appear to be more than sixteen years old, and our sun-burnt Soldiers really grieved, to see the fair faces and curling locks of their gallant young opponents, as they lay extended on the ground. They must have resisted gallantly, as some had fallen, from bayonet wounds given by our troops. There were in these woods, which were enclosed as part of the ornamental grounds of Mr. Tutin, several square holes, about 15 ft deep, with water in them. They were full of fish, which were no doubt kept there, for the use of the kitchen; each hole had a wooden cover, pierced here and there, to let in air, and hung on hinges. To save the trouble of digging graves, and as the most ready way of disposing of the dead Danes, our soldiers carried them to these holes, and when they were thus filled, dropped down the covers. We lost an Officer and about 20 men on this occasion.

August 24th. The siege actively continued, the batteries are in a forward state, & quantities of shells & mortars landing. A new battery was begun, under cover of some houses not far from the sea-shore, from which Sir William Congreve prepared to throw his rockets. Numbers of them were landed under his direction, & we anxiously anticipated the effect of these powerful engines, of which we had heard so much, even at this early period of their invention.[116] The covering parties & picquets, were cannonaded by the enemy, and lost a few men.

August 25th 26th. Great progress continues to be made in the works. Nothing new occured during these two days, but the customary sunrise skirmishing of picquets.

August 27th. Information having been received, that a body of the enemy from 3, to 4000 men had established and entrenched themselves at Kioge in our rear, to prevent our getting supplies from that part of the country, Sir Arthur Wellesly was detached with his brigade to attack them. He made a rapid night march, and at once stormed the entrenchment. The Danes were completely surprised, but recovering themselves, made some resistance, by which we lost 30, or 40, men. The result was the entire capture of this body of the enemy, of whom from 3 to 400, were killed and wounded. Fourteen hundred prisoners and sixteen pieces of cannon were taken. They appeared poor raw troops, and we could not help smiling at the indifferent figure they cut.[117]

August 28th 29th. Works rapidly advancing. Some wet weather occurring, our advanced posts pushed forwards, along the whole line, and drove the enemy's picquets out of the suburbs, which we occupied, that our troops might have cover. We had not long taken possession of these comfortable quarters, before the enemy made a sortie in considerable force, and attempted to set fire to them. They were driven back, after some loss on both sides. This kept us very much on the "qui vive" as we were not wiliing to give up our new appartments, without a good fight for them.

August 30th. The enemy again attempted to drive us out of the suburbs, & we were sharply engaged for a couple of hours after daybreak. Some of the smaller ships of our Squadron, having taken up a position nearer to Copenhagen, than they had occupied before, a flotilla of Danish gun-boats attacked them, & a smart action took place. They were open boats, having a heavy gun in the bow, with no sails, but ten or twelve pair of oars, very low in the water, and consequently exceedingly difficult to hit, from vessels as high out of the water, as our ships of war, the shot from which, constantly passed over them. Nothing could exceed the gallantry of the Danish Sailors, who continued rowing on, thro' a sea foaming with the shot from our Ships, and succeeded in setting fire to a transport which was under their protection. They then attacked the ships of war themselves, and compelled them to retire. This action took place in sight of the whole army.* As the gun boats were returning to Copenhagen, a brigade of artillery was sent along the heights of the shore to intercept them, and as they were rowing round a point, to enter the harbour, commenced a very destructive fire upon them, with Shrapnel shells, & the slaughter of Danes on board some of the boats was considerable. They never ventured out after this day. In order to get a nearer view of this engagement, I went down to a house, not far from the shore, the windows of which faced the sea, but I dared not show myself at them, fearing to draw fire from the boats on the house. I managed however to get into the attics, & there by perseverance, and the point of my sword, I contrived to push off a slate, and made a hole just big enough for my bare head to pop out, and from this position, I had an excellent view of the day's work. In coming down stairs I was struck with seeing the furniture of the house almost all of the English fashion, and amongst the pictures which hung round the rooms, were several views of different parts of England, and one or two prints of our naval victories. There was a pretty garden to the house, which was also laid out in the English style. In a drawer, in one of the lower rooms, which I either found open, or opened, I discovered some very accurate charts, & soundings of the Baltic, the Cattegat, and the entrance to Copenhagen. I thought these documents lawful prey, and sent them to Sir Samuel Hood.

*Saw them thro' a roof taking off a slate.

August 31th. The enemy cannonade our working parties and annoy us with occasional sorties. Our total loss to this day has been about 200 men killed and wounded.

September 1st. There was a smart engagement this morning in a wood behind Lassen's house. The enemy was repulsed with loss.

September 2nd. The batteries are now nearly complete. There was one on the extreme left, called the Sailor's battery. The next was that under the directions of Sir Wm Congreve. Then came the salt-petre battery. Next, one in a burial ground, which went by the name of the church-yard battery, and one on the right, in a timber yard. There was a certain anxiety observable in the countenances of the General and superior Officers which indicated some approaching serious operation. This night the house in the suburbs occupied by the left wing of the 23rd regiment took fire. It is a singular fact, that when it was occupied by the regiment we found painted on the door, 23 Dam. The house was one of a number on the bank of a piece of water, where bleaching works were established, and this house was the 23rd of the row situated on this piece of water, or as it is called in Danish, Dam.[118] The flames burst out with great fury, and were, we concluded, immediately seen from the city, for we had scarcely begun the necessary arrangements for extinguishing them, when a trumpet at the out-posts, announced a flag of truce, demanding if we would permit the fire engines & the corps to which they belonged, to come out & render assistance. As we had nothing to apprehend from such a measure, leave was given, and a beautiful corps made its appearance, with six engines capitally well appointed, who began operations without delay. Some had axes, others, saws, and all the necessary implements for pulling down houses; ladders &c. &c. A certain proportion were armed with swords, to keep off the crowd. They had brass helmets on their heads, with strong flaps of leather attached behind, so as to cover the shoulders. Their first work was to cut off the houses right & left of that which was on fire. This they did, with amazing activity and intelligence. The pipes from the engines were at the same time uncoiled, & one end carried down to the Dam. The supply of water was abundant, the pumps in excellent order, and the fire was got under in an incredibly short time. The instant this was done, they returned to Copenhagen. It appears there is a regular fire corps in that Capital consisting of six companies of infantry, and four mounted troops, with engines attached. It has its Colonel, Majors and Captains, and exercises daily. We understood also, that there is an extensive old building which is allotted for the use of this Corps, to which they occasionally set fire, & exercise their ingenuity & quickness in extinguishing it. They had contrivances of pullies, baskets and ropes by which to extricate the inmates of houses on fire, and the manner in which they practised with these, was by leaving some of their men in the old building, when they set fire to it, and getting them out, as fast as possible. I never saw so complete a security against the effects of fire, and we could not help bestowing our warmest applause on this Danish fire corps when it returned to the city. We regretted greatly afterwards to learn, that by far the greater part of them perished, in the great conflagration, produced by our subsequent bombardment.[119]

September 3rd. This night about eight o'clock the bombardment of Copenhagen began, from five batteries in each of which were ten mortars. The effect produced can scarcely be described. The hissing of the Congreve rockets in the air was a sound such as had never been heard before, and the terror they produced in Copenhagen was augmented by the great difficulty of extinguishing the combustible materials of which they were composed. Blankets & bedding were wetted with which to approach them, but this itself was too dangerous to continue, as in some of them, there were small shells, the explosion of which prevented any one coming near them, and whenever they fell upon a house they set fire to it. Perhaps the best idea that can be given of the sort of impression produced by these rockets may be extracted from a pamphlet, written by a Dane, in indifferent English, which circulated amongst our troops, shortly after the capture of the place. He speaks of mortars, shells &c. as matters of course, bad enough indeed but still a customary sort of weapon; but in mentioning the rockets, he thus expresses himself "But when I saw the air gingling with the never to be heard of inventions, carrying fire thro' the air, not to be extinguished, down upon our dwellings, oh Britain, Queen of Nations, Mother of such noble and manly sons, said I to myself, is this thy work." Perhaps no public dispatch could have testified to Sir Wm Congreve the execution done by his rockets, more forcibly, than this apostrophe of the Dane, learned in languages.[120] The Danes returned a very heavy fire, of shot & shells during this first night's bombardment.

September 4th. The fire from the batteries recommenced this evening very briskly. Lieutenant Jennings of the 23rd regiment and three men were killed this morning, just as a new battery, in front of the Church yard was unmasked. It was at day-break, & at the moment he was relieved by another officer and party of his regiment. This Officer had advanced a little in front of his party, & entered the work, where Lieut. Jennings was assembling his men, to march off. Preparatory to their doing so, Jennings ordered them to shoulder arms, on which the other Officer remarked to him, that as the sun was just beginning to peep, the light might reflect on the barrels of the firelocks and being seen by the enemy from the ramparts, which were very near, would inevitably bring a fire on the party. To this, Lieut. Jennings, who appeared exceedingly dejected, replied that it was of little consequence how he marched out—that he did not think he should ever leave the place. The Officer relieving him then asked if the enemy had been pretty quiet during the preceding six hours, the time that Jennings and his party had been in the work. He answered, that they had only fired two or three random shots, one of which had struck the ground very near him. He said no more, but the other Officer was much struck with his unusual manner, and went back to his party which he brought up with trailed arms. Lieut. Jennings moved out with his men shouldered. They had not proceeded twenty paces out of the battery, when a single round shot from the Danish ramparts was fired at them. It carried off Lieut. Jennings's head, and killed two men immediately in his rear. It was the only shot fired. Their bodies were borne off by the party, and that of Lieut. Jennings carried to his hut. It was there ascertained from his servant, that from the moment he had been warned for that duty, his spirits had completely forsaken him. He had collected together everything belonging to him, and put them with his watch and seals into a little portmanteau, which had been brought ashore for him a few days before, at the time that a small portion of our baggage was sent to each of us. He had fastened this portmanteau with a padlock, and put a direction on it to his friends in Yorkshire. He had appeared troubled and restless, for several hours before he took the command of his working party. Several Officers of the regiment had observed this change with astonishment, and had tried to rally him, but in vain. He was naturally a courageous man, and one full of life & spirits, and I cannot therefore doubt, but that he entertained so full a presentiment of his approaching fate, as to have rendered his mind incapable of admitting any other impression at the time. His portmanteau was found in the manner I have described, when his body was borne to his hut, and on the return of the regiment to England, was sent to his friends, with the direction he himself had placed upon it. It was the custom of that day, for regiments of Fusileers to wear the hair platted behind, and turned up to the top of the head where it was fastened with a small comb. Lieut. Jennings's hair must have fallen down, before the shot struck him, and was hanging by the little of his head that remained. It is in my possession, and I think I have discovered such traces of his friends, as will one day enable me to send them this sad, but very precious relic.[121]

The battery in which Lieut. Jennings was killed, was in a burial ground, laid out like a beautiful grove. From an avenue which led down the centre of it, there were little paths, diverging in all directions, on the sides of them were planted evergreens and other shrubs, with flowers between. These paths ended in spots of turf, allotted as the burial grounds of different families, and each family arranged its own spot, inclosed as it was with shrubs, according to their own ideas of taste and respect for the place. In some, were beautiful marble urns, in others, costly tombs, with willow or cypress hanging over them, and never was a scene so admirably calculated to fill the mind, with sentiments of peace and repose. The walks were kept in the highest possible order, and everything external proved the sanctity of the place, and the respect in which it was held. And yet into such a spot, man's last abode, war found its way, and the earth which covered the dead, was raised into a battery, to pour death and destruction upon the living, who had deposited them there. There was in one corner of this burial ground a sort of Mausoleum, which covered a very large vault. Some of our soldiers broke open its door & descended into it. I followed them, and as the night was rainy, we struck a light there, and remained an hour or two, as the best shelter we could have. On the sides around us, coffins were placed, which from the velvet or cloth which covered them, shewed that they inclosed the remains of some family of distinction. I took the light, to look at the inscription on one of them, It was "Emilie Gandil Fod. 7 Ap. 1780. Tod. 5 Sep. 1802." A singular and interesting occurence, this, that British Soldiers should be thus assembled, round a dim light, in the vault of a Danish family, arms in their hands, and grateful for such a place of shelter, in a dark and rainy night. It is one of those extraordinary incidents, which belong almost exclusively, to the profession of a Sailor or a Soldier. I wish I had been able to make a sketch of this rude group thus assembled in the tomb of the Gandils.

There are four burial grounds of this description, in the environs of Copenhagen, one opposite each of its gates. In the centre of one of them, is a large pyramidical tomb, on which are inscribed the names of all those, who fell in the attack on Copenhagen by Lord Nelson in 1801, the result of which, although it put an end to the Northern Alliance, and was attended with many other consequences highly favourable to England, was considered by the Danes a decided victory.

September 5th. The bombardment commenced again this evening, & the enemy returned a very heavy fire of shot & shells. The town was observed on fire in several places. The fire from our batteries, and from the Danish ramparts, resembled a constant succession of flashes of lightning, and the very firmament shook with the unceasing explosions. A Church steeple was set on fire by a shell lodging in the Belfry, and it fell, a mass of flame, with a tremendous crash, on the houses near it, and communicated flames to a whole street. The number of houses on fire, before day break exceeded four hundred. We afterwards learned, that in the course of this night, as two beautiful girls, sisters, were flying from a house, on which a shell had just fallen, a second shell fell, and exploded close to them; it blew one of them to pieces, and carried both the legs off the other, who expired before morning. The blaze of Copenhagen thus on fire, and the incessant roaring of guns, pouring destruction on other parts of the City which did not give evidence, in flames, of the effect produced by them, continued thro' the night. Day-break shewed a white flag on one of the ramparts, and our firing ceased.[122]

September 6th. A Flag of truce was sent from the enemy with proposals for a capitulation. Hostilities were ordered to cease, during the time that these proposals were taken into consideration, by our military and naval Commanders. Everything however was to remain in the batteries, ready to recommence firing at a moment's notice. The day passed with feelings of great anxiety, although we could not but perceive, that the Capital of Denmark was at our mercy, & we began already to anticipate the great prize money we should receive. No orders for firing were given during the day, and the night passed in quiet.

September 7th. Everything indicated that arrangements for the capitulation were in a forward state, not a shot was fired during the whole day. The batteries however continued manned, and ready for instant service. The servants of Officers were seen taking advantage of the day's quiet, and washing their masters' shirts and stockings, with other similar occupation. The picquets continued on the alert, but no fresh working parties were ordered, except to repair damages done in the batteries, by the enemies' shot.

September 8th. The capitulation was agreed upon, and signed.[123]

About ten o'clock in the morning, the Grenadiers of the 4th 7th 8th 23rd 32nd 50th 79th and 92nd regiments with a company of the Guards, and eight field pieces, took possession of the Citadel and dock-yard. The colours of the 4th regiment were planted in the Citadel. The number of British who had fallen, of the two services, was about 400 killed and wounded. Copenhagen had been defended by 5000 regulars and militia, 3000 sailors, and about 10,000 armed citizens. It would have been exceedingly difficult to have taken the place by assault, as the ditches are broad and deep, and the ramparts high, and in excellent order. The Dock-yard was one of the finest sights imaginable, and in the arsenal, of which we also took possession, were 16 sail of the line, 21 frigates, and many gun-boats, not exactly in a serviceable state, but in such, as to make it easy to rig them out quickly. There were also three seventy fours on the stocks, one of which was nearly finished. Nothing could be more complete, than the arrangement of this arsenal, which perfectly verified the inscription over the gate, "Quantitas, Qualitas, et Ordo." Each ship lay alongside a store-house, in the lower room of which were her anchors, masts, and spars. On the second floor, were her cables, ropes, and heavy rigging. On the third floor, were her top-sails, colours, and light rigging. There were cranes from each of these floors, from which to lower their contents into the ship. Guards were placed in each of these store-houses, and on board every vessel. In this duty the marines of the fleet took a part. Double sentries were placed at short distances from each other, all round the inside of the arsenal, which was inclosed partly by a palisade, and partly by a wall, and the gate which communicated with the city was locked and guarded. Every other possible precaution was taken against any attempts that might be made to set the arsenal on fire, during the time it was in our possession. This was by no means unnecessary as there were not wanting instances of such treachery on the part of the Danes.

September 9th. Strong working parties were sent from the different divisions of the army into the Arsenal, to assist in equipping the Danish fleet, and detachments of Sailors were joined to them, for this purpose. Sir Home Popham, the Captain of the fleet, took the command of the Arsenal and dock-yard, and assisted by other naval officers, gave the necessary directions for this being done, with the greatest possible expedition. By the articles of the capitulation, which secured to us the unconditional surrender of the Danish fleet, the British were to deliver up the arsenal, and quit the island of Zealand, within six weeks of its date, therefore the greatest dispatch was necessary, to do all our work in that time. Such however was the alacrity of the soldiers and sailors, that in the first nine days, fourteen sail of the line, were towed from the harbour to the road, tho' they had literally nothing but their lower masts in, when the fitting out began. It appeared afterwards, that we had a very narrow escape of losing this fleet, as the Crown Prince, when at Kiel, had sent a dispatch to General Pyman, with orders, that should he be compelled to surrender the city, he was to burn the fleet. The officer bearing this dispatch, was taken by some of our patroles, and Pyman never received it. Nothing could exceed the activity of affairs in the dock-yard and arsenal, the store-houses of which, were completely cleared of every sort of naval material they had contained, when we entered the place. The very ships on the stocks were taken to pieces, and brought off. The old and unserviceable ships, were destroyed, and on the 28th of October, by which time, all the ships and small craft, had been safely brought out, the last division of the British army, embarked without a casualty, and on the 29th in the morning, the British fleet with its prizes set sail for England.

During the time that we were in possession of the Citadel, none of the soldiers were permitted to enter Copenhagen; and the Officers themselves only in small parties, and with passes, signed by the General of their division. I went into the place several times, to look about me, and make purchases. The utmost gloom and surliness was depicted on every Danish countenance, and walking thro' the Streets was anything, but a pleasurable sensation. They had lost about 500 Soldiers and Sailors, killed and wounded, independent of those who fell, and were taken, in the attack of Sir Arthur Wellesly, on their entrenched Camp. Within the City, about 2000 men, women and children had perished. We thought that much blame attached to General Pyman, for not having sent out of the City as many of the women and children as chose to go, permission having been given him to do so, the day preceding the bombardment. The number of houses totally destroyed, was little short of 400, and there were few in the whole place, which had entirely escaped it's effects. The population of Copenhagen is estimated at 100,000. The public buildings are not remarkable for magnificence or beauty, but the streets are wide and regular, and the Police, excellent. The Post-man carrying about the letters, beats a large Gong, the sound of which in the streets, has a very singular effect. The King's palace forms a square, but is by no means, superb or elegant. In the centre, is a fine Statue of

Christian 4th; it was nearly destroyed by one of our shells, which struck, and injured the Pedestal a good deal. I visited a fine Museum, in which are many valuable curiosities. They appeared badly arranged, and the person who shewed them gave, in French, a miserable explanation of the collection. There was in the same range of building with the Museum, a fine collection of paintings, principally, I believe, of the Dutch school. The Traiteurs[124] of Copenhagen soon began to charge exorbitantly, for refreshments taken at their Coffee houses, by the English Officers, and the same sort of attention was quickly shewn us, in all the shops of the place, for any little purchases we might have to make, for friends at home. I did not observe much beauty in the women, but much taste and elegance in dress, and good figures.[125] The female fashions were principally French. I made several attempts to get into the Crown battery, which had annoyed Lord Nelson so much, when he attacked the place in 1801, but the jealousy of the Danes was such, that all sorts of difficulties were made, and I was not able to pay a visit to this celebrated fortress. I made however some excursions into the country, which resembles England exceedingly, and with the exception of a few miles immediately around Copenhagen, had not much suffered from the presence of so large an English army. We paid regularly for everything we wanted, and were abundantly supplied. We levelled our batteries to the ground, reembarked all our cannon & mortars, and before the stipulated six weeks had expired, little trace of our works remained.

On our return home, about six miles from Copenhagen, an eighty gun ship, the Neptune, one of our prizes, struck on a sand bank and could not be got off. The men were removed from her, and she was destroyed. It had been previously agreed, that Kronenberg Castle, which had remained in possession of the Danes during the whole of the siege, should not fire at us, as we passed it, but for fear of treachery, we kept as near the Swedish shore as possible. A sort of pier projects into the sea from the Swedish town of Helsinberg, opposite Elsinore, on which crowds of Swedes were assembled, as we passed, and we understood that the King himself[126] was on this pier, and witnessed the imposing sight of more than 800 sail of British men of war, and transports, filled with troops, bearing back to their country, as prizes, the entire navy of Denmark. The natural antipathy which these two opposite shores, have ever had for each other, is too well known, to leave a doubt, of the gratification which this spectacle afforded to the Swedish Monarch. It was Sunday, and to the surprize of the fleet, which was going at the rate of seven or eight knots an hour, with a fine leading wind, the signal was made from Lord Gambier's ship, to lay to, for prayers. At such a season of the year, and in such a sea, it was considered that the safe return to England of so valuable a fleet, having on board more than 40,000 souls, should not have been delayed an instant. When prayers were over on board the Admiral's ship, the signal was again given to make sail, and we proceeded, carrying every stitch of canvass we could set. During the 30th and 31st of October we had very bad weather and foul winds. My regiment was embarked on board the Brunswick, Captn Graves, an old broken backed seventy four, and the Danish ship, the "Heir Apparent," which vessel we were ordered to consider in our particular charge. She was manned with part of the crew of the Brunswick. As the gun-boats which we had taken at Copenhagen were not vessels of a description to send singly to England at this season of the year, and still too valuable to lose for want of an attempt to get them over the water, many of the ships of war, had one of them in tow, and no doubt had the weather proved favourable, they might, under this arrangement, have reached England in safety. One of these gun-boats was in tow of the Brunswick, with three men on board to steer. During a heavy gale on the night of the 31st a cry was heard from the gun-boat, that we were towing her under water, and calling loudly for help. We lay to immediately, and having got the men out with considerable difficulty, cut her away, and she went down. Several transports were lost, in the course of this night, and at day break we saw that only three of the men of war had been able to preserve their gun-boats, and of these three, only one I believe arrived in England. My berth, in the Brunswick, was in the Cockpit.[127] I was in a hammock, and not far from me, in a little corner partitioned off, slept the Doctor. In one of the heavy lurches given by the ship, during this blowing night, down came a pile of the iron pig ballast, with a tremendous crash. We thought the ship had gone to pieces. The Doctor got up from his bed, and in the act of closing and locking his door, said to me "God bless you my friend, take care of yourself, I won't be found by the fishes for some time to come." When the cause of the great crash had been ascertained, of course, the Doctor was not a little rallied for the wise precaution he had taken against being speedily used as bait. There was a heavy gale on the 1st of Novbr. and several ships hoisted signals of distress. Just as sun was setting on the evening of the 2nd the gale still continuing, we made Yarmouth roads, ran foul of the Cambrian frigate, and carried away her bowsprit.[128] We let go our anchor and were rubbing our hands in congratulation at the prospect of being landed the next day, when a signal appeared at the Mizen of the Centaur, which bore the flag of Sir Samuel Hood, asking, "where is your prize the "Heir Apparent", the Brunswick answered "We parted company with her in last night's gale." The Admiral hoisted "Put to sea immediately in search of her". conceive the countenances of all on board! It was a blowing November evening. The anchor was weighed and away we went, under close reefed top sails.[129] We cruized about, between the lights of the Kentish Knocks, which were frequently invisible during the squalls of that night. In one of these, when it was pitch dark, a tremendous crash was felt at the bows. Loud cries of distress followed, which sounded most lamentably in the gale, during the short moment that we were able to hear them. On we went in the roar and all was silent. We had gone over a ship, which no doubt had foundered, and every soul on board must have perished. In this wretched weather we continued beating about two days and nights longer, without seeing anything of our prize. On the third evening, provisions running short on board we put into Deal, and found her at anchor there. On the 6th of Novbr. we disembarked and marched for Colchester, where we arrived on the 13th having been absent from England, about four months, and in that time, had taken possession of the Capital of a Kingdom & brought back its whole navy. The successful result of this expedition, however little British blood had been spilled, gained for the navy & army, the thanks of Parliament. Admiral Gambier was made a Peer, and Lord Cathcart raised from a Scotch to an English Peerage. The justice and expediency of the expedition was long questioned, but as affairs in the north gradually developed themselves, the necessity of the measure, was very generally admitted, and a vote of thanks to Ministers, for their wise determination to take the step, was passed in both houses of Parliament. Napoleon himself, in an incautious speech, subsequently admitted, that he had lost the assistance of the Danish fleet, by their capture. The prize money granted to the two services, was, I believe, about a million of money. My own share as subaltern was ninety seven pounds.[130]

We found in Colchester barracks the 4th 7th and 28th regiments which had been employed in the expedition with ourselves, and had arrived there a few days before us.

II
North America 1808

An encounter between H.M.S. *Leopard* and the U.S.S. *Chesapeake* in June 1807 raised fears in Britain of a war against the United States. During a routine cruise through the Virginia Capes, the *Chesapeake* was approached by the *Leopard*. The bellicose commander of the British frigate ordered the Americans to surrender British deserters serving on board. After an exchange of fire that entailed some loss of life, a party from the *Leopard* boarded the *Chesapeake* and seized the deserters.[131] At first, Viscount Castlereagh was not sanguine about the results of a war with the United States and considered abandoning all of British North America, with the exception of Newfoundland. He soon changed his mind, however, and decided to defend the colonies. As part of his war measures, he appointed Major-General Sir George Prevost in June 1808 to succeed Sir John Wentworth as Governor of Nova Scotia.[132] The danger engendered by the so-called *Chesapeake* affair, and Castlereagh's resolve to defend British North America, also resulted in a sudden rush of troops to Nova Scotia in January 1808. The 1st Battalion/Royal Welch Fusiliers were among the troops despatched across the Atlantic. The unit marched from Colchester to Portsmouth at the end of January, and in the beginning of February sailed for Halifax. The transport carrying Browne took fully eight weeks to make the crossing.[133]

Halifax was a strategically important city, tucked away in a narrow protected waterway on the Atlantic seaboard of the peninsula of Nova Scotia. It was Britain's chief naval base in North America, and as such was visited frequently by the Royal Navy commander of the region. Halifax was also a garrison town, which, with its imposing citadel, well-built barracks and network of outer defences, comprised some several thousand British regulars. The Halifax or Nova Scotia Command was also responsible for the defence of several dependencies, which included New Brunswick, Cape Breton Island, Newfoundland and Prince Edward Island. The development of Halifax as a major naval and military point enabled the British government to use the base as an expeditionary staging area against threats to eastern Canada as well as against potential targets in the West Indies and along the Atlantic and Gulf coasts of the United States.

Halifax was also a city of some social pretensions. In 1800 it could boast over 1,000 houses, many of which were spacious and architecturally not unattractive. Some of these structures lined Argyle Street, the port's most fashionable thoroughfare. The Masonic Hall was one of the principal social centres of the city, which was fond of celebrating victories won by units of its garrison.[134] Because the port was an important garrison town, there was considerable social intercourse between Nova Scotians and the army and Royal Navy, a number of whom married local women.[135]

The reinforcement containing the 23rd also included the 7th and 8th Regiments of Foot (The Royal Fusiliers and the King's Regiment). The entire force consisted of about 3,000 men, all under the immediate command of Brigadier-General Daniel Hoghton. Once ashore, the 23rd was given the principal duty of garrisoning several of the outer forts which protected approaches to Halifax. Headquarters of the 23rd was at Annapolis Royal, some one hundred miles to the northwest of Halifax on the Bay of Fundy. Browne's company was posted to the old Eastern Battery. Located on the east side of the harbour, the work had been rebuilt as Fort Clarence just before Browne's service there. The principal feature of the fort was a massive martello tower constructed in the centre of the work.[136]

Despite war preparations in both British North America and the United States, an uneasy peace held. Peace provided Browne with ample time to attend balls and dinners which were held regularly. It also gave him the leisure to explore and celebrate the wonders of the vast trackless forests which lapped the glacis of the tiny isolated post. It was in this wilderness that Browne met the only person he befriended during his long service, a native American whom he named "Whisker Tom". These, as well as other diversions, would not last. Except for a second tour of duty in North America from March 1809 to November 1810, Browne would soon embark on a long and hard active service against the French, in Martinique and in Portugal and Spain.

VOYAGE TO NORTH AMERICA IN 1808

WHEN we arrived in Colchester barracks in Novembr. 1807, on our return from the expedition against Copenhagen, leaves of absence were granted to the usual proportion of Officers, & furloughs to ten soldiers per company. I had no particular motive, for availing myself of this leave, having seen my friends only a few months before, and remained with my regiment. We had little to do, as the weather was too wet & cold for drills, and the garrison was so large, that duties were light, to Officers of all ranks. We began to consider ourselves settled in quarters for some time to come. I was one of the mess committee,[137] and had obtained a vote, for new painting and fitting up our mess room, & I well remember how comfortable it looked, with its green walls, and dark red curtains. We laid in our winter stock of wine, voted an additional number of pamphlets and reviews, and each of us made his room as snug & tidy as possible. I undertook to teach some of the band glee singing, & the progress they made, was such, that in less than fourteen days, after they began, I produced them one evening, in the mess-room, in Calcott's glee of the "red Cross Knights." My brother Officers were delighted, and voted immediately, that a collection of the best glees should be sent for, for the use of our newly discovered singers. The band and it's improvement, became a sort of sudden hobby-horse. The subalterns subscribed for a new pair of French horns. The Commanding Officer permitted six boys to be added to the number, and the whole was put under my direction. This was amusing enough, as I scarcely knew my notes. The employment however interested me, and I was going on with great success. In anticipation of our prize money, which imagination, had made three times more than it actually proved, we invited friends to our mess much more frequently than was usual, and quite at a loss to dispose of money which we had not received (nor did we touch a half-penny of it for a year afterwards) we resolved on giving a ball, to the inhabitants of Colchester, who had never shewn us the slightest civility, but were rather remarkable for their unkindness to the military. The 4th and 28th regiments hearing of this, requested they might be allowed to join us, in this project, and by adding to the means, make it a more brilliant fête. We agreed to it, and a Major of each regiment was chosen to form a committee of management for the whole. To bring the affairs of the committee to a satisfactory conclusion, our gallant Majors found it necessary to have divers meetings at the "Three Cups" Inn at Colchester, where the ball was to be given. We could not guess, why one meeting was not amply sufficient for every purpose that was requisite, and it was only after our committee had held its third meeting, and no result reported, that we discovered, that they met over a capital supper, and the very best wines, to be paid for, from the funds destined for the ball. A stop was instantly put to this, the necessary arrangements were made, invitations given and accepted, and the ball took place. The families of Colchester were delighted with the entertainment, the daughters pleased with their gallant partners, Fathers and Mothers on the rack all the time — and we had the pleasure of discovering this means of spending our money. I do not believe, that this ball, opened a single door to us. When the bills attendant on it were paid, we found that we had still a great deal too much left of our expected prize money. My regiment was by no means satisfied, that it had only been favoured with a third share, of the expence of the Colchester ball, and we unanimously voted to give a masquerade in our mess room. This was accordingly done, and the expence was such, that we began to be almost satisfied with our performances, and that our spare cash would not prove particularly burdensome. New devices however, were not wanting, tho' on a smaller scale, to assist us in parting with what little was left, and in this sort of way we passed our time for about six weeks, and made preparations for about six months more of the same laughing careless life. Winter was in its glory — the ground was covered with snow — it was the 16th of Jany. — the mess room fire was burning unusually bright — the wine was voted unusually good, and an officer had just remarked, "this is really too comfortable to last long" — for which we thought him a croaker, when the Drum-Major came in, and delivered to the Commanding Officer a letter of Official form. A sort of chill passed thro' us all, and the blue-devils had evidently entered the mess room, with the Drum-Major. The letter was opened, and its contents were as follows: "The 23rd regiment will march in three divisions, to Portsmouth for embarkation, for foreign service. The 1st division will move by the enclosed route, on the 17th (this was the morning following) and the remaining divisions on the 18th and 19th. All Officers and men on leave of absence, to join the regiment at Portsmouth." Here was a finale to the evening's amusement. The very wind, as it whistled round the corner of the mess-house, seemed to laugh at us. The mess broke up. We sent for our servants, dispatched them to the washerwomen, and into Colchester, (at that hour of the evening) to warn those from whom furniture had been hired by Officers of the 1st division, who were to march in the morning, to attend at day-light to receive back their property. Other little bills had to be collected, and a thousand unforeseen arrangements to be made for so sudden an order of march. We inquired if any of the other regiments in the garrison, had been similarly favoured, and found it was not the case, but invitations came from them for the 2nd and 3rd divisions of the regiment, to dine with them, the days of their stay, as all our mess things were immediately packed up. The whole night was of course spent in bustle of every description, and at day-light the 1st division was under arms, baggage waggons loaded, and the usual wailings of sweet-hearts & wives, who were not allowed to accompany their Husbands, on foreign service, resounded in the barrack yard.[138]

There were about 15 Officers and 100 men on leave of absence in all parts of England, Ireland and Wales. Letters were written, ordering them to Portsmouth immediately, and here I may mention, that when the regiment sailed, which was three weeks afterwards, not a man was missing. My company belonged to the 3rd division, & on our arrival at Portsmouth, we found the 1st and 2nd on board ship. We embarked the day of our arrival. When the regiment was thus on board, two Officers of each ship, were appointed to purchase and lay in sea-stock. We subscribed about twenty pounds each, the government allowance of Bat and forage money[139] to subalterns, (twelve pounds ten,) being insufficient for that purpose. The most useful articles, were tea, sugar, coffee and biscuits. We had a tolerable quantity of port and sherry and spices of all kinds. Live sheep and pigs, fowls and ducks, with plenty of potatoes made this part of the business very comfortable. Some oranges and lemons were added in case of illness, nor was bottled porter forgotten. We purchased tin plates and dishes, and cups to drink from. The transport on board of which I was embarked, the "Royal Yeoman" was about *200* tons burthen. We were *eight* Officers and *200* men on board, besides her crew. The cabin was very small, and we slept in wooden partitions, just long and broad enough for one, fixed one above the other. There was a table in the middle of the cabin, fastened to the floor, and round it, just room for a wooden chair, which it was necessary to move, to enable us to step into our berths. This whole cabin was the most uncomfortable concern that can readily be imagined, but it was scarcely possible to be ill-humoured at it, as it produced so many ludicrous occurrences. The Officers and men were immediately divided into watches, with the exception of the Commanding Officer on board, one third of whom, were to be on deck night and day. This regulation is not strictly inforced when the weather is wet or very boisterous, as on these occasions, the men are allowed to go between decks, and only such portion remain above, as may be useful in working the ship. During the time that we remained at anchor at Spithead, there was a parade of the men on board, morning and evening, in forage caps and side-arms. After we had put to sea, the side-arms were discontinued. They were stowed away between decks with the muskets and other accoutrements. The morning parade at Sea, was merely one of cleanliness, the men appearing with bare necks and legs. In the afternoon there was only a roll-call to see that all were present, as in a transport crowded with troops, a man might fall over-board, and not be missed for some days, without some such arrangement. The men were divided into messes of six each, every man in turn acting as cook. When the Mess was of salt-pork, the cooks made a sort [of] pease pudding to eat with it. On taking it out of the Pot the six men to whom the Mess belonged, were assembled and in their presence, the Cook divided it, into six portions, but as one might contain a little more bone than the other, it was necessary, to provide against any intrigue, by which this could be assigned to one of the hungry expectants thro an unjust partiality of Mr Cook. One of the Mess was therefore blindfolded, and for further security his back was turned to the portions of Pork, which of course were rapidly cooling during this operation, and the Cook with a long stick, touching one of the portions, asked the blinded man, whose portion it was to be. He named one of the Mess, who instantly took up his portion, and moved off with it. If it was one of the bony bits, he cursed the fellow who had given it him, quite as a matter of course, and as if he had done it on purpose. This process was repeated, for five of the men, and the blind fellow took the bit that remained, for himself. With the Grog these precautions were unnecessary, as it was mixed in one common tub, and dealt out with the same Pint, to all. The grand source of grumblings, and abuse of Cooks, however, was Dumplings, which were made twice a week, and certainly most extraordinary mixtures they were, as fellows were sometimes obliged to make them, who had never before mixed flour and water in their lives. The Officers had a permanent Cook for their own Mess.

When we laid in our sea-stock, we had purchased a chess-board, and some packs of cards. The former could not possibly be used, except in fine weather, and we therefore amused ourselves principally with the cards. Play ran very high at times, and two Officers of the regiment carried their game at Cassino so far, that one lost every sixpence he had, and all his clothes and appointments; he was retiring from the table in despair, when, being a man fond of good eating, he suddenly recollected that he had a jar of pickles left, which he staked against a dollar with his comrade; luck took a turn, and he literally won back everything he had lost. Such is the usual routine of arrangements on board a transport. The comforts of these ships are I believe greatly increased since 1808, the year to which these remarks are applicable.

Before we sailed, the 7th 8th and 13th regiments also embarked. The "Penelope" Frigate, Captain Dick, and the "Banterer" Sloop of War, were appointed our Convoy. The former took on board, a new Governor for Nova Scotia, Lieut. General Sir George Provost, and the latter, General Houghton. Of these, Sir George died the day previous to that which was fixed for his trial by a Court Martial, for alledged misconduct as Commander in Chief of the Canadas, in the last American war, and the latter, was killed at the battle of Albuera,[140] at the head of the Fusileer Brigade.

We weighed anchor on the 13th of February, and were beating about the Channel the three following days. On the 17th the wind was more favourable, and we cleared the Land's-end. The breeze was fine on the 18th and thro' a fog, we could just distinguish the Isle of Ushant. Before dark, the Penelope made the signal to the Banterer that a strange sail was in the fleet, and indicated the quarter in which she was, directing the Banterer, at the same time, to give her chase. Our Sloop of war was a wretchedly bad sailor, and we could distinguish the stranger beating her hollow. The Penelope seeing this, lay to, and ordered the Ships of the fleet to keep as close as possible to her, during the night, as the stranger was certainly a French man of war or priveteer, and we thus moved on till day-light, like chickens close to the hen, with her wings out-spread to shield them from the Hawk above.

On the 19th we were in the bay of Biscay, with a favourable wind and Porpoises were rolling about us in shoals, and here for the first time, when on the watch at night, I saw that wonderful luminous appearance of the sea, of which I had so often read with astonishment. The track of the Ship, appeared a continued path of the most beautiful shining silver, and the water, as it fell back into the sea, from her chains, which had dipped into it, from time to time, when yielding to the wind, seemed as if torrents of liquid silver had been poured from them. It is said that this phenomenon is witnessed much more radiantly in the Torrid Zone, and especially in the Pacific Ocean, but even in the bay of Biscay the spectacle is magnificent. Every time that the side of the ship, as she rolls, emerges from the water, flashes of light seem to issue from the keel, and dart towards the surface of the sea. Some Philosophers, French as well as English, explain the appearance of these flashes, by the electrical friction of the water against the body of the advancing ship, but there are few points of Natural History respecting which, there have been so many disputes, as the light, thus emitted by the Ocean. Many are of opinion, that it originates from the decomposed fibrils of those microscopic animals, which exist in infinite quantities, in the depths of the sea. Cold or heat appear to have little influence upon this phenomenon, for on the very banks of Newfoundland it is often very strong, at the severest time of the winter. Sometimes too, every other circumstance appearing to be the same, it is very distinct on one night, and the following night there is scarcely any. That the saltness of the water must be concerned in it, there can, I think, be little doubt, as it is I believe, never observable on any of the great fresh-water lakes of America, nor in the Caspian sea. I have seen water in this state, rolling over the deck and leaving behind it, a track of sparkling light, and dropping from the very hand, in luminous points. I think that in my voyages across the Atlantic, I have observed the effect more vivid on dark nights, than on those of moon light.

We continued our course with varied winds till the 26th when about three o'clock in the afternoon, the Penelope made the signal of "land discovered". It proved to be St. Michael's one of the Azores. These islands are famous for their wine and fruits, and for their delightful climate. They were discovered in 1439, by a Dutch Merchant who was driven there by stress of weather. On his arrival at Lisbon, he boasted of his discovery, on which the Portuguese fitted out an expedition, took possession, and have kept them ever since. They are nine in number. On one of them, is the very high mountin called Pico.

On the 27th We passed by the remainder of the Azores or Western Islands, as they are sometimes called. We did not touch at any of them. 28th and 29th. The weather was fine and we made great progress in our voyage. The only thing of interest which now occurred from day to day, was the appearance of strange vessels now and then, to all of which, the moment they were discoverable on the horizon, one or other of our ships of war, immediately gave chase, and on coming up with them, made signals to the other, of who and what they were. The distance at which these signals are seen, and the rapidity with which communications are interchanged by them, can be scarcely comprehended by those who have not witnessed it. We saw some Grampus[141] and Turtle.

March 1st. This being St David's day, and mine a Welsh regiment, we did honour to our tutelar Saint, in the best manner that our situation would permit. The custom of the corps is, that on that day, immediately after dinner, when we are in barracks, one of the little drum-boys, rides a large goat, with which the regiment is always provided, round the Mess-room, carrying in his hand a dish of Leeks. Each Officer is called upon to eat one, for which he pays the Drummer a shilling. The older Officers of the regiment, and those who have seen service with it in the field, are favoured only with a small one, and salt. Those who have before celebrated a St. David's day with the regiment, but have only seen garrison duty with it, are required to eat a larger one without salt, and those unfortunates, who for the first time, have sat at the Mess, on this their Saint's day, have presented to them the largest Leek that can be procured, and unless sickness prevent it, no respite is given, until the last tip of its green leaf is inclosed in the unwilling mouth; and day after day passes by before the smell and taste is fairly got rid of. This may be a nasty way of making a Welsh Fusileer—and so it is, but not much worse than making a man pass thro' a dirty horse pond, in order to become a freeholder of Berwick. We could not of course, on board our little ship, render all the honours due to the day, but we had every thing dressed in Onions, and drank an extra glass of grog on the occasion.

March 2nd. It blew very hard this day and we discovered that one of our transports, the "Harriett", having on board Capt. Leaky's company, was missing.

March 3rd. The wind continues very fresh. We are, this day, by observation, fifteen hundred miles from Land's End, and about 1400 from Bermuda, which we understand, is to be our next rendezvous. We saw many of those wild and solitary birds called "Mother Cary's chickens".[142] Whenever they shew themselves, Sailors always foresee a storm. They appear singly, skimming closely over the tops of high and breaking waves, and always bear on their wings the exercrations of those on Ship board.

March 4th. It blew a gale of wind, the whole of this day & night, which continued till the 8th. On the morning of which day the "Banterer" carried away her main top-mast. Several of the transports received much damage.

March 9th. This day for the first time, we saw flying fish, one of them flew on board. A Turtle was also caught. In the evening, the rain fell in greater torrents than I ever remember to have seen it before.

March 11th. The weather was extremely hot. We were in latitude 28.49. Shoals of Tunny fish, Grampus's, Porpoises, and flying fish, were seen during the day.

March 12th. A dead calm. Our longitude was 52.33. and latitude 28.14. We got out a boat, and dined on board the Lord Collingwood, one of the regimental transports. She was the Head quarter ship, and in the evening, the other vessels got as close to her as they could, when the band began to play country dances, and the soldiers with such women as were embarked, danced till past mid night. About that hour, a light breeze sprung up, and we separated again. This little scene of gaiety was repeated whenever the fineness of the weather permitted, and an interesting one it was, that of British soldiers, dancing to their native tunes, on the bosom of the deep, in such latitudes.

March 14th. A heavy gale of wind to-day, with much thunder and lightning, which continued with more or less violence until the 20th when there was a dead calm. The storm of the preceding six days, had left so heavy a swell on the sea, that we were in danger of rolling our masts over board. At each roll, the yard-arms almost touched the water, and it was quite impossible to stir on the decks. The helm was lashed up, and we remained in that state about twelve hours. The breakage of chairs, tables, bottles &c. on board was considerable, and seasickness began again, with all its abominations. It was some days, before our stomachs recovered this rough treatment. To those who may not have witnessed a really high sea, it may convey some idea of what it actually is, by my stating that two ships are not unfrequently so near each other, as to be only separated by a single wave, and that when that wave intervenes between them, the top-gallant masts of the one, are not to be seen from the decks of the other. It can only be compared to two houses in distinct parallel vallies, with a range of mountain between them, and the effect of looking out of a ship, on the top of one of these waves, down upon another in what is called the trough of the sea, is a spectacle too magnificent for me to describe with justice.

March 20th. We dined again on board the Collingwood, &

established with that ship, a code of signals by which we might converse for our amusement. A breeze springing up in the evening, we were unable to rejoin our own ship the "Royal Yeoman" and were left on board the Head-quarter vessel for three days, consuming their stock, very inconveniently as we had now been at sea six weeks, and it began to run short.

March 21st. The "Penelope" made the signal of "land discovered" and directed the ships having the 13th regiment on board, to make the nearest Port, but thick weather came on almost immediately, and we were unable to make this land again till the 24th. It was the Islands of Bermuda or Sommers Islands. They were discovered by a Spaniard, called Bermudas in 1527, but were not inhabited before 1609, when Sir George Sommers was cast away upon them. They belong to England. These Islands are four in number, low, and very difficult for vessels to make. They are also of dangerous approach, being surrounded with rocks. The climate is said to be excellent, and indeed the Myrtle and Cedar trees with which they are covered, give proof of it. They are distant from the American coast about 500 miles, and our establishment of a capital Dockyard with all its store-houses and other conveniences offers a strong temptation to the United States in any future war to attempt its destruction.[143] This Dock-yard is the rendezvous of our ships of war on the North American station during the winter months. There are barracks also for a regiment, and there is usually one stationed there. There is at Bermudas a Whale fishery, tho' not on a large scale, and several boats were engaged in it, whilst we were off the island. We did not come to anchor, but only lay to, whilst the ships that had the 13th regiment on board, entered the harbour, as that corps was destined to remain there for the present. About three in the afternoon we continued our course for the American shore, with a fresh and fair wind.

March 28th. We saw many Dolphin to day, and a flying fish fell on our decks, whilst attempting to cross the ship.

29th. We had very heavy squalls to day and foul wind in latitude 37.50. The weather was severely cold, altho' but five days since, when off Bermudas the heat was such that we were obliged to have awnings over the decks, and even with such a screen, the pitch shewed itself between the planks of the deck, and we were greatly oppressed by it.

March 30th. In a heavy gale of wind we ran foul of the "Ocean" Transport, and as the sea was very high we were for some time in considerable danger, but we providentially got clear, with no other damage than the injury which our main rigging sustained. The Officers were at dinner in the cabin when this accident occurred, and the shock was so severe, that it upset every thing in an instant, we thought the ship had struck on a sunken rock. We instantly ran on deck, where a great scene of confusion prevailed, ordered down all the women who were screaming and at their wits end, & many of the men also, and thus succeeded in restoring order. The "Ocean" being much the larger vessel, it was thought for a few minutes that she would have got us under, and under this impression, several of our men quitted the ship, and went on board her, where they were obliged to remain until our arrival in America. Next to fire and a Sea-shore, I think running foul, the greatest danger to which vessels are exposed.

April 1st. A suspicious vessel hove in sight to windward of the Penelope, who sent the Banterer in chase of her, but she was too bad a sailor to come up with her, & rejoined the fleet, night came on and we saw nothing more of her.

April 2nd. A strong current, running a North Easterly course was very observable to-day. It is the current of the gulf of Florida.

3rd. There are strong indications of land this day. We saw sea-gulls, and sea-weed, and the water looks rather muddy. A Sloop of war, made signal by Telegraph to the Penelope, that the Rochefort Squadron, had been cruizing lately in this latitude. We thought it therefore probable, that the suspicious ship which we saw on the 1st was one of them.

4th. Wind fair, and blowing hard. The indications of land become more frequent and decided.

5th. About 4 o'clock this evening, the Commodore made the signal of "land discovered". The wind increased to a gale accompanied with snow and intense cold. At day-light next morning, we found we had lost the fleet, and to add to our vexation, a heavy squall carried away our main-yard, & it took us the whole of the next day to splice it.

6th. The gale continued with snow, and a thick fog.

7th. The weather cleared up, and we proceeded onwards in a North West direction, and about 11 at night, by the light of a beautiful moon, the sentries at the Ships bows discovered land. It was the coast of Nova Scotia.

8th. A fine Southerly wind. Halifax light-house, hove in sight about 10 in the morning. A boat was seen making for us, which proved to be a Pilot. We took him on board, & at three in the evening cast anchor, in

Halifax harbour, where we found the whole fleet safely arrived, except the "Harriett", which had been missing since the 2nd of March. She did not arrive until the 13th May, having met with several accidents which had caused this delay.

13th. The Troops landed. The 7th and 8th Regiments went into barracks in Halifax. The 23rd had their head-quarters assigned them at Annapolis Royal on the bay of Fundy, and only landed such portion of the corps, as were required to occupy the out-posts, round Halifax. Part of the Regiment had therefore to begin a fresh voyage without landing. It was not however of long duration, as they arrived at Annapolis three or four days after their departure. Before they sailed to their new head-quarters, the Regiment determined to give a ball to the inhabitants of Halifax, not one of whom they had ever seen. They did not know a creature in the place, & there was a momentary pause, owing to the difficulty of knowing to whom we could send invitations. I made known to some of my brother Officers, that I had brought out with me letters of introduction to Sir John Wentworth, the Governor whom Sir George Prevost was to relieve. The letters were from my Mother, who had known him in England, and had invited Lady Wentworth to pass some time with her in Wales a few years before, when she came to England for her health. The whole difficulty was at an end. I was commissioned to wait on Lady Wentworth, to make known our wishes to her, & ask her for a list of the families whom we could invite. She laughed heartily at our gallantry, gave us the lists we required, and away went the invitations. Every creature came, and we danced till nearly day-light, in the assembly room of Halifax, or the Free Masons' hall, I forgot which it was. We took leave of our Partners, went on board our Ships, in silk stockings and shoes, a fresh and favourable breeze sprung up, and before they could well have risen from their beds, not a trace of us was to be seen. The ball had cost us about five pounds each, & when sober reflection came over us, we could not help asking ourselves what on earth we had given it for. Halifax is a neat town containing about 5000 inhabitants exclusive of the garrison, which is usually from one to two thousand men. The houses are of wood with few exceptions, the government house is a fine stone building, with a handsome lawn in front. The barracks are very good and allowances of every kind liberal. The defences of the town and harbour appear very strong. There is a large Fort on the Citadel hill, which completely commands the town. There is another on an island about half way across the harbour, called

Georges' Island, and over the water, a third, called Fort Clarence, or the Eastern battery. There are also strong batteries at the entrance close to the Sea, and the whole of these together would render the place of very difficult capture. There was an extensive arsenal and dock-yard, which I have since understood has been broken up. At the time of our arrival at Halifax, Sir John Warren had his flag flying on board the "Swift-sure", a seventy four. She was the only line of battle Ship under his orders. The rest of his squadron was composed of frigates, and sloops of war. Halifax is the capital of Nova Scotia, and is governed by a Lieutenant Governor, and an upper and a lower house of representatives, resembling our Lords and Commons. Sir John Wentworth, who was now to be relieved by Sir George Provost, had been Lieutenant Governor of the province sixteen years. The charge of the different out-posts of the province, having been entrusted to the 23rd Regiment, Officers and different proportions of the corps, were detached to the several Forts of which these out-posts were composed, and the company to which I belonged, Captain Keith's, was sent to the Eastern battery, a fortification across the water, which was there about 2 miles across, and almost opposite Halifax, from which place we used daily to receive the parole and counter sign by Telegraph. Not long after our being quartered at this post, Captain Keith was appointed brigade Major, and I was left in command. I had under me about sixty men, and a Serjeant and twelve of the Artillery. We had a nice four oared boat attached to the post, a Corporal and four men, being its Cockswain and crew. This was our mode of communication with Halifax, & for our marketing and Mess comforts. I bought fishing lines, and used to occupy myself and the crew of my boat in fishing for my little garrison. We caught fish in the greatest abundance, and the men were capitally supplied with it. To pay for the expence of keeping up this fishing tackle, I charged the married men of the company a penny, and the single ones a halfpenny each per month. The fish we caught were Cod, Haddock, Macharel, and Halibut a large and coarse species of Turbot. Crabs and Lobsters were also in the greatest abundance. The barrack in which we lived, was on a bare rocky bit of ground, and it occurred to me that I would make a garden to it. For this purpose, instead of having an evening Parade with my men, I used to order them on fatigue for about an hour each day, and as I had masons and all sorts of trades in the company, the rough stones all about the place, soon assumed the shape of a regular garden wall, enclosing about an acre of ground in front of the Post. We got spades and pick axes from the Engineers at Halifax. The men took a hearty and good humoured interest in this little improvement, and before two months were over, I had the satisfaction of seeing a remarkably pretty garden added to the Eastern battery. I then set to work in rear of the barracks, cleared about two acres of ground and allotted it in six portions to the company to plant their potatoes in, and this too, I surrounded with a wall, made of the stones which had covered the ground.

My next amusement was to plant an avenue of Poplars from the barrack down to the little wooden Pier, from which we used to go on board our boat, and here I may gratify myself by saying, that these gardens & this Avenue of Poplars, have been the object of care and preservation by every Officer who has succeeded to the command of the Post, to the year 1828, in which I am making this little memoir, as I am assured by an Officer of rank who has lately left that country.

There were several Lakes about a league in rear of the Eastern battery, in which the Indians told me, were plenty of Trout. I have been a Trout fisher all my life, and became anxious for a better access to them thro' the thick woods, which separated them from my Post, than the sort of Indian path, which is visible one day and lost the next. Here then was work for my detachment. At ten in the morning about the time when with a favourable wind we used to hear the bands in Halifax, announce that guard-mounting was going on there, I used to have my little detachment on parade, in full dress and mounted my own guard of a Corporal and six. I then had a little drill of light Infantry manoeuvres for about an hour, and all parade duties of the day were over. There was not a sick man in the detachment. From the time that I determined to get at the Trout Lakes, of which the Indians had spoken, I used to assemble about twenty of the men, an hour after they had dined, and to work we went. My friends the Engineers in Halifax again assisted me and lent me Axes. Having made an Indian indicate to me, the direction in which these Lakes lay with his finger, I ascertained with a compass the exact point and began to blaze a path. Blazing is the term used in that country for opening out a road thro' forests, and it is done in the following manner. Five or six men are sent out into the wood in an exact line, in the direction where you mean to make the path, and each with his Axe, cuts a large slice of bark from opposite sides of the tree nearest to him, keeping the line with the trees; so marked, six more men are sent out, and the process is repeated. Half a dozen active fellows will mark about a quarter of a mile onwards in this manner in the course of a few hours.

Sometimes a bog or a morass is met with, and this occasions a great delay as trees must be felled on which to pass it. Cutting the bark on both sides of the tree is necessary to give you marks in the dark forests of these countries, by which to return to the spot from which you started. When about 500 yards is thus marked, trees are felled right and left, sufficient for the width of your intended path, and it is levelled and made good according to fancy. I had a fancy for a very good one to the Trout Lakes.

In the course of two months, my intended road was finished, and I had opened a direct line of communication from the Eastern battery to three Lakes.[144] They were not of much extent, & communicated with each other by narrow channels, in which there was some current. This made me conclude that a stream must run thro' them, and a river flow from the lower one. As I could not ascertain this by walking round the banks, the woods growing to the very edge, I made some men of my detachment carry a Canoe up, and in that we paddled along till we found the stream I was in search of. It was an evening of May when I first saw this little stream, and Trout after Trout was rising in it to the flies which were skimming its surface. Here was a discovery for a Fly-fisher. I paddled back as fast as I could, told my comrade at the barracks, Lieut. Farmer, of the happy result of my exploring expedition, & we determined to start at day-light with our rods. Off we went the next morning, with two soldiers, Havre sacks full of provisions, and Canteens full of Shrub,[145] a good flint and tinder box with two rifles, and soon arrived on the ground of our intended sport. It was a wild romantic spot, such as we read of in descriptions of the forests of America. The corner of a large Lake, had contracted itself into a narrow channel, overhung with fir and birch wood, almost to the waters edge. The stream was not very rapid, and here and there a black rock shewed its head in it. The depth varied from two to five feet. We made the two Soldiers haul the Canoe ashore, and light a fire, whilst we prepared our fishing tackle. In less than an hour, we took more Trout, than we could possibly carry back to the barracks, and determined to stop fishing and explore the stream a little. In doing this we came to a hole which was literally alive with fish, one of which we took. It was exactly like an English Herring, but a good deal larger. We afterwards learned that these fish were called Gaspereaux of which immense quantities are taken at this particular season, when they swarm in nooks and pools of rivers. Their heads and tails are cut off, and salted for winter provision. In exploring the woods we saw several tracks of Bears, and some of the red legged Partridge, which when disturbed always light on trees. My companion shot one of them. We roasted our Trout at the edge of the Lake, where our Soldiers had made the fire, drank some Shrub grog and slept for an hour or two. It was dark before we got back to our barrack, and we found that during our absence, Sir George Prevost had paid an unexpected visit to the Post. I expected to have heard that he had found fault with the absence of both the Officers at the same time, but so far from it, he had expressed himself greatly pleased with the improvements which had been made there, and in the evening, I received by a boat, an invitation to dine with him the following day. However flattering, I would willingly have avoided this as I intended to have repaired to my fishing ground again. I got home from the Governor's about eleven that night. It was a beautiful moon, and whether I was under the influence of His Excellency's good dinner, or of the free circulation of his capital wine I know not, but on my arrival at the Eastern battery, nothing would satisfy me, but an immediate excursion to the Lake. I called up two men of my company, who must have thought their Commanding Officer little less than mad, and off we set, with a rifle, a fowling piece and a fishing rod. I fished by moon-light and caught some delightful Trout. The Soldiers made a fire, I was beginning to cool, and be somewhat fatigued. Day-light had broke, and thinking it probable that this might be the scene of many a future excursion, I amused myself in planning out a hut, sent back one of the Soldiers for six men, spades and axes, and began with my remaining assistant to collect boughs of the Spruce fir, for weaving into its sides and covering it. Whilst we were thus occupied, I heard a whistle, and shortly afterwards a shot, it was evidently from a piece loaded with ball, tho it did not fly in our direction. We stopped our work, and listened for about ten minutes, but hearing nothing more, proceeded. A quarter of an hour afterwards, we thought we heard a crackling of leaves or boughs not far from us and stopped again, but all was silent. I thought this might possibly be a Bear, and we took rifle and fowling piece in hand, but as all continued quiet, and as I was aware the Bears seldom or never attack Man, we laid them down again, and resumed our occupation. In less than a minute afterwards, I heard close behind me, an odd sort of a smothered laugh, and was not a little startled. I looked round and saw a tall Indian, his rifle in his hand, and two dogs close to his legs. He appeared about fifty, a broad dark face with high cheek bones, a sort of jacket and pantaloons of blue cloth was his dress, with mocassins on his feet. He had on his head a little cap of blue cloth something like a small hat without a brim, in the crown of which was a hole, and out of it stuck some red feathers. Seeing my surprize he held out his hand without stirring from the spot where he stood, to which I replied by giving him mine. He then came forwards laughed at our work, and sat himself down on the ground with his rifle between his knees, and his dogs close to him, near the spot where our Canteen of grog was lying. I was not long in offering him a drink, and I really thought his mouth would never have left the liquor. His satisfaction was such, that his very dogs began to wag their tails. He comprehended instantly, all we were about, shewed by signs that he knew perfectly well, where we came from, shook hands with the Soldiers, over and over again, as a pledge of friendship, and looked at me, as tho' he had evidently discovered I was an Officer, and that he could not take such liberties with me. He then laid down his rifle, and began to assist us in our work. I was delighted with the acquisition of such an Artist, and his signs and movements amused me excessively. He quickly gave us to understand, that we could do nothing without hatchets, and as quickly understood from me, that I expected men with them. The party I had sent for from the barracks was not long in arriving, and they were astonished to find us and our new companion on such excellent terms. We built our hut, prevailed on our Indian friend to accompany us back to the Eastern battery, where we lodged and fed him so well, that he vowed us eternal friendship, by signs that were sufficiently intelligible. Discovering the next day, a few black hairs on the sides of his cheeks, which is very unusual with Indians I gave him the name of "Whisker Tom", by which he was known till the time of his death.[146] This took place, as I have since heard, about ten years after my regiment left America.

On one occasion not long after this, Whisker Tom, made his appearance at my Post, bringing me a present of a young Bear. I made a sort of den for it of Spruce Fir, put a leather collar round his neck, with a long iron chain, and fastened it to a strong post driven into the ground. The creature gradually became tame, and the Soldiers made quite a play thing of it. It was fed on fish and offal of every description. Some time afterwards however, it bit one of the men very severely, broke loose and was shot in the woods. My acquaintance with Whisker Tom, soon advanced into an intimacy, and he became the companion of my wandering hours and expeditions. I bought three Canoes, and learnt from him the perfect management of them. He frequently met me by appointment at the Lakes behind the barracks, and used to paddle with me to different spots, where he knew the Trout to be abundant. I never had such sport in my life as at this time, fishing on Lakes and in Streams, on which the artificial fly had never been thrown before. At length I ventured to put Masts and Sails to my Canoes, and from that moment, Whisker Tom would never enter one of them, but viewed my operations with the greatest aversion. I made my Masts of the lightest wood possible and my sails of white cotton. One of the Canoes I painted exactly like a Mackarel, and gave her the name of that fish. They were ticklish sort of things, but sailed capitally before the wind, altho' they could not bear a breeze in any other direction, making nothing but lee-way, and in constant danger of upsetting. I used to sail among the ships of the fleet as they lay at anchor, in my little Mackarel, and the Officers and Sailors would crowd upon the deck to see her. Sir John Warren was so much amused at the exhibition, that he sent me a present of a white silk ensign and pennant for her. This Admiral had heard of my constant expeditions to the Lakes, and was very desirous of reconnoitering them, for the purpose of ascertaining if they could not be made of use, as water communications with the interior, an object of some importance at that time as we were beginning to be on very uncomfortable terms with the Americans and every facility which could be given to the transport of munitions of war into the interior was well worth improving. He asked me to dine, that we might arrange an expedition for this purpose, which was accordingly done, and I have in my possession the plan which he proposed for our adoption.

We set off on this enterprize a few days afterwards, my friend Whisker Tom, and myself in the leading Canoe, four others following with the Admiral, and the Officers he had chosen to accompany him. We passed a couple of days in the survey, sleeping under the Spruce Fir, and living capitally well in every respect. The Admiral appeared exceedingly gratified with his little tour and from that time I became a constant guest at his table. I am not aware that these Lakes were ever made available for the purposes which had been the object of this inspection. When I afterwards embarked for Spain, I sent my little Mackarel with her white sails up, and her Ensign and Pennant flying, into the dock yard, as a present to the Admiral, who when he learned the name of the Man of War (the "Diadem", Captain Phillimore) on board of which I was to embark, wrote the kindest possible letter about me to the Captain, whose attentions to me in consequence, were unceasing during the time that I sailed with him.

My time was passing thus happily, and yet I could not but painfully perceive, that I was making no progress in my profession, there was no promotion whatever in the Regiment, and delightful as this roving sort of life was to me, I had a pining for that sort of service, which would bring advancement with it. Our position in America, unless a war broke out, was little better than garrison duty tho' it was certainly free from the tedium of an English barrack yard. Day however passed after day, and I never got a step by these reflections. I knew it was usual to keep Regiments in North America for a long time, and saw in the army list, the venerable names of Subalterns, who had been there some twelve or fifteen years, and still remaining in Canada, at a fearful distance from the rank of Captain, and I seriously thought of exchanging into some other Regiment. Then came Whisker Tom and my fishing rod, and I felt quite happy and contented where I was. Then again came the News-papers with accounts of the expeditions, fitting out for Spain, and this renewed the feeling of regret, that we were so far removed, from the scene that appeared to be opening there. We were not long however destined to remain idle.

Various rumours had been for some time in circulation of an intended attack against the French possessions in the West Indies, but they were repeated and contradicted so often, that we began to pay little attention to them, and perhaps the less, as there was no particular disposition in the Regiment for West-Indian service.[147] In the midst of these doubts and calculations, we received an order to prepare for active service, and for immediate embarkation.

III
Martinique 1808

Preparations for the attack against Martinique, which had been conquered by British forces in 1794, but restored to France by the Peace of Amiens in 1802, began at Barbados in November 1808. What apparently triggered this activity was the interception, during the summer of 1808, of some despatches from the Governor of Martinique, Admiral Louis-Thomas Villaret de Joyeuse,[148] to the French Government. The Admiral requested supplies and additional troops. He also described the state of the island as virtually defenceless. Among the captured documents was a complete order of battle for the garrison of Martinique. It was dated April 1808, and it was an official statement since it had been compiled by the island's colonial prefect. According to the report, the garrison contained only 2,750 regular troops and sailors, and 3,500 rather unreliable National Guardsmen. The regulars belonged to the 26th Regiment (2 Bns.), a veteran unit of the fighting in Egypt in 1801, and the 82nd Regiment (3 Bns.), a motley corps composed primarily of foreigners, refractory conscripts and 'mauvais sujets'.[149]

Prior to the decision to attack Martinique, British operations against the island (and also against Guadeloupe, which was subsequently conquered by Britain in 1810) were limited to a naval blockade. However, a chronic shortage of sailors and ships prevented the Royal Navy from maintaining an effective quarantine of the island. Consequently, Martinique continued as a haven for privateers, to the detriment of British trade. The disclosure that Martinique's defences were inadequate thus prompted Britain to eliminate this nest of commerce raiders. The commander of the British expedition was Lieutenant-General Sir George Beckwith (and not Sir Thomas Beckwith as Browne reported incorrectly in his Journal).

In November 1808, Beckwith had reluctantly agreed to the recommendation of Rear-Admiral Alexander Cochrane, that Martinique should be attacked by a combined army and naval expedition. Beckwith's unwillingness helps to explain the indecision which was reported in his council of war as late as the beginning of January 1809. Browne noted in his Journal that there was even talk of the expedition being cancelled. This, according to Browne, alarmed the troops and provided him and several of his brother officers with the excuse (as if one were really needed) to get drunk, which they promptly did at one of Bridgetown's (Barbados) notorious taverns. Beckwith, however, had good reason to hesitate in undertaking this major operation, for he had to maintain simultaneously garrisons in thirteen colonies, from St Martin in the Leewards to the north, to Surinam, well over 1,000 miles to the south, on the northeast coast of South America. He had just over 15,000 rank-and-file to defend these far flung garrisons. Had he not been promised reinforcements from Halifax for the campaign, he probably would have refused to cooperate with Cochrane. This reinforcement comprised a company of Royal Artillery and three infantry battalions, the 1st/7th Regiment, the 1st/8th Regiment and the 1st/23rd Regiment. This welcomed reinforcement was under the command of Major-General Sir George Prevost.

The Halifax reinforcements may have contributed to Beckwith's indecision regarding the operation against Martinique. There is clear evidence, according to a historian of the Royal Artillery, to show that throughout the campaign Prevost's force was regarded as an independent force co-operating with Beckwith, rather than as an integral component of Beckwith's army. This claim may well be true, though, it is not substantiated. What is certain is that because of the strength and health of the Halifax reinforcements, the bulk of the work of the campaign fell on Prevost's units.[150]

The principal operation of the campaign was the task of besieging Fort Desaix, or Fort Bourbon. Built atop, and at the extremity of, one of the steep and rugged hills which nearly envelop the capital of Martinique, Fort Royal, this most formidable work was defended by more than sixty heavy guns, forty field guns, fourteen mortars, six howitzers, and a garrison of at least 2,000 troops. The strength of this imposing fortification is evident in the Reverend C. Willyams' 1796 drawing of Forts Bourbon and Louis, or Fort de France, and Lieutenant-Colonel Alexander Whalley Light's pen and ink sketch of 1809. Light took part in the Martinique expedition as the commander of the old 25th Regiment, the King's Own Borderers, which was part of the Reserve Brigade, First Division. It was also exceedingly difficult to approach this work from the interior of the island, as was necessary, since the fort was immediately protected by a large outer work on the crest of the ridge. There were also very few draught animals to haul the guns and stores up neighbouring slopes; and, according to one authority, there were no roads to the actual sites selected for the batteries.[151] A map of the area, prepared for the Army in June 1798 by Major Charles Shipley, Commander of the Royal Engineers in the West Indies, does reveal, however, numerous roads and tracks in the general area of the siege.[152] Nonetheless, the main problem facing the besiegers was hauling over 2,000 tons of ordnance, ammunition and stores[153] from the landing beaches to positions from which an effective fire could be directed on the fort. The immense labour of landing and hauling this mass of equipment had to be performed by the troops, assisted by some four hundred sailors landed from Cochrane's ships. But on the morning of 19 February, thirteen days after this material was landed on the beaches, forty-six guns were in place and the bombardment of Fort Desaix began. During the next five days approximately 4,000 shot and 10,000 shells were fired at the sprawling fort. The bombardment continued unabated and with effect during this time. One of the shells penetrated the main magazine at 6 p.m. on 24 February, and resulted in a tremendous explosion. This precipitated the capitulation of the French later the same day, at 10 p.m.[154]

Because of their gallant resistance, the garrison of Fort Desaix was permitted to march out of the fort with the honours of war. The prisoners were to be sent to France in British transports, there to be exchanged, rank for rank, for British prisoners. Napoleon, however, refused to honour this arrangement, with the result that these unlucky soldiers were subsequently shipped instead to prisoner-of-war depots in Britain.[155] Browne described the unabashed happiness of these men as they sailed for Europe. Their evident joy can be logically attributed to the realization that they had survived the climate and were leaving the dreaded West Indies. Admiral Villaret de Joyeuse and staff, on the other hand, were sent to France, free of all restrictions.

The Martinique campaign was noteworthy for, among other things, the rapidity with which British troops and sailors achieved their objectives, and the accurate and sustained violence brought to bear on Fort Desaix by the Royal Artillery. Nine regiments were subsequently awarded battle honours for the Martinique campaign. The Royal Artillery Regiment was granted no less than two honour titles.[156]

Prevost's force arrived back in Halifax around mid April 1809, and all were given a tumultuous reception. The news of the reduction of Martinique did much to restore public confidence after the shock caused by the death of Sir John Moore at Corunna and the British evacuation from Spain in January 1809. The officers were fêted at an elaborate dinner, the high point of which was the presentation of an enormous cake in the shape of Fort Desaix.[157]

1808. JOURNAL OF AN EXPEDITION TO MARTINIQUE

NOVEMBER 27th. This day just eight months after our arrival from England, we mustered on the grand Parade at Halifax, 884, rank and file, marched down to the waters edge and embarked. The Commanding Officer had received orders to leave behind the weakly men of the Regiment, with such Officers as were least fit for active service. A hundred and ten of this description were picked out and formed into a Company. The Officers left behind were, Captain Cortlandt, who was married, Lieutenant Griffith who was an old and infirm Subaltern, and Lieut. Treeve, who was only just recovered from a severe indisposition. Just as I was stepping into the boat, I felt a large cold hand take hold of mine. It was poor Whisker Tom, I could not misunderstand this mark of his attachment, tho' his countenance was one of perfect apathy. As I squeezed his hand, I slipped a couple of Dollars into it, and lost sight of him. The 7th and 8th Regiments each leaving behind them, as we had done a Company of their invalids, embarked at the same time, with two companies of Artillery, completely equipped for active service. Sir George Prevost took the command, & General Houghton was also appointed to the Staff of the expedition. The wind was unfavourable till the 6th of December, when we weighed Anchor, with a fine fresh breeze, and as we passed close to one of the Piers, I observed sitting on it, his knees up, and head rested upon them — Whisker Tom — who remained fixed to the spot, as long as I could observe him. I waved my hand to him repeatedly, but his only recognition was, a gentle bow of the head. Before dusk we had lost all sight of land, & were once more on the bosom of the Atlantic.

December 9th. It blew a very heavy gale, this day and night and about

12 o'clock, during the time that the Watch was relieved, & the helm passing into a fresh hand, owing to some unskilful management, the Ship broached to, and was on her broad-side for about a minute in great danger, nor did she right without shipping a great deal of water, which kept us hard at the pumps for a considerable time. This was in Latitude 32.20.

13th. Continue our voyage prosperously. Our Commodore lay to the whole of this evening, for Ships astern to come up.

14th. It blew a heavy gale of wind to day, accompanied by loud thunder, and the most vivid lightning I had ever seen. It struck the Ship about 10 o'clock in the morning, having been attracted by an iron cap on the mizen-top-gallant-mast head. I was on watch supporting myself by the mizen-mast, & a man of my company close to me, was resting his body and head against it. He was struck dead on the spot. I was knocked down, as were the two men at the helm, which the mate of the Ship seeing, ran instantly to lay hold of it, or the Ship could probably have capsized. Twelve of our Soldiers on deck were knocked over. It passed also into the cabin, the door of which was open, and hurt severely Lieutenants Farmer & Wynne who were sitting there. In its passage thro' the cabin (the window of which was fortunately open, and let it escape,) it separated a rifle barrel from its stock, with which we had been shooting at Porpoises the day before, & extracted some Brass nails out of one of the Officers' Canteens. Our mizen-mast was split from top to bottom, and we hoisted a Union-Jack, in our shrouds[158] immediately, as a signal of distress. The Penelope Frigate, which was again our convoy, was not long in observing our situation, bore down towards us instantly, and remained by us till the gale had partly subsided, when she sent a boat, with a Surgeon and Carpenters, both of whom were greatly needed by us. I had suffered a good deal in my eye-sight and hearing, by the effects of the flash, & my left arm & breast had a curious shrivelled appearance. The Surgeon ordered me to be well rubbed with spirits, but I was for a long time, in a sort of stupefaction, not being able at all to conceive, what had happened to me. What I remember of the flash, is, that it was a quick & sharp explosion, exhibiting a vivid whitish light, the sound was much sharper than the report of a cannon, and more like the crack of an electric spark. The shock was that of electricity to an immense degree. One of the men who had been struck, lost his senses, and was I believe, subsequently discharged from the Regiment, as an idiot. The body of the poor fellow, who fell near me, was committed to the deep the next day. He was sewed up tightly in his blanket, in which under the soles of his feet, were placed two nine pound shot, so that when the body slid off the hatch-way, from which it was lowered towards the water, it descended at once, feet foremost, into that fathomless sea, and we had passed by, before the wave could well close over it, sailing as we then were, at the rate of ten knots an hour. This accident from the lightning occurred in Latitude 32.11.

December 18th. The weather was very fine, and the wind fair. We saw quantities of Dolphin and flying fish to day, and the beautiful Nautilus, with its azure coloured sail, was skimming over the wave.

21st. This day we crossed the tropic of Cancer, commonly called the line; but erroneously so, as the real line or Equator is in Latitude 0. whereas the tropic of Cancer is in 23.22. north Latitude. The Mate of the ship and some of the Sailors made a bungling sort of exhibition of the ceremonies which are usually practised on board ships when they cross the line. Two of them were dressed up as Neptune and his wife, seated on empty Pork casks, and near them a large tub filled with dirty water in which were a mop and a wooden bowl. They affected to issue orders that all those on board who had never crossed the Line before, should be brought prisoners before them. The messengers, who had to execute these commands, first made their appearance at the door of the Officers cabin, and made known to us the duty on which they were sent, enquiring if there were any present who had never been in that Latitude before, with a hesitating sort of look, as if in doubt, whether we would take the thing in joke, or not. Three of us good humouredly pleaded our guilt & surrendered ourselves their prisoners.

We were conducted before the God of the Sea, and his Lady, the former of whom gravely asked us our names and occupations and our object in entering his dominions. I stated that we came for the purpose of paying tribute to his Majesty, and hoped that it would be graciously received. Taking out a dollar I presented it and my example was followed by my brother Officers. The tribute money was taken by the Sea-God and he declared in a loud voice that we were thence forward at liberty to enter into his territories at all times, and to remain there as long as we pleased. The messengers then proceeded to other parts of the Ship, and we remained on deck to witness the result of their search. In about five minutes they made their appearance, bringing with them two of the crew who had never been between the Tropics before, and his Majesty aware that he not much tribute to expect from them, roughly demanded their business. They made no answer but put on that kind of laugh, which men sometimes assume when they feel that a very rough sort of joke is about to be practised upon them. The Goddess herself then repeated the question, in a voice still rougher than that of her Husband, and the same silence being observed by the culprits, His Majesty ordered them to be punished for contempt of his royal presence. They were immediately dragged close to the tub of dirty water, and well soused and mopped. They attempted resistance but it would not do, and they were certainly very roughly handled, but did not betray any symptom of sulkiness or ill-humour. I understood that the patient endurance of this ceremony, entitled the sufferer to a certificate which could exempt him from a repetition of it on any future occasion. The Messengers were then about to be dispatched for some of the Soldiers, but as we did not wish them to pass thro' this filthy ordeal, we interfered and expressed our hopes that His Majesty would consider tribute money as the purchase of their freedom of the Seas as well as our own.[159]

December 22nd. This day we met with the trade winds, which continued with us during the rest of our passage to Barbadoes.

25th. We passed our Christmas day with Cabin windows open, and only one sheet for a covering at night, finding the heat so oppressively great. The weather was beautifully clear, & the Sea a fine calm. In the evening we assembled the men, and such few of their wives as were on board on deck, we played Flutes for them, and they danced and sang songs till late at night.

26th. Weather very fine. We got out a boat, and paid a visit to one of our Transports, the British Tar. We were made to remain till dinner, and it was near midnight before we returned to our own Ship. In the course of the day we learned that the Columbine sloop of war, which had sailed with us thus far from America, was to return to Halifax the next day, when I took the opportunity of writing to Capt. Cortlandt, who with his detachment of invalids had gone to the Eastern battery, recommending Whisker Tom to his kindness, during my absence.

December 27th. The Penelope gave chase to two vessels, which proved to be Liverpool Merchant Ships. They gave her News-papers, which were sent round amongst the Transports. We read in them that France had made overtures of peace, and we also saw the first accounts of a British Army having landed at Corunna.[160] There was a very heavy and unexpected squall at night, and at daybreak the Shamrock, a three masted Schooner of war was missing. We afterwards heard that she had upset and foundered in that squall, and that every soul on board had perished.

28th. Major Ligertwood, Brigade major to the troops which sailed from Halifax, was sent on in the Rapid, Schooner, to Barbadoes, to give notice of our approach.

29th. "Land discovered" in Latitude 12.57. which proved to be Barbadoes, and about nine o'clock in the evening, we saw lights ashore, and shortly afterwards, anchored in Carlisle bay. We set our watches as usual, and those not on duty went to bed. My curiosity as to the sort of impression I should receive from my first view of a West India island, had been so intensely excited, that sleep was out of all question, and at Sun-rise I was on the deck. We were anchored close to the shore, in a deep and open bay, and almost to the waters' edge the Cocoa-nut tree shewed its tufted top. There was a sort of perfume in the air, and my eye could at once take in a new and luxuriant vegetable world. As the sun got higher, the heat became quickly oppressive, and the freshness of the scene greatly diminished. We had awnings of sail-cloth, spread over the whole decks, or the very pitch would have boiled out from the seams of the planks. Boats were soon along-side, rowed by black women, looking as disgusting as possible; but fruits of the most delicious description, with Milk too, and Spruce beer formed a part of their little cargo, and the sable venders of the latter held up the bottles in their hands, with a thumb pressing the cork upwards, but still preventing its escape, and crying out: "No pop, no pay Massa." Of course we dealt with them plentifully and they cheated us by every means in their power. To us who had just arrived from the rugged and leafless shores of North America, and its fair inhabitants, this sudden change to the luxuriance of the Plantain and the Cocoa-nut trees, and to the squalid darkness of the negro was full of interest. At noon such was the clearness of the Sea, that we were able to follow the cable with our eye in 12 fathoms water, down to the very anchor, and could distinctly see, the coral beds, and the larger descriptions of Sea-weed, which grew at that depth. The Commanding Officer went round the different ships with the Docter, and made regulations, such as he thought necessary for the mens' health, one of which was, that they were to be landed every morning half an hour, before sun-rise to bathe, and for their security against Sharks, with which the water abounded, there was a spot surrounded with high palisades for the use of the Military in barracks on the island, and to

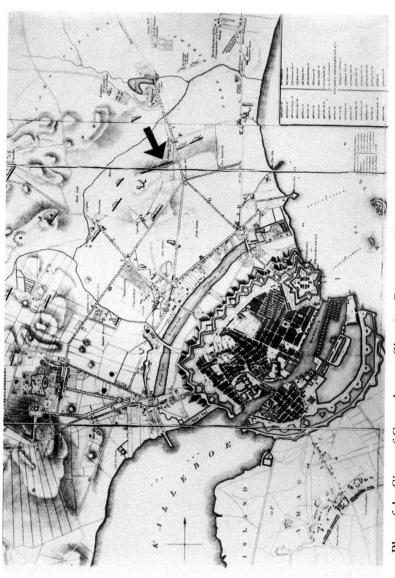

Plan of the Siege of Copenhagen, Showing Position of 23rd Royal Welch Fusiliers (1807).

A. Bucmeister, *The Bombardment of Copenhagen on the Night of 4 September 1807* (1808).

George Parkyns, *View of Halifax from Georges Island* (1801).

A Negro Market in the West Indies (1806).

which we were ordered to take our Soldiers also. Many very sage
instructions were of course given to the Officers for the care of their
individual health, and which at the time made some impression, as the
consequences of inattention to them, were held out as likely to be fatal.
We were to avoid exposure to the great heats of the day and to the damp
of the evening. We therefore selected the hottest sun of noon-day for
our expeditions on shore, and I remember being saluted by some half
naked black women in the Market place of Bridgetown the Capital of
Barbadoes, with "Ah Massa Johnny Newcome[161] go back to Shippy, too
hot for him here, kill him." In the evenings we behaved with equal
prudence, landing about seven o'clock for a dinner at "Nancy Clarkes",
the principal hotel keeper there, where we used to eat the highest
possible seasoned meats, drink Sangaree & Madeira in considerable
quantities and adjourn to a dance at some other hotel which usually
began at midnight.[162] When I first entered Nancy Clarke's house she
took hold of a button of my regimentals, looked me in the face and said
"What Regiment you belong to?["] On my telling her the 23rd, she
replied, "twenty third twenty third, Ah me shew you plenty of twenty
third in Church-yard dere." The Regiment had been in Barbadoes
about ten years before, and had lost many men and Officers by the fever.
This was Mistress Clarkes' very consolatory recollection. This sort of
life continued for about five days when one morning we heard that an
Officer of the Light Company, Lieut. Corfield, a fine healthy, active
young man, had been taken ill a few hours before. At noon he was worse,
and his head was shaved. Before Sun-set, he had died. On the morrow,
a second, Lieut. Hall was taken ill. He was sent off instantly to Nevis,
where he had some relations, and ultimately recovered. This recalled us
a little to ourselves, and prudence for a short time, was the order of the
day. We soon however grew lax again in our discipline, and a Lieutenant
of Artillery who had come with us from Halifax, disappeared after a few
hours illness. This brought us to our senses, and we behaved remarkably
well during the rest of our stay at Barbadoes. The beauty of the plants
here, and the brilliancy of their blossoms is not more remarkable, than
the bright and gay plumage of the Birds, and the very fish partake of the
dazzling changes from the sober hues of colder climates. All was new
and captivating except the human race, to which may be truly applied
Goldsmith's line "Man seems the only growth that dwindles here."
There is a sallowness of visage, and care worn expression of countenance, and an indolence of movement, observable in all classes. In

their very mode of speaking, there is a laziness, which partakes of the general lassitude.[163]

I walked about six miles into the interior of Barbadoes without observing any variety of hill or dale. My path was thro' fields of sugar, cotton, coffee, and Indian Corn. The fences were of the American Aloe, the blossom of which does not by any means confine itself as we suppose, to an exhibition once a century. It has an ugly yellow flower on a stalk about twelve feet high. Several of the fields were also divided by the prickly pear, of the size and formidable prickles of which, those who have only seen them in the flower-pots of hot houses, can form no idea. The trees with which the country was interspersed, were the Tamarind, the Date, Plantain, Cocoa-nut, Orange and Lemon, with every variety of the beautiful Mimosa tribe. The Sensitive plant is an absolute weed. I had no opportunity of judging of the sort of table kept by the Barbadians, as I was not invited into any of their houses. I visited the Church-yards and found them filled with memorials of British Officers, of all ranks, who had fallen victims to the climate. Their remains were principally a prey to the land crab, with which the burial places abound. Barbadoes is the head quarters of the Commander in Chief of the Wind-ward islands, who was at this time Sir Thomas Beckwith.

Bridgetown the seat of government is a wretched place. The houses are of wood, and the streets narrow and dirty.

January 1st 1809. Still at Anchor. The 13th Regiment which we left at Bermuda, in our passage from England to America arrived in Carlisle bay. We hear that we are destined for an attack on Martinique, in concert with other troops, expected, and that we are to rendezvous at St. Lucia. The "Junot", French Frigate, after having sailed in company with the British blockading Squadron, got into Martinique and landed 500 men there. Two French Corvettes with men and provisions have been equally successful.

January 2nd. The troops which came from America with Sir George Provost, and the 13th Regiment from Bermudas, continued on board Ship, and the men were not suffered to land, but for bathing before sun-rise. This and other precautions kept them in excellent health.

3rd. We went ahore this morning to see a Review of the 1st 3rd and 4th West India Regiments. The Officers were white, but the non-commissioned Officers and Privates all black. These sable warriors looked remarkably well in line but I did not think much of their movements, and on approaching them near, I found their appointments and general appearance anything but clean. The vapour too which surrounded them was far from fragrant, and when they formed column, it was certainly a mass of most difficult approach, to a well educated European nose.[164] The men were tall, well built fellows, which could not be otherwise, from the manner in which these Regiments were formed. The Slave trade was not abolished at the time I write, and as we had then, seven or eight black Regiments in the service, they were kept efficient, by a privilege which the Government assumed to itself, of taking out of every vessel which arrived at any of the islands with a cargo of Slaves, from the coast of Africa, eight or ten, as they might find necessary, of the finest and best shaped, to serve in the West India Regiments. For these they paid the highest price of the market, at the time of the Ship's arriving. The price of slaves varied from £60, to 120. On being oppointed to companies, the new recruits had a label hanging by a little brass chain round their necks, on which was engraved the names they were respectively to bear in the Regiment. These names were taken from celebrated Mountains, Rivers, Cities, or Fortresses, and when this source of nomenclature was exhausted, the numbers, first, second, third, &c. were had recourse to. Thus in calling over the roll of a black Company, I have heard men anwer to the names of, Gibraltar 1st, Gibraltar 2nd, London 1st, London 2nd &c. The distinguishing characteristics, of Negro countenances are so much alike, that I understood it was very difficult, for the Officers belonging to these Regiments, to become acquainted with the names of their men.[165]

4th. We hear that there is great wavering in the councils of our Generals, and that there is even a question of abandoning the enterprize altogether—that in consequence of the great supplies of men and provisions, which have lately got into Martinique, and the strength of its defences, the attack would be attended with too much hazard. We were much dispirited by this reported vacillation & could not bear the thoughts of returning to America, after so inglorious a campaign. However we had only to obey.

5th. The party on board my Ship, determined to drown grief by dining at Nancy Clarkes in more than usual luxury, and she managed a dinner for us, at about twenty-five shillings apiece. We returned on board Ship at night with aching heads and exactly that sum minus in our pockets. Had there been a ball that night at Susan Austin's, no doubt we should have attended it.[166]

6th. Captain Stuart of the Artillery, who came with us from Halifax, was taken ill this morning, grew delirious in the course of the day, and died at night. This kept us quiet for several days. I saw this evening, close to a ridge of rocks about half a mile distant, a great splashing and foaming in the water, and every now and then a large fish spring out, some feet, and fall again. Calling the attention of some of the Sailors to this curious sight, they told me it was not a very uncommon one; that it was a battle between a small Whale and a Sword-fish, seconded by another fish called a Thresher,—that the Sword-fish attacked the Whale under the belly with his horn, which made him come to the top of the water—that on his appearance there, the Thresher, a hard muscular fish, sprung out several feet, and lighting on some sensitive part of the Whale's back, made him descend to his adversary below, who in his turn pricked him up again, to be pounded by the Thresher, and that these two frequently succeeded in exhausting and killing their unwieldy victim. I cannot vouch for the truth of this curious combat, but such was the detail which was given to me. The great disturbance and foam of the water, and the springing out of a large fish, fell under my own observation.

7th. We landed this morning at day-light for the purpose of being reviewed by General Beckwith. The 7th and 23rd Fusileers, were brigaded together, and the command of us given to General Houghton. We mustered nearly 1800 bayonets. The General made a very minute inspection of the Brigade, and expressed himself much pleased with our Soldier like appearance. The Honble Colonel Pakenham commanded the 7th and Colonel Ellis the 23rd Fusileers.

January 15th. Still at anchor, and no decision appears yet to have been yet taken with regard to us. We hear many reports of the ill success of our Spanish armies,[167] and of our probable destination to Spain. We should like this above all things. This was the first day I had observed the sun-set, and I was very much struck by its extraordinary appearance. It was almost white, and conveyed to my mind an idea of heat, such as it had never before received. Notwithstanding all our vigilance and care, our men began to sicken, several were taken ill of the fever, and one died.

18th. The troops on shore were assembled this day to fire a feu de joie, in honour of Her Majesty's birthday, and several of us went on shore, to witness it. When they were drawn out, and had presented arms to General Beckwith on his arrival at the ground, attended by several other Generals, & superior Officers, he ordered them to close their ranks, and form close column on the centre. He then drew near and to the surprize of everybody, after making them an excellent speech, on the conduct and duties of Soldiers in the field, he expressed his hope to see them gallantly acted upon in the face of the enemy, and that he would give them an opportunity of doing so, in eight and forty hours. His speech was received with loud and enthusiastic cheers. We all hurried on board Ship as fast as possible, to communicate the glad tidings to such of our comrades, as had been detained on board by duty, and cheer after cheer was repeated from Ship to Ship, as they lay at anchor. Here then, was the day at hand, which we had so much desired. Whilst this cheering was going on, a Fleet of nearly 250 sail of Merchant men was passing by, and without the least knowing what was the cause of it, they answered our cheers as they went along. The embarkation of Artillery goes on very actively, and everything appears in movement and spirit. This was a little checked however by intelligence which we received, that one of our Sloops of war off Martinique, had upset in a gale of wind, & that all the crew had perished, except seven, who were saved by the Penelope.

19th. The greatest bustle is observable ashore to complete every thing for our speedy departure, and the following orders were given out. "The Army destined for offensive operations is formed into two Divisions, composed of five Brigades, and a reserve, with a proportion of field Artillery attached to each Corps, and independent of the Brigades and Park of Royal artillery, and Royal military artificers, who are not included in this order"—

1st Division

Commanded by Sir George Provost—viz:

	7th Regiment
1st Brigade	23rd Do_____ Brig: Gen: Houghton
	1st West India 5 co.
	8th Regiment
2nd Brigade	13th Do_____ Brig: Gen: Colville
	1st West India 4 Co.
	25th Flank Companies.
Reserve_____	60th Regt. 3rd & 4th Batt. Brig: Gen: Nicholson.
	4th West India.

Light Corps commanded by Major Campbell.

2nd Division
Commanded by Major General Maitland.

3rd Brigade	63rd Regiment York Rangers. Lieut: Col: Barnes. 15th & 46th Flank Co.	
4th Brigade	15th Regiment York Light Infantry Detach: 8th W. In.	Lieut: Col: Ryall.
5th Brigade	90th Regiment 3rd W: India.	Lieut: Col. McNair.

Commander in Chief Lieut: Gen: Beckwith.

Sir George Provost's division was 4170 effective rank and file, and General Maitland's rather more, making in the whole, a force of 9500 men well provided with Artillery and stores.[168]

January 20th. Embarkation of Artillery continued. The following orders were given out this day: "Upon a signal being made for the troops to land, the men will get into the boats as expeditiously as possible, but without disorder. They are to sit down in the boats, and in rowing on shore perfect silence is to be preserved. The Troops are not to load, until they are formed on the beach, nor are Bayonets to be fixed till that time, unless the landing be disputed. The formation to be effected as soon as possible. The men will fall in, in line opposite to where they disembark. They are to land in the lightest marching order as pointed out in orders of the 18th December last; but the Army from North America having joined since that period, it is left to Sir George Provost, to adopt the spirit of that order as it regards those troops who have been drawn from a climate so essentially different. In the event of an attack being made by night on any Post or Position, the advanced Picquets and Sentinels are alone to be allowed to fire on the enemy & to give notice of his approach; and the troops are to stand to their arms with celerity and regularity, and to reserve their fire. At night the Bayonet is to be particularly relied upon. Officers commanding an advance, as well as Officers commanding a support to that advance, must not allow any person to fall out to assist the wounded, who are to be left for the main body which is always well provided with surgical assistance. Music[ians], Drummers &c. are to be selected for all services not purely military. Each company is to be provided with two camp kettles."

January 22nd. The 2nd Brigade under General Colville was reviewed this morning, and made a very soldier-like appearance. Our light marching order is fixed as follows: "The watch-coat on the back, neatly folded up, with an extra flannel shirt in it[169] — the wooden cantine — the havre-sack with one third of it stitched up, to hold an extra pair of shoes, a comb, a razor and piece of soap. The men to land with 60 rounds of ammunition in the pouch, and 20 in the pocket."

23rd. Preparations continued. I was taken suddenly ill of a Cholera morbus,[170] and continued dangerously so for twelve hours, after which I gradually recovered. The men continue on the whole healthy, tho' our sick list increases.

28th. Orders given for all boats to be hoisted in at day-break, and every thing to be ready for sea the first thing in the morning.

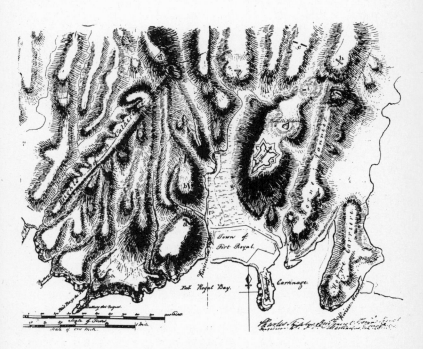

Fort Royal, Martinique. Sketch by Brig.-General Charles Shipley, February 28th, 1809.

29th. Day light shewed the signal flying to unmoor—anchors were weighed, and we sailed from Barbados against Martinique. Admiral Cochrane, and a strong fleet of line of battle Ships and Frigates accompanied us.[171]

30th. We landed at day-break this morning without opposition in Baye Robert, and after waiting nearly four hours for the disembarkation of the Artillery horses, began our march and rested that night in a sugar plantation about 4 miles in the interior. The 2nd division landed about the same time, also without opposition at Ste Luce, and a detachment of 600 men landed at Cape Salomon. The French force at Martinique consisted of about 2500 Troops of the line and as many Militia, and there were mounted in Fort Dessaix, Fort Royal and the batteries on the coast about 300 pieces of canon. The Naval force was the 40 Gun Frigate Amphitrite lying at Fort Royal, the 18 Gun Corvette Diligente at St Pierre and the Carnation late a British Sloop of war which they had captured at Marin [Martinique]. The Governor of the island was Admiral Villerret Joyeuse who opposed Lord Howe on the 1st of June.[172] When the Troops landed at Sainte Luce, the French set fire to the Carnation.

31st. We moved on this day over very steep hills and bad roads to a place called Des Rochers, and saw from thence the first of the enemy's videttes, and a strong reconnoitering party which they had sent out to watch our movements.

February 1st. We advanced to Mont Bruno, where as we had expected we found the enemy in considerable force, well posted and to all appearance resolved to defend vigorously, this very important pass of the Mountain. The action began about nine o'clock in the morning, the Fusileers leading, supported by the Light Companies which had been formed into a Brigade. Two companies only of the 23rd were at first engaged, but the opposition of the French was so serious, that the remainder of the Regiment moved up and commencing a steady and brisk fire they began to give way. Our men cheered loudly and charged them with the Bayonet. We pursued [the French] to a second hill, called Mont Sourrirè, where they rallied and received great reinforcements. We attacked again—they made a vigorous stand for several hours, and we were engaged within half musket shot. This sort of work would not do as we were expending ammunition and not gaining ground. We were ordered again to the charge, and they gave way. They did not retire far, but receiving another reinforcement from Fort Royal, tried first to turn our right, and then our left but in vain. Night was coming on and finding they could make no sort of impression on our gallant fellows, they retired about seven o'clock in the evening, leaving us masters of the heights of Desfourneaux, and Sourirè. After a close engagement of seven hours, in which the 7th and 23rd had 150 men killed and wounded and 4 Officers with about 20 missing. The French tho' inferior in numbers had been very strongly posted on ground of difficult access every part of which was well known to them. They behaved with great gallantry and acknowledged a loss on this day of 700 men killed and wounded. We slept in the Sugar canes, having very strong picquets in our front. Rain fell during the night, which wet us thro' as we had no shelter. We made good fires and cooked our provisions, troubling ourselves very little with what were to be the events of the following day. Nor did their uncertainty in the least disturb our repose.

February 2nd. A detachement of 600 of the York Rangers, under Major Henderson possessed themselves of the Battery on Pointe Salomon and made an attack afterwards on Islet aux Ramiers, which was bombarded for twelve hours by ten mortars and howitzers. The French Troops which garrisoned it, 136 men, after losing 16 killed and wounded, surrendered themselves prisoners of war. Sir Alexander Cochrane anchored with his Squadron in Fort Royal Bay, on which the French set fire to the Amphitrite Frigate and their other vessels in the harbour. They also abandoned all their forts in this quarter and shut themselves up in Fort Desaix. About noon this day we broke up from our bivouac of the preceeding night, and having received a fresh supply of ammunition moved on to the attack of two redoubts, which were immediately in our front. The enemy kept up a very destructive fire of grape and round shot, and it was determined to attempt them by storm. On approaching close for this purpose, we found a deep ditch and high palisades which it was impossible to attempt without scaling ladders, and we had not been supplied with any. There were therefore several minutes of uncertainty as to what was next to be done, and during this interval the French were pouring upon us a heavy fire of grape and musketry. The bugle at length sounded the retreat and we moved back to our old position. Our Commanders were much blamed for not having caused these Redoubts to be reconnoitered before we were ordered to attack them, and particularly that we had not been furnished with scaling ladders. The 7th & 23rd Fusileers had 5 Officers and 120 men killed and wounded on this occasion. The 8th Regiment lost 1 Officer and 11 men, and the light Brigade 1 Officer and 20 men. The loss of the enemy was also considerable.

February 3rd. Some ladders had been made during the night, & at day-break columns of attack were formed against the two redoubts, but on approaching them it was found that they were evacuated. The enemy had spiked and dismounted all the Canon, and they were of little use to us, except as commanding an extensive view of the country. I received a wound this day thro' the bend of my left arm. The ball carried away a small Artery and divided the nerve, and in passing out behind broke the bone. I was taken to a Hospital which had been formed in a sugar plantation a small distance in the rear, and continue my journal from information which I daily received there. Its vicinity to the scene of action, gave me an opportunity of almost hourly accounts.

4th. The French militia which garrisoned the town of St Pierre and its dependencies, were summoned by Lieut. Col. Barnes of the 3rd Brigade, and immediately surrendered, and the French Troops of the line having withdrawn themselves from all the out quarters into Fort Desaix, that place was invested in the following manner. General Maitland on the right extended his Division, from Case des Navires, where part of the British Squadron was stationed, to Sir George Provost's right on the heights of Sourirè, which was the most exposed part of the position. General Nicholson with the reserve, joined on Sir George's left and extended himself to Cohè, having his left flank covered by another part of the Squadron. Fort Desaix being on a neck of land was thus completely surrounded. Our lines extended from sea to sea. The enemy threw a good many shell at us in the course of the day, but without doing much injury.

February 5th. Trenches were opened and our first Battery begun. The Troops made huts of the sugar canes, having had no covering from the day of their landing, tho' the rains have been very frequent and heavy. A few tents were landed and given out.

6th. Works continued, the French made several sallies, but were uniformly repulsed. Five men of General Maitland's division were killed by a shell, and several severely wounded. The weather continues exceedingly wet, and some of our men were attacked with Dysentery, but there is no increase of fever cases. Preparations were now made to convert the sugar plantation, into which I had been carried when first wounded, into a regular military hospital, and I was borne out on some Indian corn straw, and laid in a small hut, near the house. The French

Lady, to whom the plantation belonged, treated me with great kindness, and used frequently to send or bring me broths and fruit. She sent one of her Negroes to attend me in the little hut, where I had been deposited. It was exceedingly low, and thatched with the bruised stalk of the sugar cane, after the juice had been extracted. My removal into this place, had caused me a good deal of pain, and of nervous irritability. My black attendant had left me to go to his dinner. I was lying on my back quite incapable of moving, when I saw just above me, hanging by one or two of its claws, a large Tarantula. In any other situation this creature would have been an object of interest & curiosity, but under the influence of severe pain, my imagination passed quickly in review, all I had ever read of its venom, and the deadly effects of its bite, and that I was quite at its mercy, should it let go its hold, and drop upon me. I watched the creature, with a degree of intensity that worked my whole frame into a state of fever, and my fancy had magnified it into ten times more than its reality. This state of things lasted perhaps a quarter of an hour, and I really began to believe that my senses were giving way, when in came my sable servant. I had just strength left, to shew him what had produced upon me an effect, which had evidently caused his surprise, when he displayed his white teeth in a most extensive grin, and taking off his head, a little blue cloth cap that he wore, with a bamboo that lay on the floor he poked the Tarantula into it, and bore it away. I afterwards had it preserved very carefully in a wide mouthed phial, filled with white rum and hermetically sealed. It had not been in the least injured, and when I grew stronger and the remembrance of its effects upon me had subsided, I used frequently to look at it, in the sun and admire it exeedingly. The hair with which its claws were covered exhibited, purple, green and red in their brightest hues, and never was a noxious reptile clad in such dazzling apparel. I took it with me when we returned to America, and made a present of it, to a Medical Gentleman who was forming a cabinet of natural History in Halifax, where it was considered one of the best specimens that had ever been seen. The effects however which had been produced upon me, by my intense observation of this beast were very apparent for some time to come, and shewed themselves in intermittent fever, and a change greatly for the worse in the appearance of the wound, on which some symptoms of gangrene were beginning to shew themselves. This added to my irritability, had rendered unavailing the remedies that were applied to counteract them. My Surgeon then broke to me his opinion, that it would probably be necessary for me to have the arm amputated. I told him, that if the necessity really existed, of course I had nothing to say, and was sure that I should bear it with much greater patience, than I did the pain I was then suffering. At the same time, I represented to him, how very anxious I was to preserve the limb as I was just beginning to learn the Flute. The Docter smiled, and said he feared there was little prospect of this, and the sooner it was off, the better, as should inflammation come on, in such a climate, its progress was so rapid that my situation would be one of considerable peril. I asked him however, for twelve hours more, for the sake of the Flute, to which he reluctantly consented, and left me, after filling both orifices of the wound with pure charcoal, giving me at the same time, a strong dose of laudanum.[173] I slept well, tho occasionally awakened with a sort of gnawing sensation about the wound. When the dressings were removed, next day, the charcoal was found to have made considerable impression on the gangrenous formation, and its progress was decidedly arrested. The application was repeated, and eventually succeeded. My Surgeon was exceedingly gratified with the result, and afterwards laughingly acknowledged, that I owed to my Flute alone, the preservation of my arm.

February 7th. Erection of batteries continued in very adverse weather. The French made a sortie against one of our advanced trenches, drove in our working party, and carried away some of their tools. The covering parties were also engaged this day, but with trifling loss. A French brig of war loaded with powder was taken by our Squadron, attempting to get into Fort Royal in the night, not aware that everything was in our possession, but Fort Desaix.

8th. Works continued. The picquets and covering parties were severely engaged to day. We christened our advanced battery Fort Edward, and in this work several men were killed & wounded by the accidental explosion of a shell, the fuse of which had been carelessly exposed, and some fire fell upon it.

9th. Incessant rains which render all progress in the batteries exceedingly tedious. Fluxes and fevers begin to shew themselves in the first division, but the Troops are in excellent spirits.

10th 11th. The batteries are now in a state of forwardness, the guns in their embrazures, & shot and shell landing in abundance from the Fleet.

12th. The Enemy made a feint this evening of a sally on our right, and on our forming column to resist them there, they made their appearance in considerable force on our left, and at first, made some impression on it; but we were quickly in good order again, and they were well beaten, retiring in great disorder into the Fort. In this sally, they lost an Officer, who had apparently died in a sitting posture, leaning against some bamboos. His head was dropped on his left shoulder, and he was fired at, by some of the black Troops when in that position. They supposed him to have been alive, and he was too near the French picquets, for them to ascertain the contrary.

13th. The batteries are five in number and are now nearly completed. Two smart shocks of an Earthquake were felt. The sensation to me was that of the house rocking violently, but being built of wood as most of the houses here are, it did not convey with it the idea of much danger. The people, who were all Catholics, crossed themselves most devoutly, and uttered plenty of Ave Maria's for a minute or two, but shortly after the second shock was over, they dispersed, and went laughing away to their several occupations. Earthquakes are not uncommon at Martinique, but seldom attended with fatal consequences.

14th to 17th. The rains began again, and hindered us very much. Picquets and covering parties daily engaged, and the number of casualties considerable. I was moved back into the house of the sugar plantation, which had now been converted into a Hospital, and was put into a small room, with four other wounded Officers. We were laid on the straw of Indian corn, having over it dried leaves of the Plantain, and covered with a blanket. Late in the evening, another wounded Officer was brought in, a Lieutenant Johnson of the 4th West India Regiment, and as there was not space in the room for another bed, he was put into mine, and I divided my blanket with him. He was shot thro' the thigh with a musket ball, but it was not considered a dangerous wound. We soon became good friends, and talked all night, when the irritation of our wounds deprived us of sleep. I thought him very low and dejected from the moment he was brought in, and was obliged constantly to exert myself, to keep up his spirits, by assuring him that flesh wounds, like that which he had received, were seldom long in healing. The Surgeon had reported very favourably of his condition from day to day, & frequently rallied him on the lowness of his spirits. About the seventh night, he was more than usually dejected. I was more free from pain, than I had been for some time, and having taken a small quantity of laudanum, fell asleep. It was not day-light when I awoke, and finding all still near me, I remained quiet. In a little time however I spoke to Johnson, but received no answer. As I could not turn myself without assistance, I was silent, thinking him asleep. Whilst things were in this state, I moved my arm and fancied I felt the straw and the blanket near me very wet; this made me restless, and I managed to put out my arm to touch Johnson, meaning to ask him if the straw was not wet. My hand reached his cheek, which was quite cold. I made a strong effort, threw off the blanket, and called aloud for assistance, when it was discovered, that an artery in the poor fellow's thigh, which must have been injured by the shot, had burst in the night, and he had literally bled to death, before any assistance could be rendered him.

18th. The French fired very briskly this day, and many of their shells fell into our lines, without doing much execution. The only casualty was occasioned by one which fell upon a Picquet of the 4th West India Regiment and killed 4 men.

19th. Everything is now ready, and we are told that the batteries are to open tomorrow. The enemy made a feeble sortie against our left, but were instantly repulsed.

February 20th. Our batteries began their fire, which was truly tremendous, they threw 500 shells, besides quantities of round shot, in the course of the evening. Many of the former were observed to fall into the Fort, and some were seen to rebound from their Bomb proofs. They themselves kept up a pretty brisk fire, and their shells being thrown with more accuracy than yesterday, occasioned us some loss.

21st. Bombardment continues, and the fire of the enemy is much slackened. The following orders dated the 5th inst. were circulated in the army. "The Commander of the forces has great satisfaction in requesting Sir George Provost, to return his hearty thanks to Lt: Col: Pakenham and the 7th and Lt: Col: Ellis and the 23rd and Major Campbell and the light Brigade, for the brave, gallant and resolute manner in which they drove the enemy from the heights of Sourirè, and afterwards engaged and defeated them on the 1st and 2nd Inst. surmounting in the most zealous manner, the greatest difficulties. He doubts not, but that the same valour & spirit, tempered with less impetuosity, will bring the campaign to a speedy & honourable issue."

Thanks in order were this day given to Major Pearson,[174] for his conduct in an affair of Picquets.

22nd. Shot and shell flying in all directions. The Picquets engaged with some loss. The enemy were observed taking their dead into the Fort.

23rd. Bombardment hotter than ever. The French had two field magazines blown up in the Fort, and discovered us at day break erecting another work, so near the ramparts, that they determined to dislodge us. They commenced a destructive fire on our men imployed in this work, which they kept up for about two hours, but finding that they made no impression on our brave fellows, and aware that this battery when completed, would prove very destructive to them, they sent out a flag of truce, about five o'clock in the evening, proposing a capitulation. The terms however were not approved of, in our commanding situation, and we commenced a heavy fire again, giving them time to prepare for it. They received our fire, but during the night did not return it.

24th. Day break this morning discovered three white flags upon the enemy's ramparts, signifying their wish to propose other terms. The French flag was hauled down, Commissioners were appointed on both sides, and the French garrison of 2700 men surrendered themselves prisoners of war, giving up their Eagles,[175] Arms &c. They were allowed to march out with the honours of war, and to pile their arms on the glacis. After being thus disarmed, they were to return to the Fort & occupy it as a barrack until Transports were prepared to receive them. They had lost about 900 men killed & wounded in the siege. The surrender of Fort Desaix placed the whole island in our possession, the conquest of which had occupied us two & twenty days.

25th. The Grenadier companies of the 7th and 23rd Fusileers marched in, and took possession of the North Gate, and the King's colour of the 23rd was planted in the Bouillè redoubt. The inside of the work presented a shocking spectacle of ruins, and blood, and half buried bodies, and was literally ploughed up, by the shells we had thrown into it. In the evening of this day the French prisoners embarked. They consisted of 2 Battalions of the 28th demi brigade.[176] 3 Battalions of the 87th demi brigade, and 300 sailors of the Frigate they had blown up, besides Engineers and Artillery men, making together 2600 men, adding to which the 900 killed and wounded, we have a garrison of 3500 as the original number before our attack. They were of the best French troops, and in high order. Fort Desaix had been rendered so strong by additional defences and bastions a few months before, that it was considered almost impregnable. It had 140 pieces of ordnance mounted, of large calibre. The British loss amounted to about 520 killed & wounded, of which number 328 are of the 7th and 23rd Fusileers.[177] The French Troops immediately on being embarked, tho' having so shortly before parted with their Eagles, were seen laughing and singing & dancing on the decks, just as they would have done in any little Cabaret near Paris, and in observing this, we could hardly refrain from envying their happy frivolity. The operation of greatest importance amongst them, and that which demanded immediate attention was their shaving each other, as they had on their chins a plentiful crop of about fourteen days growth. Then came the washing, and the day after their embarkation, the Transports on board of which they were, sported in the breeze one grand mass of shirts and stockings, of all colours and conditions. The chattering of the fellows it is really quite impossible to describe, and the whole scene presented much more the spectacle of elated & victorious Troops, than of men going to England as prisoners of war. They sailed the next morning, making all sorts of grimaces and bows to us. I never saw so merry a set of fellows.

The French state that the reason which principally induced their Commander to surrender so soon was that our shells had cracked and damaged in several places, the roof of the powder Magazine, and that he was in momentary dread of an explosion. On our taking possession, this was found really to have been the case, and yet when the Governor General was exchanged & returned to France, a court of enquiry sat at Paris to investigate the causes of his surrender, & after strongly animadverting on the neglect of his not having previously removed the powder into the galleries of the Fortress, he and some other of the superior Officers were stripped of their rank and honours. The town of Fort Royal which is situated under the Fort, is a pretty, clean place; it contains about 10,000 inhabitants, who profess to be much rejoiced at their having fallen under British dominion, as the stagnation of their commerce for some time past, had been most prejudicial to them. The island is beautifully diversified with hill, and valley, and streams of water pour down the sides of romantic rocks in many places. The fruits & trees are those of all the other West India islands.

We remained in Martinique till the 7th of March, when orders of thanks to the army were issued, and we embarked for America. A hospital Ship was appointed on board of which I was sent, with the other wounded officers.

March 15th. After remaining on board since the 7th we weighed anchor this morning under convoy of the Penelope Capt. Dick, and the Eolus, Lord William Fitzroy. We were becalmed off St. Pierre which looks beautiful from the Sea and appears a town of much greater extent than it actually is. A breeze sprung up in the evening, and we sailed by the island of Dominica.

16th. It blew very freshly this night, and we were under close reefed top-sails. We passed by Guadeloupe and the Saints.[178] Our Commodore lay to under the Lee of Mont Serrat to collect the Ships which had been scattered in the night.

17th. Passed by Redondo and Nevis, the latter a beautiful island. About twelve o'clock we anchored in Basse Terre roads, St. Kitts, from whence the island looks very interesting.

18th. Mr. Tidley agent to Lord Romney who has considerable estates in this Island, seeing the Flag flying by which the hospital ship was distinguished, came on board in a boat rowed by six blacks, bringing with him fruits of all descriptions for the use of the wounded. He invited me to land, which I did & passed three days with him. Nothing could exceed his kindness and hospitality. Col. Pakenham of the 7th Fusileers who had been shot thro' the neck, was also brought to his house and treated with the greatest attention. The appearance of St. Kitts is that of a highly cultivated garden, crowned with a high mountain, called Mount Misery, which is also a volcano, and smoke is not unfrequently seen, issuing from its crater. There is another high rock in the island called Brimstone hill, on which are erected barracks for a Regiment, and quarters for Artillery and Engineers.[179] The Regiment in these barracks was the 25th, old friends of ours, and they sent immediately to invite us all to dine with them on the hill. Weak as I was, I could not resist joining my brother Officers in the party, and to dinner we went. The meeting of two old Regiments who had seen hard service together, was not likely to take place without copious libations to Bacchus, and this meeting was certainly one of the most distinguished of that description. It was followed up by a similar invitation for the next day, which was also accepted, and celebrated pretty much in the same manner. Two such days could hardly be spent in this climate, without producing their consequences, and two of our Officers were taken ill of fever, and were obliged to be left behind when we sailed. One of them afterwards died. Whether the 25th left similar memorials of our meeting or not is more than I can tell. The view of the sea from Brimstone hill is quite magnificent. Half way down the rock are quantities of Monkies, established there in times long gone by, and who enjoy a similar exemption from annoyance with those at Gibraltar, and are not allowed to be shot at. They are consequently very bold and impertinent.[180] In clear weather, Antigua is plainly to be seen from Brimstone Hill.

March 19th. We removed our Anchorage from Basse Terre, to the old roads, where the water is better and the facilities of obtaining it greater. Here the Transports completed their stock of water successively. Our men began to sicken fast and the worst cases of wounds and fever, were sent on shore to the hospital of the 25th Regiment.

20th. Several of our men have died in the night, and cases of Dysentery and fever are fast increasing.

21st. Changed our anchorage again to Sandy Point, under Brimstone hill, and just before sun set, weighed anchor again for America.

22nd. Passed by the islands of Ste Eustasia, Saba, St. Martins & St. Bartholomews — saw the Virgin Islands, Santa Cruz, & St. Thomas'. Off the latter island we lay to for Ships astern to close up.

23rd. Saw the islands of Tortola, St. John's and Porto Rico. This was the last of the West Indies, of which we took our leave with no small satisfaction.

24th. At Sea, with fine weather and fair wind. The wounded men on board the hospital ship, die very fast, and I was called upon several times in the course of each day to read the burial service over the poor fellows, as they were launched into the deep. We have lost fifteen, since we left Martinique.[181]

25th. A strange sail in sight, to which the Eolus gave chase. The stranger also approached in full sail, and we were not without hopes of her proving a French frigate, and that we should see a naval engagement. But when the Eolus made the private signal, it was quickly answered by the Stranger and the vessels approached within hailing distance. After remaining in this situation about ten minutes, during which time we were proceeding onwards, the two Frigates separated, and the Eolus immediately began a telegraphic conversation with the Penelope. I was in possession of the navy signals and numbers, and made out from the flags, that our Troops had retreated from the interior of Spain to Corunna — that a battle had been fought there, in which Sir John Moore was killed, and Sir David Baird had lost his arm — that the British had been victorious, but the overwhelming numbers of the French, commanded by Napoleon in person, had made it necessary for our army to embark, and leave the country.[182] This news threw considerable gloom over us, and we prepared ourselves for further accounts of disasters in Spain. It was a great amusement to me, during the rest of this voyage to be able to read the different communications which passed between our two convoying Frigates.

30th. We have lost eleven more men since the 25th and are in latitude 26.13. and longitude 66.5. with a foul wind.

April 7th. A heavy squall of wind came on so suddenly that almost every Ship of the Fleet suffered more or less damage. In the evening the wind went down and was succeeded by heavy rain and thunder, and most vivid lightning, which is said to be almost peculiar to this latitude. Tho' the night was otherwise pitch dark, the flashes were so frequent, that I could read a book on deck without difficulty. It was the broad sheet lightning which looked as if the whole heavens gaped in fire, and forked, only occasionally. The appearance of the Fleet on a high dark Sea, exposed to view in the flashes of the lightning was most awful and interesting.

8th. Again in the latitude of Bermuda in our return to America. We passed the island with a fine fresh breeze going at the rate of 9 knots an hour.

10th. Latitude 42.4. The weather is severely cold, with a North East wind. Our poor fellows bringing their emaciated and wounded bodies from a tropical climate, give way sadly under this sudden change, and we have buried eight since the 30th of March. I was very sensible of it myself, having had several pieces of bone extracted from my arm, and was a good deal worn out, by sleepless nights, and I own that the daily occurrence of such frequent deaths affected my spirits a good deal. A child was born, during the passage, and I was called upon to baptize it. Under pressing circumstances an Officer is permitted to act as Chaplain. We understood that it had been proposed to Sir George Provost to land the worst cases of wounds and fever at Bermuda, but unfortunately he did not attend to this recommendation, and many valuable lives were undoubtedly lost by their sudden transfer in a debilitated state from the West Indies to North America in the months of March and April.

April 12th. Signal made of land discovered, and that Ships were to get into harbour as they could. We knew it to be Nova Scotia, but a thick fog came on and we dared not venture near so rocky a coast, & during the night the wind became foul.

13th 14th 15th. Becalmed in a cold raw fog. Several more of the men died.

16th. We entered Halifax harbour this evening and anchored about six o'clock after an absence of about five months, in which time we have taken the most valuable possession of the French, in the West Indies. We find that this has been the severest winter known in Nova Scotia for the last twenty years, and the sufferings of our poor Soldiers are excessive.

Dysentery soon made dreadful progress amongst them, and it was quite melancholy to see the funeral processions, leaving the barrack yards day after day. We had at one time nearly four hundred men in hospital of this disorder. Some fine weather in May however put a check to it, but not until we had lost more than a hundred men. We soon began to make ourselves comfortable in our barrack rooms. Messing was very reasonable, & the best French wines as cheap as possible owing to the prizes which were constantly bringing by Sir John Warren's squadron of Frigates, of French Merchant vessels carrying wines to Martinique & Guadaloupe. It was curious enough to see us closely wrapped up in great coats lined with fur, and fox skin caps on our heads so soon after our slender covering of Nankeen[183] in a different climate. We kept up enormous fires in our rooms, as the allowance of fuel, which is wood, was more than any Officer could possibly burn. My Barrack room was next to that of an old Captain of the Regiment, who had been with it in Holland, and in returning to England, the Transport in which he was embarked, having on board the Grenadier company & the band, was unfortunately wrecked, and very few were saved. This Captain was thrown on the Beach where he was violently struck on the head, by the butt end of a piece of floating timber. To this misfortune we attributed many singularities, for which he was remarkable. Going into his room one morning, I was surprised to see all his clothes and every thing else belonging to him, spread out upon the Floor, a sort of Alley being left from the door to his bed. On my smiling at this arrangement he very calmly pointed out to me the great advantage that it had, over the usual custom of keeping things in boxes & portmanteaus. "Now", says he, "when I come into my room & want something I have only to look round about me and see at once where it is, whilst you, I daresay, are poking half an hour or more in your box, and perhaps don't find it after all." The Captain was quite serious, and satisfied that his wardrobe was better placed on the floor of his barrack room than it could possibly have any where else. It was indeed a curious piece of Mosaic work, composed of coats, waistcoats, fishing rods & stockings, boots and swords, shoes and sashes. He told me also that there was another advantage attending this plan of his, which was, that he could count at any time, in about ten minutes the number of things he had in the world—that he then possessed 307 things, counting every pair of boots and gloves as two things. I could have split my very sides with laughter, but that he was so grave about it, and a man at all times sensitive to ridicule. His eccentricities affected every thing he did, except his military duties, in all of which he was as correct as any Officer of the corps, & exceedingly beloved by the soldiers of his company. His mode of keeping accounts with his brother Officers, partook of his general habits. For instance, had I met him in the street and borrowed a shilling from him, he would immediately walk to his barrack room, and write upon the wall, with a piece of red chalk, with which he was always provided, in large characters "I have just lent Browne a shilling" adding the date. If in the course of the week I repaid him the shilling, this was again a walk to his barrack room, and the piece of red chalk, recorded, underneath the former memorandum, "Browne has just repaid me the above," and should a delay of more than a week take place in the repayment, it was not unusual to see ones name in red letters on his wall "To remind Browne of this debt." As on leaving barracks, Officers are obliged to pay for any damage they may have done to their rooms, my friend the Captain had always a bill to discharge for the fresh white-washing of his room, which he invariably did without the least dispute. I believe his room was not unfrequently shewn as a curiosity to the Regiment taking our place in the barrack. The inhabitants of Halifax on our return from Martinique looked upon us as heroes, their own exclusive property, and were prodigal of their attentions to us; and the first fruits of them were, a determination to give us a ball, on a very grand scale. When the night arrived, we found the ball room decorated with laurel, and filled with transparencies of Battles fought, and breaches mounted, and every other description of military honour. The bands of the two Regiments of Fusileers attended, and the entertainment went off capitally. We were thus again in comfortable quarters which we enjoyed the more, from a feeling that we had done something to deserve them. We were on the best terms with the navy of the station, and had a constant interchange of dinners & civilities with them.

In the early part of this journal I have mentioned the custom of Fusileer Regiments wearing their hair in a small plait behind, and fastened with a little comb to the top of the head. This remark is applicable to the Officers only, with whom it was a very favourite distinction, as differing from the pig tails worn by the rest of the army. Powder was also used, & the hair at the sides of the face, which we called the side locks, was not allowed to grow longer than an inch, & was frizzed and rubbed up with the palm of the hand, before the powder was dusted into it. This mode of decorating the flanks of the human countenance was also the regulation with regard to the men, but they were not allowed the plait behind. Their hair was permitted to grow about a foot long, when it was turned up in a single roll which we called a club—this was clasped by a polished leather strap about half an inch wide, in the centre of which was a platted Grenade, the whole, well greased and powdered. It may well be imagined, what a tedious and troublesome operation all this was, and how much of the Soldier's time was needlessly occupied in this formidable preparation for parade. The talents of the women were very conspicuous in this head dressing of their respective husbands, and as the Officers of companies were always well pleased when they saw a smartly frizzed pate, the credit of their good humour was naturally given to the wife who had operated so successfully. The wife in her turn, held up her head the higher, from the Captain's favor to her husband, produced by his handsome side-locks; and the estimation in which the women were held by the soldiers, was not by an means derived from beauty or good conduct, but was proportioned to the degree of approbation bestowed upon the heads which they had dressed, and as casualties are frequent in Regiments so strong as they were at this time a woman of first rate talents in this department, was not unfrequently bespoken by one or two candidates for her hand, in case of misfortune to her actual lawful Lord. It was about this time that a general order was issued from the Horse Guards, for the discontinuance of the use of powder in the hair of the soldiers, and directing that their heads should be closely cropped. It is natural to suppose, that an order of this description, would have been received by the men most gratefully, and that the Officers would also rejoice at being permitted to disencumber themselves of so useless an appendage. No such thing, the order was obeyed in sulky silence by the Officers, and particularly by those, who had been distinguished, by a luxuriant plait. The Colonel himself, who was one of these, was by no means pleased with the measure. We were seated at the Mess table, when the matter was talked over, and having perhaps taken an extra glass, by way of softening our vexation, one of the Officers proposed, that we should, then and there, cut off each other's plaits with a carving knife, and make

a grand friz of them, in the fire. The first part of the proposition was
acceded to, and I can vouch for it's having been a rough and painful
operation. The question of burning and frizzing our precious locks, was
of a much more serious nature, and acceded to only by one or two old
Subalterns with whose heads time had taken its usual liberties of
thinning and bleaching. The rest of us wrapped up our discarded tails in
pieces of brown paper or pocket handkerchiefs, and carried them to our
barrack rooms. I do not think it would be hazarding much to add that
one or more of these tails could have written a curious history had the
power been granted it, of the division and distribution of its after days.

With the men the scene was far different, and the row which this
order produced in the barrack yard amounted to very little short of
mutiny. The women assembled in groupes of three and four, which after
their respective stormy discussions joined each other and added to the
uproar. They swore by every oath that a soldier's wife has no difficulty in
uttering that the order should not be carried into execution, and that
they would murder the first operator who should dare to touch a hair of
their husband's head. They felt at once, that should the barbarous
decree be carried into execution, they descended more than one step in
the scale of female perfection, and that widowhood would inevitably be
their lonely portion, in case of that event to which some of them looked
forwards with complacency, & perhaps there were not wanting those
who would rather have parted with their husbands heads, than that their
claims to preservation of caste as wives should be weakened by this cruel
docking innovation. Things were in this state of ferment when the
Adjutant waited on the Colonel to report the state of confusion which
prevailed in the barrack yard. He went there immediately and ordered
out the first company. The Regiment not giving the garrison duties that
day, he ordered a roll call of the company to see that every men was
present; which was the case as it was near the dinner hour. Having
ascertained this he desired them to take open order, and sending for
benches from the barrack rooms had them placed behind each rank, and
commanded the men to sit down. This they did in perfect silence, he
then ordered off their foraging caps and sent for half a dozen hair
cutters, of which there are always plenty in every Regiment. They were
set to work and in less than ten minutes, nothing remained but the stump
of the favourite club. The benches were then removed, ranks closed,
and the company dismissed. The women assembled in groups and
cursed and muttered, but the eye of the commanding Officer subdued

every other indication of mutiny, as he would inevitably have turned out of barracks, any of these heroines whose voice he could have distinguished. Company after company underwent the same process, and it was droll enough to see the men as they were dismissed to their barrack rooms, applying their hands to the backs of their heads, to ascertain if it were a dream or a reality. The Soldiers however soon became reconciled to this great improvement, and the Officers quickly perceived its good effects from the cleanliness which it produced. The women, I daresay, soon discovered some other foundation on which to build their hopes of perpetual wifehood, and in a few months, all the heads of the Regiment were as quiet on the subject as if such a thing as a club had never been heard of.[184]

I had a very bad attack of ague about this time, caught I believe on the lakes where I was constantly at work, with my old friend Whisker Tom, whose attachment seemed to increase for me daily. We went over our old rounds together, and had established between us a language, unintelligible I am sure to any other human being. He recommended me all sorts of remedies for my ague, but it obstinately resisted them all, and from Tertian, became Quotidian until I was reduced to an absolute skeleton.[185] It yielded at length to the constant attacks I made upon it with bark, Cayenne pepper, and Madeira, but my strength was sadly exhausted, and my spirits completely subdued. My wound was gradually healing. It will naturally be supposed that my little garden and improvements at the Eastern battery had been objects of early interest to me after our return from Martinique, & it gratified me very much to find, that the officer who was in command of the post, had not only taken them all under his particular care, but had inclosed with a wall a fresh piece of ground, and added it to one side of the garden, making his new piece, the kitchen ground of the Post, and converting mine to the pleasure, and flower garden. I paid him two visits in a little Canoe & we put our heads together for further additions to the little territory. One of my roads to the Lakes, had been made an excellent one. I found that Whisker Tom had never once visited the Post during the time I was away, although it was the usual route to that part of the interior which was possessed by the tribe to which he belonged. They were the Chictaws. I do not believe that they are a race remarkable for any extraordinary qualities either as Warriors or Huntsmen, and the taste they had acquired for ardent spirits in their intercourse with the British population, had greatly reduced their strength and diminished their numbers. Before this passion took such fatal possession of them, they used to bring to our Forts & settlements, the skins of the Bears, and other wild beasts which they had shot, and exchange them for blankets, clothing, ammunition, and such other articles as were really useful and necessary; but now they gave their skins, for new Rum and British spirits, and as well as their Squaws and children were to be seen drunk in the streets of Halifax. The consequence was, that they returned to their woods, unprovided with covering sufficient to protect them against the cold of a North American winter, and without even ammunition enough to secure their daily food, and many perished yearly from cold & famine. Such was their state when I had intercourse with them, & as I believe it has been progressively growing worse, that fine race of Indian Warriors of whom we read with respect and admiration in those records of their virtues which must be familiar to many of us, have dwindled into weakly tribes of sots, and retiring farther and farther back will perhaps be heard of in the course of half a century as we hear of the Romans and Carthaginians, now represented by orders of monks and Priests, and slaves of [. . .] the Bey of Tunis. The pathetic allusions which we still read of in our daily papers, as made by some of the remaining natives of our fatal introduction of spirits among them, cannot but be seen with interest. Poor Whisker Tom himself, faithful as he was in his attachment to me, was not proof against a glass of rum. The dexterity with which the little Indian boys made use of the bow was very remarkable, & we frequently amused ourselves with putting a glove at the top of a pole, and making them shoot at it. Their arrow seldom failed, bringing it down when placed at reasonable distances, and we used to give prizes to the best marksmen amongst them. They are very successful in bringing down Partridges from trees, and have been known, I was told, to kill six or seven, perched under each other, on different branches, knocking over the lowermost bird first. The last Papers from England inform us, that the thanks of Parliament have been voted to the army which attacked & took Martinique.[186] We are also told that our prize money will be considerable. The sum which I afterwards received as a Subaltern was about twenty pounds.[187] The Eagles of the 28th and 82nd French demi Brigades, which we had sent to England were put up in the military chapel at Whitehall, where they are to be seen with the others that were taken by the British army, at different periods of the war. The Eagles, which Napoleon gave to his Regiments, were about the size of a Pigeon with its wings displayed, standing on a wreath, as Birds are usually seen in crests. They were of silver, and screwed upon the pole which bore them, so that in case of reverse, nothing was easier than to unscrew the Bird, pocket it and save the disgrace which its capture would bring with it.

We remained in quarters at Halifax, until the 13th of October, when the out-post duty was again taken by the 23rd Regiment. Three companies, one of which was that I served in, embarked on board the Lady Delaval Transport for St. John's, New Brunswick. We remained at anchor till the 18th. When we weighed with a fine wind, & made Cape Sable before dark.

Octobr 19th. Entered the bay of Fundy which divides the British & American territories, and is remarkable for its high & rapid tides. At some places near the head of the bay they are said to rise 70 ft.

20th. Foul wind and bad weather. We are no farther than at noon yesterday.

21st. The wind continues foul & blowing fresh. We were obliged to tack all the night, in a very dangerous passage, between an island called the Grand Menan, and the American shore.

22nd. A fine fresh breeze—Passed by Grand Menan, & Passama-guoddy on the river Scudick.

23rd. We anchored at St. John's about four oclock this evening, & it was very well that we did, as our provisions were out. From our anchorage, it is a miserable looking place, the great support of which, is the Timber that it annually exports to England. There is a very remarkable water-fall at this place, about one hundred yards wide, & the fall nearly twenty feet. It empties itself into that part of the Port where the Ships lie at anchor, between two rocks, & owing to the extraordinary height to which the tide rises, the fall at high water is between those rocks into the river, and at low water from the river, into the Port. The inhabitants of St. Johns' received us with the greatest hospitality, and we were soon welcome inmates of all their houses. Major Pearson who commanded the three companies at St. Johns', appointed me to act as Adjutant, & as there was always a Town Major to the place, he desired me to take the duties of that situation also. These were, the charge of several signal stations, & particularly of one, on Partridge island, at the mouth of the river. The different guards of the place, were also mounted by the Town Major, & visited by him at night, & many was the cold walk which this part of my duty imposed upon me. There was not any pay attached to the situation, but a Captain's allowance of fuel was given, instead. The quantity which I received as a Subaltern, being quite sufficient for all my wants, I did not draw the Town Major's allowance from the wood yard, & it was bought from me, by the Commissary, who paid me for what I had saved in about eight months, more than forty pounds. Any Officer had the privilege of leaving in the stores, whatever portion of his wood allowance, was more than he found it necessary to consume, and money was always paid him for this saving. The Commanding Officer adopted a similar principle of economy for the men, and whenever the money in this saving fund was sufficient for the purpose, they received each, a new flannel shirt, or a pair of shoes. This was found to be an excellent system, and the more so, as it did not in the least diminish the abundant warmth which is necessary in the barrack rooms, during a North American winter. I bought a Canoe, gave her a mast & sail, & began to amuse myself in sailing about the river, that I might secure as much of this amusement as I could, before the formation of ice should render it impossible. I had not well indulged myself three weeks, in this favourite recreation, when one cold day, as I was recrossing from St. John's to the opposite shore, a sudden gust took my little sails aback and over I went. The tide was running rapidly out, and the Canoe was at first separated from me, but I quickly swam after her, and overtook her. She was bottom uppermost. I threw my arm round one of her ends, and called for assistance. We were fast drifting down towards Partridge island, and surveying my situation as calmly as it was in my power, under such circumstances, I had resolved, when we came abreast of it, to cast myself off from the Canoe, and swim for it. Luckily the accident had been seen from the shore, and I heard oars and voices behind me, and some one cried out "keep your hold, and don't be frightened, we are close to you." I answered, "I am not frightened, but perishing with cold, and can scarcely keep to the Canoe any longer." The boat pushed on, and I was laid hold of & dragged into it. Perceiving that my Canoe had not been secured also, I insisted upon steering after it, & it was saved. When I was landed, which was close to the Barracks, I was put into a bed between two blankets, had my body well rubbed, and a good glass of hot brandy & water, but it was some time before I could shake off the shivering of my limbs, as I must have been in the water nearly a quarter of an hour. I gave the poor fellows who picked me up, all that remained to me of my months pay, which was about nine Dollars; & I told them it was really all I had, they were perfectly satisfied, which I own is more than I was myself.

We were sitting at the Messroom table one evening when a letter was brought, to the Commanding Officer, from Major General Hunter who commanded at Frederic Town, about a hundred miles up the river, inviting him & any of his Officers who chose to accompany him, to a ball he was about to give the night but one after, in honour of the birth-day of the Queen or some other of the Royal family. None of the Officers thinking it worth while to go a hundred miles to a ball except the Commanding Officer himself, who thought he could not well decline the General's invitation, I, being his Adjutant, did not like to let him go alone, & agreed to accompany him. The river was completely frozen over, & the only conveyance we could use was a sledge. It was lined with bear skin, and fastened on all sides so closely, that the snow could not get in. There was no head to it, but we were muffled up almost to the eyes in fur cloaks, on the collars of which, during the journey, our very breath shewed itself in Icicles. The Sledge was drawn by a pair of horses, yoked abreast, which trotted at the rate of ten miles an hour. There were post houses, or stations, as they were called, every fourteen or fifteen miles, close at the edge of the river. At these places, we changed our horses. We had left St. Johns' about nine oclock in the morning & arrived at Frederic Town at seven in the evening, where we were received by Colonel Cuyler, who took us to his quarters, & entertained us hospitably. We had scarcely refreshed ourselves, when it was time to dress for the ball. General Hunter was exceedingly pleased that we had come so far to his entertainment, and invited us to remain the next day with him, but some pressing Regimental duty, made it impossible for Major Pearson to remain, and we retraced our steps on the Ice immediately after breakfast the morning after the ball, & arrived at St. Johns' to a late dinner. In our way back, we were several times severely jolted, by the sudden passage of the sledge over large cracks or fissures in the Ice, & I have been told, that at night, a dim sort of flame is sometimes observable issuing from them, but I had never any opportunity of acertaining the fact of the existence of such a phenomenon.

We were beginning to think our residence at St. Johns' rather dull, and therefore determined to give the natives a dance, & with our usual activity, decorated our Messroom with spruce fir, almost the only evergreen of the country. It was a cold snowy night & we almost began to fear that our Company could not reach us, but about eight oclock, the gingling of the bells of their sledges, put an end to our apprehensions, & we had a right merry dance, which did not finish before early the next morning. This set the society of the place in motion, & dinners & parties were given by the respective families, to those Officers who had danced with their daughters or kins-folk, and it ended by the inhabitants clubbing together to give us a handsome ball & supper, which they did, & a whole round of gaieties & amusements succeeded.

January 9th 1810. Having understood that there was a respectable lodge of Freemasons here, several Officers of the Regiment, myself in the number, resolved to dive into the mysteries of the fraternity, and I this night took the degree of "Entered Apprentice". Being sufficiently recovered from the effects of my initiation before the 12th I was advanced to the degree of "Fellow Craft" and on the 15th found myself duly qualified for a "Master Mason", to which post I was raised. We had a lodge in the Regiment, some of the members of which united themselves to that of the Town, to assist in fraternizing their brother Officers. With the step of "Master Mason" I remained satisfied until the 20th of March, when I found myself again under the influence of Masonic fever, and resolved on the acquisition of higher honours. I therefore took the several degrees of "Master Mark", "Past Master", "Most Excellent Master", and "Royal Arch", and the respect which I observed was shewn to my red apron was an ample recompence for the extraordinary trials I had undergone in the progress of my researches into the secrets of this most ancient and respectable Brotherhood. I next became a Member of our Regimental Lodge, which was called, "Number 33, of the Royal Welsh Fusileers" and was appointed its Secretary. Many men would have remained content in this exalted station, but as there were higher degrees to be acquired I determined to grasp at them; but this was attended with difficulty, as it was not easy to muster a sufficient number, according to the statutes, to confer them. On the 23rd of June however this was accomplished, & I became successively a "Knight Templar," and "Knight of Malta." The very day after this important arrangement took place, we received orders to join the Head Quarters of the Regiment at Halifax, where it had proceeded from Annapolis Royal preparatory to our embarkation for Portugal, and on the 6th of July we sailed from St. Johns' in the Lady Delaval Transport Schooner. We beat about the bay of Fundy in thick fogs and adverse winds, until the 19th when we made Halifax Harbour, & disembarked on the following day. We found that the 7th Fusileers had already sailed, and to our great surprise and mortification, understood, that we were not to follow them, until the arrival of the next English mail should confirm or annul the order for our departure. Never was disappointment greater than that which we experienced, when this arrangement was announced to us. Colonel Pakenham, brother in law to Sir Arthur Wellesley, (that brave Officer who was afterwards killed at New Orleans) had been sent for a few months before, and when he left us for Europe had faithfully promised, that he would spare no exertion to induce Sir Arthur to ask for the two Fusileer Regiments & thus to have them emancipated from the inactive scenes of a garrison life in North America, and permitted to share in the interesting warfare of the Peninsula. He had promised us too, that he would himself beg to have the command of us, and as he was a Colonel very senior on the list, we thought it probable that his brother in law, would accede to his wishes; we were all fond of him, & looked forwards with sincere delight to service under his command. When however we found on our arrival at Halifax that the 7th, his own Regiment, had actually sailed, and that our departure depended on a contingency—that the next English Packet might possibly condemn us to North American service for years to come, we were really quite in despair, & it is not possible to describe the intensity of our feelings as the usual time for the arrival of a Packet drew near. We were kept too, in that state of doubt, which prevented our making any arrangements of Mess, or Barrack rooms, of a permanent or comfortable nature, and this inconvenience, added to our other disquietudes, made us sulky and ill-tempered. At length however the well known signal from the Citadel, announced the packet in sight, and down we flew to the shore, as tho' it had been possible to see our destiny written on her very top-sails. She anchored—the Mail was landed, and carried to Sir George Provost's. In about an hour, Colonel Ellis our Commanding Officer was sent for. It is needless to say for what, or how many bottles of wine were drunk at the Mess that evening, to assist in getting off a stock which we did not choose to leave behind us. We were mustered on the Parade of the North Barracks the following morning in heavy marching order, and our immediate destiny for Portugal was made known to the men. They received it with three cheers. There still remained another cause for uneasiness. The Ships on board of which we were to embark, were to have followed the Packet from England as quickly as possible; they had not arrived. Where could these Ships be? It was the 6th of October. Just before Sun-set, the Telegraph at the Citadel hoisted the signal of "A Ship of War in sight", and shortly afterwards a second signal announced the appearance of another. They soon came up, under press of sail, and proved to be the "Diadem" 64, and "Regulus" 44, armed en Flute, for the reception of Troops. They had orders to take on board the 23rd Fusileers and carry them to Lisbon. Here then was the realization of all our hopes. The usual preparations were made, we were inspected by Sir George Prevost who took leave of us in a very flattering garrison order. Bills were collected and I believe paid, farewells were bid to Sweet-hearts, and the 11th of October 1810, saw us safely embarked for the Peninsula, nearly a thousand Bayonets, and in the best possible service order.

October 12th. The wind being fair, we were off this morning, and long before dark, had lost all sight of land.

14th. We went in chase of a strange sail. She was an American from the West Indies, and had not any news to communicate.

Captain Phillimore, who commanded the Diadem, was so exceed-ingly strict in all his regulations on board ship, that our men were getting into constant scrapes. The Officers of the Regiment also, having been used to embark on board Transports, and little accustomed to the precise arrangements, which are found necessary on board a Ship of War, were perpetually transgressing some little point or other of etiquette, and incurring the Captain's displeasure. This led to explana-tions with our commanding Officer, who endeavoured to find excuses for us, in our ignorance of man of war discipline, and a sort of coolness insensibly arose, between him and Captain Phillimore, although they did not permit it to affect their outward conduct towards each other, on any point of duty. The blame incurred by us, was more from faults of omission than of premeditated disobedience, which will be the more easily conceived, when I enumerate some of the points, to which it was necessary for us, at all times to direct our attention. Whenever an Officer came on deck from below, it was requisite for him to take off his hat, as a salute to the Pennant flying on the Main-top gallant mast head. It was also enjoined us that we should not on any account lean against the Capstan, or sit on any of the Gun-carriages. Then we were on no account to walk on the wind-ward side of the quarter deck, nor were we to assemble in groups of more than two on the deck, with various other little particularities of the same nature. It may easily be supposed how frequent would be omissions, connected with subjects of so trifling a nature particularly from men so little accustomed to similar restraints on their movements. The Capstan being a most tempting thing to lean upon, in blowing weather, even with the best intentions to the contrary, we found it very difficult to deny ourselves the support which it gave us, and our errors on this point were more frequent than on any other. One day we found it tarred all round and sure enough the flies were caught, & at the expence of a spoiled jacket, we learned to behave better in future. Traps were also laid for us on the gun carriages, into which we fell, land-lubbers as we were, to the great amusement of the crew, but upon the whole, we were good tempered fellows, and took our share of the laugh tho' against ourselves.

October 16th. We saw many Dolphin to day, and caught two. Towards the evening there was very heavy thunder and lightning. Three water-spouts approached very near the Ship. The Regulus fired at one, and it fell.

17th. A heavy gale of wind, but quite fair. We were going during the whole of this day at the rate of 12 knots an hour. A ball of fire fell close to us.

29th. From the 17th to this day, nothing particular occurred. About night fall we made the Western Islands.

30th. Saw the remarkable Peak of Pico. It is a volcanic mountain, about 8000 feet from the surface of the Sea to the summit of the Peak. There are many craters on its sides, tho' most of them are now concealed by trees. The last eruption of this Volcano was in 1718, when it destroyed most of the vineyards round about it.

31st. Past by the remainder of the Western Islands, and lay to in the evening off Graciosa, for Ships astern to come up.

November 11th. Made the rock of Lisbon, in thick and blowing weather, which prevented our approaching the shore.

November 12th. Entered the Tagus, sailing by the Fortress of St. Julian, and Belem Castle. Anchored close to the great Square of Lisbon called the Praço do Comarcio, and remained on board this night.

13th. Landed. A few days before we entered the Tagus, I had a violent attack of Jaundice, which was at its height when we anchored. This rendered it quite impossible for me to move, at the time that the Regiment landed, & I was conveyed to Belem, and put into sick quarters. It was a considerable time before I recovered my strength, and during my convalescence I employed myself in learning the Spanish language, in which I took great interest, and made rapid proficiency. I had long observed how many advantages, both of observation and promotion, Officers of the Staff had over those who remained with their Regiments, and the appointment to a Staff situation was an object of my ardent wishes. This made me the more anxious to acquire the Spanish language, as I thought it more than probable that Officers acquainted with it, would be sought for, and brought forwards, and the result proved that I was correct in this, as in the following September it was my principal recommendation, to the Staff appointment which I then obtained.

IV
The Peninsular War:
The Defensive Phase, 1810–1812

Fought incessantly over eight long and bloody years, beginning in 1807, the campaigns waged in Portugal, Spain and southern France are collectively known as the Peninsular War. Often regarded as a diverting incident to the main action in central Europe, the Peninsular War, which at various times tied down between 150,000 and 300,000 French troops, was of central importance to the course and ultimate outcome of the Napoleonic Wars. In fact, the average loss of some 300 men each day for eight years, combined with the long-term adverse effects of the campaign on French resources, probably contributed more to the defeat of Napoleon than any other single factor. Thus, what began in November 1807 as an opportunistic invasion of Portugal by the French to force that nation to adhere to Napoleon's grandiose Continental System against Britain, quickly involved the French nation in a morass in Portugal and, particularly, in Spain, from which it never escaped.

With French troops in key Spanish towns which formed a link between Bayonne in southwestern France and the Portuguese frontier, and ostensibly holding the line of communication, Spain was in fact an occupied state. This served Napoleon's ambitions well, since Spain was neither a willing nor an effective participant in the Continental System. French relations with Spain steadily worsened as Napoleon prepared for a strategic assault against Britain at Gibraltar and other targets in the Mediterranean, using Spain as a staging area. Under the guise of a friendly intervention to mediate the dispute then dividing the Spanish royal family, and to bring order to Spain's squalid and chaotic politics, additional French troops took possession of such key fortresses in northern Spain as Pamplona, San Sebastian, Figueras and Barcelona, beginning in February 1808, in order to control the passes through from the Pyrenees.

Napoleon badly misjudged Spanish popular loyalty to the

monarchy when in April he compelled all parties of the Spanish reigning house to sign away their rights and gave the throne of Spain to Joseph Bonaparte, his brother. He also under-estimated the suspicion Spaniards felt towards the French. Indeed, spurred on by the clergy, the Spanish would become obsessed with the notion that the French were the agents of the devil. All this rapidly resulted in a merciless popular war against the French, a struggle which pre-figures modern wars of national liberation. Above all, however, Napoleon misjudged Britain's ability to act decisively on the Continent.

The French army had barely enough time to settle into their new quarters when the rumble of rebellion could be heard. On 1 April 1808, the first anti-French riots occurred in Madrid. This was followed by serious rioting on 2 May in Madrid, which was brutally put down by the French. By early June virtually every province in Spain was arming. At the same time, the Junta of Seville sought British assistance at Gibraltar. London replied promptly, and 10,000 men were despatched to help either the Portuguese or the Spanish. This force, commanded by Sir Arthur Wellesley, or as one may refer to him for convenience in advance of subsequent ennoblement, Wellington, landed at Figuiera, 100 miles north of Lisbon on 1 August 1808. The main reinforcements, however, were expected to arrive some time later under the command of Sir John Moore.

For Britain, the great drama of the Peninsula opened with brilliant success, followed by farce and subsequent defeat. On 21 August 1808, Wellesley at the head of a 17,000-man Anglo-Portuguese army thoroughly defeated a French army under General Jean Junot, who lost thirteen cannon and 2,000 men. Wellington, however, was superseded in his command by Sir Harry Burrard, who, one day later, was succeeded by Sir Hew Dalrymple. These ludicrous changes in the command of the army stemmed from questions of seniority and personal tiffs. The result, according to J. Steven Watson, was to give authority to those officers who apparently lacked the will to defeat the French. The three senior British officers agreed to negotiate with the French, who requested an armistice and who were ably led by General François Kellermann. The result of the discussions was the sensational Convention of Cintra (the word capitulation was not used), the terms of which permitted the French free evacuation and repatriation by British shipping for 26,000 troops, including their baggage and booty. The inexplicably easy terms for a defeated army agreed to on 22 August 1808 provoked outrage in England. Wellington, Burrard and Dalrymple were subsequently recalled to London to face a court of enquiry and the indignation of a nation thirsting for military victory. Their departure left the command of the Anglo-Portuguese army, 30,000 of whom were British troops, to Sir John Moore. The collapse, however, of the Spanish central resistance, and the presence in Spain of Napoleon together with other competent marshals and generals at the head of a quarter of a million veteran troops numbered Moore's days in the Peninsula. Pursued by a vastly superior force, Moore retreated to the British fleet in Corunna, in northwestern Spain, where on 16 January 1809, he was mortally wounded in the final stages of an operation that resulted in the strategic retreat of 27,000 British troops from the Peninsula. Aided by Britain's defeat, the French could now turn their full attention to the further reduction of Spanish resistance.

The misfortunes of the war in Portugal and Spain did not prevent Castlereagh, the Secretary for War, from making yet another major decision. In the summer of 1809, he selected Wellington to take command of the forces in Portugal. On 22 April, Wellington arrived for the second time at Lisbon, which had never been abandoned by its British garrison. His immediate object, which would take several years to achieve, was the defence of Portugal and the establishment of a strong base at Lisbon before he could attempt the systematic liberation of Spain. One of the key elements in Wellington's plan for the defeat of the French was the use of a small, well-trained and highly disciplined Anglo-Portuguese army with a large and diffuse partisan force. Acting in concert, these two forces would immobilize the much larger French army with an insolvable strategic problem: in order to check the guerrillas, the French needed to disperse their troops in garrisons, along lines of communications and in punitive expeditions; to deal with Wellington's Anglo-Portuguese army of 45,000 British and 30,000 Portuguese troops, they had to concentrate their forces.

Another vital feature of Wellington's strategic plan was what he correctly perceived to be the inability of the French army to remain for long periods on the same ground for fear of starvation. The dazzling marching speed of the French army was paid for by the abandonment of eighteenth-century military orthodoxy with respect to the servicing of an army and supply. The French no longer relied on the traditional method of establishing supply depots. Free from this encumbrance, French armies could now appear where they were not anticipated. This freedom of move-

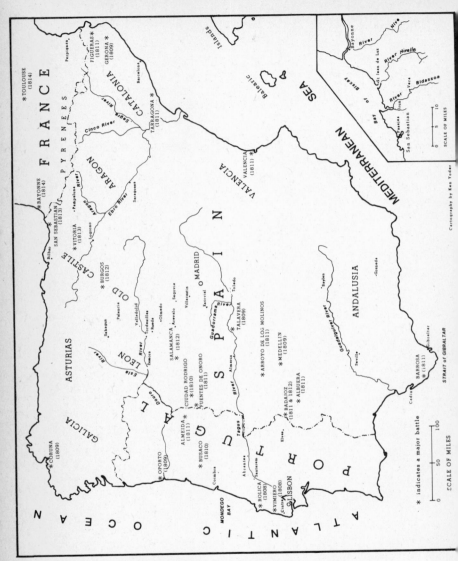

PENINSULAR CAMPAIGN: 1808–1814

ment was dependent on the French requisitioning their food in those areas they passed through or occupied. A huge army, however, rapidly exhausted all movable food within a radius of about twenty miles. An army in this predicament could not reach new food supplies without the relocation of the entire force. One counter measure to the French tactic of living off the land would be to compel them to conduct prolonged operations in a given region, which would have the intended effect of clearing the contested land of food. Thus, the French had to disperse to live, but concentrate to fight pitched battles for a short period of time only.

Wellington's strategic plan from 1809 to 1812 was to support the local forces and to make periodic expeditions from his Lisbon base and sanctuary deep into French-occupied territory to create confusion. It was not until after the capture of Ciudad Rodrigo and Badajoz, key frontier fortresses, in early 1812 (coupled with Napoleon's coincidental weakening of his forces in Spain in order to prepare for his invasion of Russia), that Wellington was able to go on to the offensive.

The keystone of Wellington's defensive strategy was the Lines of Torres Vedras, a triple line of forts across the Lisbon peninsula. The third or innermost line consisted of fortifications to protect the harbour of Lisbon for an embarkation, if such proved necessary. The two outer lines functioned as one system. They comprised natural difficulties developed in great secrecy, beginning in October 1809, by a Royal Engineers officer, Colonel Sir Richard Fletcher, and sapper officers ably assisted by 10,000 Portuguese labourers. This herculean task barred tracks, turned valleys into obstacle courses, transformed the eastern face of every hill into a formidable barrier and dammed water everywhere to inundate lines of approach. As for armaments, the Lines comprised 108 redoubts mounting 447 guns. The garrison required to man the original 108 redoubts (to which an additional forty-two were added in 1810) totalled 25,000. The last garrison troops entered the Lines in October 1810, one month before Browne arrived. When he landed he probably joined the main army which was massed around Mafra, some twenty-five to thirty miles northwest of Lisbon. In this position the army was ready to march to any threatened sector of the Lines along specially constructed lateral roads. In addition to these imposing preparations, five signal stations were constructed at intervals on dominant and intervisible peaks, a Royal Navy flotilla patrolled the Tagus, and a scorched-earth policy was implemented on Wellington's orders to deny the

French supplies of any kind.

In October 1810, Masséna's army totalling about 60,000 men came to an abrupt halt in front of Torres Vedras, whose existence came to him as a complete surprise. Realizing that the Lines were impregnable, and faced with the enormous difficulty of supplying his army from a devastated countryside, Masséna executed a tactical withdrawal in mid-November to the more prosperous region around Santarem, some forty miles north of Torres Vedras. Despite this movement and the arrival of reinforcements, the French strength dwindled to 47,000 troops. By March 1811, Masséna admitted defeat and on 5 March formally abandoned his offensive. The French had lost 25,000 men. Portugal was now cleared although not secured, since the French still occupied the three great fortresses of Almeida, Ciudad Rodrigo and Badajoz, all of which commanded the "corridors" linking Portugal with Spain. Wellington would remain on the defensive until these fortresses fell to his courageous troops during the period 1811–12. Nonetheless, the Lines of Torres Vedras had served their purpose well and Masséna's strategic retreat was undoubtedly the turning point in the Peninsular War.[188]

1810. CAMPAIGNS IN THE PENINSULA

WHEN we disembarked, the Regiment was immediately supplied with camp kettles, and other necessary equipment for taking the field, the Officers purchased Mules to carry their baggage, and provided themselves with canteens, containing a few knives and forks, spoons and plates, with a drinking tin or two, and this preparatory equipment being completed, the Regiment began its march for the lines of Torres Vedras, about 850 Bayonets, and was brigaded with the 1st and 2nd Battalions of the 7th. We were then called the Fusileer Brigade. The French Army was in front, 70,000 strong, under Marshal Massena. The force under Lord Wellington was about 35,000 British, and 25,000 Portuguese.

The lines of Torres Vedras extended from Alhandra on the Tagus, to the mouth of a small stream called the Sizandro. The line across the country between these points, if drawn directly, would be about twenty seven miles, but owing to the zig-zag direction of the vallies, the line of defence was nearly forty. Every road, which could have afforded any advantage to the enemy, had been broken up, and others had been opened, to facilitate our communications with each other. Inundations had been made wherever it was possible, hills had been scarped perpendicularly, and intrenchments formed in all directions. Every approach was commanded by cannon, and redoubts had been made, capable of offering an obstinate resistance, even should the French get into their rear, and these redoubts were well provided with provisions and ammunition. Alhandra was the head-quarters of General Hill, who commanded on the right. The Tagus was on his right flank, and gun boats were stationed in it, to give that flank additional strength. General Picton commanded on the left, his head quarters were in the village which gave the name to these formidable lines. The weakest part of the position was between Torres Vedras and the sea. Here were the inundations, which extended nearly six miles along the river Sizandro to the Sea. The centre reached from the heights of Sobral to Torres Vedras. Marshal Beresford's quarters were in the former little Town. Lord Wellington was at the Quinta de Pero Negro, about two leagues from Torres Vedras. Sobral was the principal point of defence, on this part of the line.

In the rear of this line, and nearly parallel to it, at a distance of about seven miles was a second fortified position. And again a third was established, along the mouth of the Tagus, which would have secured our embarkation, had we been beaten from the other lines of defence, and compelled to take to our Ships.

The French on several occasions, made demonstrations of attack on different parts of our formidable position, which was daily increasing in strength, from the thousands of Portuguese, who were kept constantly at work, under the direction of British Engineer Officers. Massena's first attempt was against a redoubt at the foot of the heights of Sobral, opposite to which, he had himself established one. His attack was not only completely repulsed, but we followed up the enemy in his retreat, and took his redoubt from him, which we maintained. Such demonstrations and attacks kept us constantly on the qui vive, and the Troops were always under arms before day light, with their Commander ready to direct their operations, in case of a general attack; and thus matters went on day after day, and week after week, until the 14th of December, when after considerable suffering from famine and desertion, Massena broke up from his position in our front, and retired to Santarem. Lord Wellington followed, and established his Head Quarters at Cartaxo. The French lost about 400 men in this short retreat.

In the early period of our occupation of these lines the people of Lisbon were under considerable apprehension least we should not persist in defending them, but move down to the Tagus some night or other, and embark, leaving in the lines only a sufficient number of men, to keep fires burning, in order to deceive the French; but as the position became more and more strong, their confidence increased and such was the security they felt, that parties from Lisbon used constantly to come up to see the lines, as a curiosity. The Fleet had furnished a Battalion of about 800 Sailors, and they were stationed at the Town of Alhandra. Nothing could exceed the delight of our Jack Tars, on finding themselves thus called on for land service, and the fun they used to have in this forsaken village,[189] as they sat in the streets, smoking their pipes, in venerable, velvet covered chairs, studded all over with brass nails, was highly amusing. They used every now and then, to fire a shot from their gun-boats, at the flank of the enemy, nearest the water, and on one occasion, as the French General La Croix, was reconnoitering this part of the line, one of these random shot struck and killed him. Our Picquets in some parts of the position had been on very good terms with those of the French, and there had not only been a sort of tacit understanding, that they should not fire on each other, but some of our men, had even gone so far, as to drink wine with the Picquets in their immediate front, this practice however was soon forbidden as being quite inconsistent with military prudence. Shortly after their retreat to Santarem, the enemy began to strengthen all the commanding spots, in the neighbourhood of that place, and took every other step which could indicate an intention of permanent cantonment there. They began to amuse themselves, and act plays, and invitations were even sent to Officers of our Staff, to go in, and witness these spectacles, with assurance of the perfect freedom of return. Several were exceedingly well disposed to accept these invitations, but Lord Wellington would not permit it.

Notwithstanding our advance from Torres Vedras, on the retreat of the French from their position in its front, the lines continued to be occupied by part of the British, and almost the whole of the Portuguese Army; and it was during this time that an Aid de camp of Massena's was taken in the act of making sketches of some parts of the defences. He was disguised as a Peasant, and consequently being in every sense of the word a Spy, his life became a forfeit, by the acknowledged laws of War, to the unsoldier-like nature of his ocupation. The Portuguese Government and Troops, loudly demanded his immediate death, but Lord Wellington, possibly thinking, that the prolongation of his life, added to the hope of its preservation, might perhaps induce him to make some interesting discoveries connected with the strength and condition of the French Army, would not consent to his execution, but ordered him to be sent to the Castle of St. Julian and to kept there, a close prisoner. Many attempts were made to extract from him the information that was expected, but in vain. He resisted every promise, and every threat. The Army moved on, and he was forgotten. About eight months afterwards, it fell to my lot to visit Fort St. Julian on some duty connected with the depot of ammunition there, and I carelessly asked, what had become of the French Officer that had been taken up in our lines as a Spy, and sent there. The Fort Major answered me, that he was still in a dungeon, as no final orders respecting him had been received. I asked to see him, and having been supplied with a Lantern, descended by stone steps to the spot of his confinement. When the door of his dungeon was opened, I was dreadfully shocked at the sight which presented itself to me. The vault in which he lay was filled with straw, which appeared to me quite damp. It was many feet below the tide even at low water, and the dashing of the waves was distinctly heard above. Light was received through an iron grating which opened into the Fort, and close to it a Sentry had his post. At nights, and when it rained, this grating was covered with an Iron lid. By the light of my Lantern, the poor fellow looked upwards of sixty years old, although I was assured he was not more than twenty three. He had suffered his beard to grow, which added greatly to his wretched and squalid appearance. I asked him if he wanted anything, and he answered "every thing". On my telling him that he must be aware, that death had always been considered the just fate of a detected Spy, he replied "that he was not ignorant of it, but that he obeyed the orders he had received from his Commanding Officer, and that death was preferable to the punishment that was inflicted on him." He added "that he was very anxious for some books, and a little more light, and also that an additional blanket would be very acceptable to him." I caused this last request to be granted him before I left the place, but was not so successful with regard to the books and light. I have reason to believe that this French Officer remained in his dungeon three years after I had seen him, and that his release was owing to my having accidentally told his story to a Nobleman high in power on my return to England after the peace of 1814. The fact was, that in the great arrangements and negociations of the times, this poor creature had been forgotten, and I do not believe that his release would otherwise ever have entered into the consideration of the Portuguese Government.

When Lord Wellington made his forward movement to Cartaxo, the Fusileer Brigade was quartered at Azambuja, and we remained quiet there until the 5th of March, when the French again made a retrograde march. Massena had at this time under his orders, some of the ablest French Marshals. Ney and Junot both commanded Corps — Oudinot, Regnier and Victor were at the heads of Divisions — Loison and Montbrun were also under his orders. Soult and Suchet, carried on distinct operations in other parts of Spain. Nothing could well evince the deep interest which Napoleon took in the subjugation of Spain and Portugal more than the employment of men whose names are so well known in the military annals of the times.

March 10th 1811. The French continue their retreat and leave behind a considerable number of stragglers. Lord Wellington established his Head Quarters at Thomar. We had sharp skirmishing with the rear guard of the French, which was endeavouring to gain as much time as possible, to enable them to bury such cannon as they could not conveniently take away with them. Many sick and wounded fell into our hands.[190]

As this little journal cannot detail all that passed in the different divisions of the army, it will necessarily be found very scanty in description, the observations which it embraces being confined to what could be picked up in the hurry and bustle of continued marching and counter marching, at the Head Quarters of the army, to which I was attached on the Staff of the Adjutant General. I had neither leisure nor inclination to collect the materials for book making at any future time, and am only induced to transcribe in a somewhat enlarged shape the little memoranda I made in a rough book of notes, from the pleasure I derive in retracing scenes, which at that period were so deeply interesting to me, both professionally and otherwise. I sometimes regret that I had not kept a more detailed journal, which might have been worth offering to the public.

March 14th. The enemy retire, and we continue our pursuit, taking several cannon and tumbrils. Head Quarters slept at Redinha.

15th. We halted. There was some smart skirmishing between our advance, and the French rear guard, with some loss on both sides. About this time, a circumstance occurred, which proved the efficiency of well conducted squares of infantry, however small, against the attacks of powerful bodies of cavalry. A Brigade of our light Dragoons overtook and were about to charge, on a plain distant nearly three quarters of a mile from any rising ground, a part of the French rear-guard of about 150 Infantry. When our Cavalry overtook them, they were moving off in line, under the command of a French Officer, mounted on a miserable little bit-of-a Pony, who immediately formed his Detachment into two Squares. Whilst one of these Squares retreated, the other kept up a constant fire, on our Squadron of Cavalry attempting to charge it. The horses would not face it and many of them were killed. When the retreating Square was pursued, it halted; and began the same sort of unapproachable fire; the other then commencing its retreat, & passing by the Square that was engaged, which in its turn moved off, when its partner in this conflict had stopped and faced our Cavalry. By this alternate movement in Square this little body of French Infantry defied the efforts of a whole Brigade of well mounted British Cavalry, to capture them, and gained the heights in their rear, with little or no loss. Our Cavalry could not pursue them to this high ground, on which there was a thick wood. The last man who entered this cover, was the French Officer himself, who before doing so, rode forwards a few paces, and taking off his hat, waved it in a sort of triumphant good bye. This occurrence took place in sight of both armies, and although an anxious desire that the French Detachment should be taken, was naturally felt by us, it was not possible to withhold from the gallantry and skill of its Commander, a sort of reluctant congratulation on his escape, the success of which could not but prove both interesting and instructive, to many an Infantry Officer who witnessed it.

March 16th. Head Quarters moved on to Coimbra. The place had been completely ransacked by the French, and scarcely an inhabitant was found in it. Several of its beautiful Churches had been converted into Stables for Cavalry, and were filled with straw and dirt. The doors of the Vestries had been forced open, and the drawers of the wardrobes, in which the Priests' garments were kept, had been left on the floor, the robes themselves scattered about in all directions. Altars and Images were defaced, and the marks of pistol bullets shewed that they had been shot at, as a mark. Rich silk vestments, covered with gold or silver embroidery, were used as horse clothes, and every other symbol of the

Catholic religion had been turned to similar account. And here I must acknowledge, that this evil example was not without its effect, even on ourselves, but in somewhat a different manner. The splendid robes which the French had left on the floors of the Vestries, we gathered up respectfully, and cut them into waistcoats and dressing gowns. On our days of halt and washing, it was not an unusual sight, to see Officers, whilst their shirts were drying, pacing to and fro, in front of a bivouac formed of the branches of trees, in the bedizened garments of Catholic Priests and Bishops.

The magnificent Cathedral of Coimbra, had been in a certain degree respected, but its famous University, the Students of which had long since fled, was naturally enough converted into a barrack by the French, and as naturally occupied by us, in the same capacity. Coimbra stands on high ground, is about a hundred miles north-east of Lisbon, and on the river Mondego. At this period it was not an uncommon sight, to meet parties of Nuns in most deplorable condition. They were sometimes on foot, and at others mounted, two on a mule, with the old Abbess of the Convent, from which they had been chased, at their head, bearing usually in her hand, a small black Crucifix. The enemy had no further injured them, than by turning them adrift to get possession of the convents for their Troops. Their age and squalid appearance certainly guaranteed their personal safety. Monks, in like manner, covered the roads, and I cannot say that I felt much sympathy for these fat and idle vagabonds. We furnished them however with rations, in order to secure their good opinion, and I believe, they became no mean auxiliaries, in directing public feeling and vengeance, against every thing that was French. In a military point of view the occupation of their Monesteries was certainly of some importance, as they were almost always situated on commanding ground, in the midst of fruit or Olive trees, and usually surrounded with whatever was necessary for the comforts or convenience of life. Sometimes they overlooked the fords or bridges or rivers, and were not unfrequently in situations which commanded the approaches to roads. All these circumstances made them very desirable posts for military occupation, and the Monks were accordingly dislodged, to make room for Troops.[191] Our Soldiers used to laugh heartily at these bare-headed and bare-footed Padres as they passed them on the roads, and occasionally offered them a mouthful of Rum, which the Monk never refused, and paid for, by an "Ave Maria" or a "Viva los Inglesis."

Many noble Portuguese families followed in our rear to reoccupy their houses, which they had abandoned when the enemy first advanced towards Lisbon. Their looks of despair when they viewed the altered condition of the Palace or Quinta, which they had left in full beauty, rich in furniture and comforts of every kind, and now changed into a mass of ruin and desolation was truly lamentable, and tears ran down their cheeks as they took us from room to room, telling us what each had been, and pointing to what it was. As there were not many horses left in the country, having been all pressed into the service of the Artillery or Commissariat, either by the French or ourselves, the females of the families thus venturing upon a reconnoissance of their county seats, were usually borne in a machine shaped exactly like a Sedan chair, the poles were supported by Mules, being run through a leather strap on each side of a saddle in the situation of our stirrup leathers. I never got into one of these vehicles, but they are said to be very easy, and were occasionally employed in conveying to the rear, Officers who had been severly wounded. I may here remark, that although the greater part of the horses had been taken from the King's stables for military purposes, it appeared to me, that a much greater number, were left in them, than was necessary. The Royal stables are for a thousand Horses. Those which I saw in them were remarkably sleek, and in good condition, and yet I was assured that they are never permitted to lie down; in fact the shortness of the halter with which they were tied, would not admit of it, and several of them appeared to be sleeping, as they stood. They are fed on chopped wheat straw, with very little corn.

Our men had already learned divers ingenious modes of ascertaining, where valuables or property of any description might have been con- cealed, in houses that were deserted. There being many families, who though they had fled at the approach of the French, were by no means disposed to return, whilst their villages were occupied by the English. The ground floors of the houses being usually formed of a sort of composition, when anything had been buried in them, the Soldier made the discovery by thrusting in his bayonet or ramrod, and when these told no tales to his satisfaction, his custom was to water the floor, when, any spot that had been lately disturbed, would absorb the water first, which led to the detection of many a hidden store of eatables, drinkables or linen. It was the worst plan possible, for a family to abandon its dwelling, as it was thus left entirely at the mercy of daily changing guests, but those habitations in which a member of the household remained, were always respected, and at no other charge than that of giving shelter, either to an Officer, or a certain number of Troops.

March 18th. Head Quarters moved to the Ponte de Marcella — where there was a good deal of skirmishing during the whole day. We overtook the enemy's rear guard at the bridge over the Alva at this place, and after a very sharp affair, in which they lost a hundred men killed and wounded, we took three hundred prisoners from them, and they lost nearly four hundred, in their attempts to cross at a ford, lower down the river. Their confusion on this bridge was indescribable. They threw over guns and tumbrils, and baggage, without end, their killed also, and many of their wounded. They drew up however on the opposite bank in such force, that we did not attempt to follow them. There is perhaps no scene more interesting in warfare, than the disputed passage of a bridge.

March 20th. Head Quarters, St. Marinha. There was sharp skirmishing during the whole day, with some loss on both sides. The 4th Division, in which was the Fusileer Brigade, was ordered to proceed by Abrantes, to the Alentejo, to join a Corps there, under the orders of Marshal Beresford. I was at this time sent to Lisbon on some duty connected with the records of the Adjutant General's department, and was detained there for some time, owing to which, I was not present at the battle of Albuera, or the siege of Badajos, but I am enabled to continue my journal, from the daily sources of information, which were within my reach.

March 23rd. Head Quarters, Celorico. Marshal Beresford's are at Chamusca, on the south bank of the Tagus. The enemy only shewed himself by his picquets and videttes.

April 3rd. Head Quarters, Marmeleiro — Beresford's at Portalegre. Here he was joined by the 4th Division under General Cole, which made the force under his command, including Portuguese, about 22,000 men.

4th. Head Quarters, Guarda. The light Division had severe skirmishing during the whole day, and lost 5 Officers and about 100 men killed and wounded. The French occupy Almeida.

7th. Head Quarters remain at Guarda, those of Marshal Beresford moved to Elvas. Everything quiet at the out posts.

10th. Lord Wellington offers battle near Almeida, which the enemy declines and retires, leaving in that Fortress a garrison of 1500 men.

12th. We took up a position in front of Almeida, between the Coa, and Agueda, rivers, in order to blockade that place, as it was known from intercepted letters and other information that the garrison which had been left there, was badly supplied with provisions.

20th. There was frequent skirmishing between the 10th and this day. In the Alentejo, the French take Olivenza—cross the Guadiana, and besiege Campo Maior, which after a gallant defence of a week, though manned with a very small garrison, surrenders. Marshal Beresford retook it the next day.

28th. Nothing new at Head Quarters. The 13th light Dragoons which formed a part of Beresford's force in the South, made a gallant charge on a considerable body of French Cavalry, drove them under the very walls of Badajos, killed and wounded about 150, and took 200 prisoners. Beresford crossed the Guadiana at Juramanha, and took Olivenza from the enemy by surprise, making 400 prisoners.

30th. Lord Wellington occupies a position at Fuentes de Onor, cantoning his army along the river Duas Casas, and on the sources of the Azava—the light Division at Gallegos. The object of this operation was to starve out the garrison of Almeida. In the Alentejo Beresford advances to Merida, and Talaverra Real, to cover the siege of Badajos which is undertaken by his army. This great and important Fortress had surrendered to the French on the 11th of March, before the breaching batteries were completed, and defended by a garrison of upwards of 10,000 men, of the best appointed Troops of Spain.[192] The French placed in it a garrison of 6000 men, commanded by General Phillipon. A body of 10,000 Spaniards under Blake, Balusteros, and Espanha joined Beresford about this time.

May 3rd. In the evening of this day, the French formed on the right of the Duas Casas, and attacked the village of Fuentes de Onor, in great force. It was most gallantly defended by the 42nd 60th 71st 83rd 79th and 24th Regiments, with a light Infantry Battalion of the King's German Legion. The enemy obtained momentary possession of part of the village, but were charged back by the 71st and discontinued any further efforts.

May 4th. The French made a strong reconnoissance of our position on the Duas Casas, and in the course of the day were strengthened by Junot's corps, from Alameda.

5th. The French form two columns of attack against Fuentes de Onor, and manoeuvred in front of our whole line, driving in our advanced Guard commanded by General Houston. Their principal efforts were then directed, as on the 3rd, against Fuentes, and the contest for that village continued till night fall, when our Troops still held their Post. In the course of the night they began to retire, and at day-break the whole French Army was seen in retreat. They had left 400 dead in the Village, and we had made many prisoners. Our loss on the 3rd and 5th exceeded 1400 killed and wounded.[193]

8th. The French retire to Salamanca, leaving in Cividad Rodrigo, a garrison of 2000 men. This night about twelve o'clock the French garrison in Almeda threw up three rockets in succession, which were meant as a signal to the nearest Posts of their Army that they were about attempting their escape. In about two hours after a great explosion was heard, and all our Troops who had been employed to watch their motions, got under arms and waited anxiously for orders. By and bye some Dragoons galloped back from the Out-posts and gave the intelligence that the French who had formed the garrison of the place, were already far advanced towards the pass of Barba del Puerco. The pursuit was instantly begun, and continued with such activity, that the enemy was overtaken before the whole of his Column had entered the pass. A skirmish ensued in which 150 of them were killed wounded & taken. The remainder effected their escape. In proportion as Lord Wellington had taken every precaution to ensure the capture of these men, was his disappointment great, when he found that so considerable a portion of them had escaped. The Officers therefore who were in command at the several points of the Blockade, and who had been directed by him to keep a sharp look out, as he suspected an attempt would be made to escape, were censured by him, for inattention to their duty, and amongst others to whom his displeasure was made known, was Lieutenant Colonel Beven of the 4th Regiment. He was an active intelligent Officer, who had been to England on leave of absence to be married. He had not long returned, having left his wife a very short time after their marriage, in England. Being anxious to explain to Lord Wellington his individual share of the transaction, as commanding the 4th, he wrote him a letter, mentioning exactly where the Regiment was posted at the time the French made their escape, and assuring him that it was under arms and in motion, in ten minutes after he got the orders from the General Officer commanding on the spot, to go in pursuit. It is said that Lord Wellington, after reading his letter, remarked, "that it had been a sad bungling business, wherever the fault might lie, and that Colonel Beven's letter was no excuse at all", or some such expressions as these. This was communicated to the Colonel, who walked to his hut, wrote an affecting farewell to his Regiment and shot himself. There have not been wanting those who have blamed Lord Wellington for this act of a gallant and sensitive mind, but it is hard indeed if a General commanding, cannot at his discretion, use terms of censure or of praise, on actions which may have caused him disappointment or gratification, in his military arrangments. Officers of superior rank were included in the same disapprobation with Lieut. Col: Beven, and yet they bore it calmly, and in a very few weeks nothing more was thought of the affair. The Officers of the 4th regretted exceedingly the loss of their Colonel under such very painful circumstances, and buried him with every mark of the deepest feeling and respect. I never heard anything of his poor wife, thus so soon a widow, but it is not difficult to conceive, what her situation must have been, when she was made acquainted with the particulars of her Husband's fate.

When Almeida was taken possession of, it was found little better than a heap of ruins. The explosion which had succeeded the three rocket signals, previous to the escape of the French, had destroyed the strongest bastion of the Fortress, and the works and defences of the place had been injured as much as possible. Our Soldiers were immediately set to work to repair all this, and working parties were actively engaged night and day, in this operation, as the vicinity of the enemy rendered it an object of much importance, to put the place in a state of defence without loss of time.

May 10th. The enemy retired to the woods between Espeja Gallegos, and Fuentes de Onor, and remained in position until the evening. In the night, they broke up, and retired across the Azava, covering their retreat by their numerous Cavalry.

11th. Lord Wellington put the army into cantonments on the Duas Casas.

16th. In the Alentejo, Marshal Soult advanced from Seville at the head of a force of 30,000 men, to attack Beresford who had invested Badajos on the left of the Guadiana. Beresford placed himself in position at Albuera, and here was fought one of the severest actions of the Peninsular war. Soult began his attack against the British right, on the flank of which were heights occupied by Spanish troops. These were unable to resist the attacks of the French Columns, and after a gallant resistance were compelled to abandon the Post. The enemy at the same time menaced our left, which made it impossible for the Troops in that part of the line to make any movement in support of the right. The heights which the French had gained from the Spaniards, raked and commanded the whole of the position, and it was necessary to make every effort to retake and maintain them. General William Stewart made this attempt at the head of his Division, consisting of the 3rd 31st 48th two Battalions, 57th and 66th Regiments. His right Brigade under Colonel Colborne first came into action, and behaved in the most gallant manner. Finding that their fire made little impression on the enemy's column, he proceeded to attack it with the Bayonet, and while in the act of charging, a body of Polish Lancers, which had advanced under a heavy storm of rain, and were hidden from view by it, and by the smoke from the firing, suddenly made its appearance, in the rear of this Brigade, which from this unexpected attack was unfortunately broken, and suffered immensely. The 31st being on the left, escaped this charge and kept its ground until the arrival of General Houghton's Brigade, the conduct of which was conspicuously gallant, and at its head, its brave Commander, whilst cheering it on to the charge, fell, pierced with wounds. The enemy at the same time made a strong attack on the village and bridge near it. They were ably defended by the light Infantry Brigade of the German Legion. The French Cavalry which was very superior in number to that of the British and Spaniards, endeavoured to turn our right, but was foiled in his attempt by General Lumley. At this period of the Battle, General Cole commanding the 4th Division, moved on in line, and attacked the enemy's left. This proved a most decided movement, and the conduct of the Fusileer Brigade was particularly distinguished. The enemy began to give way, and the British advanced. He was pursued across the river Albuera, which was as far as Beresford thought it prudent to follow him, in the crippled state of his army, and as he had an immense superiority of Cavalry. In the charge of the Polish Lancers, the 3rd 48th and 66th Regiments after fighting most desperately against fearful odds, were nearly cut to pieces and lost their colours.[194] In turning the fortune of the day, the Fusileer Brigade, consisting of 2 Battalions of the 7th and the 1st Batt: 23rd lost 52 Officers and 1100 men killed and wounded, and many Regiments suffered in like proportion. The Spanish and Portuguese Troops engaged, did their duty excellently well. The total loss of the British was about 220 Officers, and nearly 5000 men killed and wounded.[195] The Enemy retired after the battle, to the ground he had previously occupied, and during the night commenced his retreat on the road towards Seville, abandoning Badajos to its fate. He left a number of his wounded on the ground. On the field itself were 2000 French killed, 5 of their Generals were killed and wounded, and his total loss exceeded 8000 men. He also abandoned Almendralejo, and left many wounded in hospital there. In the muster of the British army on the following day, it was fearful to see the gaps which had been made in Regiments, by this bloody engagement. The 3rd Regiment was commanded by a Subaltern, and the 48th by a Captain. The two corps together did not muster 150 men. In the course of the two following days however, many of the Soldiers, who on the dispersion of the Brigade by the Polish Lancers, had thrown away their arms, and fled in all directions when their gallant resistance could no longer avail them, rejoined their corps, and were armed again and equipped, from the arms and accoutrements of the dead. On the 21st Lord Wellington arrived from the neighbourhood of Almeida, bringing with him the 3rd and 7th Divisions with two Brigades of Artillery. On the 25th [May 1811] he invested Badajos, on the right of the Guadiana, ordered up the Ordnance and stores for the siege and broke ground.[196] The enemy retired upon Llerena, having their advanced posts of Cavalry at Usagre, near which place, a few days afterwards, General Lumley had a very gallant affair of Cavalry, against considerably superior numbers and took a hundred prisoners. As I have mentioned in a former part of this journal, I was detained in the Adjutant General's office in Lisbon at this time, and was not in the field at the battle of Albuera. I found leisure to pay a visit to Cintra, that beautiful spot, so appropriately called the Paradise of Europe. It is twelve miles from Lisbon, and in the days of the Moors, had been a favourite residence of some their Princes, who had built a magnificent Palace there, afterwards destroyed by an Earthquake, and rebuilt by one of the Portuguese Monarchs. Traces of these active and industrious Moors are visible in all directions near the place, and their system of irrigating the neighbouring lands, is that which is in use there, to this day. In the centre of a beautiful valley, stands a steep hill, the sides of which are covered with Cork and Olive trees, and the top is crowned with a rugged rock, on which is seen an old Convent, commanding a magnificent prospect of the Sea and of the lovely vale over which it domineers. Here and there, are to be seen Monasteries of course, for never yet did the Holy Fathers neglect to fix upon the choicest scenes of nature for their residences. I could not resist the idle custom of writing my name upon the wall in the Convent at the top of the rock where hundreds of British Officers had done the same thing. There were but three or four Padres left in it, scarcely sufficient to keep the place in order. In the Palace of the Marquis of Marialva, situated about a mile lower down in the Valley, is seen the room, in which the treaty of Cintra was signed, and they shew you a large blot of Ink upon a table, which they affirm was dashed out of the pen of the French General Kellerman, after he had affixed his signature.[197] Of course I received this anecdote with considerable degree of mental reservation. A little lower down is a singular Monastery called the Cork Convent, the apartments in it are subterranean and receive their light from holes cut obliquely in the rock, which are lined with Cork to guard against the damp. The Church & Chapter house, are built over the surface. The Monks are of the order of St. Francis. There is a good hotel at Cintra, but the charges are enormously high, owing to the great influx of Englishmen & other strangers to visit this beautiful spot.

On my return from Cintra having a little leisure time on my hands, I resolved to make a tour thro' Estremadura, & in the course of it visited the town of St. Ubes, where there is a strong Citadel, & a good harbour defended by three forts. The country round about this place is beautiful, covered with Orange Groves, which at this season were full of fruit & blossom, & the fragrance was so strong, that it was scarcely possible to walk in them. There are fine quarries of Jaspar near St. Ubes. Its principal commerce is in Salt, which it sends in great quantities to America.

27th [May 1811]. The 4th Division invested Badajos on the right; the 3rd & General Hamilton's Portuguese on the left of the river, and trenches were opened, against Fort Christoval, but it was very difficult for our men to cover themselves, as the Garrison had carried away a great deal of Earth from the spot, & left the rock bare; they also kept up such an incessant fire of Cannon & Musketry, that it was most difficult for the working parties to establish themselves, however by the 3rd of June, the batteries were completed on both sides of the river & opened their fire. It was kept up with such vigour, that on the evening of the 5th the breach of Christoval was reported practicable & at mid-night the assault was ordered. The advance entered the ditch, & attempted to mount the breach, but the resistance was so formidable, that it was found impossible, & after losing many men they retired. The next two days were occupied in Connonading the breach to widen it, & being again reported practicable, a second assault was ordered. The forlorn hope advanced with the most determined resolution, but in consequence of our failure on the first assault, the enemy greatly increased in numbers, was found in the highest possible spirits, & received the attacking party with cheers. Major McGichey who led the storming party, and the Engineer attached to it were killed, & as there was not any fire, kept up from our trenches, the French mounted their parapets, & fired on our people below in the ditch, with fatal effect. The situation of our men being made known, a bugle sounded the recall, after a loss on our part of above 300 men killed & wounded. The failure of this attack, prevented any further attempt on Badajos for the present. In the mean time Marmont advanced with his army again reinforced, & made it necessary that we should retire from before Badajos, the siege of which had been converted into a blockade.

Lord Wellington ordered all the battering train to Elvas, a strong Citadel where it arrived in perfect safety. Soult in the mean time, with the remains of his army, that had fought at Albuera, joined Marmont, & gave the French a superiority over us of nearly 20,000 men, their effective numbers being from, 65,000, to 70,000 men, whilst ours did not exceed 48,000. A general action was daily expected. On the 23rd of June the enemy sent out a strong reconnoitring party of their dragoons in the direction of Campo Mayor, & made prisoners a party of our cavalry of about 70 men & 3 Officers. It is said they mistook the French for Portuguese. Our army was so well concealed, behind the hills, that the enemy gained nothing by their reconnoissance & retired. In this state of mutual observation we continued for several days, when Lord Wellington put his army into Cantonments on one side of the Guadiana, & the French General did the same on the other. The British Head-quarters were Elvas—those of the French Badajos. We remained quiet nearly twenty days, during which time Lord Wellington was silently making his preparations for the siege of Civiad Rodrigo.

August 1st. The French army began to find the inconvenience of keeping together in such numbers, from the difficulties they felt in procuring provisions, & broke up from the south of the Tagus. Lord Wellington made a parallel movement, & established his head quarters at Portalegre. The light division moved to Castello Branco.

5th. Head Quarters established at Castello Branco, & the light division at Penamacor. These movements were made without any interruption from the enemy.

10th. March continued, Lord Wellington moved to Sabugal, & sent the light brigade to Pedragao.

14th. Head Quarters, Fuentes de Guinaldo. The light division, & General Pack's Brigade, invested Cividad Rodrigo. This fortress was now beginning to be much distressed for provisions, & we had reason to believe that the French would make some great effort for its relief. Lord Wellington took up a position in front of Guinaldo, & threw up a few works to strengthen himself there, as being the best ground to intercept any supplies the enemy might destine for the place. Marmont however made a circuitous movement, in such force, that he could not be prevented sending in a large convoy. These operations occupied the time from the 14th of August till the 24th of September. And here I may record that on the 15th of August we heard that Lieut. Wynne of the 23rd had died on the 2nd at Estramoz of a fever, & of the same disorder, Capt. Keith at San Miguel, on the 30th.

Septbr. 25th. A large body of Cavalry with some Infantry and guns, crossed the Agueda this day, to reconnoitre our position at Guinaldo, & such was the rapidity of their advance, that our Picquets with difficulty withdrawn by a ford higher up the river. Our Infantry when attacked by the enemy's Cavalry which charged them repeatedly, formed into Squares which protecting each other, secured their retreat, & the light division retired in a very masterly manner, to the position in front of Guinaldo, on which the 3rd and 4th divisions were already in line. The French made no further movement on this day; but in the course of the 26th from 30 to 40,000 infantry chiefly of the Imperial guard took up a line not many hundred yards from us, where they continued to be joined by other troops until dark, from which we inferred that the 27th would be a warm day, & made preparations accordingly.

Septbr. 27th. The 4th division was very sharply attacked at the village of Aldea del Ponte, which it lost and retook several times. Capt. Cortlandt of the 23rd was killed. Col: Pearson, & Capt. Cane wounded. The casualties of the army with the exception of the 4th division were not very severe. During the night our army fell back to a position on the Coa which had been previously determined upon, followed by the enemy. On the 28th Lord Wellington offered them battle in this position, but the French having succeeded in their object of relieving Cividad Rodrigo were not disposed to attempt anything further, & drew back to Salamanca. Ld. Wellington put his army into cantonments, & the regular operations of the siege began.

In order to turn the attention of the enemy, from the necessary preparations for this purpose, which from the nature of the country, the advanced season of the year, & the difficulty of procuring transport for the battering train was replete with obstacles, Lord Wellington directed the Corps which he had left in the South, under the command of Sir Rowland Hill, to make various demonstrations. In the execution of those orders, that Officer on the 28th of Octbr. surprised a French column under General Girard, which was foraging thro' the country. General Hill made a night march, in so able a manner, that when day broke, the French Picquets who were on the look out on the flanks of the town where Girard's division had slept, Arroyo de Molinos, were seized before they had time to give the alarm, & the main body was surrounded with so much celerity, that two Generals, forty Officers, three pieces of Canon, & about 1200 prisonners with all their baggage were taken. The rest saved themselves with difficulty by flight. The French for a short time, made a feeble resistance, which cost them about 200 men killed & wounded. Our loss was from 70 to 80. The happy result of this little expedition, added to other movements made by General Hill, produced the effect which Ld. Wellington had intended, & forced Marshal Soult to concentrate his troops in that quarter.

Marmont finding a difficulty in the provisioning of his army, was at this time obliged to spread them over a large extent of country, & Ld. Wellington thought it the most favourable moment to close in upon Cividad Rodrigo. Everything had been prepared for the siege & on the 6th of Janry. 1812, a bridge was laid over the Agueda, at Salices; but the weather was too bad to move on that or the following day. On the 8th General Crawford with the light division crossed the river. The 3rd & 4th supporting. On the 9th a detachment under Col. Colbourne, stormed & took a strong work, about 500 yards from the walls, with the loss of 3 Officers & 30 men, killed & wounded. It was considered a very dashing affair. On the next day our Parallels were begun, & one of the batteries traced out. On the 14th. The enemy attacked us in our trenches, & filled up a part of them, before we were able to beat them back. Their sortie was made in considerable strength. The day following our batteries opened & a breach having been made in the Convent of San Francisco, it was stormed by the German light Infantry, who were beaten back. It was then escaladed by the 40th Regiment under Lieut. Col: Harcourt, & taken.

On the 16th a second convent, that of La Caridada was taken. The French army was now making various demonstrations for the relief of the place, which made Ld. Wellington exceedingly anxious for its capture. The exertions of the besieging army were therefore redoubled so that on the 19th two good breaches were reported practicable. At seven in the evening the 3rd division under General Picton, & the light division under General Crawford made the assault, whilst General Pack's Portuguese Brigade, made a shew of escalade.

The French defended their breaches desperately, but were at length obliged to give way, to the vigour of our attack. They fled thro' the streets, & were pursued by our troops until the whole surrendered. The number of prisoners was 54 Officers & 1370 men. The loss of the enemy in killed and wounded was considerable, our own amounted to 68 Officers & 400 men. Amongst the former we had to regret General Crawford who had so long & so gallantly led on the light division, & General McKinnon, who commanded a brigade in Picton's Division. The latter was killed by an explosion in the ditch. The capture of Rodrigo at such a season of the year, & almost in the presence of a superior army, which was deeply interested in its preservation, was one of those results, of genius & valour, which now began to attend the operations of Wellington & his army; & there was no doubt, but that the French marshals were completely out-generaled by our own leader, to whom the success of this interprize gave so much confidence, that he immediately formed a plan, for a similar attempt on the still more important fortress Badajos; and as soon as the breaches of Rodrigo were sufficiently repaired, the safe custody of the place was delivered over to the Spaniards, in order that Ld. Wellington might have greater numbers of British troops at his disposal, for future operations. The projected attack on Badajos was rendered the more difficult, because the fall of Rodrigo had been so totally unexpected by the French Marshals, they would naturally be much more on their guard for the protection of a Fortress of greater magnitude & importance. The greatest secrecy was therefore necessary, & every precaution adopted to deceive the enemy, with regard to such part of the preparations, as could not be made without observation. A Corp of about 3000 British was left on the Agueda, to keep up an alarm in the North.[198]

On the 17th of March, a bridge of boats was thrown over the Guadiana, by which the 3rd 4th & light divisions crossed & at once invested the place. The remainder of the army, under the orders of Generals Graham & Hill, were ordered about 10 leagues in advance to shew a front against Marshal Soult, who began to assemble his troops.

Badajos was at this time garrisoned by Veteran troops, under the orders of General Philippon, who had so ably defended it against our former attacks.[199] Trenches were opened on the 18th in front of a strong detached fort, called Picarini.

19th. The French made a vigorous sortie & gallantly penetrated to our very entrenchments; they were however beaten back with considerable loss; in this sortie, Capt. Potter of the 13th Regiment was killed. The weather during this time was exceedingly wet & tempestuous, so that the trenches were filled with water, & every part of our progress impeded. Our bridge of boats over the Guadiana was carried away, which made the arrival of our supplies very difficult & uncertain.

On the 25th however it had cleared up sufficiently to enable us to open a battery against Picarini, the defences of which were in a short time so completely beaten down, that it was stormed & taken the same night. The storming party was under the orders of Major General Kempt. The garrison of this little place did not surrender, until the greater part of them had fallen. We took only 80 prisoners. The assault of this little fort, caused the greatest possible alarm in Badajos, & a heavy fire was kept up from all parts of the fortress, where no doubt the impression existed that we were making a general assault.

29th. Our works were now in a very forward state, the first breaching battery opened its fire.

April 1st. Two other batteries opened, & a breach was already visible from the effects of that which commenced firing on the 29th. The enemy's fire was much slackened.

6th. Three breaches were reported practicable, & the assault was ordered for this night. There was every indication of an obstinate resistance on the part of the French, & in order to divert their attention as much as possible, & prevent them from concentrating all their strength in the defence of the breaches, Major General Picton, with the 3rd Division, was ordered to escalade the Castle, & Major [General] Leith, with the 5th division to make a similar attack on a distant part of the rampart. The 4th division under General Colville & the light under Gen: Kempt, were ordered to the assault of the two greater breaches. They were quickly discovered, & a tremendous fire was opened upon them, but they moved onwards, & descended into the ditch. On attempting to mount the breaches, they found their tops crowned with Chevaux de frise, formed of sharpened swords, which baffled every attempt of our men to remove them, cutting their hands to pieces whenever they attempted to grapple with them. Shells, Grenades, & fire balls, were hurled over the ramparts into the ditch, & made dreadful havoc amongst our people there, who, rendered desperate by their situation, tried over & over again to mount the breaches, & were as often foiled in the attempt. The number of Officers lost was so great, that everything like formation had long ceased, & but for the decided success of General Picton's attack on the Castle, there can be little doubt, that the whole would have proved a disastrous failure; but that gallant Officer, altho' the resistance he met with, was not of that determined nature which defended the breaches, owing to the comparatively small numbers of the enemy, which had been left for the defence of the Castle, preserved so boldly in his escalade, that he at length established his men on the top of the wall, & quickly strengthened himself there, by sending increased numbers up the ladders. General Leith also was equally successful in his part of the attack, & detaching a strong body of men round the ramparts, from the spot of which he had gained possession, they fell unexpectedly on the flanks of the troops who were so gallantly defending the breaches, & who appalled by this new attack, abandoned them, & thus let in the troops who were in the ditch. The garrison was soon overpowered & made prisoners. The Governor with his staff, & about 4000 men were taken. Our loss was 60 Officers and 800 men killed, 260 Officers, & 2700 men wounded.

Thus gloriously concluded one of the most important & difficult sieges, that British troops were ever called upon to accomplish. Although the gallantry of the Troops in the ditch, had not been attended with that decisive success which it so truly deserved, yet by their desperate attack they occupied so great a portion of the enemy's force, as greatly to diminish the resistance offered to Generals Picton & Leith. Hand Grenades, & fire-balls of every description were hurled over the Parapet on those below, with such rapidity as to give the whole ditch the appearance of vivid flashes of lightning renewed every instant. Lord Wellington is said to have exclaimed on seeing this continued sheet of fire, that if it was possible to picture hell on earth, such it must be. When our Troops took possession of the place, they certainly shewed mercy to all the French Soldiers who demanded it; their great object seemed the discovery of liquor wherever it could be found, & in this they were but too successful. It is difficult to describe the scenes of drunkenness & insubordination, which were the consequence of such discoveries, nor can any one except those who have witnessed it, form an idea of the state of Soldiers after a successful storm. With faces as black & dirty as powder can make them, eyes red & inflamed, & with features full of wildness & ferocity, & of the insolence of victory, after a desperately contested struggle, they break into houses, ransack every spot where wine or spirits can be supposed to lie hid, & after repeated intoxicating draughts, begin their work of plunder. Woe to that unfortunate owner of a mansion, if any such remain, who attempts to remonstrate. Discipline being at an end, the whole world seems given up to their indiscriminate rage & plunder. The interference of Officers at this moment of madness is attended with extreme danger, & it was reported at Badajos, that the Adjutant of a Regiment lost his life in attempting to check a Soldier in this lawless career. The Adjutant is said to have ordered him out of a house which he was plundering, & the Soldier replied by running him thro' the body with his bayonet. Old men have been hurled from the windows of their houses headlong into the streets, & children have been thrown after them. At Badajos, division after division was sent in to check the plunder, who so far from doing so, themselves joined in the work of havoc that was going on. Gallows were erected in several street, & Soldiers were hung upon them, but all in vain. This state of things continued for upwards of eight & forty hours after the place was taken, & every effort to put a stop to it appeared fruitless. Even the animal spirits which one would suppose, could hardly endure for such a length of time a state of this unnatural excitement, seemed more & more roused by it, & equal to fresh exertions of a similar description.[200]

Whilst our troops were in this state of insubordination Marshal Soult made some movements which indicated an approach towards the place, which created a good deal of anxiety; but this circumstance being communicated to the Soldiers, they abandoned their work of plunder & joined their colours instantly.

Leaving such a force in Badajos, as was sufficient for its defence, composed principally of Spaniards, & after giving directions for the immediate repair of the breaches, & other injured parts of the works, Lord Wellington moved forward his army, & being joined by the Troops, that had covered the siege, was prepared to give battle. Soult however, moved back on Seville. General Le Marchant's Brigade of Cavalry, followed him, & routed his rear-guard, near Llerena. I may here mention, an anecdote, connected with the plunder of Badajos, which I heard related by an officer who told me he had witnessed it.

The men brought their plunder out of the place, & sold valuable articles to the Spaniards outside for a mere trifle. When the bargain was made, & the money paid, these Spaniards moved off with their cheap purchases. At a short distance however, they were met by other parties of Soldiers who made a point of easing them of what they had thus acquired, & sold it back to them, at a smaller price perhaps than what they had before given. The unfortunate Spaniards had to undergo this process several times, tho' probably the original owners of the goods themselves. One Regiment is said to have burst into a hat manufactory, where there were a number of broad brimmed and slouched Friars hats, ready for sale; the fellows cast off their Soldiers caps, & made their appearance in the streets in this ludicrous head-dress. At his dinner table a short time afterwards, Ld. Wellington mentioned that he had passed a Soldier, outside the walls of Badajos, so exceedingly drunk & so heavily laden with plunder, that he could scarcely either articulate or move. He was about to speak to him, when a woman made her appearance, equally drunk, & heavily laden. He addressed her, asking her, what business she had there, & threatening her with instant punishment. She said nothing, but the Soldier looked him in the face, & said "Now that's what I calls right you see that we poor fellows, fights hard & gets nothing, & that these here devils, comes & carries off all as belongs to us". Ld. Wellington added, that the effect of these two creatures, thus curiously brought under his eye was so irresistably ludicrous, that it was quite impossible for him to say a word & he rode off.

Badajos being thus secured, the 1st 3rd 4th 5th 6th 7th & light divisions were put in motion for the North of Portugal, in consequence of Ld. Wellington having received information that Marmont was plundering with a considerable force in the neighbourhood of Alfaiates and Escalhos da Cima. The French Marshal had thought that in the absence of Ld. Wellington at Badajos he might make powerful irruptions into Portugal from the north. He even made a demonstration of attack on Almeida, which he knew to be in a very imperfect state of defence; but his attempt on the place failed. Leaving also some troops to blockade Rodrigo, he pushed the main body of his army as far as Castello Branco. At this place he heard of Ld. Wellington's approach to meet him, & hastily retraced his steps, & abandoned Portugal altogether. Ld. Wellington then put his army into Cantonments in the country between the Agueda & the Coa, & established his headquarters at Fuente Guinaldo. General Hill was left with the 2nd division, and a Portuguese corps to watch Estremadura. The 4th and another division were cantoned on the Douro, in the neighbourhood of

St. Joao de Pesquera, & Momento de Beira. The light division were at El Bodon, Fuentes di Onor & Nava d'Aver. A company of that division did duty at head quarters. In these Cantonments we remained undisturbed by the enemy until the month of May following. The interval was passed as busily as possible in refitting the Army. New clothing and shoes were given out—The troops were drilled as in England, & marched a certain number of miles every day that the weather would permit, in heavy marching order, to keep them in good wind. They were practised in pitching & striking tents quickly—in firing at Targets—& in cooking expeditiously. Invalids & weakly Soldiers were sent to England, & short leaves of absence were granted to such Officers as really required it. Every thing was done, to put the army into the best service state & to render it as efficient as possible. Nor were amusements wanting to enliven the Officers, when the duties of the day were over. Barns were converted into theatres, & performances of the most ludicrous description took place. At Head-quarters Ld. Wellington had a pack of Fox-hounds, & we all occasionally joined in the chase. Game was also in tolerable abundance, & those who were fond of fishing, found Trout in the Agueda & Coa. The accommodations of the junior Officers at Fuente di Guinaldo were wretched in the extreme, & they lived almost entirely on their rations. The Officers of the Adjutant & Quarter Master General's staff were however invited to dine very frequently with Ld. Wellington, & at his table drank of the best French wines, which were from time to time sent him as presents by the different Guerilla Chiefs, who had been successful in capturing French Convoys.[201] The cheerfulness or gloom of our Commander's table depended much on news which he received from England, or reports from the different divisions of his army. I have dined there at times, when scarce any one dare open his mouth except to take in his dinner, & at other times when the conversation was constant & general, & Ld. Wellington himself the most playful of the party. He would sit after dinner a long or a short time, according to circumstances, & when he wished us to retire would call for Coffee. After finishing his cup, which gave us sufficient time to drink our own, he would leave the room, & it was then expected that we should all go to our quarters. He had a small portmanteau iron bed-stead, covered with Russian leather with one pillow of the same material, & whenever anything was passing at the out-posts which led to the supposition that a movement was intended on the part of the enemy I have understood that he used to lie down on this bed-stead in his clothes, with his boots near him, ready to put on, & his cloak thrown round him. His horse, & that of his orderly dragoon were always ready saddled and ordering himself to be called on the least alarm from the advance, & with a lamp near him, he would shut himself up for the night. In case of anything occurring before day-light, to make him think his presence was necessary at the Out-posts, he would ride off, without having a single Aid de Camp called, taking with him only his Orderly Dragoon. Nothing could exceed his habits of watchfulness & activity. At nine in the morning the Heads of all departments waited upon him with their respective reports. These comprised returns of various descriptions, & the correspondence of their several departments during the preceding day, on which they had to take his instructions. Before ten o'clock all this business was dispatched, & the details of his directions were committed to the Junior branches of the General Staff.

Money was exceedingly scarce all this time, & several months pay was owing to the army, but had we received it we could not have laid it out, & living on our rations we were all getting rich. Col: Waters, Capt. Wood & myself were messed by my servant for half a dollar each, a week, besides our rations. The room I occupied was a sort of hay-loft, & I had much difficulty in keeping out the excessive cold. The hail used to get under the tiles & fall on my bed as I slept. To remedy this as well as I could I borrowed tar-paulins from the Commissary, & slung them over the spot where my bed stood. The Crevices in the walls I stopped with clay, & at last made a sort of fire place which was a great comfort. The person who kept the best table at the head quarters was the Commissary. He kept a pack of Harriers, had excellent English horses, & dined off Plate.[202] The Prince of Orange was at head-quarters during this time as one of Ld. Wellington's Aid de Camps. He was generally considered a weak young man but was not deficient in personal courage.

V

The Peninsular War:
The Offensive Phase, 1812–1814

Hard-won British victories against Masséna at Fuentes de Oñoro on 5 May and Soult at Albuera on 16 May proved to be indecisive, which led Wellington to rest his weary troops during the autumn of 1811. During this pause Wellington petitioned London with demands for supplies which he received, including a siege train. Well-equipped and supplied, he put his army in motion on 1 January 1812, in the depths of winter. Crossing the Portuguese frontier, Wellington laid siege to Ciudad Rodrigo on 8 January. Eleven days later, on 19 January, Wellington's troops stormed their way through the breaches and captured the town after a fierce fight. With a rapidity unusual for him, Wellington then marched instantly to Badajoz, which was defended by 4–5,000 French as well as German and Spanish troops. The fortress fell in a bloody assault on 6 April, and for several days infuriated British troops subjected the population to unbridled violence. These great victories (including the French evacuation of Almeida in May 1811) gave Wellington undisputed control of both corridors which enabled him to mount a strategic offensive against the French in Spain.

Despite a momentary reverse at Burgos in Old Castile in October 1812, which resulted in a costly tactical withdrawal through Ciudad Rodrigo to Portugal, Wellington's troops won climactic battles at Salamanca on 22 July 1812 and at Vitoria eleven months later on 21 June 1813. The latter success cost Napoleon Spain. The bulk of his army there streamed away in defeat through the Basque Provinces and Navarre to Bayonne, on the French side of the Pyrenees. Inevitably, the foreign troops in French service began to desert in large numbers. Units of the French army were besieged at San Sebastian and Pamplona, and subsequently in Bayonne. A French counter-offensive through the Pyrenean passes at Maya and Roncesvalles in July 1813 merely delayed the inevitable. On 7 October, Wellington crossed the Bidassoa River and invaded France itself. Fighting doggedly, the French were defeated at the Nive River and at Nivelle, 9–12 November 1813, and again at St Pierre on 13 December. The campaign of 1814 brought fresh defeats for France, at Orthez on 27 February and at Tarbes on 20 March. The last great British victory occurred on 10 April 1814 at Toulouse. Unbeknownst to either side, Napoleon had abdicated five days earlier, on 6 April, at Fontainebleau.

In order to defeat Wellington, the French had abandoned all of Spain south of the Tagus River. This concentration of forces, however, failed to have its intended effects. In addition to the superior fighting quality of the British soldier, the French were confronted with a nation in arms, not only as guerrillas, but as organized troops. Wellington had been appointed commander-in-chief of the Spanish armies by the Cortes, with the powers of appointment and dismissal of Spanish officers. Of equal import-ance, certainly, was the fact that the French never solved the strategic problem of organizing their numbers so as to deal Wellington a mortal blow. To all this must be added Napoleon's decision to invade Russia in 1812. Before Wellington had fought and won the battle of Salamanca, on 22 July 1812, Napoleon was occupied crossing the Niemen River into Russia. Troops and supplies desperately needed by his commanders in Spain would be swallowed up in Napoleon's catastrophic defeat in Russia. Napoleon, great captain that he was, knew full well what effect his invasion of Russia would have on the operations of the French army in Spain. In an effort to bring the war in Spain to an end, and thus prevent a two-front war in Europe, Napoleon offered peace in the early summer of 1812. The failure of this peace effort was to have a decisive effect on the struggle in the Peninsula.

Following his retreat from Russia, Napoleon was defeated at the "Battle of the Nations" around Leipzig, 16 to 19 October 1813, a few days after Wellington crossed into France. By 5 December Napoleon was back in Paris, pursued by an allied army. The ensuing campaign against Napoleon in northern France, from January to April 1814, coincided with Wellington's victories at Orthez, Tarbes and Toulouse in southwestern France. These victories emboldened the allies to look ahead to peace with France and a universal settlement for all Europe. Under Castlereagh's strong leadership, the allies committed themselves to a general European peace, as opposed to individual treaties, at the Châtillon Conference, 5 February to 19 March 1814, and in the Treaty of Chaumont, which was agreed to on 9 March 1814.

The last action of the Peninsular War was the spirited French sortie from Bayonne, on 14 April 1814, four days after the great battle of Toulouse. With the final capitulation of the commander of the Bayonne garrison in May 1814, the war, variously called the "dirty war", the "badly begun" war and Napoleon's "Spanish ulcer", was at last over.

The fighting in the Peninsula was at an end, but not for many Peninsula veterans. Several thousand were quickly dispatched to fight the Americans, who had declared war on Britain in June 1812. There was even talk of sending Wellington to command the army in America. Peace came on Chrismas Eve 1814. The news of the peace came too late, however, to save several hundred British soldiers who died needlessly in the abortive attack at New Orleans on 8 January 1815.[203]

Early in June it was evident that preparations were making for breaking up our winter quarters. The first indications of movement were an attack made by Sir Rowland Hill on the bridge of Almaraz. This bridge over the Tagus near the town from which it derives its name was the most convenient line of communication between the French armies on the North & South of that river. It was a bridge of boats defended by very formidable Têtes-de Pont & other strong works connected with a Castle at Miravete. The destruction of this bridge was an important object. Sir Rowland made a night march with about 1800 men & at day-break surprised the enemy's works. Such was their alarm at this unlooked for attack, that their defence was comparatively feeble, & the bridge was taken possession of with all the works & stores connected with it. It was immediately destroyed, & our troops retired. Our loss was about a hundred & fifty killed & wounded. As soon as Marmont had heard of Sir Rowland Hill's movement towards the Tagus he sent a force to meet him, but it was too late to save the bridge. Ld. Wellington was exceedingly pleased, at this second successful enterprise of Sir Rowland's.

On the 13th of June [1812], head quarters left Fuente Guinaldo. The right column of the army composed of the first, 6th & 7th divisions was commanded by Sir Thomas Graham. The centre, was formed of the 4th 5th & light divisions under General Leith. With this column moved head quarters. The left column consisted of the 3rd division with the

Portuguese Brigades of Generals Pack & Bradford was commanded by General Picton. Sir Stapleton Cotton commanded the cavalry, the greater part of which moved with head-quarters. The total strength of this part of the army moving under the immediate orders of Ld. Wellington was about 45,000 men. We slept the first night at Quadrapero, the 14th at Cabrillas—the 15th at Aldequella la Bovida—the 16th at a small house under a hill, a league beyond Carneiro. Here we fell in with the enemy's advance of Cavalry, & had some skirmishing, we took seven prisoners & had four men wounded. We crossed the Yeltes river this day, & the Tenebron on the 15th. The former is a rapid stream.

17th. Approached the banks of the Tormes, & reconnoitred the river. Two fords were found, one at Santa Martha, about two miles above Salamanca, & the other a league below it. The latter a very indifferent one. Halted on the banks for the night.

18th. We cross the Tormes in two columns one at each of the fords. The French army had abandoned Salamanca, but had left in some strong works there a garrison of 800 men. These works were constructed, round a Convent, of solid masonry were loopholed, palisaded, & stockaded, & had two ditches round them. They were not to be reduced but by regular approaches. They were reconnoitred by General Clinton, to whose division their capture was entrusted, & batteries were immediately erected against them. On the following day, their defences being a good deal injured by the fire of these batteries, an attempt was made to carry them by escalade, but it failed. General Bowes who headed this attack was killed, & we had also upwards of 100 men killed & wounded. The rest of the army was in Bivouac on the right bank of the Tormes, Cavalry picquets having been sent some miles to the front, without meeting the out-posts of the enemy. On the 21st information was received that Marmont having drawn considerable reinforcements from Valladolid & his garrisons on the Douro was moving forwards to relieve the forts in Salamanca. Ld. Wellington immediately advanced with his army, & took up a position on the heights of San Cristoval to cover the place, leaving the 6th division to prosecute the siege of the Convent. Marmont encamped his army closely under us, & we had a complete view of them.

The two armies continued thus closely together with no other hostile movement than skirmishing of the picquets for several days. On the 25th the French endeavoured to gain a height on our right, which if in their possession would have greatly endangered that flank. The 7th division under General Hope was ordered to resist this attempt which they did effectually, driving the enemy to their original position. On the 26th another Battery was commenced against the Forts in Salamanca. Marmont on the same day crossed part of his army over the Tormes at the ford of Huerta, & threatened our rear. General Graham was sent over the ford of Santa Martha with the 1st & 7th Divisions, & closing upon the enemy, they retired and recrossed the river, remaining in bivouac on its bank.

27th. Part of the Convent was this day set on fire, by red-hot shot from our batteries, & a practicable breach was also made, but just at the moment that the Troops were about to assault, a white flag was hoisted, & terms of capitulation proposed by the Garrison. There was however a difficulty in the terms, & the batteries began again to fire, & under their cover the storming party advanced. The French did not offer much resistance & the place was carried. 28 Officers, & 706 men, were made prisoners of war. They were immediately marched off for Lisbon. 36 pieces of Cannon & a great quantity of stores & clothing fell into our hands. The works were immediately destroyed. On the 28th Marmont having been made aware of the surrender of the Forts, began his retreat this night, taking the main road to Valladolid. Our advanced guard pursued. Ld. Wellington moved forwards on the following day with the whole army, which encamped in the neighbourhood of Orbada, three & a half leagues from Salamanca, were Head Quarters remained that night.

30th. Moved to Fuente la Pena, three leagues, still on the road to Valladolid. Met with the enemy's outposts & drove them in.

July 1st. Advanced to Alejos, three leagues, skirmished with the enemy's Cavalry & took some prisoners.

2nd. Moved on to Villa Verde, three leagues. Came up with the enemy who Cannonaded us. Had a sharp skirmish with their rear guard, & took 26 prisoners. Several deserters come in.

3rd. Halted this day at Villa Verde. Ld. Wellington reconnoitred the banks of the Douro, & found the enemy in force at Roueda.

4th. Advanced on Roueda, on which the enemy retired over the bridge of Tordesillas. Head quarters remained at Roueda until the 15th when having learned that the enemy had marched towards Toro, about four leagues down the other bank of the river, & was crossing his army there, Ld. Wellington began to retire & arrived at Nava del Rey at six oclock this evening. There was a bridge at Toro which had been destroyed. On our arrival at Nava information was received that the enemy had crossed over two Divisions which were already nearly six miles on our side of the river. The Army was immediately put in motion by its left during the night, & day light found us as follows. Portuguese Cavalry at El Pinero—6th & 7th Divisions at Fuente la Pena 3rd Division & Spaniards at Castrillo—5th Division, Tordesillas—4th & light Divisions at Castrajon. The rest of the Cavalry at Alejos, & onwards near our right flank. The 1st Division was in reserve at Carnizal, to which place the baggage was ordered. Ld. Wellington reconnoitered some rising ground near this village, & appeared to wish to act defensively. We saw little of the enemy this day, but in the night, the right of our Cavalry, was driven in upon our Infantry very sharply & the enemy's whole army was found to have crossed at Tordesillas. Marmont it appeared had changed all the movements he had made down the river during the day, had counter-marched at night, & had quite succeeded in clearing away everything from the point at which he was desirous to cross. He manoeuvred capitally. Many Officers thought that he might have performed this operation more simply, & with much less fatigue to his men by crossing at once at Toro as he had threatened; but it was not possible that he could have been aware of Ld. Wellington's defensive system. There was in fact, little difference in our respective forces. Marmont had been reinforced with Bonnet's Division, & the capture of the Salamanca Forts had given us our 6th Division, which had been employed on that duty, besides other reinforcements, which balanced the enemy's accession of Bonnet. He therefore had a right to expect attack if he attempted the passage at Toro, & would have risked being thrown back on the Douro, with a bad line of retreat if beaten. Between four & five on the 18th we galloped off from Fuente la Pena, hearing a sharp firing in the direction of Castrajon, & much uneasiness was felt for the 4th & 5th Divisions which were retiring from that neighbourhood. We found both parties Cannonading each other near that village, & the French advancing rapidly & in force.

The Cavalry had some skirmishing and two or three of our Squadrons, 11th & 12th did not behave well. They were close to Ld. Wellington & would have lost the two guns attached to them but for the bravery of the Horse Artillery. Marshal Beresford was nearly taken in endeavouring to rally them. The French did not derive any advantage from this momentary disorder & the Infantry Divisions retired by

Tordesillas to cross the Guerena towards Canizal. The passage of this rivulet was very awkward from the heights on the enemy's side commanding the Fords. The Infantry had been suffered to remain close to the stream to procure water & were exposed to a Cannonade from which they suffered. We thought this stream would probably have been the seperation of the army's for the day, but by three in the afternoon the enemy had crossed over a force of cavalry & infantry on our left, in that straggling imperceptible manner so peculiar to the French, that made us disregard it, & the more so, as his main movements seemed directed towards the contrary flank. He manoeuvred mixing Infantry with Cavalry & at length approached very near our left with two or three Battalions & guns. Ld. Wellington ordered General Cole to attack with a Brigade of the 4th Division (the 27th & 48th) in line, supported by a Portuguese regiment in column on each flank. The enemy stood & fired little. They were very firm until within fifty or sixty paces, when our fellows gave them the Bayonet with cheers, routed the column & left of the French about 80 dead & 100 prisoners besides wounded. Our men charged at too great a distance, their ranks were in confusion, & they were so breathless & exhausted when they came up with the French, that they could scarcely use the Bayonet. It was ascertained from the prisoners that these two Battalions of ours had charged six of the enemy, about 3000 men, & that their force across the stream, & at hand to support consisted of two Divisions which had concealed themselves in the inequalities of the ground. General Cole hastened back to his Division after this creditable affair, & before the enemy's superiority could annoy him. Our Cavalry, probably owing to the roughness of the ground did not make much of the enemy's broken column. The French sent to be permitted to carry off their wounded who lay on the ground half way between the hostile armies. There was afterwards some Cavalry skirmishing, & in a charge by the enemy, the Hussars were broken, but saved by one of our heavy Regiments which cut up a good many of the French. The army then took up its ground for the night—the 4th 5th & 6th Divisions in front of Canizal as in an advanced position, the remaining Divisions thrown back to the left towards Parada de Rubiales. The forenoon of the 19th passed without movement, but about twelve oclock the enemy made a march by his left, & we followed in a parallel direction to our right, taking up ground in front of Cabeza de la Valissa upon a vast extensive plain. It was dark before the Troops could be placed & some did not reach their ground till midnight. It seemed as if the enemy had decoyed us to equal ground, & from his concentration that the morning would bring with it a decisive battle. At day-light the 20th we were drawn out in order of battle in successive lines, the reserves in column, having a wide plain of more than a mile to our front, & the same distance to our rear. The enemy was on the ridge of heights on the opposite bank of a branch of the Guerana stream, formed in columns. The two armies could see each other very distinctly. After an hour or two of expectation, he opened out into column of march, of two lines, moving on the outside of the rivulet by Morguera, Cotorillo & Revilla de Cantalpino. We moved in open column of two lines within the stream, leaving Mollorido on our right by Cantalpino & Hamillos. Our left halted in the neighbourhood of Pitiega, & right, a good deal in front of Cabazeavillosa, in the direction of Puebla de Escalonilla. The enemy in the evening took up his ground parallel to us & not far off. The 6th Division & two Brigades of Cavalry were detached by Aldearubia to Aldealingua upon the Tormes, securing the right of the Salamanca position north of the Tormes. The enemy also sent two Squadrons into Huerta. These movements were the conclusion of a day of great interest, & which must have been full of instruction to Officers of all ranks. The sight of two well-equipped armies of nearly 50,000 each, marching in two parallel lines within artillery range, & frequently cannonading & skirmishing with each other, was the most beautiful & magnificent military spectacle that could possibly be witnessed. The heads of the two armies marching in column were seen moving towards the Tormes each pushing for a ford of that river, the French, for that of Huerta—& the English, for that of Santa Martha—The route of the British was through a valley, & that of the French on the heights overlooking them. The day was beautiful—a bright sun & a gentle breeze to which the colours of the British floated as they moved below, whilst the Eagles of the French were glittering above. Wherever a point projected a little into the valley, the French ran out a few pieces of Artillery upon it & connonaded us as we went on. These plunging shots did not do us much mischief. The order of the two armies was as regular as if at a review. Each watched his adversary most jealously for a fault which neither could discover. Of these two gallant armies how different was the condition at the same hour of tomorrow! Here for the first time I observed the experiment made of following the French example of mixing light troops with our Cavalry & I believe its good effects became generally felt & acknowledged. By degrees the breeze died away, & the

day became excessively hot & sultry & as great part of the march lay thro'
corn, & ploughed fields, the troops were much fatigued; some Divisions
having marched more than seven leagues, & had been under arms an
hour before day-light. The left of the army had an alarm in the evening.
General D'Urban's Portuguese Cavalry the colour of whose clothing
was very similar to that of the French, making its appearance unexpectedly, was fired at by mistake, & lost a man or two.[204] This alarm caused
more effect than it ought, & looked as if the confidence of the Troops
was somewhat damped; but it might have been the effect of their
excessive fatigue. During the night, the baggage was sent to the rear &
the Troops marched at day-light for the Salamanca position. Head
Quarters slept this night at Cabeza de la Vallissa. I well remember, that
on that night, the Officers of the Adjutant General's department had
taken up their quarters in the church of that village, & supposed that
they had settled themselves till morning. Our horses had entered the
Church with ourselves as a matter of course. We were seated under an
image of the Virgin Mary before which a lamp was burning. Our table
was the Bier, on which the garment of a Priest was spread for a table
cloth, our chairs were the flag stones, which as the Bier was low, was no
inconvenience. Our Canteens & tins of Grog were before us on this
table. A dim light at the distant end of the aisle shewed the spot where
our horses were feeding with their saddles on. We were busy con-
gratulating ourselves on our comforts, & not a little amused with the
singularity of our position, when a horseman gallopped up to the
Church door. It was an Aid de Camp of Sir Stappleton Cotton's who
commanded the Cavalry. He alighted, & approaching us, said he was
exceedingly sorry to disturb us, but that having been sent by his General
to look out for quarters for himself & his staff he had found none but
those which we occupied & he therefore invited us to move out & find
accommodations elsewhere. As it is the custom of the service when an
army is in the field, for senior Officers to turn out their Juniors whenever
they are in want of quarters we had nothing to do but to obey. Had we
been permitted to occupy some other corner of the Church we should
have been very grateful for the indulgence; but on our hinting at such an
arrangement we were told that the General's staff, orderlies, & horses
were so numerous that it would be difficult to lodge them all in less space
than the whole Church, with any degree of comfort to himself. We
therefore sulkily bridled our horses & led them out. The night was dark,
with occasional showers; but seeing several fires blazing under a wall of

the Church yard we made for them, & found a group of Spanish Muleteers carousing by their blaze, whom we displaced to make fresh fires for themselves elsewhere, & took possession of their warm births. We were soon rolled up in our cloaks & fast asleep. An hour before day-break we were on horseback & rode to the out-posts where there was no appearance of the enemy placing himself as in the first advance before our position, nor did he make any movement in the early part of the morning. The weather was very dark & threatening rain, & two villages were on fire by design or accident on his line of march, which, together with the haze made his manoevres very indistinct—until about two at noon his movements were decidedly on Alba de Tormes. The whole army, excepting the 3rd Division, a British, & the Portuguese Brigade of Cavalry, were ordered across the river & occupied some strong ground covering Salamanca on the Southern side; but not placed in position as the movement took place late & the night was exceedingly dark. A body of the enemy's Calvalry pushed forwards to Calvarasca d'Ariva, & the situation of the army was not quite the best to receive the enemy in case he attacked at day-light. Much of this imperfection in the arrangement was attributed to the orders of march having failed to be delivered in time. The Provost Marshal of Head Quarters also caused much confusion, he had been sent to clear Salamanca of baggage & stragglers, & to expedite his mission he called out that the French were at the gates & a scene of confusion ensued which it is not possible to describe. The night was full of alarm & annoyance. A great part of the cavalry were during the night lying down in Squadrons with the bridles in their hands. By degrees the night grew darker & stormy, thunder rolled tremendously over our heads, & vivid flashes of lightening made the scene most imposing. Two great armies were on the ground under this rage of the elements waiting only for sufficient light to begin their work of blood. At length several horses were struck by the lightening which so terrified the remainder that they charged over their reposing riders, & having broke loose in every direction so near the enemy's posts, that it became a serious apprehension whether they could be collected before the morning. Many dragoons were so bruised & wounded as to be unfit for duty, & long after day-light from eighteen to twenty horses of General Le Marchant's Brigade were missing. Head Quarters were this night at a little village called Penillas, at the foot of the Arrepiles.

It has been almost necessary to enter into a vast quantity of detail, connected with these movements to enable one to follow them on the map. The incertitude in which we were kept by the enemy as to his real direction cannot but be observed. We were also greatly harrassed by being in constant readiness, & then racing at a late period to counteract his manoevres. Independant of the extreme risk of the system in an open country, this haste to retire before an equal army certainly lowered the spirit of our Troops; altho' of all others, perhaps they are the least liable to be influenced by the morale of the French, & as to Marmont's movements, I am inclined to think that the credit which he gained with our army for the style & effect of his manoevres was principally to be attributed to his having discovered the secret of Ld. Wellington's system of conducting operations, that of declining attack; & therefore while Marmont equally declined to attack in front, he was certain, by flank manoeuvres in a plain country to turn us out of every position we took up, with impunity. No particular preponderance of force had occurred to give him this advantage; but a principle on our side of refusing offensive operations. Thus he obliged our army, equal in Infantry & superior in Cavalry to retire from the defence of the Douro to behind the Tormes almost without a shot; & this by the simplest means. His great care should have been not to rouse the Lion's wrath by treading too close upon him, & had he not assumed too much upon our passiveness we should have turned upon him, until we came to our old haunts upon the Agueda.

His arrogance & an inadvertency of ours were the causes which led to the glorious & happy change in our affairs at Salamanca, where we gave him a complete overthrow & obtained a decided victory.[205] On the morning of the 22nd [July 1812] The enemy began skirmishing with his cavalry opposite our left, where the 1st 7th & 4th Divisions were placed—the remainder were disposable for any event, & the 3rd Divisions with General D'Urban's cavalry were on the right bank of the river at the Ford of Santa Martha. Ld. Wellington had ordered the baggage to east Castro, five leagues in the rear, & every department had made its arrangement for a retreat. Marmont's movements were very undecided for some hours, & he began the day by a good deal of skirmishing opposite our left & centre—at length, he shewed large columns of Infantry & Cavalry on the skirts of the woods from Alba de Tormes, & in a direction that outflanked our right. Ld. Wellington appeared only to delay retiring in the hope that he might be attacked, & when the enemy were gaining ground to the right he said "We must be off as fast as we can, or fight him."

Whilst it was a doubt, from the closeness of the enemy's manoeuvres whether Marmont would attack or not, he had by degrees, inclined two or three Battalions thro' the standing corn, & undulations of the ground, close to an isolated hill on our right, & got near it so suddenly, that he was in possession before we could occupy it, & we had only just time to secure a second hill of the same description—but I must now attempt to give an idea of the ground.

The left of our position was [.?.] upon the Tormes about three miles above Salamanca, & covering the Ford of Santa Martha, almost a perfect plain—the centre was woody ground & very favourable to us—the right was strong with three hills, of which the two farthest were those I have mentioned; being very peculiar features—standing up very high by themselves, without connection, narrow & flat at the top, & in most places inaccessible from the ruggedness of the ascent—a stream running thro' a broad valley marked out the line of our front; & I should imagine the extent of this ground to the water might be about four miles. Farther on to our right there were several very advantageous knolls, upon which the enemy was circling round us—his ground was excellent with the advantage of a wood to cover all their movements. The hill on our right, which I have said the enemy carried by surprise was very important to the compactness of our position, & rendered fresh dispositions necessary. The enemy's possession of it, hemmed us in so unpleasantly that it was resolved to retake this hill, & attack the enemy, if not very generally, at least to liberate ourselves from an encroachment that threatened the safety of our retreat. The attack of this hill was on the point of moving off, when it was perceived that the enemy had brought up a very heavy column to support his acquisition, & Ld. Wellington balanced, I believe from the hope that the French Marshal having this hill, would attack us, & indeed all his dispositions now looked very like it. The intention of repossessing ourselves of the hill was therefore given up or deferred, & the 3rd Division was ordered to occupy a hill about two miles in rear of our right which was necessary for our retreat, & to recover the retiring of the other columns. The 1st & 4th Divisions with General Pack's Portuguese Brigade were brought further to our right—the 5th took the ground of the 4th the 7th on the left, & the Light, in reserve. By the time this change was completed the enemy had made great progress. We cannonaded his columns near the steep hill with effect & they retired, taking up ground as in position. This was about twelve o'clock & he was gaining upon our right flank very fast. Ld.

Wellington then found that the enemy would be able to inconvenience his retreat exceedingly if he delayed any longer, & that he must attack or retire. Marshall Beresford's opinion was asked & he was against an attack, considering the strength of the enemy's position, that the river was almost upon our rear, & also upon the principle which had hitherto made Ld. Wellington decline acting on the offensive. Sometime elapsed, during which there was some Cavalry skirmishing for the hills further on our right which the enemy obtained. Every instant our situation became more & more critical, & the feelings of those Officers of the army, who from their situation had been enabled to observe all the movements of the enemy & the consequences which they threatened were anything but confident or comfortable. It was then proposed to attack the enemy's left with the first division, that Pack's Brigade should retake the hill, & that the remainder of the army should advance upon the enemy's centre. This attack from its plan, was more for the object of unshackling ourselves, than for deciding the fate of the two armies. However, the enemy was so close that all partial plans required correction, before they could be acted upon, which was rendered doubly necessary by the very rapid changes of the enemy's movements.

This plan was therefore deferred, apparently, because the enemy was bringing down his cannon, & threatening to attack us. The two parties then commenced cannonading each other, & it became evident that we must submit to be very much incommoded in our retreat, or be forced to fight. At about two, or rather later, a fresh disposition was made for a general attack; & nearly at four the armies stood as follows: the 3rd Division on our extreme right, with D'Urban's Portuguese cavalry attached to it—Le Marchant's heavy Brigade of Cavalry close to a little village the name of which I have forgotten—on their left, was Bradford's Brigade of Portuguese Infantry, & in the rear of these were Don Carlos's Spaniards—the 5th & 4th Divisions in the centre, each forming its second line, with the 6th Division in reserve. Pack's Portuguese Brigade was to attack the hill occupied by the enemy—the 7th Light, & 1st Divisions with the remainder of the Cavalry were on the left—whilst these dispositions were making, the centre was very warmly cannonaded, & stood it remarkably well, sending out a considerable line of sharp shooters. The enemy also appeared to be moving Infantry down, but I should suppose rather for the purpose of supporting his artillery, than from any intention of positive attack. This arrangement made, the 3rd Division was to attack the hill occupied by the enemy's left, sweeping round it, & pressing along the flank, whilst Bradford's Brigade, the 5th & 4th Divisions with the cavalry, were to advance against the enemy's centre—the left was refused & is to be considered as a reserve.

When the 3rd Division was in motion, the enemy immediately marched some strong columns to strengthen the hill, which they occupied before our people could ascend it—but nothing could withstand the bravery of this division, or the intelligence of its Commander Packenham; & fighting to maintain its fame in presence of both armies who were anxiously looking on, it signalized the commencement of the action by routing everything before it; & was admirably seconded by the Portuguese Cavalry under D'Urban, who charged the enemy's Infantry when shaken, with great success, & also made two successful charges against their Cavalry. When the 3rd Division had thus commenced the action, Bradford's Portuguese, & Le Marchant's heavy Cavalry were put in motion, & almost immediately after, the 5th 4th & 6th Divisions—the battle then became general, excepting on our left; but the vigour & ardour of the 3rd Division having formed its front upon the enemy's flank, gave Bradford & the 5th Division great assistance, & the heavy Cavalry charging the enemy as he was in disorder & retiring made this part of the action not doubtful for an instant—the 4th Division & Pack's Brigade were not so fortunate. The former after driving the enemy from a hill, which he had warmly contested, were in their turn charged by five Battalions of Infantry drawn up six deep, & probably would have withstood even this tremendous fresh formation, had not some Squadrons of French dragoons charged the Portuguese in flank, & broke them, which also for a moment, disordered the Fusileers, & the five French Battalions succeeded in retaking the hill—the Fusileers rallied instantly to their colours at the foot of the hill & regained their order. The 5th Division had passed the right flank of the 4th Division, & had in the same manner as the 3rd brought up its right, & took everything in flank & rear; it was thus in rear of these five French Battalions, who were still holding the hill, & behaving very gallantly— The Portuguese Brigade of the 5th Division from being on the left took these Battalions of the enemy completely in flank; but there was so much hallooing that instead of charging they began firing which was as dangerous to the British as to the French. Marshal Beresford & his staff put a stop to this firing, & he was making a disposition to charge the enemy in flank, which these Regiments, the 3rd & 15th Portuguese were not very willing to try—a few companies made a sort of shabby charge which these French troops would scarcely have regarded but that the 4th Division again attacked & the 5th took them in rear. They then moved off & the greater part were killed or taken prisoners. About this time Marshal Beresford received a shot in his left side, it was a severe wound, the ball was I believe afterwards extracted somewhere near the shoulder blade. General Pack's attack on the hill did not succeed—his Brigade was repulsed after conducting itself very gallantly & losing nearly a 3rd of its numbers—this hill if decently defended was almost impregnable. It was now beginning to grow dark, & the Divisions that had attacked drew up in two lines nearly at right angles across the line occupied by the enemy's centre. He had still a very good retired position & Ld. Wellington ordered it to be attacked by the 6th Division, meaning that the 5th & 4th should give a flank assistance, whilst the three Divisions of our left were advancing upon the enemy's right, & outflanked the hill which the 6th Division were to carry. Ld. Wellington himself conducted the three Divisions of our left, viz. the Light, First and Seventh and before the attack by the 6th became very hot this body of our Troops had turned tho' at some distance the enemy's new left. It continued however to make an obstinate resistance against the 6th Division which at length did carry it; but the Troops of that Division were not quite satisfied with the mode of attack by which they were brought up in front & then halted to fire at an enemy who had better ground. The advance of the Left met with little or no opposition some of our Cavalry on this flank had an opportunity of charging successfully, & it being now between nine & ten o'clock the action was considered over, & the enemy in rapid retreat & in great confusion. The night & the woods thro' which the road to Alba de Tormes lays, made it difficult to follow up our victory, & the best way to avoid the uncertainty of night operations even against a defeated enemy, appeared, it was understood, to Ld. Wellington to move by his left upon Huerta, at the angle of the Tormes, by which he had a shorter road than the enemy, to fall upon him the next morning—the justice of this movement may be seen on the map, & that our line was shorter than that of the French to Penaranda. The light Division which led, had no guide, & after marching till near mid-night found itself at Calvarasca d'Abaxa where it was halted for the night. Some Officers were of opinion, that if the whole army had marched upon Huerta, the enemy must have been brought to action the next day, or if he had been followed up, by pressing with all our force upon the Alba de Tormes road, that he could not have crossed the river without great difficulty & loss. Ld. Wellington's arrangement of intercepting the French Army by moving upon Huerta seemed an Excellent combination, but it failed, for want of guides. About midnight Sir Stapleton Cotton received a severe wound from one of our videttes whose post he was crossing, the man being ignorant whether it was friend or foe. Our night movements having thus failed, when day broke & our army crossed the Tormes in pursuit, the French were pretty far advanced in their retreat, but the heavy German Cavalry fell in with their rear-guard, which it charged, taking & destroying the greater part of them.[206] Before noon on the 23rd everything was over for the day, & we had time to ascertain the result of yesterday's action. We had taken 6000 prisoners, 20 pieces of Cannon, 4 Eagles, & 2 Generals, & the loss of the enemy was about 12,000 men. Our own loss about 5,200, killed & wounded.

This victory appeared to give us everything on our side of the Douro, in the provinces West of Madrid, & as General Santo-Cildes was somewhere on the North side of that river, we hoped to be able to cross it, this campaign. King Joseph, we heard was about to leave Madrid with reinforcements, but we did not apprehend much from his presence. We were not able to make much more of our pursuit of Marmont, as our Commissariat was left far in the rear, our arrangments previous to the battle not having been made for an advance.

The 22nd was however a great day, & will probably be the cause of inducing Ld. Wellington to change his system from the defensive to the offensive, in which it is evident to the whole army, from the style of his attack, that his real genius lays. The manoeuvring of all the divisions was most creditable to them, the Cavalry, particularly the Brigade of poor Le Marchant who was killed, behaved remarkably well, & the results of the 22nd gave fresh hopes & confidence to every individual in the army.

On the 23rd Head Quarters remained at Tortillas, where a few prisoners were brought in, & about twenty deserters from the enemy's ranks made their appearance. The army moved the next day to Flores de Avila, it was a march of six leagues on the track of the retreating French. We took some stragglers & passed many who had died of their wounds, [as well as] carts, baggage &c. We were badly off for provisions here & in order to give time to the Commissariat to come up with supplies Ld. Wellington halted, the 25th & sent off his dispatches for England.

An Officer of the Adjutant General's department rode back from this place to take a survey of the ground on which the battle had been fought, to assist him in bearing the field in memory. He saw there a beautiful young woman running wildly with her hair loose about the spot from which the 3rd Division had first attacked. She was looking about with earnest anxiety & a distracted air amongst the dead, & those of the wounded who had not yet been removed. She stopped at every corpse, the greater number of which had already been entirely stripped by the Spaniards or women of the army. & he afterwards understood that her name was Fitzgerald, & that she was searching for the body of her Husband, a young Lieutenant who had lately joined the 88th Regiment & had been killed in the action. There was also seen on the field of battle a large white Poodle dog running thro' the groups of French as they lay dead, which at length stopped at the body of an Officer, & after smelling at it for a short time, lay down & howled piteously. It remained near the body all night, & the next day was seen sitting before the door of a house in Salamanca, from which position it would not move. It was the house where a Lady lived, whom the French Officer was in the habit of visiting very frequently, & to whom he was to have been married. I saw this dog at the door of the house, where it was recognised by several who knew it. I did everything in my power to obtain possession of it, but it was not possible. It was admitted into the house & to my applications for it, I received for answer, that it would not be parted with.

The number of the Prisoners taken in the battle had been so great that it was not possible on the night of the Victory to make the necessary arrangements for their being immediately marched to the rear;[207] & it being difficult to find at once a place of sufficient security, they were collected together on a little angle of the river where the stream was very rapid & deep. A Portuguese battalion & a few Cavalry were left to guard them. These Troops formed a semicircle round the prisoners, a few sentries being also placed at the edge of the stream to fire at such, as should attempt to cross by swimming. I understood from an Officer who was one of their guard that night, that they were at first very silent & sulky, but that in less than an hour, tho' without food or the prospect of any, as were our own Troops, they were as merry & gay as if they had been going to a dance; they only intreated that they might not be left to the escort of Spanish Soldiery, from whom they had everything that was cruel & inhuman to apprehend. I believe however, that they were given in charge to part of the Division of Don Julian Sanchez, who in conducting them to the rear, behaved to them with humanity.

It was at this period that Ld. Wellington first made the acquaintance of Dr. Curtis, who has since become so celebrated, for his publication of the Duke's letter to him, on the Catholic question. He was at that time, a Priest in the Irish Convent at Salamanca, & rendered the army good service by his zeal & activity in their favour. Many Officers of the army were familiar with him, & he was full of attention to them, whenever his assistance could be useful. Whether these circumstances had any influence on his subsequent appearance in Ireland, as a Roman Catholic Bishop, I know not. I remember him well at the time of which I write, & he was considered a man of much talent & information.

The character of the women, Wives of British Soldiers, who in spite of orders, threats, & even deprivation of rations, had forced themselves in numbers, (from the dêpots in the rear, appointed for them), to the sides of their Husbands, now began to exhibit a fearful and melancholy change. All ideas of conduct or decency had disappeared—plunder & profligacy seemed their sole object, & the very Soldiers their Husbands evidently estimated them in proportion to their profiency in these vices. They covered in number the ground of the field of battle when the action was over, & were seen stripping & plundering friend & foe alike. It is not doubted that they gave the finishing blow, to many an Officer who was struggling with a mortal wound; & Major Offley of the 23rd Regiment, who lay on the ground, unable to move, but not dead, is said to have fallen a victim to this unheard of barbarity. The daring & enterprize of these creatures, so transformed beyond anything that we have heard of in man, is not to be described. They had no hesitation in engaging themselves three or four deep to future Husbands, & according to the activity in mischief, of each, was the number of candidates for her hand, in case of disaster to her lawful Lord; & one of them has been heard to reply to a Soldier, who offered himself, as successor to her then Commanding Officer: "Nay, but thou' rt late, as I'm promised to John Edwards first, & to Edward Atkinson next, but when they two be killed off, I'll think of thee."[208]

July 26th. The Army advanced in pursuit of the French to Aldea Seca, four leagues on the main road to Valladolid and bivouacked. On the 27th advanced to Arrevalo 1½ leagues—the 28th to Almedo—the 29th to Mojados, 3 leagues—the 30th to Boacillo, from which place Ld. Wellington and some of the Staff with two Squadrons of Cavalry rode into Valladolid, distant about 3 leagues. The French had abandoned this City, leaving behind them 800 sick, 17 pieces of Cannon and 20,000

shot and shells. After giving some directions relative to the sick &
wounded French, & also for establishing the military police of the town,
Ld. Wellington rode back to Boacillo; & it plainly appearing that there
was little chance of overtaking the enemy, who were retiring in full speed
towards Burgos, our Commander recrossed the Douro on the first of
August, & established his Head quarters at Cuellar, where he remained
5 days, both to refresh the Troops and to determine what was necessary
to be done against another French Army which was moving from
Segovia, under the command of King Joseph, & was believed to be from
15 to 20,000 men. Ld. Wellington decided on a rapid movement against
them & on the 6th moved on to Mozon Cillo, 5 leagues. On arrival there
he found that King Joseph having got intelligence of this advance against
him, had abandoned Segovia.

7th. Entered Segovia — 4 leagues, found there 27 pieces of Cannon &
several mortars, a great quantity of powder had been blown up, & many
stores destroyed. This City was once a very strong place, it occupies part
of the sides of two hills, with the intervening valley, thro' which runs the
river Eresma; it is surrounded by a wall having towers at intervals. There
is a magnificent Roman Aqueduct here which supplies the place with
water. It is upwards of a mile & a half long & supported by near 200
arches. In the castle there had been some very rich tapestry, & other
valuable ornaments, which had carried off by the French. They had
made equally free with some fine paintings which had been in the chapel
Royal. On the 8th Head Quarters moved to the beautiful Palace of San
Ildefonso. It is most romantically situated, at the foot of the Guadarama
mountains. There are remarkably fine fountains and water-works in the
gardens, which we lost no time in setting to work & were much gratified
by their magnificence. The Palace was built by Phillip the 5th & a town
was speedily formed to supply the wants of a Court. It became afterwards famous for an excellent manufactory of plate-glass, which continued at work even in these scenes of war, & I saw a very fine plate cast
at the establishment there, at which operation Ld. Wellington was also
present. It had been for some time a practice which was daily rather
gaining ground than otherwise for Officers of different degrees to
appropriate to themselves little memorials of the houses in which they
had been quartered & of course a Palace offered a considerable variety
of choice. This sort of appropriation was called "making." For my own
part, I had not hitherto met with anything I particularly coveted, nor was
there indeed at San Ildefonso any object within my reach of peculiar

attraction; but I thought it a pity to leave a King's palace without carrying off some proof positive of my having lodged in it, & by way of a first essay in the art of "making", pounced upon a blue silk counterpane, which had covered me the preceding night. Being in no small dread of detection as this rising art had not yet found its way to the General Officers or heads of departments, I rolled it up tightly in an old Bearskin mattrass on which I used occasionally to sleep, & packed it on my mule with my other baggage, which was on the day following. I had flattered myself, that this proof of my profiency in "making" would have accompanied me to my fire-side in England, & I little dreamed that I was destined to carry it some scores of leagues for the benefit of some Frenchman who probably picked it up, when I was compelled to disencumber my baggage of it in our subsequent retreat from Burgos in October following. This unforeseen result had upon the whole a salutary effect upon me as my future predatory habits were confined to trifling articles, & those only of real utility. From displays which I saw on my return to England after the Peninsular campaigns were at an end, others had managed much better than myself in this respect.

The army crossed the Guadarama mountains by the pass of Nava Cerrada, at which village Head Quarters remained for the night 10th of August. The advance had some sharp skirmishing with the advance of King Joseph's army.

11th. Moved on to Torre Ladrones 4 leagues, pushing in the enemy's outposts. 12th. Advance to Las-Rosas, 2 leagues. King Joseph here made a reconnoissance, & attacked a small body of Portuguese Cavalry, to which were attached 3 guns of a horse brigade under Captn. Dynely, so sharply that the Portuguese gave way and the guns were taken. Captn. Dynely was made prisoner with his guns after behaving very gallantly. I understood that he made his escape during the course of the following week & rejoined the army. The Portuguese were luckily supported by two Squadrons of heavy German dragoons, in whose rear they reformed. The Germans moved briskly against the enemy, drove them back with some loss, & I believe recaptured the guns, but not before their horses had been carried off, & the gun-carriages so injured as to be rendered unfit for immediate service.

13th August. Accounts were received at the outposts, that King Joseph had abandoned Madrid the preceding night, moving with his army on the great road to Toledo, & leaving 2 strong battalions in the fortress of Retiro, & a small work belonging to it, called fort La Chine.

The army immediately moved on to Madrid, & took possession of the Capital. When Ld. Wellington approached with his staff, in the group of which I rode, a deputation of the principal Authorities & inhabitants came out to meet him, admidst loud & continued acclamations from thousands who had joined this procession. They had already found time to decorate the gate thro' which he was to enter, as a triumphal arch. The streets were lined with well dressed persons of both sexes, waving handkerchiefs and vociferating, "Vivan los Ingleses", & "Viva Fernando settimo". The windows & balconies were filled with people, principally females elegantly dressed, repeating the acclamations of their friends below in the streets. Garlands & tapestry were suspended from all parts of the houses; the stirrups of the Officers, as they rode along, were taken hold of, & they were gently stopped to be saluted with every possible expression of good will & joy. Many were taken into the ice and lemonade shops by the rejoicing citizens of this delivered capital, & made to partake abundantly of these delicacies, nor would any money be received in payment. The inhabitants contended with each other, who should take the British Officers into their houses, nor would there have been any need of the usual process of issuing billets, but for the necessity of the address of every Officer being known at Head Quarters. For three successive nights the city was brilliantly illuminated, & British Officers were seen in all directions with Spanish Ladies leaning on their arms, who were pointing out to them, the different habitations of their Grandees by the light of the lamps. Priests & Monks too joined in this festive scene. Portuguese & Spanish Officers also, mixed abundantly in it, & the whole presented one of the most curious & interesting spectacles I ever beheld. The whole city was in a sort of confusion of joy for several days.[209]

Immediately on our entrance, Ld. Wellington invested the Retiro with a sufficient force, & began works against it. On the 15th preparations were made for carrying it by storm, when the French sent out a flag of truce, & agreed to capitulate. We took possession on the following day, finding immense stores, 180 pieces of canon, 20,000 Muskets, & one Eagle; the number of prisoners was about 2000. Permission had been given to the garrison to march out with the honours of war, but they were to deposit their arms & accoutrements on the glacis. Here I saw them assembled for that purpose, rage was strongly depicted on their countenances, & many were beginning to knock off the butt-end of their muskets, by striking them violently against the ground. This was not put

an end to without considerable difficulty.[210] They were marched thro'
the streets of Madrid, under a strong escort of Spanish Guerillas, a
compliment purposely paid to the nation. The French were all the time,
imploring to be taken out of the custody of these Spaniards, & that a
British escort should be given them to Bilboa, the place of their
embarkation for England. They seemed perfectly well aware, of the ill
treatment and cruelty to which they would be subject in Spanish hands;
possibly feeling that they had well deserved it. It was not however
convenient to detach a sufficient body of British to guard these men, &
they were marched off under the same guard that paraded them thro'
Madrid. On the day following their departure, accounts were received
by Ld. Wellington that the Guerillas were murdering all those who
lagged behing thro' weakness, & that the treatment which these poor
Frenchmen were receiving was of the most barbarous description. An
Officer of the Adjutant General's department was immediately
detached to enquire into the truth of this statement, that Officer was
myself. I came up with the escort about 7 leagues from Madrid. on the
road side for 3 leagues before I overtook them, I saw many bodies of
French Soldiers, dead. They had been pierced with spears and evidently
murdered. I was exceedingly shocked to find how true the report had
been which had reached Ld. Wellington. I rode on to the front and told
the Officer commanding for what purpose I had been detached from
Madrid, & with how much pain the Commander of the forces had
heard, of the cruelties of which the troops under his orders had been
guilty. As I was speaking to him, the French almost shed tears of joy at
hearing the purport of my mission. They assured me they had done
everything in their power to behave orderly & to give as little trouble as
possible to their escort, that they had had no food since they left Madrid,
were so weak that they could scarcely march further, & yet dared not lag,
as those who fell out of their ranks were immediately murdered. They
literally clung to me, & besought me to leave them no more until they
reached the end of their march, & I sincerely regretted that I was not
able to comply with their wishes. Before I left them however, I had them
moved up into column as closely as possible, & prevailed on the Guerilla
Commandant to address his troops in the hearing of them all. He
commanded them to desist from practices which had given so much
pain at Head Quarters, & on no account to be guilty of any repetition of
them. I assured him that should a single instance recur of similar
barbarity, his Corps would be disbanded as unworthy to serve with the

Spanish Armies, & that he & his Officers would be held personally responsible for every life that was lost, from the time that I took my leave. Having thus done all that was in my power I returned to Madrid, & had afterwards the satisfaction of learning that the prompt attention which Ld. Wellington paid, had the desired effect, & that these poor Frenchmen reached Bilboa without a repitition of the horrors, which had disgraced their first days' march under a Spanish guard.[211]

During our stay in Madrid which continued to the 1st of Septr. the army was placed in cantonments & every thing done to refresh & re-equip it with the utmost activity. Ld. Wellington & his staff were quartered in the palace, from which King Joseph had removed most of the valuable articles of furniture but still every comfort remained. The staff of Head Quarters were billeted in the immediate neighbourhood of the Palace as being most convenient for public business. Ld. Wellington gave frequent large dinners to the Spanish Generals, & Guerilla Chieftains, inviting always a proportion of British Officers to meet them. Several balls were also given by him, at which all the beauty of Madrid was assembled, & it almost appeared that we were at Madrid for the sole purpose of amusing ourselves, whilst in fact we were in the midst of hostile armies, the observation of which & preparations for meeting them, were the constant objects of our Commanders anxious thoughts. At one of the dinners to which I have alluded, an anecdote is related of the Empecinado, one of the most distinguished of the Guerilla leaders. A large boiled Trout was placed before him, served up in the English fashion, with a folded napkin under it; some one at table sent his plate to this chieftain for a slice. After having cut thro' the fish, he was observed to labour hard at something more, & at length succeeded in putting on the plate of the person who had sent for the fish, that portion of the napkin which lay under the slice, having by dint of perseverance got thro its several folds with great neatness. This was too good a joke not to be taken advantage of, & several of the Officers present, instantly sent for fish, each receiving his due proportion of the napkin underneath. The Empecinado was afterwards made aware of his mistake & enjoyed the joke as much as any body at the table. At these dinners I had opportunities of seeing, the leaders of those Guerilla bands, who had most distinguished themselves—Espoy-y-Mina, Morillo, the Pastor, the Empecinado, Don Julian & others. Don Carlos d'Espagna, Abisbal, Alava, Wimpfen & many other Spanish Generals of note were also to be seen at these entertainments. These latter were generally men of good family, but the Guerilla chiefs were mostly men of low birth, bad manners & butcher like appearance. There was at this time at Head Quarters a very amusing fellow called Fuentes. He played the guitar prettily & sang droll songs to it. This quality procured him occasional invitations to Ld. Wellingtons table, where he used to exercise it. He had afterwards an appointment given him in the Spanish Commissariat. Fuentes was a laughing good tempered creature, who would come to our quarters to play & sing to us in an evening & his Spanish wit & drollery never failed to put us in high good humour; he would drink grog with us & eat of anything we might happen to have provided it were well seasoned for him with garlic, of which he used to eat such quantities that nothing but his musical & amusing qualities rendered him bearable in a room. He never could be induced to come & see a Cannon shot fired, & had not the least hesitation in confessing, that he believed himself to be an arrant coward. Whenever the baggage of the army was sent to the rear, preparatory to an action, Fuentes never failed to accompany it, & was not unfrequently found to have taken up his quarters even a league or two further back.

The Prince of Orange continued still at Head Quarters, acting as Aid de Camp to Ld. Wellington, & became popular by his quiet & unassuming manners. I may here mention that when in 1814 the Revolution in favor of his family took place in Holland, he left us at San Jean de Luz.[212] A British sloop of war was sent there to receive him, & the boat which put him on board was rowed by British Officers. In the house in which I was myself quartered at Madrid before I was removed with others of the head quarter staff into the Palace of the Prince of peace, was a priest, who was certainly disposed to shew me every sort of attention. He used to come to my bed-side very early in the morning with a cup of the best chocolate that ever was tasted, two pieces of the whitest bread toasted and a glass of the coldest water; entering my room with his "Benedicte" he approached the bed with all reverence, enquired with becoming earnestness how my excellency had slept, & whether I was disposed to accept the poor refreshment that it was his happy lot to offer me. Nothing could be more gracious & condescending than the reception I always thought it my duty to give the worthy monk, thus bearing his morning tribute to a hungry English Officer in the capital of his country, & who was receiving the offering with as much apparent unconcern as a longing stomach could make appear on the countenance. I did not wish to appear too much delighted, but rather that he should think this daily attention quite a matter of course. His obsequiousness & my condescension would have made no bad scene in a comedy.

Whilst at Madrid we used sometimes to amuse ourselves with comparing the different things we had "made" since last we had had an opportunity of meeting for such a purpose—but in truth our means of transporting baggage were so limited that these transfers of other peoples property were at this time confined to articles of clothing & real necessaries. I must however admit that a sort of an itch for stealing occasionally prevailed over the principle of honesty, & on entering a house when in want of almost all the comforts of life as we sometimes were, the eye wandered round a room as it were mechanically to see if it could meet with any object that would supply our deficiencies. The sleeve of a shirt hanging out of a drawer, naturally led to the feeling of comfort which such an addition would make to a wardrobe that barely covered a gentleman's back, & the tempting situation of the worthy hosts chemise giving evident proof that his drawer was too full, was sometimes pointed out in significant silence to a soldier servant who needed no farther hint, & the attention of the servant to his masters wants was usually discovered in an unexpected change of linen; no enquiry was made as to the source of the supply, and credit was naturally given to the servants ingenuity, the proof of which was received with internal gratitude, but not acknowledged. The most fortunate of all "makes" certainly was when by happy accident an Officer was quartered in the house of a Padron of about equal dimensions, so as to enable him to step into his hosts shoes or boots. This was indeed a welcome discovery. The spaniards, the lower floors of whose houses, were usually made of an earthy composition, used to bury their household goods, linen &c underneath them but our Soldiers soon borrowed from the French, the ingenious practice of watering these floors, & the water sinking first in the part where the earth had been last disturbed, discovered the treasure which was then brought to light & disposed of as circumstances made desirable. In return for all the fêtes given by the D. of Wellington, the authorities of Madrid thought it necessary to arrange their great national exhibition of a Bull fight, in which of all others the Spaniards most delight. The place in which this spectacle takes place in Madrid, is within the area of a sort of unroofed theatre, there are three tiers of boxes one above the other, with a certain portion about the centre of the second tier more sumptuously decorated than the rest & which is usually occupied by the Royal family. On the occasion of this exhibition, this portion was set apart for the D. of Wellington & his staff, who attended in full dress, as did all the Spanish authorities, & their families. The area below was covered with a soft sand, & the lower tier of boxes was separated from it by a wooden partition about seven feet high, over which the persons in the lower boxes could see from their benches, which were placed so as to give them this advantage. at one side of the area is seen a large pair of folding doors, one of which communicates with a sort of den inclosing the Bull. The animal is let in to this den singly, from other dens where they are kept preparatory to this national exhibition. At the moment appointed for the purpose, a trumpet sounds, & a man on horseback fancifully dressed, with a lance in his hand, enters the area from the other folding door. The horse is usually a poor one for which little money is given by the municipality as it seldom recovers from its rencontre with the bull. When the man, thus seated, has made a tour or two round the area, & bowed to the spectators, he puts himself in an attitude of defence opposite the other folding door, making a flourish with his lance. A second trumpet sounds, when the door of the den containing the bull opens & out he springs, wild with fury, as it is customary to goad & provoke them in their dens by every possible means. Those which I saw at this fête, were of a mouse colour, rather small but beautifully proportioned & full of fire & activity. After shaking himself, the Bull gazed round about him, & began to paw the ground & to bellow. The horseman approached with his lance in his hand, the bull continued pawing the ground apparently not observing him, then suddenly turning his eyes up, looked at him, shook his head & made a fierce rush at the horse. This, the rider parried & being very dexterous in the use of his lance, received the bull on it piercing him in the shoulder. The bull drew back wounded, but instantly rushed on again, the horseman missed his thrust with the lance, but changed his position so instantenously, that he himself escaped, but the horse was dreadfully gored. The Bull withdrew his horns and again pierced him in the belly, the rider still remaining in his seat, but this last stroke was too much for the poor animal & he fell. The horseman sprang over the partition between the area & the lower tier of boxes & escaped. Another trumpet was the signal for the entrance of a second horseman, who rode gallantly up to the bull, but the creature appeared rather tired, & did not attack this enemy, with the same fury as the first, & the man had opportunities of piercing him several times, & greatly fatiguing him. Having done this a trumpet called him off & he retired thro' the folding door by which he entered—I believe the horseman on these occasions is called the Picador. Then enters a man on foot dressed in a fantastic manner, with a cap on his head hanging down on one side, a pointed dart like an arrow in his right hand, & a sort of red shawl hanging like drapery from his left arm. He approaches the bull who plunges at him. When about to do this, the man turns quickly, & offers him the red shawl at which the animal instantly darts. On striking the shawl his eyes are for the moment covered with it, & at that time the man, who is called the Banderillero sticks the arrow into him, it penetrates the skin & hangs down from it. The Banderillero is then supplied with another, & when that is similarly transfixed, a third, and so on till the bull is seen with a dozen or more of them hanging from different parts of his body. Sometimes there are fire-works & crackers in these darts, which are so contrived as to go off from time to time worrying and irritating the animal more & more. The efforts which he makes to disengage himself at length exhaust him a good deal, & when thus wearied the Picador retires. Then comes the Matador armed with a short sword in the right hand, & a Red shawl as before hanging over his left arm. He moves towards the bull presenting the red shawl, the animal darts at it, as the Matador lowers his left arm, which thus brings the bull before his right hand, with his head & body curved towards the lowered shawl. The Matador seizes this moment & plunges the sword up to the hilt between the shoulders in a place which he knows to be mortal, & the animal drops instantaneously. The sword is left in, the Matador mounts the carcase & bows to the audience. He is answered by loud clapping of hands, & "Viva el Matador" from all sides. A Trumpet sounds—two mules, beautifully caparisoned abreast trot in, having a rope attached to them which is fastened to the bulls horns, & at another sound of the trumpet the mules drag him off—another trumpet, & another bull enters instantly. The same process is repeated. I observed that the Ladies took particular pleasure in this spectacle, & whenever a horse was gored & fell, were loud in their applause; & a Spanish Lady sitting near me, to whom I remarked that I was glad to have had an opportunity of witnessing this Spanish national amusement, said to me "that it had been a very dull & stupid exhibition as not a single man had been killed." Such accidents as the death of the Picador & Matador are not very unfrequent, as the red shawl sometimes fails to divert the attention of the animal from the man, & the horse-man himself has occasionally been gored to death, when by the fall of his horse upon him, he has not been able to leap over the inclosure, which divides the area from the lower tier of boxes in sufficient time. At the exhibition which I have described, a bull in his fury sprung over this fence without touching it, & the people on the seats who fortunately saw him approaching had only just time, to open right and left, & thus escape being crushed. He broke both his legs on the spot where he alighted, & was thus rendered incapable of doing injury. Two bulls were also baited with dogs on this occasion, but it was by no means a spirited contest, nor did it appear to excite so much interest as the other.[213]

1st Septbr. Ld. Wellington having intelligence, that strong French armies were moving on Madrid from different quarters marched with four Divisions against General Clausel who was advancing to the Douro. About 10,000 Spanish Troops accompanied him & formed his left. About 5000 men were left in Madrid & Sir Rowland Hill watched Soult on the Tagus.

Head Quarters occupied the Escurial. It is about seven leagues from Madrid. It is not so handsome a Palace as that of San Ildefonso, but is famous for being the burial place of most of the Spanish Monarchs, & was built by Phillip the 2nd to commemorate a victory gained over the French near St. Quentin in 1557. Its shape is that of a Gridiron because St. Laurence on whose day the victory was gained, was broiled to death on such an instrument. The Royal Sepulchre is called the Pantheon, being in imitation of that building at Rome.[214]

2nd Septbr. Halted at Villa Castin seven leagues on the road to Arravelo.

3rd.—Marched to Arravelo seven leagues and a half.

4th.—Halted at Olmedo four leagues. Here we heard that the enemy's outposts were at Boacilla, & remained one day to reconnoitre them.

6th. Moved to Boacilla five leagues, drove in the enemy's Cavalry videttes after some sharp skirmishing.

7th. Approached Valladolid found that the enemy had closed the gates, & placed some light Infantry on the wall near the Puerta de Toro; our Light Infantry closing upon them they abandoned the walls & gates, & the latter were quickly forced open. Our Troops entered before the enemy had quite time enough to retire from the place & the 12th Light Dragoons with a party of Guerillas had some skirmishing with a Squadron of French cavalry in the town. They retired by the bridge over the Pesuerga which having been ruined, was blown up as soon as they were over. On the other side of that stream which tho' narrow is deep &

difficult to cross, we saw the French army drawn up in line of battle. Before day-light the next morning however, they had retired. Valladolid is 2 and a half leagues from Boacilla. Here we remained until the 10th waiting the arrival of Castanos & his army which was to have joined about the 6th. This City is surrounded by strong walls, there are more Monasteries and Nunneries in it than in any City of Spain that I can remember. It was formerly a Royal residence, & the Royal Palace which still remains is immensely large. There is also a large building of the Inquisition which has no windows but merely holes to let in the light, the effect of which is most gloomy & barbarous.

10th. Ld. Wellington thought it better to advance by easy marches, than to wait any longer for Castanos, & established His Head Quarters at Cegales two leagues, sending his advance across the Pesuerga by the ford of Santa Maria & the bridge of Cabizon.

11th. Moved on to Duennas 3 & a half leagues. Saw nothing whatever of the enemy.

12th. Marched to Magaz 2 leagues. Near this place we found one of the French outposts & drove it in.

13th. Torquemada 2 leagues. Had some skirmishing here & took some prisoners.

14th. Cordevilla one league. The enemy retired on our approach.

15th. Revilla Pallajera 2 & half leagues, the enemy were here in considerable force, but they retired in the night without exchanging a shot. The slow movements of the last five days had been occasioned by the non-arrival of Castangos who by some mistake had conducted his army by a wrong route.

16th. Moved to Pampliega 2 leagues: here Castangos joined with his army. They were about 10,000 men badly clothed and equipped & still worse in discipline. The men themselves were in general, fine stout looking fellows, but had the appearance of not being more than half fed. In a position about a league from Pampliega, the French army was seen drawn up in three lines, their flanks & centre covered by Artillery. Their Cavalry in Squadrons. On the right bank of a stream falling into Pesuerga, called the Adaja, where the country was flat & well adapted to Cavalry manoeuvres. The numbers of the French were about 30,000 men, as Clausel had been joined by General Souham, who brought with him 10,000, and being the senior Officer took the chief Command. Up to a late hour at night, the enemy shewed no diposition to abandon his position & Ld. Wellington resolved to attack them at day-break. The plan of attack was given out, baggage was sent to the rear, & every arrangement made for a general action. But when day broke on the following morning it was found that the French had decamped leaving their fires burning.[215] I had gone to bed the night before after arrangements for the attack had been made when I was sent for to the Quarter-Master General's Office, where I received from Sir George Murray a letter which I was to deliver immediately to the General Officer commanding a Division of Spaniards on our left. I had also verbal instructions as to the part which this Spanish Division was to take in the attack, & enjoined to see that the orders contained in the letter to the Spanish General were punctually obeyed. The night was so dark that I had some difficulty in finding him & his division. When I had made them out, I proceeded to the Generals quarters & gave him the dispatch. He & his Aid de Camp were sitting smoking together in the cottage of a wretched village, which had been completely destroyed by the Spanish Soldiery. Doors, windows, & furniture had been used as fire-wood, & the confusion & noise round the General's quarters were such as to be hardly described, which seemed to give the General no sort of concern. He read his letter which had been written in Spanish by General Alava a distinguished Spanish Officer attached to Head Quarters; [he then] immediately shook me by the hand, said he was very glad to see me, & assured me that his division whilst employed in the contemplated attack should implicitly obey any orders that I might be charged with. He then gave me some cigars & put before me some spirits & water, & as I spoke Spanish pretty fluently we were soon excellent friends. He appeared to me as if my arrival had relieved him from a weight of responsibility of which he most willingly divested himself. This General's name was St. Pol. He was a fat goodnatured man who looked much more like a monk than a General Officer. I must however do him the justice to say that he had his division under arms an hour before day-break on the following morning altho' all my efforts to check the great noise with which this formation was accompanied were quite ineffectual. They marched off however in tolerable silence but when it was made known that the French had decamped of which I was first informed (because seeing the fires of their picquets burning I was not aware of the fact) by a note in pencil sent me by Ld. Wellington himself which I have still in my possession, nothing could exceed the tumult of these Spaniards. They swore & called the French every name of reproach that was possible, using every term of opprobrium to which they felt that they themselves could possibly lay claim. Liars, Thieves & Cowards they were who dared not face brave Spaniards. One would have supposed they had been fighting a desperate battle & gained a complete victory. St. Pol proposed to halt his division & that they should pile arms & go to sleep. I pointed out to him that the troops on his right were moving forwards & that he would be expected to accompany their movements, which he ordered his division to do. The whole army halted about mid-day. St. Pol also halted his division in the middle of a small plain. I then shewed him a wood a little distance on his left thro' which it appeared that a stream ran, & recommended him to take his division there for the advantage of wood & water. He did so, expressing to me his grateful thanks for my having pointed it out to him & assured me of his eternal friendship. I then left him & rejoined Head Quarters.

On the 17th of September Head Quarters moved to Frandovines two & a half leagues where we had some skirmishing with the enemy's cavalry.

18th. Villa Abilla 2 leagues. We saw nothing of the enemy this day.

19th. Villa Toro. 1 & a half leagues, & 2 miles from Burgos into which city we entered. The enemy had retired leaving in the Castle a picked garrison consisting of 2 Battalions of the 34th. Regiment, the 130th & the Guarde de Paris, 2500 men with ammunition & Provisions in abundance.

The main body of the French army retired to Briviesca where it took up a position. The Castle of Burgos is on a hill of a conical form, it commands the town entirely, has three walls & ditches, the two inner ones of which are stockaded & palisaded. There was also an old convent on the hill which was converted into a barrack, & divided from the castle by a deep ditch palisaded, over which was a draw- bridge to keep up the connection. The hill on which the Castle stands is in some measure commanded by another hill from which however it is separated by a deep valley. On this other hill, the French had made a strong horn-work, which was mined. On the top of the castle were six eighteen pounders, which were pointed upon the horn-work so as to command it completely. There were altogether 28 pieces of cannon mounted in the castle & its works—2 mortars & 4 howitzers. These works were reconnoitered immediately on our arrival & the storm of the horn-work was ordered to take place at night by parties of the 42nd & 79th Regiments, under Majors Dick & Cocks. The work was carried after considerable difficulty & with a loss of 380 men killed & wounded. The city of Burgos being so completely under the guns of the Castle was found untenable for Head Quarters & they were removed to the little village of Villa Toro, & preparations were made for a regular siege. The 1st & 6th Divisions with the Portuguese Brigades of Generals Pack & Bradford were employed on this service. The 5th & 7th divisions with the cavalry moved to the front to observe the enemy & established themselves at Monasterio, Villa Fria & the neighbourhood. The Spaniards also took up a position in the same direction.

20th. Trenches were opened under a heavy fire from the enemy which caused us considerable loss.

21st. An attempt was made this night to carry a work at the foot of the hill on which the Castle was situated but it failed & we lost about fifty men killed & wounded.

22nd. The trenches continued without interruption, except one unsuccessful sally from the enemy, until the 30th.

Octobr. 1st. Three guns were mounted on our batteries—24 pounders. They were the only heavy guns we had, we called them Thunder, Lightning & Nelson.

4th. We attempted with these three guns to make a breach in the wall below the Castle, but the great weight of artillery which the French brought to bear upon us silenced them in about an hour. In the evening of this day a mine that had been run under the wall was fired with excellent effect. A capital breach was made on the top of which the 24th Regiment gallantly established itself. The next day the French sallied out & destroyed the lodging we had made before there was time to repulse them. We reestablished ourselves, but with considerable loss as two of our battering pieces had been rendered unserviceable & we had no means of resisting the tremendous fire from the castle. The heavy rain which fell, also greatly impeded our progress. On the 8th the garrison made a strong sortie drove back our troops & destroyed all our works between the second line & the wall. The following day some howitzers arrived with which we battered the defences of the castle with some effect. We received a report that the enemy having received reinforcements of 10,000 Infantry & 1500 Cavalry and being joined by the army of the North, 12,000 men under Caffarelli, were concentrating their force near Pancorvo. This made Ld. Wellington the more anxious for a vigorous prosecution of the siege, in which we had made little progress for the time that it had occupied us, but yet almost as much as could have been expected when our very insufficient means are con-

W. D. Cribbs, *Officer and Private, 8th West India Regiment,*
c. 1803-1812.

British Siege of Fort Bourbon, Martinique, February 1809 (1809).

St. Clair, *British Camp near Villa Velha, Portugal, 19 May 1811* (1812/13).

British Troops Storming Ciudad Rodrigo, Night of 19 January 1812 (1813).

sidered. On the 16th an attempt was made to carry a breach that had been made by the howitzers, & after a sharp contest, the second line was carried. Some men of the German Legion penetrated even the 3rd line, but the garrison attacked so vigorously that our men were driven back. The enemy in our front were now moving on, & on the 18th there was sharp skirmishing near Monasterio.

19th. The French drove in our Cavalry & advanced in great force.

20th. A last attempt was made this day to storm the Castle, but with no better success than before. Our loss was very severe, the siege was then abandoned & the French General Breton was left to reap all the laurels of our repulse. Our loss during the siege was little short of 2000 men & 60 Officers killed & wounded. The ill success which attended this affair was entirely owing to the very inefficient means with which it was attempted.[216] Before abandoning the siege we buried our heavy guns, which was in fact hardly necessary, as they had been rendered quite useless. On the night of the 21st we began to retire on the road to Valladolid by a forced march, & Head Quarters were established at Frandovines.

22nd. The enemy pursued & we had some sharp skirmishing. Head Quarters halted at Calle del Camino two & a half leagues.

23rd. Retired to Cordevilla $5\frac{1}{2}$ leagues, the enemy in pursuit. Their Cavalry in a large mass were rapidly approaching our rear guard, in which they had already occasioned some disorder,[217] when the 1st & 2nd light Infantry battalions of the Kings German Legion, threw themselves into squares, & in the most gallant & determined manner resisted & repelled every attempt of this formidable body of cavalry to break them. The French experienced considerable loss, & our rear guard got clear off. This was one of several occasions on which I had an opportunity of observing the inefficacy of cavalry attacks on squares of Infantry.

24th. The army retired to Duennas, 5 leagues. Here, the 5th division had a very sharp engagement with the French advanced guard supported by a strong force of artillery. Our loss was not much short of 500 men. We halted the next day at Duennas, in order of battle, the enemy closed up, but did not attack us. Our time was occupied in mining two bridges over the Carrion river at Palencia, & also those at Duennas, & Villa Muriel. There was also a bridge over the Pisuerga ordered to be similarly prepared. The bridge at Duennas was destroyed. Those at Palencia were gained possession of by the enemy before the mines could be exploded & the mining party at the bridge over the Pisuerga were so rapidly attacked by some of the enemy's cavalry who beat in the covering party whilst they were at work, that they were all made prisoners.

26th. Head Quarters were at Cabezon 4 leagues where the army crossed the Pisuerga. The enemy pursued us closely. The ground about Cabizon is particularly favorable for Military position, & as the only bridge across the river was mined & strongly barricadred Ld. Wellington determined to remain here until all the sick & wounded & stores could be safely moved from Valladolid.

29th. We recommenced our retreat through Valladolid to Boacilla 4½ leagues, blew up the bridge at the former place & saw nothing of the enemy this day.

30th. The army retired to Rueda on the Douro 5 leagues. The enemy moved down the river & by swimming over a body of men above Tordesillas surprised a picquet that had been left at the bridge there, got possession of it & occupied the town, & also the village of Toro.[218] Head Quarters however did not move from Roueda, until it was ascertained that Soult had united his army with that of Souham & Joseph Bonaparte, making a force of 75,000 Infantry & 15,000 Cavalry on the right-bank of the Douro, while Ld. Wellington's whole force did not exceed 50,000 Infantry & his Cavalry did not muster more than 4,500 Sabers. In this state of things it was impossible to remain longer where we were, as the enemy was in a position to cut off our communications with Portugal. General Hill who had been left with the 2nd 3rd 4th & light divisions & 5000 Portuguese with an equal number of Spaniards in the neighbourhood of Madrid, being too weak to oppose Soult, had been ordered to retire, & join Ld. Wellington at Alba de Tormes, 4 leagues from Salamanca, which he did by a march through the pass of Guadaramma, as leisurely conducted as our own had been from Burgos; the enemy making frequent demonstrations of attack, but never putting them into execution.

6th November. Head Quarters were established at Tordesillas del Orden 5 leagues on the road to Salamanca & on the 7th they moved to Petiaqua 4½ leagues.

8th. The army in its retreat entered Salamanca 4 leagues. We found that General Hill had safely arrived at Alba de Tormes, which the French attacked in great force, but the town had been so strongly barricadoed & was so well defended by the 28th 50th & 71st Regiments that after cannonading it sharply, the enemy desisted from further attempts & manoeuvered higher up the river. From the 9th to the 15th

Ld. Wellington remained at Salamanca, closely observing the French who did not appear inclined to press him, but on the latter day they passed their whole army over the tormes at Galisancho about 3 leagues higher up than Alba. Ld. Wellington drew up his army in line of battle on the position of the Arrepiles on the very ground where the enemy was routed on the 22nd of July. Here we waited battle not doubting that the great numerical superiority of the French would certainly induce them to attack. They did not do so however but moved round our right flank so large a column as to threaten communications with Portugal & Ld. Wellington then thought it prudent to retire, & Head Quarters slept this night at Carneiro 3½ leagues.

16th. The enemy pursued but in small force with Cavalry only & some light Artillery. They made some prisoners & having succeded in penetrating between the line of march of two of our divisions they captured Sir Edwd. Paget our second in command with one of his orderly Dragoons. He had been riding to give some orders to the rear division & being very near-sighted did not perceive that it was French Cavalry approaching him until it was too late for him to escape them. The weather was dreadfully severe incessant rain, intense cold & constant hail storms. Head Quarters remained for the night at Aldequela de Bovida 3 leagues. On the 17th we moved to Cabrillas 3 leagues, seeing but very few of the enemy, & on the 18th the army crossed the Yeltes & Tenebron rivers, which were so swollen by the rains of the last three days as to be scarcely fordable. Head Quarters reached Cividad Rodrigo 6 leagues where it remained till the 24th when Ld Wellington moved to*   the army went into winter
quarters on   the neighbourhood of
Moime   General Hill took his corp
towar   Quarters there. Castanos
retu   French cantoned
th   Valladolid.
&   as
at Segovia—Soult at Toledo—& the Count D'Erlon (late General Drouet) who superceded Souham in the command of the army of Portugal had his Head Quarters at Valldolid. The army of the North under Caffarelli returned to Burgos & that neighborhood.

Thus ended the campaign of 1812, the result of which no doubt disappointed the expectations of the people of England after the brilliant

* Blank area indicates missing portion of the page.

manner in which it had commenced, a result which certainly would have been of a very different character had we not attacked the Castle of Burgos with means so very inadequate to its reduction, which independent of the severe repulse that we met with there, caused a delay in our ulterior operations which checked for the moment the patriotic impulse of the Spaniards & gave time to the French to assemble armies of such strength as made it next to impossible for us to cope with them. Retreat was the inevitable consequence & we found ourselves at the conclusion of the year on the exact spot from which we had started at its beginning.[219] The feeling of superiority however with which the French armies had been impressed with regard to us and our allies the Portuguese & Spa*   decided change. Their career of suc   eat. and their movements had   s energy which mark the   & in the same prop in its established a feeling of equality at least, if not of something more with our adversaries. The losses of the French in the course of this year may be estimated pretty nearly as follows. I am speaking merely of that

Cividad Rodrigo		3,000 men	Prisoners
Badajos		5,000 do.	do.
Salamanca Forts		800 do.	do.
Battle 22nd July		7,000 do.	Prisoners
Do. do.		1,600 do.	
Do. died of wounds		1,500 do.	
Valladolid		700 do.	Prisoners
Madrid		2,500 do.	do.
Guadalascara		900 do.	do.
Cuenca		1,000 do.	do.
Astorga		1,200 do.	do.
Tordesilas		300 do.	do.
In different skirmishes		1,000 do.	
Killed & died of wounds in the whole campaign	say	6,000 do.	
At the siege of Burgos		500 do.	
Total		33,000	

* Blank area indicates missing portion of the page.

part of the French army opposed to the operations of the Duke of Wellington.

The loss of the British & Portuguese may be calculated pretty nearly as follows in round numbers, the exactness of which can however be perfectly ascertained by a reference to the Gazettes of the day in which every detail is given with the greatest accuracy.

	K. & W.	Prisoners
Rodrigo	1,900	
Badajos	5,000	
Battle 22nd July	5,000	
Burgos	2,000	
On the retreat		2,000
	13,900	2,000
Of these will be again fit for duty	7,900	1,000
Leaves	6,000	1,000
	1,000	
Total	7,000	Lost in 1812.

Of the loss of the two armies from sickness & other casualties it is hardly possible to form a correct estimate. It must probably have been pretty nearly alike in proportion to their respective numbers.[220] The Spanish troops were I believe on the whole more healthy than our own altho' neither so well clothed nor fed. They had always however a good many men in hospital from sore feet owing to their being so badly shod, a complaint which at times also greatly reduced our own numbers. We had devised a partial remedy for this by making such men as were without shoes put their feet on the fleshy side of the hide of a newly slaughtered bullock, cut out what was sufficient to enclose them and sew them up, keeping them so until a supply of shoes arrived. The sufferings of the army during the three days before we reached Cividad Rodrigo were indeed bitter. No one can imagine all we suffered from cold & wet & hunger. The continued rain made it impossible to light fires, & our clothes were so wet that it made us feel the cold much more severely—add to this the want of proper nourishment; but in these cases of extreme suffering, the mind breaks forth in all its splendor, & supports the miserable prison in which it is confined with an elasticity and energy sufficient to convince any man that he bears about him the germ of immortality, & that there is a spirit within him which must have been breathed upon him by the great Author of our existence—this it was that gladdened many an hour of privation & hardship & lightened up the frame in its moments of darkness. How greatful ought we to be for this support, & how unworthily do we usually express our gratitude. Nevertheless let us humbly trust that the simple prayer of the Soldier finds its way into the presence of its great captain when offerred to him with sincerity of heart. I have seen such homage paid to him who was our shield in the day of battle, & have ventured to hope that it was not altogether unacceptable, nor unheard, as unvarying protection was afforded us, & continued victory followed the pathway of our colors. Two days before we arrived at Rodrigo the army retreated thro' a considerable wood of oaks into which pigs had been driven to eat the acorns that had fallen from them. Our hungry Soldiers began to fire upon these pigs to kill them for the sake of the Pork, as no provision had been served out. This firing at the pigs at length became so serious as to ressemble skirmishing at the out-posts, & kept those divisions that were out of the wood in continual alarm. Ld. Wellington therefore issued a most severe order to prohibit it, making death itself the penalty of disobedience, & Officers were detached in all directions to put a stop to it. Late in the evening, I was returning to Head Quarters thro' the wood with another Officer of the Adjutant General's department, when we saw a cavalry Soldier trotting off with half a pig before him, bleeding as he went along. The man looked round, & it was immediately evident that he knew he was acting in disobedience of orders as he increased his trot. We soon however came pretty close to him, when he set off in a canter with his half pig before him, & we after him with our swords drawn. The real fact was, we wanted his pig & he wished to keep it. Ours were the best horses & we gained upon him, calling out to him to stop instantly, which however he did not seem the least inclined to do. We got still closer to him, when he once more looked round, & seeing the case was desperate let drop the half pig which lightened his horse & he changed his canter into a gallop & was soon out of our sight. Our object being gained we immediately stopped, divided the half pig with our swords, each taking his portion on his pistol holsters covered with his cloak. I never eat better pork, the relish for it having been greatly increased by the chase after its original owner the cavalry man. My brother officer of the Adjutant General's department, had not time allowed him to enjoy his portion, as he was detached that same night to a considerable distance on a particular service.[221]

When we reached Cividad Rodrigo, our halting place, we had the comfort of finding ourselves once more under cover. It was about nine o'clock of a dark rainy & chill November night, when we entered the gates. As it was too late for us to be regularly billeted on the inhabitants we went into any houses we could find open with teeth chattering & stomacks loudly complaining of the ill-treatment they had received for several days past. I knocked loudly at a door in a small street which was at length opened to me. Inside were the remains of a fire on the hearth, & in a bed, the side of which was almost blocked up by a chest of drawers was one who had evidently jumped in after opening the door. By the dress which lay on the drawers I knew it to be a Padre. "Holloa my friend", I said (in Spanish), "tumble up, I am cold & wet & hungry— make a good fire—lend me a shirt—give me some meat, & let me lie down in your place". He was a great over-grown fellow who appeared exceedingly little inclined to move, & began a conversation with me from his bed. This however did not answer my purpose as I told him, & engirding my sword from my waist, it gave him a hint by the noise that it made, that it was necessary he should be a little alert. He said that he had nothing in the house, to which I replied, that I had little doubt, of being able to find plenty of everything, as I had been used of late to know pretty well the sort of places, where household conveniences were kept. Rather than give me the trouble of a search of this description, which might have led to the discovery of more wants than I had announced to him he found me all I had asked for, tho' not without much affected difficulty, & many solemn assurances of his great poverty of which I believed just as much as suited my convenience. He made a good fire & had an omelette smoaking upon it, in a much shorter time than I could have hoped for, which in spite of the quantity of garlic that had entered into its composition, I greedily devoured. I next permitted him to air one of his clean shirts for me which I put on & jumped into his bed, taking my sword with me as a bed-fellow, & telling him to keep up a good fire & not disturb me. I had placed my wet clothes over a chair near the fire & seeing them begin to smoak famously I hoped to have them quite dry when I awoke. Laying down my head I was thankful for the luxury I was enjoying, forgot the past with all its miseries of hunger wet & cold & was just beginning to sleep, when an Orderly Dragoon rapped at the door who it appears had been thumping at every door in street for me, told me the Adjutant General wanted me immediately & rode off—This moment was to the best of my recollection that of the greatest bodily misery & mental vexation I ever remembered. I could scarcely prevail upon myself to believe that it was a reality. However I had nothing to do but to rise. It occurred to me, that the countenance of the Padre was very much brightened up at the prospect of being so soon rid of his unbidden guest, & I could have found in my heart to have abused him for the unequivocal expression of his countenance, but for my conciousness that I had on my back an excellent shirt of his whilst I left him in return a miserably ragged one of my own. With considerable difficulty I put on my half dried smoking clothes—tied round me a sash that was more like a wet rope than anything else—burst one of the only pair of boots I had in forcing it on my foot, & in this truly happy condition, sallied forth to search for the Adjutant General's quarters, leading my horse by the bridle which had been shut up in the next house to the Padre's that had no door to it. This in a place as large as Rodrigo was not a thing to be at once accomplished. However I made for the main Guard which was in a Square close by and found that my Chief was quartered at no great distance. As I went along I was constantly endeavouring to keep myself in good-humour (in truth to little effect) by repeating to myself "what can't be cured must be endured". I found Col. Waters the head of the Adjutant General's department very unwell & so fagged & knocked up as scarcely to be able to speak. He said he had been sent for by Ld. Wellington but was too ill to obey the command, & desired me to wait upon him immediately to receive his orders. Off then I went on a fresh search for the Commander in Chief's quarters which I was not long finding, nor did he keep me waiting an instant after my name was announced. He was in a terrible ill-humour, & his countenance was full of anger & vexation. I wished myself well out of the house even before he began to speak, & my feelings of body & mind were anything but enviable. He began abruptly "Where is Col. Waters?" "He is very unwell Sir." "There are a great number of stragglers left on the road, are there not?" "I believe there are Sir." "Believe! you know it, do you not, what numbers should you think there are?". "I should think more than a thousand Sir". "Then you must set out immediately & endeavor to collect & bring them in, in the best way you can, & when you return, come to my quarters and report to me what you have done". What is life without pleasure thought I, as I went out shivering in my half dried clothes. The rain & sleet were still continuing & the cold increased as the night advanced. Having received such an order as this from the Commander of the forces himself, no time was to be lost in obeying it, & I bethought myself how it could best be done. I first rode to the main guard where I left my horse, & seeing a dozen long Spanish waggons with a covering made of a sort of matting peculiar to that part of the country which had arrived with provisions in the course of the evening, I took a dozen Soldiers from the Guard & put one into each of them. I next sent for a Commissary who was quickly found, made him get some biscuit & some wine, & put a little into each waggon for the immediate use of such poor fellows as I might find on the road unable to proceed from want of food. Whilst I was doing this, a Docter passed by who was going to the main Guard to ask for a Sentry for some medical stores. I laid hold of him without hesitation, told him the orders I had received from the D. of Wellington, & directed him to assist me in the execution of them, as it was probable that medical assistance would certainly be necessary. He appeared a good deal annoyed at having been seized upon in that unexpected manner, at a time when he was making arrangements for his night's rest, but like myself had no alternative but to obey. Putting him into one of the waggons, & myself into another, I ordered the drivers to proceed on this delightful expedition. It was about eleven at night. We left Rodrigo by the gate thro' which we had entered a few hours before, & I proceeded along the road (which we found it most difficult to trace from the extreme darkness of the night) towards Salamanca. My intension was not to halt before day-break, or until we should be near some of the enemy's posts, to be ascertained by falling in with some of our own Picquets opposed to them. Day began to break as I entered a small village called Spirito Santo, & there I directed the Drivers to turn the horses heads again to Rodrigo. As the Sun broke out, I never can forget the sight of horrors that was exposed to my view. Groupes of women & children & drum boys lay perishing with cold— some had already died in a sort of rolled up posture—others were not yet dead, but convulsed with a sort of hysterical laugh which sometimes precedes death—there were stout soldiers too, who had breathed their last by the roadside on that bitter night, & many a gallant spirit, that would have been unmoved in the thickest fire had been bowed down by cold & hunger. The ground on the right & left of the road was a sort of common on which a stunted heath grew, & it was in the bushes that the dying & dead were discovered. The Soldiers whom I had brought out in the waggons, & myself looked out for them, & carried such as were unable to move to the road, there placing them in the waggons under the care of the Docter, who administered the biscuit & wine that we had brought out with us, in such quantities as he thought most judicious. It is indeed difficult to detail the sad scene of suffering & death that I witnessed on this night—but I was deeply thankful that I had been sent out on the duty which I was performing, & thus made the instrument of saving many lives. I took back in the waggons 120 men, & collected together about a hundred more who were able to walk after having received some refreshment. Those whom I thus took charge of, were almost all British. I was obliged to leave behind many Portuguese who I fear perished. What could I do?—I had not the means of assisting more & gave the preference to my own Country-men. On my return to Rodrigo, where the General Hospital was established & took the whole of the sufferers there, were some of them as I afterwards learned, became ideots. I then went to Ld. Wellington's quarters, to report my return & the result of my mission. He thanked me, & asked me to dinner. I would have given the world to have made an excuse to the invitation, but knew not how to do it. My next care was to find out the Friars house again, which for a long time I was quite unable to do. When at length I succeeded I found it occupied by several Officers with whom I sat down got something to eat & drink, told my adventures of the past night, & shortly afterwards jumping into the Padre's bed soon fell asleep, as happy & as light-hearted as if I had been the Tenant of the softest couch in King Joseph's palace at Madrid.[222]

I think it was about this time that I began to remark the different effects of a continued war-fare like that of the Peninsula on the character of the Officers & common Soldiers. The latter appeared to me, to become daily more ferocious & less fit for return to the duties of citizens, & I sometimes apprehended that when they should be disbanded in England after the restoration of peace, the country would be over-run, with pilferers & marauders of every description. The Officers on the contrary seemed to become more thoughtful & humane, & more anxious to exert themselves in softening the misery with which they were surrounded. In the performance of this duty they never appeared to spare themselves, & an Officer quartered in an house, whenever such a luxury was afforded, insured considerate conduct & protection to all its inmates. This was so well known to be the fact, that there was a constant endeavor on the part of the Masters of houses to have Officers billetted upon them.[223]

In all the cold & rain of the last three days of the Burgos retreat, Ld. Wellington was on horse-back with the troops from sun-rise to sun-set, sharing all their privations & encouraging them by his presence to proceed cheerfully on their march. It had the happiest possible effect both on Officers & men, & some were heard to exclaim, "Never mind this ugly weather, we shall soon be back again, & that's the fellow as will shew us how to lick the French."

It was somewhere near Rodrigo that a Dragoon & his horse were said to have ridden over a precipice when the army advanced in the preceding year, & I understood that about this time, their skeletons were discovered by an Officer of the light division who was out shooting. The horseman was in his saddle, the horse & himself both on their sides; the leather of the accoutrements was quite rotten—the iron of stirrups & bit, rusty—the bones of both completely bleached—some of them broken, but close to the parts to which they belonged. The horse appears to have been killed as instantaneously as his rider.

At this period the Spanish Guerillas annoyed the French exceedingly, intercepting their correspondence & cutting up their communications with unceasing perseverance, & so great was their number & activity that even a single letter sent by one French General to another was necessarily escorted by a Squadron or more of their Cavalry. They frequently made prizes of wine & other things coming from France for the use of the French Commanders, & sent presents of them to Ld. Wellington at whose table they proved most acceptable acquisitions. To guard against the enterprizes of these daring & successful bands the French at length established small fortified posts at the distance of a few miles from each other along the main roads. These they fortified & loop-holed, putting in them small garrisons of Infantry to protect their communications. These small detached posts were kept constantly on the alert, & yet with all their vigilance several of them were surprised & taken.

Freneda where Ld. Wellington established his Head Quarters on the 24th of November was a miserable village on the confines of Spain & Portugal not far from the Agueda river. The accommodations of every kind were as wretched as it was possible to conceive & supplies of every kind for the Officers of Head Quarters, beyond our bare rations of bread, meat, & spirits, very difficult to be obtained. One or two Suttlers it is true established themselves there, but their stores of every kind were bad, & the charges for them enormous. There were hard Dutch pine-apple cheeses so salt as to be scarcely eatable, & so hard that the teeth could with difficulty penetrate into a slice, the price of which was a dollar a pound. Dutch butter too was of pretty nearly the same quality & dearness. This Suttlers however had Tea, sugar, & Tobacco, & sometimes tolerable cigars, which were in great demand. They grew enormously rich & saucy as every sort of protection was afforded them, & no bounds put to their extravagant charges. Amonst them there was a woman named Antonia. She was a stout lusty person of rather a jolly countenance, dirty enough, but one who in the midst of her filth, always wore a massy gold necklace, to which a cross of the same metal was attached & a pair of long pendant ear-rings. This Antonia was the greatest cheat of the whole set, & amassed a considerable fortune by her attendance on Head-Quarters, to which she was attached [. . .] for several years, her goods becoming worse, & her prices more exhorbitant each succeeding campaign. There were several candidates for her hand amongst the Gentlemen Suttlers but she steadily declined the honor of any alliance with them.[224]

Ld. Wellington was in the habit of giving audience to the heads of departments at nine o'Clock every morning. They brought with them reports of every-thing new that had occurred connected with the duties of their respective officers, during the preceding day. I mean of course the ordinary details of the service, as anything extraordinary was reported to him immediately on its being made known to the chief of the department in whose province it lay. He used to read these reports carefully over, & give the necessary directions connected with them. The whole business of the army seldom occupied him more than an hour, such were his habits of business & decision. He always invited to his table some of the Officers of the Adjutant & Quarter Master General's department at Head Quarters.—Occasionally also, some of the Medical & Commissariat Staff, & Commanding Officers of Regiments stationed at no great distance. General Officers whom business of any kind brought to have an interview with him were invariably pressed to dinner & to stay the night, & a spare quarter was reserved for guests of this description. His Stable was oeconomically but well served under the superintendance of Colonel Collin Campbell, who was Commandant of Head Quarters. Including his Aids de Camp he usually sat down to dinner from twelve to sixteen persons sometimes more. The Cook was a good one & the wine principally furnished by the Guerillas, excellent. Lord Wellington was temperate at his meals, & drank at most from half a bottle to a bottle of Claret. There was no want however of abundance of wine at his table, & his guests might take just as much as they pleased. The dinner hour at Freneda was five O'Clock. About half past eight Lord Wellington used to call for coffee, of which a cup was taken to each person at table. When this had been drunk he retired, & it was the signal for every one else to leave the house. He would then read or write in his bed-room for about an hour, & then go to bed. As at Freneda we were some distance from the enemy's out-posts. he was able to undress himself, but when the French were nearer & that there was any possibility of movement or attack he was not in the habit of taking his clothes off, but used to change his linen & boots & lay down in a sort of Russia leather bed on iron legs, which fitted into a moderate sized portmanteau & was carried on the back of a mule. He had no Sentry at his door but always two orderly dragoons at hand with horses saddled & themselves ready to mount at a moments notice. He was ready at all hours of the night to receive reports of any interest from the out-posts and whenever they were of a suspicious nature with regard to any movements of the enemy, would mount his horse & gallop off to the advance without ordering any of his Aids de camp to be called, & attended only by one of the Orderly Dragoons, & it has occasionally happened that when his Staff awoke in the morning they learned that their chief had been on horse-back & with the picquets of the army hours before. He had at Head Quarters a pack of hounds from England & hunted two or three times a week with such Officers of Head Quarters as chose to join in the chase. These were not many, as few could afford to have English horses, & our Spanish or Portuguese steeds were not equal to the work. There was no want of Foxes, but it was a difficult & rocky country to ride over. He went out shooting every now & then, but did not appear fond of it, as he was a very indifferent shot. He was seldom or never ill. For myself I had so many duties to perform in the Adjutant General's department as to have little time for amusement. I managed however to go Fly-fishing at times & many is the fine Trout I took out of the Agueda. The room I lived in was over an old Cow-house, to which I ascended by a flight of stone steps on the outside; my bed was on the floor in a corner, & as the snow used to come in through the tiles of the roof, I got a couple of tarpaulins from the Commissary, & suspended them over it which completely sheltered me; & a mason made me a fire-place in another corner. Two other tarpaulins on the floor served me for bed-side carpets. There were a bench, table & two stools, & the rest of the furniture was supplied from my canteen. My messmates were Col. Waters & Captn. Wood, our Messman was my servant who drew all our rations together with his own & gave us breakfast, dinner, & supper for two dollars a month each. We had however some extra wine of our own as we always took care to keep our Borachio's full whenever there was opportunity of buying it. This arrangement experienced occasional interruptions, as my servant was not the most sober man in the world, & it has happened that when we assembled for dinner, we found our Cook drunk under the table, & no preparation whatever made for our meal. The man I believe made a good thing of messing us, because of our dining so frequently with Lord Wellington. A Private in the 68th Regiment called John Green was at this time Captn. Wood's servant, & waited upon us at our mess. I mention his name because he has since written rather an interesting little book called "the vicissitudes of a Soldier's life". After dinner we used to smoak cigars & drink grog till bed-time, which was always an early hour, & sometimes sent for Fuentes, whom I have recorded in a former part of this journal, to play the guitar & sing to us. The Prince of Orange was at Head Quarters, acting as one of Lord Wellington's Aids de camp. There were attached to him, two very gentlemenlike & agreeable men one a Fleming, Baron de Constant, the other an Englishman of the name of Johnson, who had been with the Prince at College. They were both very fond of music, & used to visit me occasionally in an evening & sing Spanish duetts & trios. We never gamed nor do I remember to have seen a pack of cards at Head Quarters. Nine O'Clock was our usual hour of going to bed, & sun-rise that of our getting up. We were all in the highest possible health & spirits, & never knew what a tedious or dull hour was. The man who lived in the greatest style & luxury at Head Quarters was the Commissary. He had four or five English horses & eat off a service of plate, a French Cook, & the best wines made his table a frequent resort of those who had no other access to these enjoyments. Like many others of the same department, he joined the army on a mule, & as poor as Job, but in the course of a couple of years contrived to amass considerable wealth. I have heard it said that remarks were sometimes made to Ld. Wellington on the rapid manner in which Commissaries got rich, & that his reply was, that the only control which he could exercise over them was that in which the provisioning of the army was concerned, & that if they did their duty in that respect he required no more—that the Treasury at home had decided on the mode in which their accounts were to be kept, & had sent out Commissaries of accounts whose duty it was to see that those forms were rigidly attended to, & that whether they made money or lost it was no concern of his. The fact certainly was that there were many means of making money at the entire command of the Junior class of Commissaries which several of them found it difficult to resist. For instance the mode of collecting corn, where the army was not in contact with the enemy, was, by detaching one of these Officers some distance to purchase it. He was furnished with dollars & as a voucher of the price which he had paid for the grain he was required to produce a certificate from the Alcalde of the place where he had made the purchase stating what was the market price of corn on that day. Now in most instances the Alcaldes of Spanish villages were men who would sign anything for a dollar, & therefore his certificate was usually just what the Commissary might choose to dictate to him. Another great source of gain of this description was this:— The Muleteers of the army many of whom were owners of from ten to twenty mules, were paid a dollar a day for each Mule, & were likewise furnished with a ration for themselves & their animals. Money was occasionally so scarce that the army was without pay for eight months together, & of course the Muleteers or Capatazes as they were called, shared in the general deprivation of money. Driven to despair many of them deserted taking with them all their Mules. Thus all their arrears of pay were forfeited, but these arrears were drawn by the Commissary when the day of payment came, & remained in his own pocket. A third arrangement by which a great deal of money was made by those who had any money at their disposal (& few but the Commissaries were in this situation) was the following. Dollars were so exceedingly scarce & so difficult to be procured that such of the Capatazes as had large sums owing to them, were literally paid by bills on the Treasury. They knew not what to do with these pieces of paper, which they were unable even to read, & willingly offered them for half their value to those who had money to purchase them. Pay-Masters and Commissaries alone had the means of taking advantage of this state of things. The heads of the Commissariat department had not similar opportunities of realizing fortunes, as they only directed purchases to be made by their juniors, through whose hands alone the money passed.

As the Spring months came on they brought with them my favorite amusement of Trout fishing, & as I was never without my rod & pocket book during the whole Peninsular war I began to prepare for sport in the Agueda—Nor was I disappointed, as I took many a dish of remarkably fine Trout in it. There were some remarkably large stepping stones in the river about two miles above Head Quarters, on which people could pass over when the water was low. Taking my stand on them I never faild catching some fine fish. My Fly was rather large with a dirty red body & brown wings. I used the same fly afterwards in the Bidassoa with similar success. Returning home one evening rather later than usual over a wild & rugged country I encountered a pack of wolves crossing my path, at a lounging cantering pace. I hardly knew at first what to think of it, having nothing in my hand but my fishing rod—but I stood still & they went by without appearing to notice me. I conclude they were not particularly hungry as these animals when wanting food are exceedingly fierce & ravenous. They have been known to penetrate the very centre of Head Quarters, & to attack the Commissariat Bullocks (even when under the protection of Sentries) whose torn & bleeding sides have exhibited in the morning deep marks of the Wolf's voracity. Horses have been attacked in like manner when at their picquets, & Mules have been literally devoured in a night attack of these enterprising animals, but I never heard of an instance of a human life having been lost in this manner, nor even of a man having been attacked by them. Vultures hovered round us in great numbers, & of enormous size. They grew so fat on the dead, both men & beasts, . . . [that] it was with some difficulty they could get on the wing when fully gorged. but it was next to impossible to get sufficiently near to shoot them, as they invariably placed a Sentinel to give timely notice of any suspicious approach. When in the air they soared about in circles, higher than the eye could well distinguish them, altho' they probably had a distinct view of everything on the ground that was attractive to their appetite.

Ld. Aylmer was at this time the head of the Adjutant General's department an excellent Officer much respected & beloved. He was exceedingly methodical in all his arrangements & appeared fully to enjoy the confidence of Ld. Wellington. The Officers of the light division which was cantoned at no great distance from Head Quarters amused themselves with performing plays during the winter. They first of all fitted up an old chapel as a theatre, but a Priest representing to Ld. Wellington the pain with which he saw this appropriation of the building it was forbidden; & they selected a barn for the purpose. The performances were excellent, & we frequently went over from Head Quarters to be present at them. The different divisions of the army were drilled & exercised & marched out in heavy marching order from fifteen to twenty miles whenever the weather permitted. The equipment & material were put into the best possible order, & everything done to render the troops as effective as possible in preparation for the ensuing campaign. Ld. Wellington reviewed them by divisions & expressed himself exceedingly gratified with their good & Soldier like appearance. Strong reinforcements also arrived from England & everything appeared to contribute to render us more formidable both in discipline & numbers then we had ever yet been.[225]

Spring advanced & the month of May brought with it dry and warm weather, on the 22nd of that month the army was put in motion & the following was its strength on taking the field.

British

Cavalry	6,500	Lt. Genl. Sir S. Cotton
1st Divn.	4,120	Sir Thos. Graham
2nd Do.	7,030	{ Honble. Wm. Stewart under Sir Rowland Hill
3rd Do.	3,800	Sir Thomas Picton
4th Do.	4,200	Sir Lowry Cole
5th Do.	3,900	{ M: Genl. Hay in the absence of Sir James Leith
6th Do.	4,200	{ M: Genl. Pakenham in the absence of Lt. Gen. Clinton
7th Do.	4,000	The Earl of Dalhousie
Light	3,000	M: Genl. Charles Alten

Portuguese

Cavalry	1,4000
With 1st Divn.	none
—— 2nd Do.	2,8000[226] & 5,000 Amarantes Division
—— 3rd Do.	2,200
—— 4th Do.	2,500
—— 5th Do.	2,300
—— 6th Do.	2,300
—— 7th Do.	2,200

—— Light Do.   1,800
—— Parkes Brigade   2,000
—— Bradford's Do.   2,400

Making a total of British & Portuguese of about 70,000 effective men. There were some divisions of Spanish Troops cooperating, but I do not exactly know what was the amount of their numbers.[227]

Staff of the Army

Qr. Mr. General	M: Genl. Murray
Dy. Adgt. General	Lord Wellington
Commd. Artillery	Lt. Col. Dickson
Do. Engineer	Sir Richd. Fletcher
Inspector of Hospitals	Dr Mc Gregor
Commissary General	Sir Robt. Kennedy
Military Secretary	Lord F. Somerset

Of Artillery there were 4 Brigades in reserve, & a Brigade with each division—British. Of Portuguese Artillery there were 3 Brigades, making a total of 106 pieces of Field Artillery, including 1 Brigade of eighteen Pounders on Field carriages, & 5 Brigades of Horse Artillery.

CAMPAIGN OF 1813.[228]

22nd May. Marched from Freneda in Portugal to Cividid Rodrigo in Spain 6 leagues—saw nothing whatever of the enemy.

22nd. Tamames—4 leagues, only one French vidette appeared who was driven in. We halted here one day that Ld. Wellington might make reconnoissances.

25th. Matilla—a small village near Salamanca. Here our advance had a slight skirmish with some French Cavalry.

26th. Entered Salamanca from which place we had been driven by the French the 15th Novr. last year. The enemy shewed some force here, & not retiring so quickly as Ld. Wellington expected, he ordered General Fane's Brigade of Cavalry to cross the Tormes supported by General Hamilton's division of Portuguese Infantry & to attack them. The day was intensely hot. The French did not wait the attack but moved off & were vigorously pursued—300 prisoners were taken, many of whom were drunk & a complete route of the French division commanded by General Villatte took place. Head Quarters returned & slept at Salamanca, where they halted three days.

29th. Miranda de Douro 9 leagues. Two Pontoon bridges were thrown over the river a little lower down than the town, & the army was occupied two days in crossing over.

30th. Carvajales near the Esla. The enemy shewing force on the other bank of this stream, the two German regiments of heavy Cavalry & the Brunswick Infantry, crossed it lower down than where the enemy was posted, in which operation they had about thirty men drowned. The French were dislodged & the whole of this part of the army crossed the Esla the next day.

During these operations on the Douro and Esla, Sir Rowland Hill's Corps consisting of the 2nd Division, Hamilton's Portuguese, & Morillo's Spaniards moved on the other bank of the Douro, direct from Salamanca, & on the main road to Valladolid in order to clear that part of the country from the enemy.

1st June [1813]. Zamora. We were received by the inhabitants of this place with every demonstration of joy. We, marching in as the French moved out, to which circumstances alone we were well aware these indications of welcome were owing, as Zamora had always been remarkable for its decided partiality to the French.

2nd. Toro. The enemy as usual awaited our arrival, & did not retire till after some pretty severe skirmishing. We took up our quarters in the place & had made ourselves pretty comfortable for the evening, when to our great surprise the enemy returned in force, to ascertain no doubt what strength we had in the town. We attacked them & after a sharp affair made prisoners 260 men of the French 3rd Hussars, with their horses & appointments. The men themselves were fine Soldier-like looking fellows but their horses were indifferent & in bad condition.[229] We halted at Toro one day.

4th. La Mota—Fell in again with the enemy, who retired after a little skirmishing.

5th. Castro Monte—Saw nothing of the French this day. When Joseph Bonaparte became fully aware of all these movements he concentrated his troops so as to cover Burgos in the neighborhood of which are many fine military positions. Ld. Wellington therefore determined to manoeuvre him out of his position & marched in the direction of Palencia. Castro Monte is about 9 leagues from Valladolid.

At this place I heard that an English Officer had been left behind by the enemy when they retired from that City, & that he had been long ill in bed unable to move. From the description that was given me of his person I thought it more than probable that it was an old Brother Officer, who had been taken on Lord Hill's retrograde movement from Madrid, & I determined to ride over there to ascertain the fact. Thinking he would naturally be in much distress for want of money, I called on Ld. Fitzroy Somerset the military Secretary, & asked him for six doubloons to give to this Officer whoever he might turn out to be, which he immediately gave me on my signing a receipt for them. On my arrival at Valladolid I made every enquiry to ascertain where the Officer was lodged, but was for a long time completely unsuccessful. At length however one of the police of the place undertook to conduct me in my search, & at length in an obscure quarter of the city, & up several pair of stairs, in a miserable room which had not been cleaned out to all appearance for ages, & on a yet more miserable bed, I discovered the object of my expedition. As I had thought more than probable, it turned out to be Lieut. Farmer of the Welsh Fusileers. It was sometime before I recognised him, as his countenance & whole frame were frightfully changed by rheumatism. His body was literally doubled up, & appeared to have stiffened in that position, & his beard which had not been shaved for weeks covered the greater part of his countenance. When he saw me, he literally burst into a loud hysterical laugh, & I thought the poor fellow was mad, but when he recovered himself, he told me that the sight of a friend & brother Officer was so sudden & unexpected, that it quite overpowered him, that he was very ill & had been much neglected, a fact which it was very unnecessary in him to represent to me as it was sufficiently indicated by his appearance. As I had not much time to spare, the distance back to Head Quarters being considerable, I went to the Alcalde & procured him a billet on an excellent house, got four fellows who carried him on his bed into it—had him deposited in a large cheerful room, looking upon the great Square of the town, & recommended him strongly to the kindness & attention of the owner of the house, who assured me that he would do everything in his power for him. I then gave Farmer the six doubloons I had brought, the value of which was about twenty guineas, & sending for a Barber to shave & clean him instantly, took leave of him. I afterwards had a servant & linen sent to him. The next I heard of him was that he had safely arrived in England, but continued a cripple. He had been a remarkably handsome young man, tho' inclined to corpulency, & was a particular friend of mine, because we had been quartered together for some time, at an out-post in N. America. On my return to England after the Peninsular war, I was pleased at the reception of a very grateful letter from his Mother Lady Farmer, acknowledging the great service I had been of to him at Valladolid.

June 6th. Advanced to Ampudia, the enemy's rear-guard retiring before us, without skirmishing.

7th. Entered Palencia, a beautiful City, on the Carrion River. the enemy had retired, & we saw nothing of them.

8th. Head Quarters moved on to Amusco, a small village.

9th Advanced to Melgar de Fernamental—no enemy in sight—halted here one day.

11th. Moved to Castroxeriz—where we halted 24 hours to give time for the arrival of supplies. From this place a reconnoissance was made on Burgos, which was ordered so suddenly, that a French Division which formed a Corps of Observation on some heights near the place, retired in disorder, & passing thro' Burgos, blew up the Castle & works connected with it—It was done so clumsily, that many men were said to have lost their lives by the explosion.

13th. Villa Diego—here we again came up with the rear-guard of the French, & had some skirmishing in dislodging it from the position it occupied.

14th. Moved to Massa—here we learned that the French had retired across the Ebro.

15th. Head Quarters were established at Quintana, a small and most romantically situated village on the Ebro, near which there is a narrow bridge. The army crossed by this bridge, the descent of which, & subsequent ascent of the high ground on the other side of the river, is of the most striking & singular character. It almost resembles a winding staircase, overhung with immense rocks—The clattering of the horses hoofs, & rolling of the Artillery over the surface of this rock—the long irregular line of glittering Bayonets—the different uniform of British, Portuguese & Spaniards, with here & there an Officer on horseback mingled with the ranks—the singularly storm-like appearance of the Sky, as the sun was setting, when this passage of the army took place, rendered the scene more beautifully impressive than anything I can remember—That so many of England's Sons should be assembled in so wild a spot, to shed the blood of men, who had never offended them at the call of their King & Country, & that the human mind can be wound up to such a pitch of eager enthusiasm as then filled the breasts of these gallant men, is a fact well worthy the regard of those who have made human character & passions the subject of their speculation & research. The gallant & imposing spectacle of this passage of a far famed stream, under such circumstances would have made War a vision of romance to a passer by—or a magnificent subject for the pencil of the Painter—all its horrors would have been lost sight of in the admiration which such a scene would certainly have excited. An admiration, the effect of which, even at this distant period from the event itself, is awakened afresh, from its mere record by so feeble a pen. Lord Wellington himself appeared full of the interest which the sight created, & it was remarked by those near him, that he was in the highest spirits possible. Before midnight the whole Army had crossed. My lodgings this night were on the basement floor of an old Tower, which had been used for some years as a shelter for Cattle or Sheep. Captn. Eckersley of the Adjutant General's Department was my companion—As the Commissariat was in the rear & had not yet made its appearance, we were badly off for provisions, & to add to our embarrassment my Brother[230] paid us a visit, caused no doubt by a similar deficiency in his own Havresack. Thus situated, I thought our best rescource might be the river, & as I never moved without a fishing rod as part of my Baggage, I went down to the stream, & took half a dozen excellent Trout, which we broiled, & thought the most delicious fish we had ever tasted. This old Tower looked upon the Bridge & the winding passage through the rock, by which the Troops passed—My Brother left us after partaking of our meal, to overtake his Regiment, which had gone by an hour or two before. At daybreak, I amused myself again with my rod, & took fish for another Day's dinner.

June 16th. Head Quarters moved to Medina del Pomar. Here was a large plain, on which the Army encamped for the night. A small stream ran through it, which was quickly laid under requisition for washing & cooking purposes.

17th. Advanced to Quincoces, saw nothing of the French.

18th. Berberena—The enemy's rear-guard retired at our approach without skirmishing.

19th. Subijana de Morillas—Here our advance met with resistance, & there was sharp skirmishing thro'out the Day. We found that King Joseph's Corps had joined the French army, from Madrid. It was composed of 18,000 men—Mashal Jourdan, Chief of the staff. The French Army thus mustered nearly as follows:

Army of the North	25,000	Count d'Erlon
Army of the King	18,000	Marshal Jourdan
Army of the South	17,000	Genl. Drouet
Cavalry	5,000	Pierre Soult
	65,000	

20th. June. The greater part of this Day was passed in making reconnoissances on the French position, as they now appeared to have taken one up, as if to stand & fight a battle—They fired on our reconnoitring parties, & resisted the attempts of our picquets to drive in their out-posts. Enough had however been observed, to enable Lord Wellington to make his dispositions for attack. The City of Vittoria was in sight, at a distance of perhaps a league—King Joseph assumed the command of the whole Army & appointed Count Gazan his Quarter Master General. The Country immediately about Vittoria is flat—but intersected with deep narrow roads—the winding stream Zadorra, & some prominent ranges of elevated ground—

The French position was as follows—Their centre occupied the left bank of the Zadorra, in 3 lines, occupying also a singularly shaped hill called "La Altura de los Ingleses", so named from it's having been the height from which Edward the Black Prince poured down with his British, & routed a French Army, in former days—On this hill, they had planted a battery of 6 field pieces, which completely commanded a narrow bridge over the Zadorra, by which alone, that stream could be passed, by the 4th Division which was in front of it. The enemy's right was posted on a range of heights, above a village called Abechuco, in front of the river—& their left thrown back in rear of the stream occupied also, in force, the mountainous range of La Puebla. By this arrangement they covered the roads from Madrid, Bilbao & Logrono—Their General Clausel was detached with a strong Division at Logrono, which made it necessary for Lord Wellington to send the 6th British Division under Genl. Pakenham, to observe his movements—The main road to Bayonne was also covered by a strong French Division—& it could be observed that large Convoys were moving along this road towards France, as if to disencumber the Army, & make it more moveable, preparatory to a general Action, of which the results could not be foreseen. Singularly enough the French had not destroyed, nor even mined the narrow Bridge over the Zadorra, in the centre of their position.

Such was the ground ascertained to be occupied by the enemy, by the reconnoissances made on the 20th. June—Their Cavalry was in Brigades & distributed pretty equally along their line—their Artillery very numerous, & observed to be posted on every knoll & rising ground.

21st. June. The Day broke beautifully—a bright Sun & clear sky, which as the dawn advanced shewed the glittering arms of the French on the same positions as had been occupied by them yesterday. They were under arms, & Officers galloping about in all directions with here & there a group, as if assembled round some Chief & receiving his directions—All being prepared, the British got the order to attack every part of the enemy's line about eight o'clock. Sir Rowland Hill moved up the strong heights of La Puebla, against their left, & met with great resistance, & considerable loss—There it was that Lt. Col: Cadogan fell at the head of his Regiment the 71st—Sir Thomas Picton & Col: Cole, the gallant Commanders of the 3rd & 4th Divisions, briskly attacked the Centre, & in advancing upon the Zadorra, discovered some small wooden foot bridges, in addition to the narrow stone bridge, which the enemy had neglected to remove, & which were very useful in enabling them to pass their Corps over, which they did, under a heavy fire, which occasioned them severe loss. They established themselves, & drove back the French, who fought gallantly, & disputed every inch of ground—I rode up the "Altura" & beheld from it's summit, Sir R. Hill gradually gaining ground & pressing the French. The British centre having made good its attack, moved on with increased energy & rapidity, & drove all before it, whilst at the same time, Sir Thomas Graham who had been charged with the attack of the enemy's right posted on the heights above Albechuco succeeded completely, & was forcing the French from the ground which commanded the road to Bayonne, when the King sent a strong force to occupy the Villages of "Gamarra Major" & "Gamarra Menor" on the Zadorra, the possession of which places would still have preserved his communication with Bayonne. seeing this, & knowing the importance of cutting him off, from this road, Sir Thomas caused those places to be immediately marched upon & attacked, by the 5th Division under Genl. Oswald, & Longa's Spanish Corps—Both attacks succeeded—The French were driven out at the point of the Bayonet—but again rallied, were reinforced & attempted Gamarra Major in which they did not succeed, but continued to occupy strong ground in it's rear, until the success of the attack on the Centre enabled the 3rd & 4th Divisions to detach troops to the assistance of Genl. Oswald, who then drove back the enemy from their position behind Gamarra Major, occupied in their place, the main road to Bayonne, & drove their right, in confusion on their centre, leaving open to their retreat, only the road to Pamplona, The success of Sir Rowland Hill, & of the centre, led by Sir Tho. Picton & Sir Lowry Cole had been complete—& the whole French Army was in full retreat & discomfiture—leaving behind everything that could impede a rapid flight. Their Cavalry alone seemed to preserve something like formation & order, & formed a rear-guard for the fugitives. The British pressed on rapidly— The French threw away Arms and Accoutrements, knapsacks, havresacks, & canteens, & thus lightened of every load, nothing could catch them. Of their Materiel, the Victors took possession of 214 pieces of Cannon—400 Tumbrils filled with ammunition—2 or 3 million of Ball Cartridges—whilst the enemy took off with them a single gun & one Howitzer. The gun was taken from them on the following Day, in an attack made on their rear-guard, before it could enter the gates of Pamplona into which Citadel the French Army retired in as great a state of disorganisation as it is possible to conceive. The scene which discovered itself in the streets of Vittoria & in all the Lanes & Outlets from that City, as the enemy fled thro' them, beggars description: All the Baggages, Carriages, Mules & Equipage of King Joseph & his Court— the Military Chest which had arrived with the arrears of pay for the Army of the Centre only a few days before, & contained some Millions of Dollars in Silver & Doubloons—Coaches with their Coachmen on the Boxes or Postillions on the Horses, flogging & swearing to the utmost extent of their lungs—Ladies with imploring arms, or outstretched Infants thrusting themselves from the windows of these Coaches, or descending from them to the ground—others on Horseback or on Mules, endeavouring in vain, to extricate themselves from the mass of impediments that blocked up their way, & to gallop off— Spanish girls, the Mistresses of the fugitive French, who had been either carelessly or purposely left behind with the baggage—all these mixed up with Cannon, Tumbrils, drunken French Servants, the wounded, the dying & the dead, may give some faint idea of the conquered ground, on which a great battle has been fought & won. Such are the relics of the vanquished, when forced to quit the field with a rapidity such as that which was pressed upon the French at Vittoria. Of their persons we could not lay hold of above 5000—their flight had been so effectual, disburdened as they were of every thing that could impede it.

A friend of mine, Captn. During, of the Adjt. Genl. Department seeing what he thought a smart young French Officer riding off, gallopped after him, to stay his flight, when on getting alongside, it proved to be a beautiful Catalonian girl, who had been Mistress of a French Colonel, for two years—She implored our Captain's mercy who sent her to his baggage—She exchanged Masters with admirable & cheerful composure, & remained attached to the Captns. Suite, until the entry of the British Army into France the following year. This was by no means a solitary instance of such arrangements—& shortly after the battle of Vittoria, Spanish Guitars were gaily sounding in the English Camp, & Spanish girls singing extempore praises of the immortal Wellington, with the same zeal & energy, as had no doubt so lately called forth similar strains, in honor of the great Napoleon—oh! human nature what a Weathercock thou art!

Matters were going on thus flourishingly, when as I was accompanying a Squadron of the 18th Hussars in pursuit of the enemy, who were flying as fast as possible, we overtook a line of Carriages & baggage, which offered so much temptation to many of the Soldiers of the Squadron, that they could not resist falling to the work of plunder,[231] whilst others with their Officers continued in pursuit—The Squadron was thus considerably weakened in number, a circumstance which was observed by the French Rear-Guard, near which we now rapidly approached—They suddenly detached a Body of Cavalry from it, which falling on the few of the 18th—who were in advance, killed some, wounded others, & took some prisoners—In this last lot I was myself included, my Horse having been killed, & my Head cut longitudinally with a Sabre, so as to knock me over—When I rose I saw half a dozen French Dragoons occupied in securing me & emptying my pockets, one of them having off with my cocked hat. They called me all sorts of opprobrious names in all the range & vexation of a vanquished Army, & one fellow to whom I was given in charge, got off his horse to look for a cord to fasten my wrist to his stirrup. Luckily he could not find one, I, shewing him that I was wounded declaring at the same time, that I could not possibly make any successful attempt at escape, he ordered me to lay hold of his stirrup leather, swearing that the instant I let go, he would cut me down, accompanying his threat, by putting his broad-sword as close to my skull as he decently could. He continued muttering oaths & curses, deaf to all my entreaties for a mouthful of wine or water, as my lips were parched, & clotted with dust & blood. A Serjeant & three men of the 18th were killed at the moment I was wounded, & likewise four Privates of the same Regt. were in custody of the Gendarmerie, whom we overtook, & they joined the party which formed my Escort. They were the French 4th Dragoons, in dark green uniform & brass helmets, the lower part of which were covered with tiger skin, about four inches deep—a remarkably fine Corps. Nothing could equal the expression of rage & indignation in which these men indulged, abusing King Joseph & all their Generals & vowing revenge in every shape. It was now about six o'clock in the evening of a hot, sultry day, & my thirst was excessive. Shortly afterwards, a cloud of dust was seen behind us which rapidly came nearer. then were heard voices & the gallopping of Horses. soon their heads were visible & then they passed to our right flank, still almost covered with dust. our Escort consisting now of about a 100 men, Gendarmerie included, began to trot sharply. Shots were fired by the strange body of horse, & I discovered the blue uniform of our Cavalry. They came within about thirty yards along-side the French, & sharp skirmishing began. The enemy then placed me & the other Prisoners on the side next their opponents, that they might see where their countrymen were as they fired. This sort of work continued for some minutes, & I could not imagine why our fellows did not charge, little aware at the moment, as I afterwards ascertained that there was a deep narrow road between them & the French which their horses could not leap, & of which the enemy were also aware. Men were wounded on both sides. At length the deep road became more open, & our Soldiers were preparing for a charge on the French, when the fellow who guarded me, swore a tremendous oath, that if he could not keep me he would put an end to me, & lifted up his sword for the purpose of carrying it into execution. I flinched, caught the blow just above the Hip, & taking advantage of his stroke having failed started off, ran with full speed towards my Countrymen, with several shots fired at me in vain; & when I found myself safe in their possession, fainted—whether it was fatigue pain or joy, which caused this revulsion in my blood,—I know not— probably a mixture of all three. The French gallopped off, & their other prisoners escaped also. The party who had rescued us, belonged to the 15th Hussars, & was led on by Captn. Thackwell. It was not long before

I was in a Surgeon's hands, my head was shaved & dressed, meat & drink given me, in moderation. & I was left on the ground, in charge of a Serjeant of the Regt. who had orders to see me safe into Vittoria, report my situation to some one of the Medical Staff, & then rejoin his regiment immediately.

As I thus lay on the ground, numbers of the French Civil Employee's were still endeavoring to effect their escape on Horse-back flying over the plain. I told the Serjeant I had lost my Horse, & knew not how I should supply his place, my other Steeds being with the baggage, wherever it might be. He quickly answered that he would certainly not be long in supplying me with one. A French Commissary soon afterwards, mounted on a very pretty long-tailed Chestnut Horse, was seen approaching at a sharp trot, looking around him on every side. My Friend the Serjeant saw in this Gentleman just the victim he intended. off he flew, quickly overtook Commissary, knocked him off his Horse, felt his pockets, left him on the ground, & taking his Horse by the bridle cantered back to me, with this most acceptable present. It was not without great difficulty & pain, that I was able to mount, whilst the Serjeant led the creature by the bridle. We went back slowly to Vittoria; it was near nightfall. Within about a mile of the place, we discovered a small line of dark coloured Waggons with covered tops, surrounded by British Soldiers & Spaniards. Some of the covers of these waggons had been torn off, & men were on the top throwing down small square boxes, & filling their pockets with something or other, which we did not at first clearly ascertain. As we approached it appeared that these Waggons were the French Military Chest, full of Dollars & Doubloons, & that the Soldiers & Spaniards were busy helping themselves to these treasures, with which the road was covered, by the breaking to pieces of the boxes as they were thrown to the ground from the Waggons. It was too tempting a scene for my Conductor, to pass without a remark. For myself, I was in too great pain to be much interested by it. The Serjeant however mournfully said "Ah! your Honor, if you were but well enough, just to be able to sit your Horse for a minute, & remain quiet, what a tight Day this would be for me—by the Powers, but it would be my making for ever". "Why my Lad, I owe you no trifle for this Horse on which I sit, & I care not if I remain a minute or two whilst you help yourself, as so many others are doing". "Now the Lord love your Honor for that kind word" says my friend as he sprung from his Horse (fearing perhaps that I should change my mind) of which he gave me the Bridle at the same time. & to my great astonishment & satisfaction I saw the Serjeant, in an instant, as hard at work as the busiest of the plundering group, filling pockets, Havresack, boots & the crown of his cap. Then he ran to his Horse, which I was holding in infinite pain, & began filling his Holsters. At length, when I conclude he had satisfied himself, that he had not other hole in the world then at his command that could contain another Dollar, he quietly said to me—"Now your Honor, I've done—but it would it not be a pity for your Honor to leave this spot with empty pockets? if you could but sit for another minute or two, Faith I'd fill every spot of you with silver." I was not long in giving him an apparently reluctant answer, just to let him understand that he might do with me what he pleased. Before my answer was well out of my lips, off he ran & was back in a minute with both hands full of Dollars, which were stuffed into the pockets of my Coat. Then came a second supply & a third, till both Pockets were filled, & the Fellow then literally thrust a hand-full into my trousers, though as they were not hermetically sealed at the bottom they again tumbled on the road. We were both literally crammed with this money, & I really could scarcely comprehend for a time whether the Serjeant had stuffed me for my own advantage, or for want of convenience to bear off the Treasure. but he quickly relieved me from all doubt on this point by saying, "at all events your Honor if you have got a hard thump today, you have got your pockets well lined with Doubloons". I own that stiff & sore as I was I felt the comfort of this remark as we rode into Vittoria. I was not however free from apprehensions of my pockets bursting & that my prize would be scattered in the streets. It was night when we entered the City, & the Serjeant knocking at the door of a respectable looking House, declared me by signs to be a wounded English Officer & begged I might be taken in which was done immediately. I was shewn up-stairs to a very comfortable room. The Serjeant stripped & put me to bed; some Chocolate was brought me. & he then went to see after my Horse, & to look for a Surgeon to bring him to me. All this was done in about an hour. I was bled[232] & had a draught, which greatly composed me. The Serjeant had a Mattress brought into the same room, to lay down in a corner saying he would start to join his Regiment at Day-break. I had lain in bed about two hours, when I heard the Serjeant rise. He approached my bed. I asked him what he wanted. He replied, "I thought your Honor might be asleep, & I just intended to go out for an hour, & look about me, amongst all the fine things I saw lying on the roads as we came in." I do not want anything I said, & you may do what you like only remember your Regiment at Day-break. Away he went. Before Day-break he returned & I heard a sort of rattling & arranging of things near his Bed. Just as the Sun was rising, he came once more to me & said, "Well, your Honor, I'm off & I'm mighty glad to see you doing well & in good hands. I found a few trifles on the road last night & I'm leaving some for your Honor". With this, he laid on my Bed a Watch, Chain & some Seals, a Spying glass & a writing Desk, an inkstand which had evidently formed part of the writing-case, & several Necklaces & Trinkets. "Much good & long life to your Honor, & keep the things for I've got as many as I can carry. but how the Devil I am to carry my Dollars I hardly even think of. Faith, I'd give twenty of them for a Pound". He left me and I never saw the Serjeant more. The next day I raised myself in my Bed & looked for my Coat, which the careful old Soldier had placed under my pillow. I felt the pockets — all was right — they were hard & full. I counted them, although to do so I was obliged to put myself in a most painful position. There were 470, or nearly 120£! The Serjeant must have sacked at least double that Sum.

I remained in Vittoria under the hands of the Surgeon only ten Days, & then thinking myself sufficiently strong for duty, set off for Head-Quarters which were established not far from the foot of the Pyrenees.

Vittoria was made a Hospital Station, & was soon crowded with sick & wounded British Officers & Soldiers — The conduct of the Portuguese Troops in the battle of Vittoria had been admirable: Nothing could exceed their gallantry & discipline, & their loss was in full proportion to that of the British.[233]

I well remember when we had passed through Vittoria, seeing amongst other Ladies, who were descending from their carriages, in great alarm, the Countess Gazan, Wife of the Quarter Master General of the French Army — As I passed her, she declared to me in a scream, who she was — I recommended her to re-enter her carriage, shut the door, & remain quiet — She said she would — There were, a Nurse & two little children of hers in the next carriage to her — It appears, that after I had ridden on, she left her carriage, & in the hurry of the moment, lost the Nurse & Children, one of them she afterwards found the same evening — but the other was missing. She was taken to Lord Wellington's Head Quarters, & remained there some Days, every exertion was made to discover her Child, but in vain — For a day or two, I was told, her sorrow was great — The Officers of Head Quarters shewed her attentions, & her grief began to diminish — in a few days more her spirits returned—she was cheerful—gay—In about a week, little more was said by her on the subject of her missing Child, & she was sent in to her Husband, with the Nurse & the remaining little one, apparently quite reconciled to the loss she had sustained. The Child was afterwards found, & restored to her. It had been seen on the ground, crying, by an English Cavalry Soldier, who took it up before him, carried it so for several Days, fed it with part of his ration, & had taken an amazing fancy to it—The Soldiers of his troop also made a great pet of it, & he parted with it at length, not without great reluctance.

In the baggage of the French Army which fell into the hands of the Victors was found the Baton de Mareschal Jourdan. It was sent by Ld. Wellington to the Prince Regent who in return transmitted to our glorious Commander the Staff of an English Field Marshal.

King Joseph himself, with difficulty escaped, some of our Dragoons having at one time, almost surrounded his Carriage; but he contrived to get off. I heard, that such had been the confidence, with which the French spoke & thought of beating us, that they had ordered their dinners in Vittoria, to which many of our Civil Departments, who came up, after the Battle, sat down in stead. They had wished the "Padrones" of their Quarters merely a good morning, & told them to have every thing prepared for them in the evening as usual. Numbers of the inhabitants of Vittoria had sallied out in the evening of the 21st when the Armies had passed by, to join in the plunder—& all the Civil Departments having now come up, got the greatest part of the booty, the Troops themselves who fought & won the battle being in full pursuit of the enemy. British Paymasters, Commissaries, Purveyors, were hard at work & made a most successful Campaign of it before the necessary guards arrived which were sent back as soon as Ld. Wellington had been informed of the extent & value of the Booty. These guards certainly saved a good deal, but much had been already disposed of, & there is reason to believe that a single Officer of the Paymaster General's department (Capt. Ackersley) was sent on the track of the mule which bore away this treasure, but did not succeed in capturing it, & as the fact was not positively traced to the very person alluded to, though there was no doubt of it, he could not be meddled with. Large sums were carried off by others, in comparison of which my little 120 was not worthy of notice. Soldiers wives were seen for weeks after the action in muslins, three of four gowns one over the other, trimmed with fine lace, several pairs of earrings dangling from their ears, reticules, watches & fans as part of their costume. The contrast of these decorations with their brazen tanned faces and brawny arms was ludicrous enough. I have heard that upwards of 500 Spanish Damsels passed into the hands of the civil Branches of the service, who had followed the victors in time to rob them of their spoil. These fair ladies were speedily reconciled to this change in their position, caused by the fortune of war, & remained with their new masters until the army passed the Pyrenees, when the vast increase of baggage which had been occasioned by such recruits, calling for Ld. Wellington's interference, he issued an order before we entered France, that they should be sent home and numbers returned into those parts of Spain from which they had originally joined the French Army. Some, however, contrived to absent themselves for a few days and then reappeared with the baggage as before, but by far the greater part were disbanded. They were attired in every sort of dress that can be conceived, some in jackets above & petticoats below, others as hussars, some again in habits, others in muslin with large straw bonnets. They were found laughing and singing along the whole line of march, perched for the most part on the panniers that were slung over the mules. They had almost all guitars, which they accompanied with pretty voices, the muleteers themselves joining in chorus, whenever their airs admitted of one, which most of them did. Ld. Wellington himself, angry as he was to see such an increase of baggage, could not help smiling as he passed them to their loud "Viva Wellington" saluting him as he went by.

Sir Thomas Graham's Corps made an unsuccessful attempt to intercept Genl. Foy, who had retired by the great Bayonne road. He made shew of a stand at Toloso, but Sir Thomas blew in the Gates with Artillery & followed him hard, until he crossed the Bidassoa into France.

Clausel also escaped, by marching on Saragossa, & passing into France by the Pass of Jaca. Sir Rowland Hill followed up the successes of the 2nd Division, & pushed the enemy through the passes of the Pyrenees into their native Country.[234]

The movements of Head Quarters, in the interval between the 21st of June, when I received my wound, & the 1st of July, when I rejoined the Army, were made to me, to have been as follows:

June 22nd. Advanced to Salvaterra—skirmished with the rear-guard of the enemy, & took from him the only gun he had left.

23rd. Echarre Aranaz—Again skirmishing with the French rear-guard, as they retired—Took very few Prisoners, as the Gendarmerie collected, & beat in all the stragglers.

24th. Trurzum. Here, the enemy appeared inclined to make a stand having a river to cover them, on the banks of which they had placed their remaining Howitzer, but the passage of the stream was soon forced, & they retired: rapidly in disorder. We took some Prisoners, & several Deserters came in confirming the report of the great disorganization of the French army.

25th. Head Quarters at Orcoyen a village about two & a half leagues from Pamplona, in which the French, in retiring into France, had left a considerable Garrison. Halted here one Day, for the Commissariat to come up, and the men were also in great distress for Shoes, many being foot sore, & unable to proceed. To remedy this, in some degree, (for there [are] no Shoes at hand) whenever a Bullock was killed, the men who were without shoes, used to cut out of the fresh hide, as much as would cover their feet & bind above the Ancles, the fleshy side inwards—then stitched it up, & wore it as long as it would last together—

27th. Head Quarters Tafalla—We saw nothing of the enemy here, but they left some dead behind them, on whom Vultures were performing the last Offices. There were numbers of these Birds, the largest & fattest I ever saw, so fat indeed, that when surprized it was with difficulty they could rise, without having taken some half dozen immense hops, with their wings expanding more at each, until they had them at full stretch, & they then soared off, describing circles as they mounted, until the eye could scarcely discover the small speck they occupied in the Sky. They were very wary, & it was most difficult to get a shot at them. They used to hover over us, & accompany us in our movements, ready to pounce down on any horse or mule, or Soldier, who might die on the march. There were also Wolves, in great numbers, near the frontiers, exceedingly fierce and daring, which have been known to attack the Bullocks of the Army in the night, even when under the charge of Sentries, in herds of twenty or thirty together, making the most horrible noises possible. Our very Cavalry Horses have been attacked & grievously torn by them, at their Pickets, & pieces literally taken out of their flanks. I do not however recollect any instance of a man having been attacked by them.

28th. Caseda. We made forced marches yesterday & to-day, in hopes of cutting off Genl. Clausel, who was endeavouring to rejoin the French army by a circuitous route.

30th. Monreal—Here we discovered, that it was a vain attempt, that

of trying to catch Clausel, as he was a full day's march ahead of us[235]—
We retraced our steps therefore towards Pamplona.

July 1st. Head Quarters—Huarte about a league from Pamplona.

This fortress which was well garrisoned & provisioned, had been
blockaded by the 4th & 6th Divisions, since the Day that the French
Army passed through, after their defeat at Vittoria—All idea of turning
the blockade into a siege, appeared to be at an end, if Ld. Wellington had
ever conceived such a plan—& the British Divisions were relieved in
the duty, by Carlos's Corps of Spaniards, Strengthened by a Divison of
O'Donnel's Army—& thus enabled the 4th & 6th Divisions of British,
to march on France with the rest of the Army.

In the mean time Sir Thomas Graham, with the left column moved on
St. Sebastian, the enemy retiring before him with constant skirmishes—
He immediately invested that strong Fortress, in which the French had
left a picked Garrison of 2000 men, under an able and gallant Commander. The Centre of the Army & Head Quarters moved up the Valley of
Bastan, in the Pyrenees—whilst the right, under Sir Rowland Hill,
directed its course along the Valley of Roncesvalles. When the centre &
right had passed thro' their respective Vallies, they were to effect a
junction & establish their communications on the Pyrenees, thus
covering the Spaniards who were blockading Pamplona, & at the same
time Sir Thomas Graham & his Corps, who was to undertake the siege
of San Sebastian.

3rd. Head Quarters Ostiz. Saw nothing of the enemy.

4th. Lauz. Here we had sharp skirmishing, as the French did not
seem disposed to quit the place, before they had ascertained the force
with which we were advancing in that Valley. We drove them out
however, but the evening was far advanced before this was done, & it
was night when we got into our Quarters. There was a deserted House,
into which I felt my way, & putting my Horse into one of the lower rooms
& shutting the Door, I went out for a light. Having procured one, I went
up stairs into a room covered with Indian Corn Straw, of which I
collected some into a corner, & laid me down to sleep. In about an hour,
there was an alarm at the Outposts, & I was groping my way down-stairs,
by the way, as I thought that I came up, when down went my right leg
into a hole & I fell. I found I was wet up to the hip, & hastily withdrew the
leg, which operation was succeeded by a strong ranced smell. I felt the
limb, & found it very slippery, & discovered that I had fallen into a long
Oil jar, which the Spaniards of these Vallies are in the habits of inserting

into the floors of small landing places off their stairs, into one of which recesses I had inadvertently strayed, in my luckless descent this night: my Boot was full, my Trowsers steeped, no baggage at hand, nor likely to be for another Day at least—weather broiling hot. I was not relieved from this mess for nearly two Days afterwards. No one could approach me, as the smell was overpowering, & not unlike that of a Dog who has rolled himself to his heart's content in Carrion. Oh! the luxury of pulling off those Boots, putting on another pair, & a clean pair of Trowsers.

The Valley of Bastan, which War was thus desolating, appeared the very emblem of Peace & Happiness, save where our tracks & those of whom we were in pursuit, had left such deadly impressions. The Mountains which inclose it are of all shapes, wooded here and there, studded with Orchards, principally of Apple Trees, which were at this season loaded with fruit. An abundant stream runs thro' the centre, & at small distances from its banks, whitewashed houses of different sizes, according to the circumstances of the Owners, gave an air of cleanliness & comfort to the scene, such as I had seldom witnessed before. The Men are well built, tall & stout, & in place of Hats, wear on their Heads, a dark blue worsted Bonnet wove without a Seam, such as is seen in some parts of the Highlands of Scotland. The Women are also tall, fair & comely, they wear their hair exceedingly long, tied in one long tail, platted behind & nearly touching the ground, the whole is combed off the face & twisted in this tail. It has a very sigular appearance to a stranger, & it is with difficulty, that the eye becomes reconciled to the singularity. The Cyder is excellent, & the bread beautifully white & good. The weather was delightful, when we were in these romantic Valleys. It was however exceedingly difficult to keep up the communication of the several Divisions which were in the three passes of Maya, Bastan & Roncesvalles, on account of the high Mountains which separated them. The Cavalry had almost all been sent to the rear, both because of the inutility of that force in mountainous regions, & of the difficulty of finding them Forage. The Allies were at this moment divided into the three Corps occupying these Vallies, widely separated from each other—the besieging Army of St. Sebastian, & the blockading force at Pamplona. How clear & able must have [been] that Head, which directed the daily movements & operations of an Army thus situated.

July 10th. Head Quarters Zubieta. The Centre of the army being moved to the top of the Pass of Maya & encamped on the Pyrenees.

From this spot we first discovered the Ocean, after so long a separation from it, and the feelings it excited were truly enviable. We looked down upon France as on an immense plain—Saw her Troops in bivouac on a strong position, with a river in its front—Troops, whom we had followed in a splended succession of Victories, from the Shores of the Tagus, where they bullied us to the utmost, & where all were desponding but our Commander himself who even at that time of trial and doubt, was full of confidence in his Army and himself. What a proud moment for him, thus to see France as it were at his feet. British Frigates were cruising near the Shore, & their glasses could no doubt discover the Colours of English Regiments unfurled to the Breeze, on the summits of the Pyrenees. Not a Ship of France could venture to shew itself, & we saw our gallant Vessels the undisputed Masters of the waters, & thus a strong appui to the left flank of our Army. Lord Wellington established the best sort of communication in his power, with the detached Corps of his Line, and then moved to his left, in order to have a more easy & shorter intercourse with Sir T. Graham's Corps at St. Sebastian.

July 11th. Head Quarters Ernani—About four leagues from St. Sebastian. Halted here one day, in the course of which Ld. Wellington rode to that place, taking with him some of the Staff of Head Quarters, in order to make a reconnaissance of the Fortress. St. Sebastian is built on a narrow Isthmus, which runs out into the Bay of Biscay, the length of which is about a quarter of a mile, and by which alone it can be approached. It is surrounded by strong Walls, the foot of which is washed by the Sea, except at the neck of the Peninsula. At high water vessels of Burthen can come almost close to these Walls, but their is generally a heavy swell dashing against the rocks, which makes the approach difficult & unsafe. There is however a small Harbor, into which Ships can run. The Town is completely overlooked & commanded by the Castle, the paths leading to which are very narrow, & commanded from above. The Garrison consisted of 2500 picked Troups under Genl. Rey, a distinguished Officer, & Deserters from the place stated that they were amply furnished with Ammunition & Provisions. The streets which are broad and handsome, & flagged with white stone were reported by the same Deserters to be barricadoed at intervals, & trenches dug across them, everything seemed to indicate a most determined resistance. Sir T. Graham had about 9,000 men under his orders before the place. The weakest part of the defences appeared to be the left Flank, which was in a certain degree commanded by sand hills, from which at a distance of about 1800 feet almost the botton of the wall could be seen. On these hills, batteries were erected, regular approaches not having been found necessary, & occupying too much time. The battering train being at hand, Guns were soon mounted & the firing began.

In this interval, a change was made in the command of the French Army. Napoleon greatly vexed no doubt, at the continued defeat of his Marshals in succession, dispatched Marshal Soult, to assume the command of the French Armies in Spain, with the Title of "Lieutenant of the Emperor". This Marshal had long been considered the ablest & most enterprising Officer of Napoleon's Armies, & therefore a better selection could not have been made, for the purpose of retrieving the honor & the losses of his Forces in Spain. Soult on taking the command, issued flaming proclamations, & took most active measures to recruit his Army, & improve its moral & discipline. He expressed his determination instantly to force the English back over the Ebro, lest their feet should pollute the soil of France, & that he would undoubtedly celebrate the Birthday of His Imperial Master (12 August) in Pamplona, & relieve St. Sebastian before that Day. Other portions of his proclamations were filled with illiberal & false accusations against Ld. Wellington & the misconduct of his Troops in the countries they had marched over. The general Orders he issued to his Army, were in a still more abusive style, which we had an opportunity of ascertaining, one of the Orderly books of a Regiment, having been brought in by a Deserter. It is worthy of remark, that amongst other directions, he ordered all Regiments to send their Eagles to Bayonne.

July 13th. Head Quarters returned this Day to Zubieta in the Valley of Bastan.

14th. San Estevara. Here intelligence reached Ld. Wellington that Marshal Soult was preparing to move forwards & attack us, and measures were accordingly taken to give him a proper reception. We halted here the 15th July.

16th. Lesaca. On arrival here, we find, that two breaches having been reported practicable at San Sebastian, Sir T. Graham ordered the assault of the place. The storming party was of 2000 men, including the 1st 4th 38th & 44th Regiments. The springing of a Mine under the glacis, was the signal for a general onset, & the Troops sprang forwards, in the highest possible style & spirit. In attempting to mount the breach however, so heavy a flanking fire was brought to bear on them, that they were unable to face it, & after a severe loss, retired into their trenches. One great cause of failure, was said to have been the want of a sufficient reserve, to support the storming party, who had at one time actually carried the Breach, but their numbers falling shorter every moment, from the destructive fire kept upon them, they were unable to sustain themselves there, which would have been otherwise, had they been supported by the presence of a strong reserve. Our loss was exceedingly severe. One hundred & thirty Officers & upwards of a 1000 men, were killed & wounded in this unfortunate assault.[236] Much blame was given to the Commander of the siege,[237] but whether with good reason or not, I cannot pretend to judge. Ld. Wellington was evidently much disappointed with the result of the attack, which I had an opportunity of ascertaining, as I dined with him this Day, & he scarcely spoke a word to any one at Table. This Table, in fact, to which I was in the habits of being frequently invited, was pleasant or gloomy, in exact proportion to the good or ill success of projects, carrying into effect at the time. If matters went on badly, Ld. Wellington preserved so determined a silence, that no one ventured to interrupt it, & we were all heartily rejoiced, when he called for Coffee, the usual signal for wine drinking to cease, & immediately after taking it, he used to retire, & we were expected to do the same. But whenever all was going on well, no one was more cheerful, or full of anecdote & good humour. He would sit later than usual, ask some goodnatured question of every one, & make the evening as pleasant & sociable as possible; nor have I ever seen more gaiety & fun than on such occasions. At times he would relate anecdotes of Indian Campaigns, the recollection of which appeared to interest him exceedingly, & which of course was highly acceptable to us, & it appeared to me, that he took peculiar pleasure in old Indian stories, as was particularly apparent, when an old Officer who had served with him in the East (Col: Shawe) came from England, to pass a month or two at his Head Quarters. We then had constant stories of what had been the events of those Days, & all this helped the evenings off most agreably. The Officers of the Adjutant & Quarter Master General's Department, in the former of which I held my Staff Appointment, were usually invited in turns, to dine with Ld. Wellington. The Dinners were good or indifferent according to the place we were in, & the possibility of obtaining anything more than the rations, but the Wine was always good, being principally French, which had fallen into hands of plundering Guerilla parties, who sold it afterwards, & not unfrequently sent to

Head Quarters a quantity as a present to the Commander in Chief. I remember the circumstance of a Butcher in London sending him an immense round of Beef, cased in sheet Lead & soldered up. It was three weeks on the passage, but arrived at Head Quarters, as good & fresh as possible.

Head Quarters remained at Lesaca, until the 25th July, at Daybreak of which Day, Soult attacked in two very strong Columns, the passes of Maya & Roncesvalles.[238] The attack on the former was conducted by Count D'Erlon, at the head of 15,000 Men, & that on the latter by Soult in person who led on a Corps of nearly 40,000 men. The British force which guarded the Pass of Maya was very inadequate to resist so serious an onset, & the 50th 71st & 92d Regiments suffered very severely in their gallant tho' unavailing defence. They retired in good order on their reserve, which formed & offered further resistance, but the French Corps which pressed on, was infinitely too numerous to be long withstoood by such inferior numbers, & our Troops were compelled to retire several miles, after a loss little short of 2000 men killed & wounded. In the Roncesvalles Pass, Soult moved against the advance commanded by Genl. Byng, & at the same time directed a strong force to attack a part of the 4th Division which occupied the Bridge of Arcola. They fell back on the remainder of that Division, & the whole took up a strong position for the night, against which Soult pressed no further at the time. He then pushed Byng's advance & drove them back, as well as Morillo's Corps of Spaniards, which had been detached by Genl. Byng to cover a road, the possession of which by the enemy, would have turned his flank, & rendered his post untenable. These Troops & Genl. Byng backed on General Cole's Division, who retired to Lizoain & halted there. Sir Rowland Hill then retreated before the enemy in his front, to Trueta, where he took up a strong position. Genl. Picton on being acquainted with all these operations, moved up instantly with the 3rd Division to Lizoain, & took the command of the Troops there. The enemy attacked him, & he retired in excellent order to some strong ground, & remained there all night. Ld. Wellington, during this time, was nearly at the left extremity of the Line, for the purpose of rapid communication with St. Sebastian, & our Troops were already in full retreat through the passes of Maya & Roncesvalles, overpowered by superior numbers, before he could arrive with that part of his Army, & take the personal command & direction. In his rapid movement to reach Picton & Cole, he had a very narrow escape of being taken, the road by which he had passed, having been occupied by French Cavalry, a few minutes after he had gone by. On this Day, the 25th July, my Brother who commanded a Company in the 23rd Fusileers, in the absence of its Captain, received a shot, which severely wounded him in the thigh. The ball lodged near the Hip, & has never been extricated.[239]

July 27th. Picton not liking his position in this mountainous district, where communication is so difficult, & all the passes & bye-roads so much better known to the enemy, than they could possibly be to the British, began his further retreat. & the Corps under his orders were already in sight of Pamplona, in which the French Garrison was blockaded by a Spanish Corps. Lord Wellington stopped for a short time at Elmendoz, ordered the further retreat of the retiring Corps to be stopped, & Picton instantly put them in fine position & order of battle; in which the Commander of the Forces found them, when he joined. He immediately ordered up a Corps of Spaniards, to support them, & on receiving reports from the other Divisions of the Army, resolved at once to dispute every inch of ground with Soult, whose great object was the relief of Pamplona, which he had announced in a proclamation some Days before. Our Army was dejected at the prospect of his being able to realize his threats; but Ld. Wellington appeared full of confidence, & quickly restored it to the Troops. Our loss had been very severe in the last two Days, & that of the enemy no doubt in proportion. We soon found the effects of the orders our Commander had given to the different Corps, by their concentration, to oppose Soult, who made a halt, & took up a position.

July 27th. Head Quarters Lizazzo. There was very sharp skirmishing at the outposts of each Army this Day, & Soult seemed more determined than ever to relieve Pamplona, which was now in view of both Armies, & the French were in Telegraphic communication with the place. Such was the confidence of the French Garrison of their speedy relief, that they actually illuminated the Town, to shew the joy they thought so near realization, & this illumination was seen from the tops of the hills where we were posted. The Garrison was already beginning to feel the effects of a vigorous Blockade, in many privations caused by a scarcity of Provisions, & had been on short allowance for upwards of a week. When they perceived our retreat & the French Army actually in sight, to effect their deliverance, their joy knew no bounds. They attempted a sortie or two from mere wantonness, in which they were driven back with loss. They discharged Cannon, sent up Rockets and shewed a constant sort of intercourse with their approaching Deliverers. The British Army was however in position between them & their hopes, & had to be overthrown, before their joy could be complete. Lord Wellington sent very strict orders, for the Spanish blockading Force to be doubly vigilant, lest a successful sortie should endanger our rear. The English were posted on a range of heights, & the French on another opposite—a narrow Valley was between them. The Picquets of both were half way down, & the Sentries at the bottom quite close to each other. As the evening of the 27th closed in, every thing indicated a fierce and bloody morrow. The Troops slept on their Arms, the fires of each Army, dimly burning, & at length expiring. It was a warm sultry night—& many a brave fellow, on that wild spot of the Pyrenees, was then sleeping his last sleep on Earth. There was an occasional challenge of Sentries heard, both of the English & French Army. I held my Horses Bridle as I lay on the turf, with some companions around me, & our discourse was entirely occupied with the probable result of the Day following, which we all knew would be one of severe conflict. We gradually dropt off, asleep, ready for the call of an instant, & wrapped in our Cloaks for a while forgot the fatigues of the Day that was passed, & the probable events of that which was to come.

It is impossible to conceive the position of two hostile Armies, more wild & romantic & interesting, then that which was thus exhibited on the night of the 27th of July. Soult, having successfully driven us back from the tops of the Pyrenees, looking down on France, as our next conquest, resolved to set free the French Garrison of Pamplona, actually in sight, & Ld. Wellington equally resolved to prevent his doing so, & at the head of his victorious Troops, full of confidence & resolution. He was in excellent spirits, & visited every Post & Picquet of the Army, before he laid himself on the Turf, to wait the next Sunrise.

28th July. The Baggage of Head Quarters was sent to Villalba—At Daybreak, the French were observed, formed in Columns of attack & ready for Battle. These Columns were very deep, & headed by Grenadiers of their Army, who moved steadily onwards, in the most imposing masses I ever beheld. The British fully prepared, were formed in two Lines, & remained in silence, looking on the French advancing Force—The Enemy's Grenadiers in their Bear-skin Caps, with red feathers, & blue frock coats appeared the most warlike body of Troops possible. As they moved on, they threw out their Skirmishers, which were met by British light Troops, & thus the work of this bloody Day

commenced. Their Skirmishers were quickly supported by reinforcements, which caused similar strengthening of our own. Then began the
Artillery, from both sides, & shortly afterwards, the solid masses were
hotly engaged. The crash of the two Armies was fearful. I never
remember to have witnessed so tremendous an onset. The French
persevered most gallantly in spite of the vast numbers they were losing
every moment. At one time they had nearly gained the Hill on which the
British second Line was formed, when three Cheers & a rush
announced the charge of the Fusileer Brigade, which completely upset
them. The Fusileers halted for breath—the French reformed & came
on again, with the utmost fury & determination. The other Brigade of
the 4th Division made a similar charge & again the enemy was
overthrown. After a short pause, they again returned to the disputed
ground, which French gallantry never more conspicuous, endeavoured
in vain to get possession of. They were repulsed by the British at every
point, & the slaughter was dreadful, the whole ground was covered with
bodies & Grenadier Caps. They fled across the Valley which had
separated the two Armies, at Day-break this morning. British Troops
followed, & again established their Picquets on their old ground. It was
now about eleven o'clock—An interval of an hour took place, both
Armies looking at each other, whilst the Skirmishers were still smartly at
work, & heavy cannonading going on. About noon, the French again
formed their Columns of attack & moved against us, if possible, more
desperately than before—They crossed the Valley, & when nearly at the
Crest of the English position, to which they had driven our Picquets,
were again charged by the bayonets of the gallant 4th division, & literally
pushed down at their points, into the Valley below. In this repulse of the
enemy, Captains Stainforth & Walker of my Regiment, the 23rd
Fusileers, were killed, & Ld. Wellington in his Dispatch home, said that
much as he had always been satisfied with the 4th Division, it had that
day surpassed all its former gallantry. Even this did not put an end to this
bloody day, although the loss on both sides had been very severe,—
About 2 o'clock, the French were once more seen, forming their masses
of solid Columns, & shortly afterwards, they pressed on once more to
the attack—The British Bayonet was again brought into play, with the
same decisive & terrible effect as before—Soult was seen in the centre
of his Columns, directing & animating his Men, & Ld. Wellington
equally active, & every where present, encouraging all by his coolness,
courage & decision—wherever he shewed himself, confidence

attended him—He never doubted the result of the Day's action—We had now lost upwards of 4000 Men, & the dead bodies of the French, covered the ground more thickly than I had ever before seen strewed on a field of battle—Their defeat was complete, but we could not descend from our heights, whilst they remained on theirs, so that when night put an end to the conflict, each Army was seen on its original ground with the valley between them! A spent Musket Shot, struck me on the Collar bone, during the last attack, but only made a tumor, & I was not obliged to quit the field. This Day, was the most desperately fought of any, in which I had been engaged, & the night was passed by both Armies, it might be said under arms. Those who slept, did so, on the turf, with their accoutrements on, & their Muskets by their sides. The disappointment of the French Garrison in Pamplona, at the non arrival of their Comrades, to relieve them, as had been so confidently promised, may be conceived—No more illuminations were seen, but several rocket signals were exchanged, during the night. They attempted also a sortie against the Spanish blockading Force, but were repulsed—We were now all suspense & anxiety, as to what the morrow would bring forth. The French watch-fires burned brightly on the hills they occupied, & groups were assembled round our own during the night. The appearance of the night-fires of two Armies so near each other, is singularly beautiful—Their extent, the brightness of some & the dimness of others—the glittering of arms, as they pass by the blaze, & the shadows of those who are assembled round, have a very imposing effect, & an occasional bugle, sounding the relief of a guard, or a picquet, with its echo, in mountainous districts completes the interest of such a scene. I believe it was in the course of the Actions of the last two days, that I first remarked the singular similarity that exists, in the dying movements of Birds and of Men, when badly wounded. I have observed a Soldier, mortally wounded, by a shot through the head or heart, instead of instantly falling down, elevate his Firelock with both hands above his head, & run round & round, describing circles before he fell, as one frequently sees a bird shot in the air, flying round in circles as it falls to the ground. & in like manner, Men, when badly wounded seek for the shelter of a stone or a bush, to which they betake themselves, before they lie down, for support & security, just as birds, or hares do, when in a similar state of suffering.

29th July. Day broke—Both Armies were under arms. The French Garrison in Pampluna, who had witnessed all the events of yesterday, made no further attempts at rejoicings or illuminations—Ld. Wellington had been rather uneasy this day, in consequence of the Army wanting ammunition, from the immense quantity which had been fired away yesterday in action. He was certainly desirous, that the Action should not be renewed whilst this deficiency continued. Fortunately a fresh supply arrived at the Camp, at night, & the Army was busy filling pouches with Ammunition. The Soldiers themselves had been anxious on account of their pouches not being filled with Cartridges, & the honest & gallant joy was so loudly expressed in Camp when the supply arrived, that the French might have heard it, in their lines. A renewal of the Action was now wished for, in the morrow, & Ld. Wellington determined to be the attacker, in case Soult should decline the honor. It appeared afterwards from Deserters, that the French had been themselves in want of Ball Cartridge on the 29th otherwise the Action would have been renewed. As the practice of burying the dead, had been omitted by both Armies for some time past, the eyes had for ever before them, the sight of unburied Comrades, undergoing the different changes & progress towards putrefaction—This, which had formerly been looked upon as a reproach, had lost all its power of exciting the feelings, although the appearance of the dead almost implored for burial. The Soldier who survived had not time sufficient for this purpose, under Arms from an hour before Sunrise constantly until dark, except at the interval of Cooking, & not unfrequently the whole night, his own wants were so urgent as not to leave to his consideration, the decency or propriety of burying his Comrade. The 29th of July passed away without fighting, except a slight skirmishing along the Line; but as the Troops were under arms all Day, they were much fatigued.

30th July. From movements making in the French position, Ld. Wellington at once determined that they were preparing to retire. He gave immediate orders for a general attack on their Line & the British moved on rapidly. The enemy was attacked, just as [he] was beginning to retire, which caused much confusion in his ranks, & a total rout of every part of his line ensued. The pursuit commenced immediately, & about 1500 Prisoners were made. In our progress over the ground, which had been occupied by the enemy on the 28th we were really astonished to observe the number of their dead, numerous as we had been led to suppose them. The French Division taken, stated their loss since the 25th to this Day at 14,000 men, killed, wounded & prisoners. We continued our pursuit of the enemy the whole Day, & took a considerable quantity of Baggage & stores. Head Quarters remained this night in a wood near Lanz. Sir Thomas Picton's Corps had been the right of the Army, & moved up the pass of Roncesvalles, which route had been taken by the enemy. Sir Rowland Hill, during the Actions of the Pyrenees, had been detached to Lizazzo, with the 2nd Division only, to watch the movements of a French Corps under the Count D'Erlon, which was endeavouring to pass by the flank of our position, & turn it. He was very superior in number to Sir Rowland Hill's Division, which nevertheless took up an excellent position near Lizazzo, covering the road which led past our flank to Pampluna. Here he was repeatedly attacked & met with severe loss, but he repulsed the attempts of the Count d'Erlon until he was reinforced by the 7th Division, when the Enemy desisted from further operations in that part of the field. On the retreat of the other part of the French Army, the Count d'Erlon moved off, in the direction of St. Estavan, & was immediately followed by Sir Rowland Hill's Corp, which made some prisoners. By these operations Sir Rowland became the left of the Army, & Sir Thomas Picton the right—As we moved on however, to our old position on the Pyrenees, these two Corps changed their ground, & Sir R. Hill became as usual, the right of the Army. In our pursuit of the enemy, we observed from an eminence, a Convoy approaching through the valley of Bastan, which track had not been taken by any part of the defeated Army. They were moving on in perfect confidence, & as carelessly as possible, with provisions for their Army, which they had every reason to believe, was near Pampluna. Our Troops which in this valley were few (only one Brigade, under B. Genl. Byng) took off their Packs, & waited the approach of this Convoy, which was escorted by about 1,000 men, & when sufficiently near, they set off at full speed down the hill & attacked them, routed the whole escort, took many prisoners, & the whole of the Convoy—Brandy, Pork & Biscuit. The Prisoners taken, had not heard a word of the result of the battles near Pampluna, & to their ignorance on this subject they owed their capture. The provisions proved a most welcome supply to Genl. Byng's Brigade, & to the 4th Division which afterwards arrived in the Valley of Bastan.

31st July. Head Quarters at Trueta. Met with a Patrole of the enemy's Cavalry, & found from one of them who deserted, that Count d'Erlon's Corps had halted at St. Estevan, on the banks of the Bidassoa, & that Sir Rd. Hill was moving on the road from Lizazzo to St. Estevau, to dislodge the French from that place. Ld. Wellington moved the 4th Division out of the valley of Bastan, towards St. Estevan in order to second, by a flank attack on the enemy in that place, Sir R. Hill's movements against their rear—The march of the 4th Division was so rapid & well conducted, that the French Generals were just going to dinner at St. Estevan, when the near approach of the British was made known to them. They had caused the roads from Sir Rwds. Hills Columns only to be watched, & were not prepared for a movement against their flank. They ordered their Troops under arms, & began an immediate retreat to the pass of Vera, leading into France, which pass, is the nearest to the Sea of all the Pyrenean passes, excepting the main road near the Sea from Irun to St. Jean de Luz. They were pursued, & their baggage overtaken. As their march was close on the edge of the Bidassoa from St. Estevan to Vera, they threw into the stream a great part of their baggage & medical & other stores. Horses, Mules & Men fell into the river in all directions, many were drowned & a great quantity of the baggage of the French Corps taken. It was literally composed of what they had robbed, at the different places they passed thro' after the battle of Vittoria. Sheets, Counterpanes, spoons, forks & every article of household furniture that was portable, had become a new baggage to the French Army, & it was remarkable enough, how quickly they had compensated themselves for their losses on the 21st of June. Head Quarters remained this night at St. Estevan and halted there one day.

August 1st. St. Estevan. Saw nothing whatever of the enemy—& moved on towards Lesaca.

August 2nd. Head Quarters remained at this place the whole of this month. The troops were encamped on the passes of Roncesvalles & Maya, & communicated with a hill opposite Vera, which town was not occupied by either the French or English. It is situated close beneath a range of hills on the French side of the Bidassoa, & which range was yet in possession on the enemy, who employed himself night & day in erecting lines & batteries to secure their position. The Outposts & picquets of the British were close to Vera, on the Spanish side of the Bidassoa. The enemy thus remained in position, on a range of hills, at the foot of which ran the river, on whose banks their Picquets & Videttes were posted in great numbers. During these operations in the field, Sir Thos. Graham's Corps consisting of the 5th Division, 2 Portuguese Brigades, & part of the 1st Division, prosecuted the siege of St. Sebastian, the occupation of which became very necessary for the security of the left flank of the Army, during further operations. Fresh batteries had been raised & the approaches ran as near the enemy's work as it was possible, & on the evening of the 30th of Augst. inst. a breach was reported practicable. The following day the 31st was determined on for a general assault, & the garrison who had established a telegraph communication with the French Army, from the Castle of St. Sebastians to the enemy's Camps on the heights above Vera, were seen making signals constantly on the 30th Augst. About mid-night after this day, intelligence was received from the Outposts, that the French Army was under Arms, & formed in Columns, was moving down from the heights of Vera towards two fords over the Bidassoa, the one a little below Vera, & the other opposite San Marcial, & close to the main road from Irun to San Sebastians, with an evident intention to gain that road & relieve the garrison of the besieged if possible. The British got under arms immediately, & moved down towards the fords, to dispute the passage of the river with the French. The latter however, were already over, & meeting the British Columns obliged them to retire to a position about a league in the rear, where they formed & waited for the attack of the French. The enemy moved on, but when they had reconnoitered the British Position they halted, & a very sharp affair took place, between the advance of the French, & a Brigade of the 7th Division. the latter were obliged to retire after considerable loss, particularly in the 51st & 68th Regts. they retired in good order, & united themselves with the remainder of this part of the British Army in position. The French did not attack it, tho' they again reconnoitered this position. These operations took place between that column of the French Army, which crossed the Ford a little below Vera, & the British troops which had been sent to oppose their passage. In this part of the field, the British force was one Brigade (M. Genl. Inglis) of the 7th Division, & the Portuguese Brigade of the 4th Division, which had been detached in support of the Brigade of the 7th Division. The French who crossed at this ford, were in 3 divisions, about 15,000 men—The gallantry of the British in keeping this body in check, with so inferior a number, was very conspicuous. In the mean time the enemy who had crossed opposite San Marcial about a league lower down the river, than the ford below Vera, had passed the river in boats, & large rafts made of pontoons, & on a pontoon bridge, (which was sunk afterwards by the tide coming in rapidly). This body of the enemy consisted also of 3 Divisions. The Troops opposed to them were the Spanish Army under O'Donnel, about 10,000 men. the 1st Division, & the two British Brigades of the

4th Division, were held in reserve to support the Spaniards, should it prove necessary.

The French crossed the river, & attacked the Spaniards, who were on a hill, in an excellent position, & defended by Lines & batteries, which had been the work of several weeks past. The Spaniards were full of confidence in their works & position, & resisted gallantly three attacks from the enemy, with an interval of about an hour between each attack. Their conduct on this occasion was good, & this was the only time I ever saw the Spanish Army behave like Soldiers. The 31st of August is one of their proudest days. They lost about 2500 men killed & wounded. When the French moved on to attack them the third time, the Spanish General sent to Ld. Wellington, to beg he would allow the 1st or 4th British Divisions to assist them—to which Ld. Wellington replied that he meant the glory of that day to be entirely Spanish. Their conduct in repelling the two former attacks of the enemy had been admirable, & he would not have tarnished it, by allowing any other Troops to claim a part of it, that the 1st & 4th Divisions were so posted as to prevent the possibility of disaster, even tho' the Spaniards should yield to this third attack of the French. The Spaniards were not assisted & repulsed the enemy alone. The French Army had thus passed the Bidassoa to attack the British, & if possible to relieve St. Sebastians, which was but 10 miles distant from this scene of action. They had failed in their object completely, & now began to think of recrossing the river, & regaining their former position on the heights above Vera—During & after the Action this day (in which [. . .] the Spaniards lost about 3,500 men) the rain had descended in torrents incessantly, & the river was swelling so fast, that the French in repassing by the spot, which had been only knee-deep in the morning, had so many men drowned that they could no longer persevere in passing the remainder of their Army by that ford, but directed the force which had not been able to cross, towards a bridge close to Vera, in order to pass there. Exactly opposite this bridge, on the other bank, was a fortified house, with a ditch & a wall, & the walls loop-holed. This house seemed exactly as a tête de pont, to the bridge, & nothing could pass the bridge, but under a warm fire from the house. Ld. Wellington, foreseeing from the tremendous rains & swelling of the river, that the enemy would not be able to pass over all his men by the ford below Vera, & that consequently they would be obliged to make for the bridge, had ordered part of the 95th Regiment & a Portuguese Regt. of Cacãdores to make a push, & if possible, throw themselves into this fortified house, which commanded the bridge, & after entering it, to barricade themselves in it. The attempt succeeded perfectly—so that when the French Column, about 8,000 men, arrived at the bridge, and began to pass over it, the two Regiments in the fortified house opened a tremendous fire upon them. The French had no means of avoiding it— they ran over the bridge as fast as they could, exposed the whole time, to the fire from the house which they had not time to attack, as Ld. Wellington had caused two British Divisions to march after them towards the Bridge. The French passed the bridge and lost 1,200 men & 2 Generals, killed & wounded in doing so. The 2 Generals killed were La Martiniere & Vandermasen.[240] The total loss of the enemy this day, in the passage of the Bidassoa, & attack of the British & Spaniards in their positions exceeded 8,000 men. The rain continued all the night, which was consequently pitch dark. Ld. Wellington had fixed his Head Quarters at an iron Forge situated in a lonely & deep valley of the Pyrenees, at the edge of a narrow & rapid stream. A Spanish Peasant had undertaken to guide us to this spot, & we began our march over a steep & winding path so narrow that we were obliged to dismount, & lead our horses in single file. The Guide led the way, then some of the staff. The Duke himself also dismounted, & such was the darkness & insecurity of the path, that we took hold of the tail of the horse in our front. I had that of the horse of the Marquis of Worcester, then, one of the Duke's A. D. Camps. There was an occasional clap of thunder & flash of lightning, which only rendered our darkness still more obscure. We proceeded in this manner, about two hours, & at length heard the stroke of a hammer & saw a distant light, we also heard the sound of falling water, & this turned out to be a small cascade greatly increased by the heavy rains which fell directly in our path. Some of us clung closely to the part of the path, immediately under the fall, & were drenched, if it were possible still more—others in attempting to avoid it, the darkness being very great, fell over the side, dragging their horses upon them. Of this number were Sir Edward Pakenham & Captn. Eckersley D. A. A. Genl. They were hurried down a steep slope of shingle, & having been stopped in their descent by trees, clung to them, until day broke, exposed all night on so comfortless & dangerous a spot to the rain, which fell in torrents—they were not hurt. The rest of the party proceeded onwards, & were safely conducted by the guide to the Forge, where immense fires were lighted, & all got ready for the next day's work.

When the skirmishing of the Picquets, a short time before the battle of

San Marcial, gave notice that a serious affair was going to begin, the Judge Advocate of the Army, Mr. Larpent was seized with a wish to see a fight; he & a Commissary, Mr. Jesse climbed a small hill, thinking to look down on the fight below. They were so intent on what was passing, & so secure as they thought, on this high spot, the approach to which was thro' a wood, they did not observe a company of French Voltigeurs[241] (who had been sent by the French General to take possession of this hill) creeping thro' the wood, & in the midst of their contemplation of the scenes below, they were made Prisoners. It rained terribly, & when they came to the banks of the Bidassoa they were made to mount the carriage of a gun, & were passed thro' on it. As we gave the French a good beating, they retired, & Mr. Larpent, & the Commissary were made to march all night in the rain, until they reached Bayonne.

The assault of the town of St. Sebastians took place, during these operations in the field, on this day [31 August 1813]. After a most severe & obstinate resistance, the French were driven from the breach, & the British got into the Town, which was on fire in all directions. The French fled out of the Town & retired into the Castle. A scene of plunder now took place, which can seldom or never be prevented when a place is carried by assault, & had the enemy made a sortie from the Castle, whilst this was going on, there cannot be the smallest doubt, but that they would have recovered the Town without any difficulty. Our loss in this assault was 2,300 men, & in the actions in the field this day 3,000.

Head Quarters moved this night to Articuza, a small village about three miles from Lesaca. The French had thus lost the City of St. Sebastians, & had been defeated in a general action on this day. The Castle of St. Sebastians, was however not yet taken.

1st Septembr. [1813]. Head Quarters moved again to Lesaca, where they remained the whole of this month. The Army had need of rest, & remained encamped as before on the Pyrenees, on the passes of Roncesvalles & Maya, looking down upon France & the French Armies, who employed themselves night & day in raising works & batteries, destroying roads & bridges, & fortifying every knoll & spot of ground that they supposed would impede the entry of our Army into France. On the 8th of Septbr. the Castle of St. Sebastians, which was threatened with assault, capitulated.[242] The Garrison were prisoners of war, & 1,700 men. They had lost 700 men killed & wounded in the last assault, & had during the seige sent 500 wounded by boats into France, which boats had returned with fresh troops, in spite of all the care of Sir Geo: Collyer, who with a small squadron watched the sea-side of the Castle. Our left flank was thus secure, & the Troops which had been employed in the siege, now moved up to Irun, to be ready for future operations. The whole town of St. Sebastians was burned to the ground, except nine houses. The French certainly set fire to the place, & the whole odium of the loss of this beautiful City, fell to the British. A Spanish Garrison of 2,000 men was sent into the place, & British Engineers were immediately ordered there, & the repair of the breaches was undertaken & completed in a short time.

At the siege of this place, it will be found on a reference to a sketch made on the spot, that our Breaching Batteries were established near a small stream which emptied itself into the Sea, & which at high water was not to be forded. The first attempt to take the place was unsuccessful, owing to its having been begun too late, & when the tide had already commenced flowing. We lost in the breach a great many men & Officers, & as the tide came in it ascended the breach, & carried away the dead & such of the wounded as were unable to move. There were lying on the breach, rather high up, two British Officers, the one of whom was shot thro' the body, the other in the thigh—They had lost much blood & were unable to move, & the tide rising fast, had already covered part of their legs—During this time, a tremendous fire was kept up by our batteries, every shot of which, must have passed close to these Officers. In the midst of this fire, a French Officer suddenly shewed himself on the breach, from the Town side of it, with a white handkerchief in each hand—Our firing instantly ceased. He then caused four or five French Grenadiers to ascend from the Town, & they went down the outer part of the breach, where the two British Officers were, lying, half covered with the tide. The Grenadiers bore them on their shoulders into the Town, & the French Officer, when on the point of retiring, took off his Cap to our Batteries & made them a low bow, he then disappeared, & our fire recommenced. The gallantry of this French Officer, & his humanity, were made known to the D. of Wellington, & when the place was taken, I was sent in to count the Prisoners, & to make enquiry for the Officer. The French Commandant sent for him, & I was sitting in the Castle with the Commandant, expecting every moment the appearance of a fine Soldier-like looking fellow, as the daring achiever of the deed, when the door opened, & in came with a swimming air, an old little creature, upwards of fifty, taking snuff, & as shabby as old Elwes. He was announced to me as the Man. When I complimented him on the deed, & said the D. of Wellington had sent me for him, he answered with the most perfect nonchalance "Bah Monsieur ce n'est q'une bagatelle—c'est une petite chose que j'ai eu l'honneur de faire mille fois dans ma vie". I took him to the Duke, with whom he dined. He was restored to liberty immediately, & sent to Bayonne by Sea in a boat furnished by Sir Geo: Collyer. The Duke gave him in writing, a paper assigning his release to be owing to the gallantry of his conduct.

Our first attempt to storm St. Sebastian had failed, owing to its having been undertaken an hour or two too late for the tide. The bodies of those who fell were carried out to Sea, brought back to shore, stripped by women & Spanish Peasants, & again carried out. There is but little current in that part of the Bay of Biscay, on which St. Sebastian is situated, so that these bodies remained nearly about the same part of the coast, & were brought near the shore by the flowing tide, & carried out as it ebbed. In about three weeks, they became phospherous & luminous, & were distinctly seen at night, floating on the waters, as so many dim pale lights—painful & affecting beacons to the Soldiers who were still employed at the siege, & after the Town was taken by storm, & the French retired into the Citadel where we immediately attacked them. they could not venture out to bury their dead, but used to roll them over different parts of the Battlements, & they were thus strewed on the side of the hill on the different spots to which they had rolled.

The Army remained encamped on the Pyrenees until the 10th of October. On the 2nd of October the Garrison of Pampluna sent out proposals for capitulation, to the Spanish Army which blockaded them. They were at the last extremity of hunger, & aware of the defeats which had attended the Army, that Soult had led to their relief, they had no hope whatever of escape. Horses, Dogs, Cats, & every animal in the place had been eaten. The terms were acceded to, the Garrisons prisoners of War, & the place & Citadel delivered up to the Spaniards.[243] Thus was the right of our Army rendered more secure, by the surrender of this important fortress, the army began to prepare immediately for further operations in the field.

10th Octobr. Head Quarters moved on to Vera, the light Division & the Spanish Division attacking & carrying the heights, & driving the enemy from all his works to the Mountains of La Rhune, which is the highest point of this part of the Pyrenees. On the top of this mountain where there are the remains of a Convent. The French maintained themselves for several days. Sitting on a stone at the foot of this hill after it was carried, I passed by Col: Barnard of the Rifle Corps, who had just received a severe shot in the breast. I asked him if I could be of any service to him, to which he very faintly replied in the negative, as a Surgeon had been sent for.

I may here mention, when I was rejoining the Army of the Pyrenees, on the 25th July after the wound I received at Vitoria on the 21st of June—I passed by the road side a small bivouac made of a couple of sticks & a blanket, & I saw a wounded Officer lying there, attended to by a Servant. Such sights were too common to attract attention & I rode on. On approaching the army I found there had been a skirmish in the morning—that my Brother had been severely wounded, & that the little bivouac, I had so carelessly passed contained him. His wound was very severe, & his recovery most tedious & painful. The ball has never been extracted.

During the time that Head Quarters were at Lesaca, & before our successful attack on the height of Vera of which an account has just been given, a negotiation was entered upon for the exchange of Mr Larpent who had been taken prisoner when gazing on the field of battle at San Marcial, & I was sent in several times with a flag of truce to endeavour to effect it. but as Mr Larpent had called himself Judge Advocate General, the French believed he ranked as a General, & would not accept in exchange for him, a Commissary who had been taken some time before. However after proper representation as to the mistake, I was sent once more, took the French Commissary with me, & received the Judge Advocate in exchange. It appeared he had been terribly frightened when taken, & his health must have suffered very much, for he was miserably meagre when I received him from the French. The negotiations for his exchange, took place in one of the passes of the Pyrenees, & I was uniformly blind-folded & conducted up a rugged path, no doubt, to make me report afterwards, that the approach to these lines was very rough & difficult. But the last time I went in, the handkerchief that was bound over my eyes was tied so high, that with a little effort, I could see below, & also a very little to one side. I did not fail to avail myself of this, & I made several observations on the strength of their works & forts as I was led past them, & which afterwards proved useful. In particular, I was able to observe that they were without ditches, owing I suppose to the difficulty of making them quickly in the rock. After having been conducted to the General's hut who was very civil to me, & gave me some Beer, a liquor I had not tasted for some time, he began to ask me questions as to the state & number of our Army. Of course I added at least 10,000 to their number, & represented their state as everything that was fine. He laughed & said he knew that we were without shoes, & that the number I stated was exaggerated & that as a Staff Officer I should have known better. I then asked him, whether Staff Officers in the French service, who were sent with flags of truce, were in the habits of giving information as to the real strength & state of the French Army to an Enemy's General? He took the remark good humourably & shortly afterwards let me go. The French Officer who then took charge of me to lead me to the Out-Posts, where I had left my horse with the Trumpeter who came with me, to announce me as a flag of truce, & prevent my being fired upon, bound my eyes again, & not tight, so that I had opportunities of making further observations. When we came to the spot, where the French Sentries were placed, he unbound my eyes, & there I found several French Officers assembled who asked me, if I would sit down, & have some bottled beer with them. I consented, & we all sat down together under a tree, drinking beer, & as gay & sociable as could be, as if we had known each other all our lives. Nothing could equal the fun we had & the stories they told me. I stayed with them some time, & before we parted, they asked me whether the Duke of Wellington intended to attack their position shortly, or if he did not think it too strong to attempt. I replied, that as they knew very well, the manner in which we had taken Badajos & St. Sebastian, they could not seriously think that we considered their position too strong to attack, but that I was not at all aware of the Duke's intentions. They all laughed at this, & asked me if the Duke knew the position was defended by the gallant & invincible 28th. I said that I saw by their buttons, that was the number of their own Regiment, & that admitting their gallantry, which I had witnessed in another part of the World, as I had been present at Martinique when two of their Battalions & their Eagles were captured, I had little doubt of seeing the other two equally well taken care of. One of them, then said thoughtlessly, that we treated our prisoners badly in England, & I assured him he was mistaken, & that the representations made on that subject, were incorrect, & merely written in foreign papers, to please Bonaparte. An Officer quickly said, he supposed I meant the Emperor, to which I bowed. Before we parted, it was proposed, that I should take down their names, & they mine, & that we should agree to be kind to eath other in case of our being made prisoners by either party.

Two days afterwards, we attacked the position, & after some hard work it was carried, & a number of prisoners taken. At nightfall, & when the action was over, I rode to the fortified house near the Bridge of Vera over the Bidassoa, to count the prisoners, in order to enable the Adjutant General to make a correct report of them. On my entering the house, I was saluted with, "Ah voici notre Ami, notre cher Capitaine Browne," & I discovered that all but one of them, with whom I had conversed so gaily two days before, were prisoners. I shook hands with them, rallied them a little on the fate of the invincible 28th, & assured them of the pleasure I should feel in performing my promise to them. They were sent to Passages to be embarked for England, & I wrote to the Commandant, recommending them to his particular kindness. He was exceedingly attentive & good to them, & saw them provided with an excellent Transport & every comfort, when they were embarked, & they wrote to me a very grateful letter, now in my possession, before they sailed.

Riding back to Head Quarters after my interview with the French Officers in the fortified house, I heard a sort of groan at a short distance from the road side, proceeding as I thought from some bushes about fifty yards off. I rode to the spot, & saw a French Officer on his back apparently dead. I got off my horse to feel his hand, when he feebly opened his eyes, & repeated the same sort of moan, that had caught my attention as I was riding by. I could discover no wound, when on attempting to raise him, I saw blood at his back, & discovered that a musket shot had struck him near the spine, which had so paralysed him as to prevent his moving from the position in which he had fallen. His cap was lying near him, & his head having rested upon the ground, was already in possession of maggots, which were crawling in numbers, & had eaten into that part which touched the earth. I concluded he must have fallen, in a sharp affair of out-posts, which had taken place, three or four days before we carried the heights of Vera, & that his body had not been found before I was led to it by the groan which I had heard. I got four Soldiers to carry him to our hospital, where he lingered nearly a week without food or articulation.

During the time that the light Division was engaged near Vera, with the enemy, Sir Thomas Graham's Corps (the left of the Army) crossed the Bidassoa, at a ford near the mouth of the River, & which is passable at low water only. This ford is exactly opposite Fonterabia. It had not been guarded sufficiently by the enemy, who doubted a possibility of the passage being effected at that place. The ford is broad, & the men were in places breast high. The guns were dragged under water by ropes. When the enemy were aware that a serious passage had been effected by this ford, they collected & opposed the Column of Sir Thos. Graham, which nevertheless advanced, & after some severe skirmishing proceeded to Andaye, which is on the main road to St. Jean de Luz, & distant about two leagues from that place. A communication was then formed with the light Division on the right, who now taken position, on the heights above Vera, from which they had driven the enemy. The French retired to their bank of the Nivelle, which River runs close to the town of St. Jean de Luz, where there is a bridge over it. There is also another bridge over this river, near Ascain, about two leagues higher up. The loss of the British in the passage of the Bidassoa this Day & in the attack of the heights of Vera, was about 900 men, & of the Portuguese not so many. The line of the British Army was now, with its left wing resting on the Sea, its Centre upon the heights of Vera, & its right on the tops of the Roncesvalles pass. Of the enemy, his right, was on the Sea, at St. Jean de Luz (his advance in front of this place & close to Andaye) his Centre near Ascain, & his left at St. Jean Pied de Port. The river Nivelle was in front of his position & ran nearly along the foot of it. Works & batteries were thrown up in every direction, & the whole attention of the enemy was evidently taken up, in rendering their new position as formidable as possible. He worked night & day. Sir Thomas Graham here gave up his command; his eyesight having suffered so much as to render his absence necessary. Sir John Hope assumed the command of the 1st Division & left Column, & became second in command of the Army. About this time, considerable reinforcements & detachments arrived from England, which the great losses sustained by the Army, in the operations of the last 3 months had rendered highly necessary. Head Quarters remained at Vera till the 10th of November, & this interval was occupied in reconnoitring the different roads which led into France, & preparing the Troops for fresh marches—refreshing the horses—repairing the Artillery, & in the different Regiments, the Tailors & Shoemakers were at work, refitting everything for a fresh campaign. The men were drilled & exercised, & whenever the weather would permit they broke up from their encampments for the day, & marched for a league or two—then returned, pitched their tents again, & occupied themselves as usual. The Army was in excellent health.

About this time I was sent into the French Lines with a flag of Truce with two of their Captains who had been severely wounded. One had had his leg amputated above the knee, & the other below. These operations had been performed with so much skill, that it was considered sufficiently safe to send them to their friends in ten days after they had taken place. They were exceedingly grateful for the treatment they had received. The Regiment at the French Outposts was one of the Corps of the Duke of Nassau, which afterwards came over to us in a body. I had much conversation with several of their Officers, who appeared heartily tired of the service in which they were engaged.

A considerable body of our Troops being encamped on the Pyrenees in sight, & within gun-shot of the French picquets, every sort of temptation was thrown in the way of our men to induce them to desert. Printed papers in English, German, Spanish, & Portuguese were found without our lines, & the effects they produced were not altogether unsuccessful.[244] The weather was cold & raw, & the duty of the Outposts severe & those who had any cause for discontent, of whom there are always plenty to be met with in an Army, thought they saw a remedy for discontent in quitting their Colors. They were miserably disappointed. A Deserter, is ever suspected, even by the power to whom he deserts, & after the Enemy's General had gained from these culprits, all the information they were able, they were thrown into the same prison with their Country-men who had been taken prisoners in the honorable discharge of their duty, & exposed to all the reproaches & contempt from them which their unsoldierlike conduct deserved. These Deserters, were afterwards formed into a Corps & marched in the depth of Winter against the Allies—many of them perished, many deserted again to the Allies, & the remainder have been delivered up to their Country, since the Peace. The Soldiers who deserted from the Enemy to the British, were most of them enlisted into Regiments serving in the West Indies, & out of them have been formed the 7th & 8th Battalions of the 60th Regmt.[245] The Spanish Army which had been occupied at the Blockade of Pampluna, were now enabled to advance to the Pyrenees, since the surrender of that Fortress, which was delivered up in the highest possible order & immediately garrisoned by 3,000 Spaniards.

The strength of the Allied Army at this time, actually under Arms & in the field was,

Cavalry	British	7,000	
Do.	Portuguese	1,000	
Infantry	British	35,000	
Do.	Portuguese	19,000	
Do.	Spaniards	16,000	
Artillery	British	2,000 men & 70 pieces of Cannon	
Do.	Portuguese	400 do. & 24 do.	
Do.	Spanish	200 do. 14 do.	

This was the Army under the command of the Marquis of Wellington. The Army had abundance of provisions, but were badly clothed, & forage for the Horses & Mules was exceedingly scarce & of bad quality.

10th of November. The position of the enemy on the right bank of the Nivelle having been reconnoitred, & the weather for the last three days, having become more favorable, Ld. Wellington determined to attempt this day the passage of the Nivelle, & to drive the enemy from St. Jean de Luz. The attack began at day-light.[246] Sir John Hope's Corps moved on the main road from Andaye to St. Jean de Luz, & was very severely cannonaded from the forts & redoubts constructed by the enemy on that road. Several of these redoubts were taken in succession. The attack of the Centre began by an advance of the light Division against Petite La Rhune, which had been occupied & kept by the enemy from the day on which they were driven from the Mountains of La Rhune itself. The Light Division moved on to the attack covered by their advanced Skirmishers, & such was the rapidity of their movement, that they captured the whole of the Tents of the enemy's encampment on the Hill, which the French had not time to carry off. The 4th & 7th Divisions moved against the position of Sara which the French had made exceedingly strong, & after an obstinate engagement, this strong Fort was carried, & a Redoubt in which was the 1st Battalion of the French 88th Regiment was surrounded. The Spanish Corps of General Downie following in rear of the 7th Division, the care of this Redoubt, in which the French Battalion had been thus inclosed, was entrusted to them, & the British marched on in pursuit of the retiring enemy. The Spanish General immediately sent a flag of truce into the Redoubt, proposing to the French Commander, to surrender, & a apprizing him that he was surrounded by 4,000 Spaniards, & totally cut off from all communication with the French Army. The Frenchman sent for answer, that tho' he were surrounded by the whole Spanish Army, he & his men were resolved to perish with their Arms in their hands & to sell their lives as dearly as possible, rather than surrender to the Spaniards, but that if a single British company were sent to him, he, with the Battalion under his command would immediately lay down their Arms. In vain the Spanish General represented the insult thus offered to him, & threatened to carry the Redoubt by assault, & put every Frenchman to the sword that was found in it. The French 88th Regiment manned the Parapet & were prepared to receive the Spanish Assault. The drums and trumpets of the Don sounded the Assault, & everything was bustle & confusion in the Spanish Ranks—The Officers hollorring out to their men, not to *come* on, but to *go* on, & the men—very unwilling to shew so much disrespect to their Officers as to take the lead & this continuing, until the Spaniards found themselves at the end of their assault, *further* from the Battery than when they began it. The French coolly pointing their muskets over the Parapet, & looking at them. This scene was repeated, & all attempts to induce this Spanish Division to close with the enemy having entirely failed, a Company of the 43rd was sent for, to whom the French immediately laid down their Arms, on the sole condition, that when disarmed & Prisoners, they should be marched to the rear by a British escort, which was granted them. The Battalion consisted of one Colonel 42 Officers & 700 men. They were immediately sent off to the rear under an escort of the 18th Hussars, & remained that night in the fortified house near the bridge of Vera, on their route to Passage for embarkation. Sir John Hope had thus advanced on the road to St. Jean de Luz, whilst the 4th & 7th Divisions, the former commanded by Sir Lowry Cole & the latter by Ld. Dalhousie, carried the position of Sara & moved on towards St. Pee. The 6th Division in the mean time moved from the pass of Maya to Urlache, & carried, in the most determined & gallant manner, a range of fortified heights, the right of which rested on Sara. They therefore, after carrying these heights closed upon the column of the 4th & 7th Divisions. Sir Henry Clinton commanded the 6th Division. The 3rd Division under Sir Thos. Picton, moved down from the pass of Maya, at the same time with the 6th Division & directed its march to Zagarramundi, which place it occupied after a sharp skirmish. The Corps under Sir Rowland Hill moved on Cambo, from the pass in the Pyrenees where it had been encamped, & also met with considerable opposition. Every part of the British line was warmly engaged, & the French disputed obstinately every knoll & rising ground—but were compelled to give way, after immense loss—night came on, & the position of the British Army after this day's victory was as follows:

The Right on a height near Cambo—the Centre near the village of St. Pee—the Spaniards at Ascain, & neighborhood—the Left in front of Andaye, but had not occupied St. Jean de Luz. The Nivelle had been passed, & the enemy had already crossed the Nive, to the banks of which river our Cavalry followed, that night. The enemy however, still held the village of Cambo, on the left bank of the Nive—and St. Jean de Luz, but they evacuated the latter place on the following day, after a fruitless attempt to burn the bridge over the Nivelle, which separates the Town into two parts. Sir John Hope's Corps then moved up to St. Jean de Luz, & his advance was sent on as far as Bieritz, about 2 Leagues from Bayonne. Sir Rowland Hill also drove the enemy out of Cambo & across the Nive on the following day, two hours before day-light of which day an Officer of the Quarter Master General's department & myself were ordered to repair to an old ruined Convent on the top of Petite La Rhune to be ready to observe the Sun-rise & send down an instant report, if we observed any change to have taken place in the enemy's positions from those which he had occupied on the preceding evening at sun-set.[247] We were conducted to this old building by a Spanish Peasant. It was so dark, that we could see nothing before us, but the path appeared perfectly familiar to him, & we arrived within the Convent walls in perfect safety. Just as the Sun was rising, we climbed up an old Turret, which had once supported the Convent Bell, & as day-light gradually appeared it opened to our view the most magnificent spectacle that it is possible to conceive in a bird's-eye view of the two hostile Armies. The French occupied the same ground, on which they had bivouac'd for several preceding days, with the report of which we instantly descended to Ld. Wellington. The loss of the British in the action of the 10th was 4,000 killed & wounded, in which were 200 Officers. Col: Bernard of the 95th was severely wounded in the attack of the light Division on the Petite La Rhune—Head Quarters moved to St. Pee.

11th Novbr. Head Quarters, St. Pee. The position of the British Army this day, was as nearly as possible, as follows—

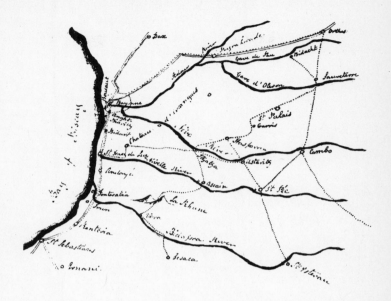

2nd Division & Portuguese Do.	at Cambo
3rd 4th 6th & 7th	at St Pee, Ustaritz, &c
Light Do.	at Tyatyce &c
1st & 5th Divisions	at Biaritz
Spaniards	at Ascain
Head Quarters	St Pee

12th Novbr. Head Quarters moved to St. Jean de Luz. This is a considerable Town, & is about half way between Bayonne & St. Sebastians. It is preserved from the incroachments of the Sea, by a considerable wall which is built on the Sea-shore, on the top of which is a pleasant walk.[248] Ships of burthen, cannot enter the Fort of St. Jean de Luz, but are obliged to go to Socoa, about a mile further, & on a point of land that juts into the Sea. Here is a good basin capable of holding about

20 sail of Ships of from 200 to 400 tons burthen. It is dangerous for larger vessels to attempt the entrance of Socoa. There are excellent Pilots here, who put to Sea on the approach of Ships. Socoa is defended by a stone Fort & Castle, with a battery for nine pieces of Cannon. It is surrounded on the land side, by a ditch and wall, over which there is a draw bridge. On the other side, the foot of the Fort is washed by the Sea. There is no approach for Boats, on account of the very high Surf. St. Jean de Luz is not defensible against an army. The people in the place do not generally talk French, but the Basque language, which is one of the most difficult perhaps in Europe. The road from Bayonne to this place, & from St. Jean de Luz to Irun is excellent. There is a good Fish-Market here. The enemy were at this time at work in Bayonne, adding to its strength on every side, & occupied in the formation of a Fortified camp, between the Nive & the Adour, across the neck of land near which the former river joins the latter. Head Quarters remained at St. Jean de Luz until the 23rd of February, during which time, the enemy were constantly on the alert, & creating alarms on every point of our line. On the 8th of December, it was ascertained that Soult had arrived at Bayonne, & that he was assembling all the force he could spare from observation of the ford over the Gave de Pau, & Gave d'Oleron, & that he had declared he would drive the English out of St. Jean de Luz, which Lord Wellington, had declared by proclamation a free Port, & which was immediately resorted to by Vessels from the Coast of Spain, with all sorts of provisions & stores for the Army. The Duc d'Angouleme[249] also had arrived & was at work printing proclamations, exhorting the French to shake off the yoke of an Usurper, & to join the Standard of their Ancient Kings. These proclamations were printed, but Ld. Wellington being aware, that negociations for peace were at that time impending at Chatillon,[250] would not permit their circulation. He did not object to their being printed & held in readiness for such time, as their being issued might be prudent & allowable; but until it was officially announced, that the negociations at Chatillon were at an end, he would not permit any proclamation against Bonaparte, with whom the British Government were then treating as the Emperor of the French. Ld. Wellington's own sentiments were however decidedly favorable to the Bourbons. Soult made all his preparations for attack on the 8th of December, & on the 9th at day-break, moved on with his masses of Infantry & attacked the 1st & 5th Divisions, who were on the main road from St. Jean de Luz to Bayonne, at Bidart.[251] These Troops made a

gallant stand, but were obliged to give ground to superiority of numbers for a short distance. The enemy moved on as far as the Mayor's house of Bidart, where we had a strong body posted in a wood. In this wood, there was a terrible carnage; a gap in a hedge which led to it was taken by the French, & retaken many times, & a small house in the wood shared the same fate. The French had occupied this house in the morning, & under its cover had formed unseen by the British, a strong body, which afterwards gained the wood. At night fall, the wood & the house were retaken, & it being thought adviseable, to pull down the House, to prevent the enemy availing themselves again of its cover to form their Columns, in the event of their being able to drive us from it, it was taken down during the night, & at day-light not a trace of it was left. The enemy missing the house, were evidently surprised at its removal. Our loss on the 9th was about 900 men. The enemy gained ground, early in the day, & kept it until about three o'clock, when they were driven back, & each Army occupied its position of the day before.

10th Decbr. At day-break this morning Soult renewed the attack & moved a Column to our left, along a slip of land, close to the Sea-shore which was divided from the main road to Bayonne by a small Lake, which was situated below the house of the Mayor of Biaritz. The object of the enemy was evidently to get possession of Bidart, which from Bayonne, would have been a position for the French, as it is upon a hill, looking from the road to St. Jean de Luz from Bayonne, & would have been an important post to the enemy. The position of the left of the British & the right of the enemy on this day was as follows:*

The enemy moved his Columns on both sides of the Lake opposite the Mayor's house, & at the same time on their left of the main road from St. Jean de Luz, to Bayonne. They were here opposed by the 1st & 5th Divisions, and on the day, as on yesterday a considerable affair took place near the Mayor's house. The 4th Division was continued under Arms the whole Day ready to move to their left, to the support of the 1st & 5th divisions, should circumstances render that movement necessary. About noon however, the Enemy, not having succeeded in his attempts on the Mayor's house, gave up the contest, & both Armies, once more moved back, & occupied their respective positions, before the battle of the 7th & remained quiet for the night.

11th Decbr. Day-light this morning discovered both Armies under Arms, the British expecting to be attacked. The French Skirmishers

* Sketch map overleaf.

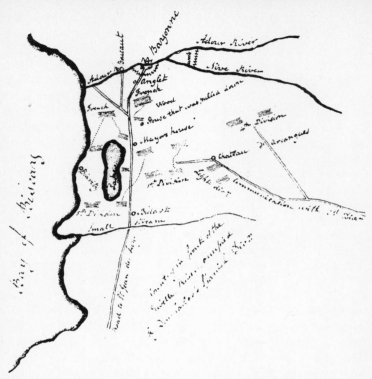

moved on & began their fire, which was returned by the light Companies
of the Guards, who were posted at & near the Mayor's house. This light
firing lasted until mid-day, when the enemy's advance retired, & the
French Army began to cook. Not anything more was attempted this day,
but the line remained under Arms.

12th Decbr. The Armies remain, as at Sun-set yesterday evening, but
it was observed that movements were taking place in the Columns in
their rear. Ld. Wellington in order to ascertain the nature of these
manoeuvres, ordered the advanced Troops of the French to be driven
in, which they were, & the enemy was found to be occupied in moving
large Bodies of Troops into Bayonne; our pressing him however, caused
a halt in these operations, & he drew out his line, supposing our
intentions to be more serious than in reality they were. Our troops
pressed on, & gained the village of Haut Anglet, within a mile & a half of
Bayonne. This was too close to the enemy's work to render any further

Officer, 31st Light Infantry, 1812.

Pierre Leroux, Chasseur, 1st Light Infantry, 1809.

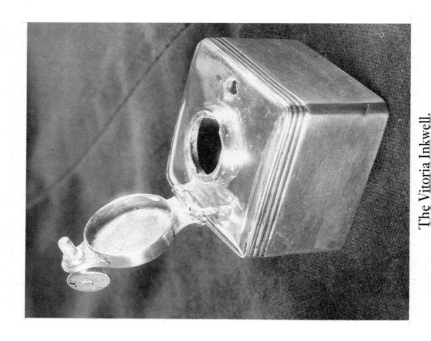

The Vitoria Inkwell.

Bookplate of Sir Thomas Henry Browne.

British Troops Storming St Sebastian, September 1813 (1813).

T. W. N. McNiven, *Sir Henry Clinton and Staff Before Bayonne, December 1813* (1813).

advance, at present prudent. Nothing further passed this day, but a Staff Officer arrived from the right of the Army, with the intelligence, that the position of Sir Rowland Hill, who was across the Nive, advanced close to Bayonne in that direction, had been well reconnoitred by Marshal Soult this Day. The 6th Division was immediately ordered across the Nive, & to form a reserve to Sir Rowland Hill's Corps, & to act as circumstances should require. The 4th Division also broke up from their Camp, on the right of the Major's house, & moved to Ustaritz, where there is a bridge over the Nive, & from which place they might be able to act in concert with the 6th Division if necessary. We began also to throw up batteries & entrenchments to cover our position near the Mayor's house, which was now rendered weaker, by the movement of the 4th division from its right.

13th Decbr. This morning during a thick fog, the enemy moved out of Bayonne, & attacked Sir Rowland Hill, in a most desperate manner, & in the first hour, succeeded in driving him back. But having been reinforced by the 6th Divn. coming closer up in his rear he assumed the offensive, & the Brigade of M. General Barnes, consisting of the 50th 71st & 92nd Regiments, charged the enemy in so gallant a style with the Bayonet, that he began to give way. This blow was quickly followed up by General Pringle's Brigade, & the French now fled in all directions. Their loss was immense. The ground was as thickly strewed with dead, as at the battle of the Pyrenees on the 28th of July. They continued their hasty flight into Bayonne, pursued by Sir R. Hill as closely to that Citadel, as their works & batteries would allow. This was the second occasion on which General Barnes had eminently distinguished himself, by his cool bravery & determination. Having been left by the 50th Regiment for a few minutes he remained in the middle of the road with his hat in his hand, & called to them to advance again. The Men immediately obeyed the voice of their General, & he headed them in a successful charge. The 6th Division arrived too late, to take any part in this day's action, which was gained by Sir Rowland Hill's Corps exclusively. The loss of the British this Day, had been about 2,000 men, & now ended the series of actions, which had been fought on the 9th 10th 11th 12th & 13th of December, on which days, the two Armies had been constantly under Arms and engaged with more or less severity. The loss of the British during this time exceeded 6,000 men, whilst that of the French was about the same number. They lost 3,500 in the action with Sir Rowland Hill on the 13th. On the 9th Sir John Hope personally

& highly distinguished himself. Seeing the 47th Regiment yield to the pressure of a considerable body of the Enemy near the Mayor's house, he flew into the hottest of the fire, & with his hat in his hand cheered the Men, led them back to the front, & by his own personal courage & efforts at this important moment, preserved to the British the town of Bidart, which, once occupied by the Enemy, could not, from its very commanding position, have been regained without considerable difficulty & loss, & the possession of it, would have secured to the Enemy that very advantage, which had been decidedly the object of his attack on the 9th. Sir John Hope was wounded in the instep, & tho' in great pain, did not quit the field, & was on horse-back again, the following morning, at the head of his Corps. His conduct this day, endeared him more than ever to the Army, in which his character already stood high. The enemy had now retired into Bayonne & its outworks, & employed themselves night & day, in adding to the strength of the place. Bayonne is a fortification of the first class by Vauban, & the Citadel is in the highest possible state of preservation. The Troops which were at this time destined for the Garrison of this place, & its fortified Camp, were the 3rd Division under General Abbé, which was about 6,000 effective men. the services of this division were exclusively given to the defence & duties of the Camp. a provincial Battalion formed of the 118th 120th & 122nd French Regiments was also attached to General Abbé's command, to assist his division in their duties. The Garrison of the Citadel, & work of the Town was of 9,000 Men, & the Governor of the place was General Thuvenot. There were provisions as the French themselves said, for a year in the place, which being exceedingly strong, & garrisoned by about 17,000 Men, Ld. Wellington foresaw at once, how much time would be lost, & how many lives must necessarily be sacrificed, if the siege of the place should be undertaken. He resolved therefore, that when the Adour should be passed,[252] so as to enable our Troops to get at the other side of the Town, a blockade should be established, & the troops which were to form that blockade were to consist of the 1st & 5th Divisions, General Bradford, & Pack's Portuguese Brigades, Ld. Alymer's Brigade, & Don Carlos's Division of Spaniards. Head Quarters was moved back again to St. Jean de Luz. The weather had become so very severe, as to prevent all idea of operations for the present. The roads, except the main road to Bayonne, became almost impassable, & in the transport of provisions, on Mules, from the Fort of Passages & from St. Jean de Luz to the several divisions on the right of the Army, a great number of these animals perished, from the depth of the roads, the scarcity of forage, & the extreme severity of the weather. The roads of communiciation were literally so deep, as to be nearly impassable, & the dead bodies of the Mules in all directions added to their difficulties. The Troops went into Cantonments as near their respective positions, as the vicinity of Villages or Houses would admit. The cavalry went to the rear, beyond Pampluna & their Head Quarters, were established at Tassalla. It was quite impossible to find forage for so large a body of cavalry in the front. Once more then, the Troops were in houses, & the great work of Shoemaking & mending, & repairing Clothes began. Grey watch-coats that were worn out, & in holes, were cut up to mend red coats. The Army was in a terrible plight for want of Clothing, & the Men had every Color on their backs, that would have done Harlequin credit.[253]

A considerable quantity of clothing, had however arrived at Passages from England, & small vessels were despatched from St. Jean de Luz to bring it to the latter place. As it arrived the different Corps or Regiments were allowed to come down from the lines of St. Jean de Luz, where they arrived successively. The day they marched into St. Jean de Luz, they halted, the day after they clothed from head to foot, & the day after that, they began their march to the Army. This operation lasted, until nearly all the Army were newly clothed. The scene of this operation was not a little amusing, & the wit of the Soldiers, at thus changing as it were their skins, was exerted to the utmost. Caps, Jackets, Trowsers, everything old, was thrown away,[254] & the Army soon appeared as gay as it had ever done. The men became comfortable & warm, & the quantity & quality of the vermin, they thus got rid of, was sufficient, as they themselves owned, to cause their becoming fat & plump in a very short time. The Town of St. Jean de Luz, became thus a sort of depôt of the Stores & clothing of the Army. Shops were established in every House, & every sort of comfort & necessary very soon arrived from England, & so great was the number of Speculators who arrived, that their competition rendered the price of Articles much more moderate, than the necessities of the Army would otherwise have forced them to pay. Houses were let by their owners for very large sums, & a single room, fronting a Street would produce six Dollars a week, for the purpose of being converted into a Shop. The Officers of Head Quarters, & those whose duty called them, or kept them at St. Jean de Luz, were of course quartered upon the inhabitants & paid nothing for lodgings. The two Brigades of

Guards were billetted in the place, as well as Head Quarters. Their strength was about 3,500 Men. General Howard was in command of one Brigade & General Stopford of the other. By this time a much better understanding prevailed, between the Troops & the inhabitants of this part of France, than at our first entry into the counry, owing to the strict discipline established by Ld. Wellington & to the great activity of the Provost Marshals of the different divisions of the Army. The powers of the Provost Marshal of an Army are very considerable. He has life & death in his hands, & in case of his seeing a soldier in the act of plundering, there is no need of Court Martial or evidence, but with his Cord ready, like his early Prototypes, Trois Echelles & Petit André, the culprit is suspended on the nearest Tree.[255] Such extensive power, is considered necessary to prevent that system of plunder, which if permitted, would not only tend to arm an exasperated population against an Army, which like ours in Spain, professed to come as Allies, but the discipline of the Army would soon have an end, & the ranks be deserted. I have never heard of an instance, where the exercise of this power, has been thought to exceed what discipline & the moral existence of an Army required. It was had recourse to in frequent instances, after we crossed the Pyrenees, into France as friends of the Bourbons, but the necessity for it gradually diminished, as the Men ceased from plundering. Morillo's Spaniards plundered a good deal at Morales; three were taken in the act. The D. of Wellington ordered the Division to assemble, & form in Square which he entered with some of his Staff, caused these three men to be produced, marched round the Square, & shot by their Comrades.[256] The Spaniards were white in the face with astonishment when commanded to put this order into excecution, but the Duke remained steady in the midst of them, it was carried into effect, & he rode slowly away.

During the time we were in winter quarters in St. Jean de Luz, we had Divine Service every Sunday in a field near the Sea. The D. of Wellington & all the Officers of Head Quarters attended. A Hollow square was formed by a Brigade of Infantry quartered in the Town, & under the Colors of one of the Regiments, was placed a big drum for a reading desk. A Serjeant acted as Clerk & Prayers were then offered up. The attention of Officers & Soldiers was exemplary, & doubly so when Psalms & Lessons were selected alluding to our situation, or to the uncertain tenure by which we held our lives. There was something affecting in the simplicity of this form of Worship, the most reverent we had it in our power to show to Him, who had been our constant Protector. The same service was performed every Sunday when we were not fighting, with every Brigade & Division of the Army. It is singular enough that most of our great battles were fought on Sunday— Salamanca, Vitoria—Albuera—Badajos—Orthes & Thoulouse. I do not remember ever to have seen the Sacrament adminstered on any occasion of Sunday Divine Service.

The French Officers who were taken prisonners in the Peninsular war, were for the most part ungentlemenlike men, tho' there were some exceptions, & as they were encouraged by Napoleon, to break their Paroles; they considered their word of honor as a mere form and made no sort of scruple of acting as if it were so. The Adjutant Genl. of our Army, drew up a written form for a Parole of Honor, which he required every French Officer to sign, before he was sent to the rear, if he wished to go without a guard. It was part of my duty to receive the signatures of this paper, as everything relating to prisonners of War is in the department of the Adjutant General. Even these written Paroles were frequently violated, & the little anecdote I am about to relate, shews under what aggravated circumstances such violation could take place. In the Action of the 12th December, we made many Prisonners, & amongst the rest a Chef de Bataillon,[257] an elderly Man, who appeared very much dejected. Head Quarters were at that time in St. Jean de Luz. His appearance interested me, & after he had signed his Parole, I asked him to come & breakfast with me. He did so, and I was otherwise kind to him. The following day it was ordered that they should be sent to the rear, to Vitoria under an Escort, as there were a good many Soldiers prisonners also, who were to be sent at the same time. When the order for moving was announced to the Chef de Bataillon, he most earnestly requested to see me, & the Provost Marshal having brought him to me, he burst into tears, said that his Wife & Children were at Bayonne, that they depended entirely on him for support, that he felt quite sure, that if he could send a letter to Marshal Soult by a flag of truce, he would be immediately exchanged, & he conjured me by everything that was dear to me to allow him to remain at Head Quarters, until an answer to his letter, should be received from Bayonne, which was but 65 miles distant. I represented to him the impossibility of my acceding to his request, as the order I had received from the Adjutant Genl. to send him & others from Head Quarters was peremptory, & that my Commission would be forfeited by disobedience of these orders. He threw himself at my feet, wept bitterly, & shewed such marks of absolute despair, that having just ascertained, that a Flag of Truce, was going in with letters, I gave him leave to write his letter, & it was sent with others. I then told him that I took upon myself to permit his remaining, until sufficient time should elapse, for his receiving an answer, & that I considered two days, as the utmost I dare allow him. I represented to him that should he attempt to escape, & break his Parole, I should immediately lose my Commission, & begged of him to keep as quiet as possible. He professed his gratitude in the most affecting manner, & went away. I had him afterwards to dine with me, & desired the Provost Marshal to attend to his comforts. The next morning I sent for him again to breakfast with me, & after long expectation of my quest, I found, that during the night, he had succeeded in procuring the dress of a Peasant, & had made his escape. The name of this fellow was Joubert. I immediately went to Sir E. Pakenham the Adjt. General, & related to him the whole circumstance. He was good enough to promise me not to mention it to the D. of Wellington, & told me, he hoped it would be a warning to me for the future, strictly to obey my orders, & not to listen to the tales of such unprincipled fellows, as most of the French Officers were. The conduct of this man, was of great disservice to other French Officers who fell into our hands on future occasions

14th December. General Hill established his Head Quarters at Cambo, with one Brigade in front of that place. The bad weather continued, which rendered the arrival of supplies for the army very uncertain & insecure. The surf was so high on the coast from Passages to St. Jean de Luz, that the small craft could not always venture out; & on them we were greatly dependent for provisions, as the state of the roads had rendered the Mule Transport so difficult. During our stay in St. Jean de Luz, Ld. Wellington determined, that when the weather would at all permit, he would attempt the passage of the Adour, & he rode out constantly to reconnoitre such parts of the country, as would lead to its banks—& also the river itself below the town of Bayonne, where it empties itself into the Sea, & where it is about one hundred & twenty yards across. Perhaps there are few rivers where passage for a body of Troops, could be attended with more difficulties than the Adour. The right of our Army, in order to cross to their front, had to pass the Gaves d'Oleron & de Pau, both deep streams, before they could arrive at the banks of the Adour. Bodies of French Troops defended the Fords over the two Gaves, which the rains had also rendered more deep, & rapid than usual, & the roads which led to the Fords were in the most dreadful state.

Below the Town of Bayonne, where the left of our Army, must necessarily have passed, in order to facilitate the operations of the right of the Army, the river was exceedingly broad, & influenced by the rise & fall of the Tide to a great degree. The mouth of the river moreover was so near to the town of Bayonne, where there was a Garrison of 17,000 men, that the attempt to pass the river so near this large body, would of course, be attended with great risk & difficulty. Ld. Wellington was not long however in forming his plans. St. Jean de Luz was distant from the mouth of the Adour, along the shore, about two leagues & a half. A plan was laid for boats to enter the mouth of the Adour, for the purpose of forming a bridge over that river, a little above the place where they should enter, & that every material should be immediately prepared for the purpose. Admiral Penrose, who had relieved Sir George Collyer on his station, was sent for & consulted on the subject. The Admiral & Ld. Wellington rode together without any suite so that they should be the less an object of observation, to the mouth of the Adour, that they might form an accurate judgement of the breadth of the river, it's rapidity & the effect produced upon the stream, by the rise & fall of the Tides. After a mature consideration, the following plan was determined upon, for the construction of the intended bridge. Forty two boats of the country, each having two Masts, & about ten tons burthen, were to be collected. They were to cross the bar at the mouth of the Adour, when the weather should render it possible, which occured very rarely. They were to be moored with their bows to the stream, a little below the village of Boucaut, on the opposite bank. Another Anchor was to be thrown out from the Stern of each Boat, to keep her steady, when the tide entered the river; being thus moored, head & stern they would remain firm. Over these boats, two large Cables were to be thrown, resting on their decks, & secured to their masts on the inside, but not tied tightly to the Masts. On these Cables planks were to be laid, & having holes bored in them for the purpose, they were to be tied down to the Cables. On each side of the river was to be erected a strong Windlass, for the purpose of taking in whatever slack might be caused on the Cables, by the operation of the weather or other causes. The passage was to be between the Masts of these boats. A Boom was to be prepared, to be thrown across the river, above the Bridge, & to be defended by three Gun-boats, in order to stop any Fire-Ship or combustible Body which might be sent down the river by the enemy, for the purpose of affecting the destruction of the Bridge. The sketch which follows may convey some idea of the formation of the Bridge, protected by the three Gun-boats and the Boom in front of them.

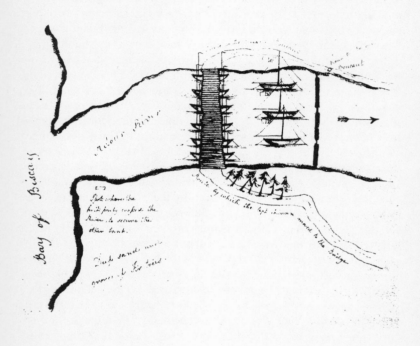

Each boat on leaving St. Jean de Luz, was to contain the planks and materials to connect her with the next boat, & on their being moored the bulwarks of the boats were to be cut away, so as to give a Level for the Cables and planks to rest upon. The Boom was also to be constructed at St. Jean de Luz, & when completed to be towed out of that harbour, & to be lashed, in three or four pieces as most convenient to unite afterwards with little loss of time, to the sides of some light Transports (three Brigs) which were to enter the Adour, at the same time with the little Fleet. Such were the preparations which occupied the attention of all ranks, during our stay at St. Jean de Luz. Soldiers and Sailors (of whom forty were sent from the Squadron under Admiral Penrose) assisted in rigging out the Boom, preparing & stretching the cables.[258]—On the right & centre of the Army Sir Roland Hill's Corps was occupied in mending the roads in his front, & Sir Lowry Cole was busied with the 4th Division, in the same manner. The roads were so very deep, that the only means of repairing them, was found to be with Boughs, Trunks & branches of Trees, & the progress of each work was very tedious. The roads of communication however were much benefited by it.

In the mean time the reverses of the French Armies in the North,[259] began to make considerable impression, & in proportion as these reverses became more serious, the opinion of the people in many places, began to waver, as to the possibility of their keeping their ground much longer. Every means was resorted to by the French Generals to keep these events as secret as possible, but letters from their Comrades who were in the field with the Emperor, from time to time, made them acquainted with the true state of affairs, & by no means contributed to rouse the spirits of the Army in our front, which had been beaten so frequently. The foreign Troops in the French service began to desert in considerable numbers, & on the 16th of December, two entire Regiments, viz: two Battalions of the Nassau Regiment, came over to us in the night, with their arms and equipments complete. Their Adjutant had been sent into the British Lines, about two hours before, to prepare us for the arrival of these two Regiments. They were in front of the 4th Division, & Sir L. Cole when he received the message from their Commander, put the 4th Division under Arms, to guard against surprise, & by this Division they were received. These two Regiments were about 11,000 Men of a remarkably fine description, & all old Soldiers. They marched to Passages on the following day, & were embarked for England, for the purpose of proceeding to their native country through Holland, where the revolution in favor of the Statholder had now declared itself. They sailed two Days after they had quitted the French, & arrived in Holland on their route home, in one fortnight from the time they had come over to Ld. Wellington's Army. There was another foreign Regiment viz: that of Baden also in our front. Marshal Soult alarmed at the defection of the Nassau Regiments, had the Regiment of Baden marched to the rear, where they were disarmed, & sent [as] prisoners to the interior. His precautions were right & justifiable. It was certainly the intention of the Regiment to have come over to us, the very first opportunity which should present itself. The name of the Commander who brought away the two Nassau Regiments, was Col. Kreuse. He stated that he had received positive orders from his Sovereign, the Prince of Nassau, to quit the French Army and go over to the British, the moment he should find a proper occasion. This order had been sent to him, & delivered by an Aid de Camp of the Prince of Nassau. Colonel Kreuse was well known to several Officers of the German Legion, with our Army. The desertion from the foreign Troops in the different Regiments of the Line, became very considerable, after the arrival with us of the Nassau Regiments, Poles, Germans, & Italians, came over to us, seven & eight a day, frequently.[260] The disasters of the French Army at Leipzig had previously been made known to us, in the hollow of a Cane which was thrown over the Bidassoa to one of our advanced Sentries on our bank of that river.

Everything being prepared for the passage of the Adour, & the weather proving favourable, Ld. Wellington after inspecting all the preparations on the left, & giving the necessary instructions, proceeded to the right of the Army, leaving Sir John Hope in command of the left to put into execution which had been determined upon as the operation of that part of the Army. His presence on the right was the more necessary, as the obstacles in front of the Gaves d'Oleron & de Pau, which Ld. Wellington had resolved to pass in order the more effectually to divert the Enemy's attention from Sir John Hope, & thus to render his operations the less difficult, were very considerable. These two Gaves, which empty themselves into the Adour, near Peyrehorade were very deep, the roads to them very bad, & the enemy shewed a determination to oppose the passage. On the 23rd of February, the fleet which composed the Bridge, protected by two Frigates, & some Sloops of War, appeared off the mouth of the Adour, & about the same time Ld. Wellington began the advance of the right of the Army, making his Head Quarters Hasparren. He crossed the Gave d'Oleron with the Troops, & established himself at Sauveterre, pushing the advance to the banks of the Gave de Pau, almost opposite the Town of Orthes, & remained with the right of the Army in this position, until the 26th of February. The little Fleet on the left, in the mean time, & on the 23d of February, after cruizing close to the mouth of the River for a length of time, without being able to discover its entrance, owing to the very high Surf which broke at some distance from the shore, sent off several boats for the purpose of ascertaining the exact point they were to make for, to enable them to enter the river. Two Men of War's boats were sent off to make the attempt, but both were unfortunately upset, & their Crews perished. Captn. Elliot of the Martial, Brig of War, lost his life in one of them and Mr Bloye, Master's Mate of the Lyra. A boat from a Transport, shared the same fate. At length, a Flag was brought down on the shore, & hoisted exactly opposite the spot, which seemed the least subject to the constant & tremendous Surf, as a point for the little Fleet to direct itself upon, & one of the boats which was to form the bridge, at length ventured thro' the Surf & after almost disapperaring, & when every one thought she was gone to the bottom, she rose again, & entered the River. Her Crew had tied themselves to the Masts, & were not washed away. Her entrance into the river was greeted with three cheers by the Troops, & she received a reward of 50 guineas, which had been decreed to the boat which should first enter. The Crews of the Boats outside, heard the cheers, & concluded she was safe in the River, pushed on for the spot, where she had ventured in, & after a most anxious & perilous passage thro' the surf which breaks on the bar, at the mouth of the River, the whole of the boats got in, except three which perished in the Surf. Two Transport Brigs with stores for the Bridge, also got in, & a third was dashed on shore in making the attempt: her cargo however was equally of use, as she was thrown on shore, at a very convenient spot for taking out her stores. The Gun-boats also effected the passage in safety, & the whole proceeded about half a mile up the river, protected by the troops, to the spot assigned for the bridge to be laid. Anticipating the arrival of the bridge on the 23d, Sir J. Hope had, on the night of the 21st caused Pontoons to be brought to the left bank of the river, & at day-break he commenced passing over some of the Guards, near the mouth of the river, in these Pontoons, for the purpose of taking up a position on the other bank, under cover of the Artillery on our bank, & thus securing both sides of the river for the free entrance of the boats on the 23d. He had succeeded in passing over about 500 Men of the Guard under Col: Cotton, by about 3 o'clock on the evening of the 22nd, when a column was observed coming out of Bayonne, on the same side of the river with those men who had been passed over, for the purpose of attacking them. This Column was about 1,500, & were advancing rapidly upon the 500 British, who were thus separated from the main body of the left Corps of the Army, & on the opposite bank of the river. It was not possible to pass over any Artillery or Cavalry in these small pontoons. Sir John Hope therefore sent over a number of Rockets, which had newly arrived with our Army, & the 500 British having put thermselves in position, within range of the Guns on our bank of the river, made little works for throwing off the Rockets, & waited the approach of the French, who advanced in one Column, covered by their Skirmishers. The Enemy advanced as nearly as was thought proper to try the effect of the Rockets, which were then discharged at the approaching Column. It was thrown into confusion, & dispersed in all directions, beginning a hasty & irregular retreat. Our Men advanced from their position, & made about 20 prisoners from the Enemy's retiring Column. Several Men were found killed & dreadfully scorched with the Rockets, & the Prisoners expressed themselves to have been exceedingly alarmed by them. In truth they gained much in the good opinion of the Army this day, as a great prejudice had existed against them previously, particularly in the mind of Ld. Wellington. It is but just, at the same time to mention, that tho frequently brought into Action afterwards, it was never with the same effect, & on the whole, the prejudice stands unremoved.

On the arrival of the Boats to form the bridge, whilst some were mooring & preparing, in their proper stations, others were employed in passing over Troops, Cavalry & Artillery & the whole of the left Column were passed over on the 24th. The Enemy not choosing to make any further attempt to oppose the passage. The Troops when crossed, began to move on towards Bayonne, & took up a position there. Sir John Hope established his Head Quarters, at Boucaut, on the right bank of the Adour, opposite to which place the bridge was to be established, the formation of it now proceeded quietly, & was completed in two days, thus establishing a communication with the Troops which had remained on the left bank, & extending by these means the circumference of the Blockade of Bayonne. The direction of this bridge, & its subsequent management & care, were entrusted to Major Tod of the Staff Corps.

Thus on the 26th of February, Ld. Wellington was on the bank of the Gave de Pau, having crossed the Gave d'Oleron, & Sir J. Hope had passed the Adour below Bayonne. A further concerted operation was then decided on. Ld. Wellington rode to the Head Quarters of Sir J. Hope, from the right of the Army, & expressed in strong terms, his approbation of Sir John's measures & their great facility which their success had given to his future operations. He then left Sir J. Hope & returned to the right: his Head Quarters at Sauveterre. Sir J. Hope had in front of the position which he had occupied near Bayonne, a range of heights, called "Les Hauteurs de St. Etienne", which prevented his observing the Enemy's movements in or near the Town, & which he considered as essentially necessary for him to carry, & he resolved to attempt them on the night of the 26th of February, the same night, that Ld. Wellington on the right assembled the Troops on the banks of the Gave de Pau, with the intention of crossing at day-light or during the night. Sir John Hope began his attack about mid-night. The Enemy resisted gallantly, but were not able to keep the heights, which were carried principally by the German Legion, whose loss was 450 men killed & wounded on the occasion. Their conduct was most brilliant, & gained for them the thanks of Sir J. Hope, & the approbation of the Army.[261] They established themselves so well on these heights by day-light, that the French seeing they could not be driven from them, but with exceeding loss, did not attempt to do so. From these heights, every movement of the enemy near the town was very discernible, & the importance of their possession fully appeared, & justified the successful attempt which had been made to gain them, notwithstanding the attendant loss.

The Army was at this time divided into three Corps. The left Corps under Sir J. Hope, consisted of the 1st & 5th Divisions, Ld. Aylmer's Brigade (which was the 62nd 76th 77th & 85th Regts.) two Portuguese Brigades, one under the command of M: General Bradford (the 13th & 24th Line & 5th Caçadores) & the other under Br. Genl. Campbell (the 1st & 16th Line & 4th Cacadores) a Division of Spaniards under Don Carlos, & a proper proportion of Cavalry & Artillery. This Corps was about 20,000 effective & was left to blockade Bayonne, where the Enemy had left a Garrison of 17,000 Men. The right Corps of the Army was as usual under Sir Rowland Hill, & consisted of the 2nd Division, a Division of Portuguese under M: Genl. Lecor, & a Division of Spaniards under the Guerilla chief Murillo, with Cavalry & Artillery in proportion. The right Corps was about 14,000 Men effective. The centre Corps was under the command of Marshal Beresford, & was formed of the 4th & 6th Divisions—The 3th & 7th Divisions were not included in any Corps, but distinct by themselves, as was also the Light Division. Lord Wellington having crossed the Gave de Pau on the evening & night of the 26th of Febry. made the necessary preparations for attacking the position of the Enemy, which covered the town of Orthes, on the 27th.[262] About 9 o'clock the 7th Division supported by the 4th began the attack, & about the same time Marshal Beresford directed the Brigade of Fusileers in the 4th Division, to carry a height on which were posted two Divisions of French. The difference & superiority of the Enemy's numbers on the height made the attack fruitless, & the Fusileers were repulsed. They again attacked, & were supported by the 6th Division; after considerable opposition from the Enemy, they succeeded, & the height was carried. The French however kept possession of the main point of their position, & would in all probability not have been forced from it, had not Sir Rowland Hill (whose Corps did not cross the Gave de Pau at the same time with the other Troops) crossed in rear of the Enemy's left, which rested on the river, & established himself on a range of hills in their rear, & on which he began immediately to deploy his Columns, which were consequently forming line in rear of the French, & threatened their communications. The enemy perceived the consequences of this manoeuvre, & lost no time in moving from his position. They preserved admirable order in their retreat, & their rear-guard, was so ably commanded by General Count Reille, that it was quite impossible to attack it with any chance of making an impression. The Hussar Brigade pursued very closely, & took some prisoners. The 10th Hussars, made two excellent charges and brought off from the Enemy's rear about 120 prisoners. The French took the road to St. Sever, & continued their retreat pursued by the British, the whole night. Some hundreds deserted the Enemy during the night. Their loss was about 3,500 killed & wounded, & that of the British & Portuguese 3,200. About 400 prisoners were taken. Lord Wellington was struck by a spent ball on the left hip in the middle of the engagement. He was greatly bruised but did not quit the field. The Spanish General Alaves was wounded slightly, close to Ld. Wellington, who did not feel much inconvenience from his contusion until the 28th & 29th when he was feverish & unable to sit his horse. He soon recovered or appeared to do so, & was on horse-back again to the great joy & satisfaction of the Army, who were very uneasy at the report relative to his wound having been exaggerated, which made him doubly anxious to shew himself to the Troops, the moment he was able to ride.

Febry. 28th 1814. The desertion from the French Army was this day exceedingly great, upwards of 300 Deserters arrived at the British Head Quarters, independent of those who took the nearest road to their homes. Head Quarters were established at St. Sever for a few days, on the 29th Inst., the 28th having been passed at a village between Orthes, & St. Sever called Hagenau. St. Sever is a beautiful town, near the banks of the river Luy, over which there is a bridge about half a mile on the road from St. Sever to Aire [–sur–l'Adour], & the village looking to that point is an excellent position, & difficult to be turned except from a considerable distance. The French in their retreat had burned this bridge, & Sir Rowland Hill's Corps, which was at this time the advance of the Army, crossed the Luy at a ford, about 500 yards down the stream, from the Bridge, where also two boat-rafts were afterwards established. the swelling of the river from the rains, having rendered this ford no longer passable, every exertion was immediately made to repair the bridge, which was not completed before the 10th of March, owing to the breadth of the stream, & the effectual distruction of the Bridge by the Enemy. Sir Rowland Hill's Corps however moved on, carefully following & observing the manoeuvres, & on the 5th of March, (the anniversary of the Battle of Barrosa[263]), the enemy having taken up a strong position in the Town, & on the heights of Aire, which is 5 leagues from St. Sever. Sir Rowland Hill having received instructions to establish himself in Aire, if it could be done, without much risk & loss, ordered the attack of the place, which was commenced by General Hamilton's Portuguese Division, supported by General Barnes's Brigade in reserve. This attack was on the Enemy's left. His right was at the same time attacked by the two other Brigades of the 2nd Division, under Major General Byng & Col: O'Callagan of the 39th Regt. The Portuguese Division who headed the attack on the Enemy's left were repulsed & fled with disorder, until Genl. Barnes with his Brigade moved on, & after checking the pursuit of the Portuguese by the French, attacked them with such vigor, & so much skill, that he entirely restored the battle on the left, & gained complete possession of the heights on that side of the field, the Portuguese rallying & forming in advance again, a support to Genl. Barnes's Brigade. This was the third occasion on which Genl. Barnes's eminently distinguished himself, & confirmed the high opinion which had been formed of his talents & courage. The two other Brigades, had also succeeded in their attack, & had gained the Town, which was hastily abandoned by the French, who left behind them their wounded, & considerable Magazines of Corn, flour & wine in their Stores.

Aire is on the Adour, which is about 60 yards wide near the Town & not fordable. There is a good wooden Bridge about 3 miles higher up the stream than the Town. Sir R. Hill, having made Aire his Head Quarters, on the capture of the place, Ld. Wellington continued his, at

St. Sever, & the Army occupied the different villages & buildings in the neighborhood. A supply of Shoes had become highly necessary for the Army, & a little rest was also desirable, as they had been constantly marching & skirmishing by day, & watching by night, since the 22nd of February. Head Quarters moved on the 10th of March from St. Sever to Aire, on which day the Bridge over the Luy at the former place had been completed. Sir R. Hill advanced his Head Quarters to a small village about two leagues in front of Aire, on the road to Toulouse through Rabastiens, called St. Mont. The enemy occupied the country immediately in our front, & were constantly employed in creating alarm, & keeping the British on the alert day & night, which harrassed the Troops exceedingly, as it was intended. Soult had never given repose to the British of any duration, but always threatened attacks, or made indications of movements on our flanks or in other directions, & by every means, which an excellent General could devise, rendered our situation as restless & harrassing as it was possible. Sir John Hope's Corps, had by this time completely invested Bayonne, which it was determined by Ld. Wellington not to besiege, but to blockade. The strength of the place, which is an excellent work of Vauban's, & the numerous garrison, making a Siege of the works, a matter of much doubt as to the result, and a certainty of very great bloodshed. Sir John Hope established His Head Quarters at Biaritz which is near the Sea, about three miles from Bayonne in the direction of St. John de Luz, a very centrical situation for the Commanding Officer of the blockading Army, after the establishment of the Bridge over the Adour opposite Boucaut. The duty on the right bank was taken alternately by the Guards & the German Legion, & on the left bank, by the 5th Division & Ld. Aylmer's Brigade. A Division of Spaniards under Don Carlos & one Brigade of the 5th Division had the Blockade on the neck of land between the Nive & the Adour. Some works were thrown up, & trenches made, to add strength to the Posts of the Blockaders, & a few Guns were placed to command several points, from which a sortie might be expected. The French were exceedingly jealous of any movements near their works, & even fired on single Officers & Sentries, who passed within Gun-shot. The Blockade however was solidly & firmly established, & the surrender of the place was left to be decided by the good or ill success of the future,[264] with the active part of the Army under the command of Ld. Wellington. Head Quarters, remained at Aire until the 18th of March when they moved to Viella a small village on the road to Tarbes, which route had been taken by Soult. The movements of the French General towards the Eastern coast of France were now apparent & his reasons for pursuing this course in preference to any other were evident. As Soult retired from before Ld. Wellington towards the East, & was drawing the British Forces after him, he had two particular objects to answer. The first was that he daily approached nearer to a junction with Marshal Suchet, who was withdrawing his Army (35,000 effective, & in excellent order) gradually from the Eastern Coast of Spain, & part of which was actually within seven Days march of Soult's force, having been detached to keep the communication open between Soult & Suchet. Soult therefore might reasonably calculate on a junction with the other Army when Ld. Wellington should have followed him to Montpellier — for however notorious it was, that Marshals Soult & Suchet were at decided variance with each other yet a sense of common danger, & a regard for Military character would have speedily united them, [when] that became a measure of necessity. Soult's other reason was, that in the actual state of affairs in France, it was a material object to prevent Ld. Wellington from penetrating directly into the interior, by drawing him on one side, & moreover the Country from Toulouse towards the East of France is mountainous & woody, abounding with excellent military positions & the roads indifferent. He was therefore for these several reasons, acting the part of an excellent General, by taking this track, altho' he abandoned the right, & left Bourdeaux & the navigation of the Garonne open from the interior. The sentiments of the inhabitants of Bourdeaux were not of that decided turn in favor of the Emperor, which could lead Soult to expect much from them, in the event of his Master experiencing a reverse; & aware that a Division under General Decaen was in possession of the Forts which guard the entrance into the Harbor, he decided on abandoning Bourdeaux, which was taken possession of by Marshal Beresford in command of the 4th & 7th Divisions on the 12th of March, in the midst of the acclamations of the inhabitants in favor of the Bourbons. This City, the second in the Kingdom having been secured, the 4th Division & the Marshal returned to the Army, & Ld. Dalhousie was left governor of Bourdeaux, with the 7th Division some Cavalry & Artillery. Ld. Dalhousie was not idle in command, but confident of the friendly disposition of the inhabitants of Bourdeaux; he undertook to drive the French from the Forts which guarded the entrance into the river, & gained military possession of that part of the Country between the right bank of the Garonne & the Dordogne &

which was then occupied by detached Corps & some Regiments of General Decaen's Division. His Cavalry he stationed at intervals to protect the communication between Bourdeaux & Ld. Wellington's Army, & which was repeatedly interrupted & inconvenienced by French Guerilla Corps, the formation of which in our rear had been ordered & greatly encouraged by Soult. A Regiment of Dragoons, the 7th Hussars had their Head Quarters at Mont de Marsan on the Adour, thro' which town the main road passed from Bourdeaux to Toulouse & the East. Ld. Wellington by enforcing good conduct from the Troops & seasonable proclamations, to which he added weight by making severe examples of those who acted in defiance of them, in a short time caused the dispersion of these Corps of Guerilla's by making every village near which they were seen or stationed, pay for the support of a strong body of Spanish Troops, which were made to advance into those towns in the neighborhood of which the Guerillas were. This made it the interest of the different Villages to repress the Guerillas, rather than by encouraging them, to render themselves liable to the support of the Spanish Troops. Ld. Wellington also gave permission to every Town in his rear to form a City Guard for the preservation of its police, which was to act under the orders of the Mayor, & was to consist of many or few numbers, according to the size of the Village or the necessity of the case. The Mayors were held responsible for this command. They were empowered to arrest & send prisoners to the nearest Division of the British Army, all stragglers or Men committing irregularities in the rear of the Army, & to make any police regulations they pleased, transmitting them to Ld. Wellington for his approval. These marks of confidence had wonderful effect on the inhabitants of the villages who were mostly in this part of France tired of the war, & glad to hope for any change. It is worthy of notice, that the Civil Guards thus permitted in our rear, all armed, & whose number were not less than from 12,000 to 15,000 men, never in a single instant acted beyond the power entrusted to them by Ld. Wellington; nor did the Mayors in command of these Armed Detachements ever abuse the confidence placed in them, but were of most essential service to the common cause by having the means of protecting their own property in rear of the Army from stragglers, whose sole object is plunder & irregularity. In many instances where British Troops could not be left, they furnished guards over the stores or other Military property. This disposition of the people, which had gained much strength from the continued reverses of the Emperor contributed greatly to the success of Ld. Wellington's operations, by leaving him under no anxiety for the rear of his Army & his communication with his Flanks.

18th March. Head Quarters moved on this Day from Aire to Viella, where the rear-guard of the enemy was met with, & a slight skirmish ensued. On the 19th the Army moved on & Head Quarters were established at Mourbourget. The advance of the Troops moved on through Vic Bigorre & a very sharp affair took place. The country round about this town is a perfect flat covered with vines, into which the enemy had thrown a whole Division to act as Skirmishers to Light Troops, & it was a matter of great difficulty to drive them out, owing to the impossibility of discovering whether our flanks would be secure in driving them out or not. Sir Edwd. Pakenham seeing that the skirmish, which had now cost us nearly 500 men killed & wounded, would in all probability last until night, put himself at the head of the British Light Troops, under the Command of Col: Keane of the 60th 5th Battn. & charged through the Vines, until he came to an open space, close to which stood the town of Vic Bigorre. No time was lost in the arrival of the 3rd Division, which supported by the 6th Division, drove the French thro' the Town & established a Bivouac on a rising ground about half a mile from it, where the remainder of the Troops also took up a position for the night, the Picquets of the Enemy being posted as closely as circumstances would admit. Head Quarters moved on to Tarbes on the 20th, & in the neighborhood of that place there was a very sharp affair in which was lost about 200 men. Tarbes is a large & populous town, & the seat of a Prefecture. It contains about 15,000 inhabitants, the greater part of whom had deserted the place, during the continuance of the skirmish. On the 21st the [army] moved on & Head Quarters were established at Tournay, about two leagues & a half from Tarbes, the rear-guard of the enemy retiring before us, & not shewing any disposition to come to action. On the day following, the 22nd of March, Head Quarters at Galan, three leagues in advance of Tournay, & on the 23rd they moved on again to Bologne four leagues in advance of Galan to Toulouse. The rear-guard of the enemy continued to retire without fighting, & the inhabitants had now ceased to abandon their houses, the consequence of which was, that there was abundance of provisions for the Army, & from the regularity of the payments on the part of the British, the greatest good order prevailed between the French people & the Army, who observed the most exact discipline. From Boulogne

Head Quarters advanced on the 24th of March to L'isle en Dodon three leagues, & on the 25th to Samatan, not meeting with any opposition from the enemy. During this continued advance of the British Troops, the Spanish division under General O'Donnel, better known by the name of the Conde d'Abisbal, followed in the rear, & committed so many depredations, that Ld. Wellington found it necessary to make some severe examples, & several Spanish Soldiers were hanged by his orders, which had a great effect on the rest, & assisted materially in restoring order. The Spanish Troops pretended to murmur at the death of their Comrades, but were soon convinced of its necessity. The Conde D'Abisbal was a very zealous partizan of the British, & used every endeavour to preserve discipline amongst the Troops. On the 26th of March Head Quarters moved to St. Lys, three leagues from Samatan, & four & a half from Toulouse. The rear-guard of the enemy was here met with, & a few shots exchanged. Head Quarters halted here on the 27th to give the Army a day's rest, & to receive supplies of provisions from the rear. On the 28th the Army again advanced, & Head Quarters were established at Seysses, two leagues from St. Lys. The Garonne ran about two leagues from this place under Toulouse, & was about 120 yards broad, no ford, & the enemy occupying some heights on the other banks, & still keeping two Divisions on our side of the river with the bridge of Toulouse in their rear for a retreat in case of being pushed by the British, & on the other side of the Bridge had been erected a Tête de Pont on which four pieces of heavy Cannon were mounted. The necessary arrangements for crossing the Garonne making it probable that some time would be expended before they could be complete, the Army was placed in Cantonments, such part only remaining encamped as were necessary for the immediate duties of the outposts. Sir Rowland Hill's Corps was established in & near the town of Muret, & on his immediate left, the Corps of Spaniards under the Conde d'Abisbal. Sir Rowland Hill's right rested on the Garonne. The 3rd Division rested at Grenade, & the 6th at Lequeran. The 4th had remained at Coudon & the neighborhood of Mont de Marsan, since they had returned from Bourdeaux with Marshal Beresford. This division was now ordered to join the Army, previous to the passage of the Garonne, & the active operations that would follow. The cavalry was stationed in proportions with the infantry. On the 6th of April it was resolved to throw a Pontoon bridge over the Garonne in the night, near the town of Muret, & every preparation was made accordingly. The Troops were to be on the march from their several cantonments an hour before day-light, towards the spot where the bridge was to be thrown over. The Pontoons were moved down to the river in the night, & two of them were launched into the river. A rope was passed over, as usual, & several more Pontoons were launched, when after some consideration, it was found that we had not a sufficient number to cross the river at this place, & a countermand having been sent to the Troops, the Pontoons were again taken up with the greatest expedition & moved off, but not before an alarm had been given on the French side of the river, which was followed by some French troops coming down to the water's edge. They had discovered that we were about some movement there, but had neither seen nor heard anything, as it afterwards appeared, to induce a belief that an attempt had been made there, to throw over a bridge. Violent rains succeeded this attempt, & rendered for a few days any further effort at crossing the Garonne, quite out of the question.

The troops remained in the several cantonments, & were employed in making frames with barrels in them, to assist the Pontoons, in the event of their not proving in sufficient numbers for the passage of such other part of the river, as might be afterwards selected for the passage. Another brigade of pontoons was ordered from the rear, there being two brigades one of which had moved with the Army, as they were a very great encumbrance & addition to the baggage, & it had been always supposed that one brigade of 18 pontoons would be sufficient for every purpose.

On the 6th Head Quarters moved to Grenade, on the evening of which day another attempt was made to establish a bridge over the river about a mile & a half higher up than Grenade. This attempt proved successful, & the 3rd 4th & 6th divisions with 3 brigades of artillery, & 3 brigades of cavalry were passed over. Violent rains came on & it was found inpracticable to pass over any more troops, & the bridge was taken up with great difficulty owing to the rapidity of the current. The Army was thus divided without the possibility of one part rendering assistance to the other in case of an attack from the enemy, who had it in his power, by means of the bridge of Toulouse, to attack whichever part he chose with the whole of his Troops. Whether he was ignorant of the state of things, or for some other reason, he did not make any movement, & on the 8th of April, the river having subsided, the whole of the British Army was passed over, (the bridge being reestablished) except the Corps of Sir Rowland Hill, which took up a position in front of, & to watch the bridge of Toulouse, which position they immediately strengthened with some small works & Abbatis. It was most important to have this post well secured, to prevent the enemy detaching over the bridge any force that could attack or interrupt the communications with our rear & supplies. The Army advanced on the 8th nearer Toulouse, on the right bank of the river, & the enemy was found in position, on some very strong & commanding ground, the strength of which had been greatly added to by trenches & works, & they were occupied in every direction in making batteries & redoubts. They had left a brigade of Cavalry in advance of their position, about a league, which was driven in, & on this occasion the 18th Hussars distinguished themselves, by charging a French Regiment of Cavalry, whom they put to entire rout & literally overset them, taking about 80 prisoners with their horses, & they continued the pursuit so eagerly & so closely that they drove the Enemy over a bridge which crossed a stream at the foot of a French position, which stream tho' narrow, is exceedingly deep, & not fordable except in the dry weather of Summer. The occupation of this bridge was of material importance, & a Brigade of the 4th Division was immediately advanced to retain possession of it, & to strengthen it for the night. This bridge was afterwards one of the points by which the British debouched and formed previous to the battle of Toulouse, & without its possession, the crossing the Stream over which it was built would have been a matter of the greatest difficulty, as the banks were very steep and sandy, & the water deep with a very soft bottom. There was another bridge about a mile higher up the stream & nearly opposite the centre of the enemy's position, & also another beyond that. These two Bridges had French picquets upon them & were both mined, one of them was carried before the mine exploded, on the evening of the 9th but was retaken.

10th April. The battle of Toulouse[265] commenced about 8 o'clock in the morning, by the passage of the 4th & 6th Divisions under the orders of Marshal Beresford, over the river Ers, at a narrow bridge near Croix d'Orade, which had been secured the previous day by a gallant charge of the 18th Hussars. Beresford moved up the stream on its left bank, & attacked a small village called Montblanc, which was but feebly defended. He then when nearly opposite the centre of the enemy's fortified position formed in column of attack. The 3rd. & light divisions were on the right, to threaten the City in that quarter or to support the Spaniards, under Freyre, if necessary, which troops were to attack the enemy's left. Here they were repulsed, & driven back with some loss.

The light division moved up quickly to their assistance, & the French who had advanced on our right flank in pursuit of the Spaniards, were driven back. Beresford's attack in the mean time, was made with determined courage, in face of a most severe fire of grape & round shot. The 4th division turned the enemy's left, & thus enabled the 6th to make good its ascent up the steep hill on which stood an old Convent called Mont Calvinet, which had been strongly fortified. They carried this work at the point of the bayonet, & established themselves on the summit of the hill, the French retiring down the other side, towards the bridges over the Canal, which surrounded the part of the City which the heights overlooked. The 3rd division under Picton, did more than Ld. Wellington had required from its Leader, & without effecting much good, met with severe loss.

Sir Rowland Hill on the other side of the Garonne, by a sharp attack on the suburbs, kept the enemy too well employed in that quarter to enable him to detach any troops to support Soult. General Pack's Portuguese Brigade attacked & carried two redoubts in the Centre of the position & on the left of the 6th Division. The enemy made great efforts to recover them but were driven back with loss. Thus routed in every direction Soult took up a position from the Canal to a height called La Pujade, but was immediately attacked in it, by the 4th & 6th Divisions supported by a body of Spaniards, & driven completely over the canal.

The victory was now won, but our loss had been very severe, as nearly 5,000 British & Portuguese were killed & wounded, & the Spanish loss was also considerable.

The French lost Generals Taussan & Lamorandière, several others were wounded & taken,[266] & 1500 men. They carried off their wounded, but the number of dead left on the field was very great.

Soult withdrew his force the next day, within the city, & appeared resolved to defend himself there. Ld. Wellington instantly prepared to surround it on every side, to prevent his escape. He could have distroyed this beautiful place from the heights, from which we had driven the enemy, but Ld. Wellington would not fire a gun upon it. Soult quickly discovered, that he and his whole army would inevitably be captured if he remained in Toulouse, & in the night of the 12th he withdrew his Army entirely on the road to Castilnaury, which gave him an open communication with Suchet. On the morning of the 13th Ld. Wellington entered the place, amidst the joyous cries of the people. The white flag was hoisted, & "Vive le Roi" resounded from every part of the

City. On the evening of this same Day, Colonel Cooke arrived from Paris, to announce the downfal of Bonaparte, & the restoration of the Bourbons, to the throne of their Ancestors.

The Head Quarters of the Army remained in Toulouse, until the acknowledgement of Lewis XVIII was universal in France & the Army & the French Marshals had taken the Oaths of Allegiance to them. Preparations were then made for the return of the British Army to England, & several Regiments were sent in Boats down the Garonne to Bourdeaux for embarkation.

In the mean time in order to hasten the conclusion of the war between Great Britain & the united States[267] a reinforcement was ordered to be sent from the Pe[n]insular Army to Sir George Prevost—This reinforcement consisted of six Brigades of three Regiments each, with a Staff & Artillery in proportion. The following was Ld. Wellington's general order, relative to this force.

Toulouse 16th May 1814.

No: 3 The following Regiments being destined for a particular service, are to be formed into Brigades & Divisions, as follows, & to be commanded by the General Officers as set down for them.

Lieutenant General Lord Hill to command.

Lieutenant General Lord Hill to command.

1st Division			14th Regiment of Light Dragoons
Lt. Gen. Sir H. Clinton, K. B.	Major Genl. Barnes	3rd Foot 1st Battalion	
		27th . . . 1st	
		37th . . . 1st	
	Colonel Keane	4th . . . 1st	
		44th . . . 1st	
		57th . . . 1st	
	Col: O'Callaghan	39th . . . 1st	
		58th . . . 1st	
		85th . . .	
2nd Division			
Maj. Gen: Kempt	Major Gen. Power	5th Foot 1st Battalion	
		27th . . . 3rd	
		28th . . . 1st	
	Maj. Gen. Robinson	9th . . . 1st	
		76th . . .	
		88th . . . 1st	
	Maj. Gen. Ross	40th . . . 1st	
		60th . . . 5th	
		81st . . . 1st	

Lieutenant Col. Cairncross, Six companies Royal Artillery.
Lieut. Col. Burgoyne, Detachment Royal Engineers,
Major Colleton, ... do . . . Staff Corps,
The following Officers are appointed to the Staff of this Corps.
Lieut. Col. Bouverie, Deputy Adjutant General.
. . . . . . Stovin,   28th . . .
. . . . . . Tryon,   88th Foot.   } Assistants Adjutant General.
Major During, King's German Legion
Captain Browne, 23rd Fusileers, Deputy Assistant Adjutant General.
Lieut. Col. Jackson, Coldm. Gds. Deputy Quarter Master General,
. . . . . . Abercromby 28th Foot   }
Major Montgomerry, 50th . . .   } Assistant Qr. Mr. Generals.
Captain Forest,   3rd . . .
. . . . Dumaresq,   9th . . .   } Dep. Assistant Qr. Mr. Generals.
Lieut. Evans,   3rd Dragoons

Lieut. Col. Goodman, 48th Regiment, Acting Deputy Judge Advocate
Major Anevyl   4th Foot
Captain Smyth   95th . . .
. . . . Blair,   91st . . .
. . . . Wylly,   7th Fusileers   } Brigade Majors
. . . . Blakeney, 66th Foot
. . . . Campbell, 64th . . .

A complete Squadron of the Cavalry Staff Corps is to accompany this Force, should there be sufficient means of Embarkation. This Corps is to be attended by four Brigades of Artillery with their Equipments. They are besides to have on board, three Brigades of Nine Pounders Artillery, & one Brigade of Eighteen Pounders, with two Brigades of Mountain Guns.

There must be six Companies of Artillery, & a proportion of Ordnance Stores.

The Officers above mentioned are forthwith to join their several Brigades, & Divisions, in the neighborhood of Bourdeaux, & they are to embark as soon as the Senior General Officer with them will be informed that Transports are ready.

The Field Marshal has no intimation of, or authority to give them any order for their Destination.

An expedition was at the same time planned against New Orleans, & a further one, on a larger scale, for other operations against the Coast of the United States. Part of the reinforcement enumerated above, sailed direct from Bourdeaux to Quebec—& the other expedition against New Orleans, went on its destination under the order of Sir Edwd. Pakenham.

The third & larger Force, destined for the same quarter, & which was to have sailed from Portsmouth, was afterwards countermanded. To the Staff of this last Army, the writer of this Journal having been transferred, he obtained leave to return to England by Paris, where he remained a fortnight, & then went to London, reported himself to Lord Hill, & called on him daily for orders, until it was officially notified that the expedition was abandoned.

The remainder of the Pe[n]insular Army embarked at Bourdeaux, & returned to England, having been in the Field, the greater of them since 1808—& lost in the many Actions in which they took part [   ] Officers & [   ] Men—having driven the French, led on by their ablest Marshals, from the Lines of Torres Vedras near Lisbon, to the right bank of the Garonne at Toulouse after [   ] pitched Battles [   ]Sieges & Skirmishes[268] without end.

VI
1815–1816

On May 30 1814, the powers of Europe signed a peace treaty with France. This document confined France to her boundaries of 1792. During the 1814 campaign in France, the powers agreed to convene an international conference at Vienna after defeating Napoleon. The Congress assembled in September 1814 to settle the political shape of post-Napoleonic Europe. All the states of Europe sent representatives. However, all important questions were decided by the four victorious great powers, Russia, Prussia, Austria and Britain. In the midst of these talks, Napoleon escaped from Elba, where he had been exiled, and landed on the Riviera coast of France on 1 March 1815. Agreeing to contribute 150,000 men each to the army for defeating Napoleon, the allies met Napoleon in Belgium at Waterloo, where the Duke of Wellington won a great victory on 18 June 1815. Napoleon abdicated a second time and for a second time was exiled, this time to distant St Helena in the south Atlantic.

On 8 August 1814, nearly three months after the French sortie from Bayonne, Browne received word from the Horse Guards that his appointment as Deputy Assistant Quarter Master General for the expedition to North America had been confirmed.[269] When this order was subsequently countermanded, Browne applied for and received a well-deserved leave of absence in England. The May 1814 peace with France produced the inevitable retrenchment in British military spending. As with a number of other regiments, the parsimonious actions of the government resulted in the reduction of the 2nd Battalion of the Royal Welch Fusiliers. In October 1814, while Browne was on leave, the fit men of the 2nd were incorporated into the 1st Battalion. The whole of the officers were placed on half pay, however. This included Browne since he had received his commission in the 2nd Battalion. Upon Napoleon's escape from Elba, Browne accepted an appointment as aide-de-camp to Lord Stewart, then British ambassador at Vienna. As a result of this assignment, Browne was not present at Waterloo. He did, nonetheless, accompany Lord Stewart to Paris in 1815.

1815

I NOW for the first time since I entered the Army obtained two months leave of absence, during which period the second Battalion of my Regiment, into which I had got my company was disbanded, & I was placed on half-pay.[270]

I had not however been at home more than five weeks before Napoleon made his escape from Elba; this event called the Army into Active Service again, & I went to London to endeavor to obtain employment. There I found a letter from Lord Stewart, our Ambassador at Vienna on whose Staff when Adjt. Genl. in Spain, I had served, informing me he was about to take the Field with the Austrian Armies, as General Officer, & offering me the appointment of his Aide de Camp.

At the same time I heard that Col. Torrens the Adjt. Genl. had gone to Brussels to see the Duke of Wellington & arrange with him the Staff of his Head Quarters. Wishing to be appointed to that Staff, where I should be in the midst of my old Comrades of the Penninsular, I kept Lord Stewart's letter unanswered until the return of Col. Torrens from Brussels. I saw him at the Horse Guards after his return, & asked him if my name had been included in the list of Staff for the new Head Quarters of the D. of Wellington, to which he replied in the negative. I then answered Lord Stewart & accepted the appointment he had offered me. I called on Ld. Castlereagh who gave me Dispatches for his Brother, & others for the D. of Wellington, which I was to deliver as I passed thro' Brussels. On my arrival there, I saw the Duke, who shook me by the hand & said, "Ah! Browne! I am glad to see you at your old post again!" to which I replied in astonishment, "I wish Sir, I had been appointed to my old post, but having called on Sir H. Torrens, when he returned from your Grace, to enquire whether I had been thought of, for my old Pe[n]insular situation at Head Quarters, he replied in the negative, & I then accepted an offer I kept by me unanswered for some time, made me by Ld. Stewart of the situation of his Aid de Camp, & am going to him to Vienna.["] The Duke replied "this is impossible Fitzroy (Ld. F. Somerset was present) shew me the list of names Torrens took with him to the Horse Guards, for appointment to the Staff of my Army." It was produced, & opposite my name "indispensably necessary at Head Quarters"—I was quite cast down when I saw how the Horse Guards had served me—The duke was much annoyed—said it was not the first time he had been played a trick in that quarter, & that he would resent it, by not taking the Officer appointed in my place, but would appoint one himself—"however" he added shaking me again by the hand "I see how it is, & as far as I can be of use to you hereafter you shall not be a sufferer—I wish you would take some Dispatches for me to Blucher who is at Liege & on your road to Vienna, & that whilst I am getting them ready, you would see Genl. Barnes (the Adjt. Genl. at Brussels) tell him I sent you to him to talk over with him the arrangements for the Adjt. Genl. Department, which were adopted in Spain, & which I wish to be continued here." I went to Sir E. Barnes, dined with him, told him all the regulations of the Adjt. Genl. Department which had been adopted in the Pe[n]insular, & left him about ten at night; I returned to Head Quarters received my Dispatches for Blucher from Ld. F. Somerset, & saw the Duke again, who parted with me in the kindest manner. I found Blucher in bed, in a little village about 4 miles from Liege. His Aide de Camp Count Nostiz slept in an outer room, with a lamp burning, which he took up when I went in, & accompanied me to the inner room, where the Marshal was sleeping on a Mattrass on the floor.

It was at the time when the Saxon Troops had mutinied, because Blucher wished to incorporate them in the Divisions of the Prussian Army, in place of leaving them to act in a body as he had no great opinion of them. This, they resented, mutinied, & compelled Blucher to leave Liege, & retire to the village where I found him. He made me sit down whilst he read the Duke's Dispatches by the light of the lamp, then shook me by the hand, & finding I was going to Vienna dictated a letter to his Aide de Camp Nostiz to Ld. Stewart, & gave it me to take to him. He said he would answer the Duke's Dispatches in the morning.

Blucher disarmed the mutinous Saxons, & sent them to the rear. The King of Saxony, afterwards offered them to the D. of Wellington, but he declined their services, unless his friend Blucher would give them a character, which he would not, & they consequently remained in Garrison, during the campaign which followed.

I went on to Vienna & was altogether ten night & nine days going from London to that City—travelling night & day—I was greatly fatigued.

I found Ld. Stewart preparing to take the field in a few days, every thing packing up, & time we were to start for the Austrian Army immediately. I made my preparations as quickly as I could, & we set out for Heidelburg, where Schwartzenberg was, in a week after my arrival.

Soon afterwards the Emperors of Russia & Austria, & the King of Prussia arrived, & moved with the Austrian Head Quarters, for the rest of the Campaign. The Emperor of Russia had his two Brothers as his Aides de Camp. Platoff, with his Cossacks, was also at Head Quarters.

We remained at Heidelburg about a fortnight, which time the Troops of the great Powers were rapidly advancing towards the Rhine—& an army of 30,000 Bavarians, under Prince Wrede, also joined the confederacy against Napoleon.

The D. of Wellington in Belgium was also receiving daily reinforcements from England, & France was at the same time pouring out her thousands to range under the Standard of the Emperor.

On the 5th June, we moved onwards in the direction of Strasburg, where there was a very large garrison under General Rapp. as we approached that place, we fell in with the French Patroles & advanced Posts, & severe skirmishing took place. The Russian reserve of 80,000 men were drawing near & a forward general movement of the whole line was made. Strasburg was invested, & we were already in contact with large bodies of the enemy, when on the 23d June we received the account of the great & eventful battle of Waterloo; & on the 26th a Courier arrived with the news that the D. of Wellington & Blucher were in Paris, & that Louis the XVIII was proclaimed. Our business was over. Ld. Stewart left the Head Quarters of the Allied Sovereigns, & I went with him to Paris. The English & Prussians were in occupation of that Capital. Paris was devided into Districts, & English & Prussian Officers placed in charge of them.

It was a singular & proud sight, that of British Troops encamped in the Bois de Boulogne & Thuilleries Gardens, in the very heart of Paris—Our bugles sounding the reveilleé & retreat, & the French Capital under Martial Law.

We remained some weeks in this military possession of Paris. Arrangements were then made for the removal of the Troops & the occupation of France for three years by 150,000 Allied Armies, of which the D. of Wellington was appointed Generalissimo.

I returned to Vienna with Ld. Stewart as his Aide de Camp, & was afterwards appointed private Secretary to the Embassy. The reduction of the 2nd battalion of my Regiment having placed me on half-pay, my military career was thus brought to a close.

I had been exposed to much danger, by Sea & by Land, & had suffered considerably from fevers & illnesses contracted in various climates & from wounds received in the field, but in 1816 had returned safely to the home I left in 1806—

Appendix A
BIOGRAPHICAL NOTES

List includes most of the persons cited by Browne in his journal. The entries for each are limited to some principal service events.

Abbé, Général Louis Jean. This skilful divisional commander fought British troops as well as Spanish guerrillas. He was present at the principal battles fought in northern Spain and southern France in 1813.

Abercromby, Colonel, Hon. Alexander. The son of Sir Ralph Abercromby, he took part in the Helder expedition (1799). He was present at Talavera (1809), Bussaco (1810), Arroyo dos Molinos (1811) and Almaraz (1812) in the Peninsula before being appointed to Wellington's staff in 1813 as Assistant Quartermaster-General. He retained this appointment in the Department to 1814 and then served on Wellington's staff at Waterloo (1815).

Alava, General Miguel de (1771–1843). He replaced General Romana as Spanish liaison officer with the Duke of Wellington. He continued his service as a member of the Duke's staff during the Waterloo campaign as Spanish Commissioner. Prior to his British service, he served aboard a Spanish man-of-war at the battle of Trafalgar in 1805.

Alten, General Sir Karl, Count von (1764–1840). A distinguished Hanoverian soldier, Alten transferred to British service in 1803. During the Peninsula campaign, he served with the King's German Legion, the successor body to George III's Hanoverian army, and commanded the famous Light Division after the death of its original commander, Robert Crauford, in 1812. With the reconstitution of the Hanoverian army, Alten became a field marshal. In Wellington's words, Alten "was the best of the Hanoverians".

Aylmer, Major-General Matthew, Lord (1775–1850). He entered the service in 1787 as an ensign in the 49th Foot. He served in the West Indies and was present at the Helder (1799) and Copenhagen (1807). In the Peninsula he was present at Talavera (1809) and other important actions. In July 1813, after service as Deputy Adjutant-General to Wellington's army, he was given command of an independent brigade.

Baird, General Sir David (1757–1829). A popular officer, Baird served with distinction in India, from 1780 to 1802. He commanded a division at Copenhagen in 1807. After this service he joined Sir John Moore in Portugal where he lost an arm at the battle of Corunna, on 16 January 1809. This proved to be his last active service in the field. In 1820 he was appointed Commander-in-Chief in Ireland.

Ballesteros, General Francisco (fl. 1810). A Spanish general and Captain-General of Andalusia. Jealousy at Wellington's appointment as Commander-in-Chief of all Spanish armies by the Cortes led him to make an abortive bid for power in October 1812. This failure led to his incarceration in North Africa.

Barnes, Major-General Sir Edward (1776–1838). This brave and talented officer commanded a brigade at the capture of Martinique (1809) and throughout much of the campaign in the Peninsula, where he was twice wounded. He was present at Bussaco (1810), Vitoria (1813), the Pyrenees, Nive, Nivelle (1813), and Orthez (1814). During the Waterloo campaign (1815), he served on Wellington's staff as Adjutant-General. He was subsequently made a Knight Commander of the Military Order of the Bath.

Beckwith, Lieutenant-General Sir George (1753–1823). Beckwith entered the army as an ensign in the old 37th North Hampshire Regiment in July 1771. He distinguished himself during the American Revolution and the wars of the French Revolution and Napoleon. Twice during the 1793–1815 war command of the Windward and Leeward Islands devolved on Beckwith, in 1805 and again in 1808. He served as Governor of Martinique after its capture in 1809. In 1814 he received the rank of General and, following the final defeat of Napoleon in 1815, he was appointed Commander-in-Chief in Ireland.

Beresford, General William Carr, Viscount (1764–1854). He served under Sir John Moore throughout the Corunna campaign of 1808–09. Because of his outstanding gifts as an organizer, he was selected by Wellington in 1809 to train the Portuguese army. In that capacity he raised the famour *Caçadores* regiments which earned Wellington's praise. On 2 March 1809 he was promoted Marshal in the Portuguese army. He served as the Master-General of the Ordnance from 1828 to 1830.

Blake, General Joachim (1759–1827). Born of Irish parents at Malaga in Andalusia, in 1808 he was given command of the (Spanish) Army of Galicia. Although considered to be an officer of great ability and courage, he suffered several defeats and was finally captured in 1812.

Blücher, Field Marshal Gebhard Leberecht von, Prince of Wahlstadt (1742–1819). A crude, wild, hard-drinking soldier, as well as a fine, if limited, fighting commander, whose career began at the age of fourteen. Nicknamed "Alte vorwärts" ("Old Forward") by his Prussian soldiers, it was due to his doggedness that his troops arrived at Waterloo at the crucial moment, thereby turning an indecisive battle into a decisive victory over Napoleon.

Bonaparte, Joseph, King of Naples, then King of Spain (1768–1844). Napoleon's respected elder brother, he accepted the crown of Spain in 1808 without enthusiasm. The first constitutional monarch in the history of Spain, he unsuccessfully tried to make himself acceptable to the Spanish people who regarded him as an intruder. Decisively defeated at Vitoria on 21 June 1813, he retired to France. The following year, however, Napoleon made Joseph commander of the Paris National Guard.

Bonet, Général Jean Pierre François, Comte de (1768–1857). He first joined the French army in 1786. A veteran of many battles, his service in Spain began in 1808. In July 1812 he succeeded briefly to the command of the French Army of Portugal. After the second Bourbon restoration, he became Inspector-General of Infantry.

Bouverie, Sir Henry Frederick (1783–1852). He entered the army in 1799 as an ensign in the Coldstream Guards. He served in Egypt (1801) and at Copenhagen (1807). In 1809 he was sent to the Peninsula where he was present at the Douro (1808), Talavera (1809), Salamanca (1812), Vitoria (1813), the Nive (1813), and Orthez (1814). He also held several staff appointments during the Peninsula campaign.

Bowes, General B. F. (d. 1812). This officer served in the Peninsula and was present at Vimiero (1808). He was later killed leading an attack against one of the fortified convents of Salamanca (1812).

Bradford, General Sir Thomas (1777–1853). He entered the army in 1793 as ensign in the 4th Foot. After serving in the expedition to South America (1806), he served in the Peninsula at Vimiero (1808) and Corunna (1809). In 1810 he took command of a Portuguese brigade and commanded it successfully, particularly at Salamanca (1812). He was severely wounded at Bayonne (1814).

Breton, Général Jean (See Dubreton).

Browne, Lieutenant-Colonel George Baxter. Younger brother of Thomas Henry Browne, he entered the army (23rd Royal Welch Fusiliers) in 1806. During his service in the Peninsula, he was wounded at Badajoz (1812) and Roncesvalles (1813).

Burgoyne, Sir John (1782–1871). He entered the Royal Military Academy, Woolwich in 1796 and was gazetted to the Royal Engineers in 1798. During the Peninsular War he assisted in fortifying the Lines of Torres Vedras (1810), took part in the sieges of Badajoz (1811, 1812) and Ciudad Rodrigo (1812), directed the reduction of the forts of Salamanca (1812), and was commanding Royal Engineer at the siege of San Sebastian (1813). He achieved some notoriety during the Crimean War (1853–1856) as a result of his insistence on reducing the Malakoff in the siege of Sebastopol.

Byng, Field Marshal Sir John, Earl of Strafford (1772–1860). Prior to his move to the Peninsula in 1810, Byng saw considerable service which included Copenhagen (1807) and Walcheren (1809). Soon after his arrival in the Peninsula he was given command of the 2nd Brigade in Sir Rowland Hill's 2nd division. He was present at many of the major battles in Spain and distinguished himself at the battle of the Nive River (1813) in southern France. He commanded the 2nd Guards Brigade at Waterloo. Byng later commanded in Ireland, from 1828 to 1831.

Cadogan, Colonel Henry (1780–1813). After serving in Scotland, the Channel Isles and Curaçao, he served as an aide-de-camp to Wellington in 1809. He was given command of the 1st Brigade of Sir Rowland Hill's 2nd division. At the battle of Vitoria, on 21 June 1813, he was mortally wounded leading the 71st Highland Regiment up the slopes of the Puebla Heights.

Caffarelli du Falga, Général Marie François Auguste, Comte de (1766–1849). Enjoying a variegated career, which included service in the Sardinian army from 1785–1792, he assumed command of the French army of the North in the Peninsula in 1812. The following year he became Napoleon's aide. In 1815 he rallied to Napoleon's side upon the latter's return from Elba.

Campbell, Lieutenant-Colonel Sir Colin (1776–1847). After considerable service in India (1802–1806) and Copenhagen (1807), he served as Wellington's senior aide-de-camp in the Peninsula. Campbell took part in most of the major campaigns of the war. After becoming a major-general in 1825, he served as Governor of Nova Scotia (from 1833) and Ceylon (from 1839).

Castaños, Francisco Xavier, Duke of Bailen (1756–1852). Born in the Spanish province of Biscay, his greatest victory during the war in the Peninsula was the capture of the French garrison at Bailen in July 1808. In May of the same year he was appointed commander of all Spanish troops concentrated in Andalusia.

Castlereagh, Robert Stewart, Viscount Castlereagh, Second Marquis of Londonderry (1769–1822). This distinguished statesman first entered Parliament in 1794. Until 1805 most of Castlereagh's time was devoted to Irish affairs. In that year he was appointed to the War and Colonial Offices. He also served as Foreign Minister from 1812 to 1822, and masterminded two coalitions against Napoleon. Castlereagh was the senior British representative at the Congress of Vienna and later championed the Congress System as a way to reduce international tensions. An unpopular figure during his last years, he committed suicide in 1822.

Cathcart, General Charles Murray, Earl (1783–1859). Cathcart saw service in several campaigns, including the Walcheren expedition (1809) and the Peninsular War, 1810 to 1812. He was Quartermaster-General of the British army from 1814 to 1822. Commander-in-Chief in Canada from 1846 to 1849, he was made a full general in 1854.

Clark, Nancy. This celebrated freed black woman owned one of Bridgetown's two hotels in 1806 or 1807. Her business apparently ceased operations in 1812, when it may have been destroyed by fire.

Clausel, Maréchal Bertrand, Comte de (1772–1842). A hard-fighting and gallant French soldier, Clausel saw considerable service in Italy, Saint

Domingue (as Haiti was then called), Holland and Dalmatia, before being posted to the Army of Portugal (1810–1812). Although wounded at Salamance (1812), he took over the command from Maréchal Marmont and launched a telling if hopeless counter-attack. He served with distinction throughout the final campaigns of the Peninsular War in southern France. After Waterloo he commenced a political career which included the appointment of Governor-General of Algeria in 1835.

Clinton, Lieutenant-General Sir Henry (1771–1829). First commissioned in 1787, Clinton served in Holland (1788–1789). In 1793 he became an aide-de-camp to the Duke of York. His service record included a stint as a liaison officer to Field Marshal Alexander Suvorov's Russian army in North Italy. After serving as Adjutant-General in India from 1802 to 1805, he was again attached to the Russian army and was present at Napoleon's great victory at the battle of Austerlitz, 2 December 1805. In the Peninsula he served Sir John Moore as Adjutant-General and commanded the 6th division under Wellington.

Cochrane, Sir Alexander Forrester Inglis (1758–1832). Admiral; served with credit on several stations, including the West Indies and North America. Government posts included governorship of Guadeloupe, from 1810 to 1813.

Cocks, Lieutenant-Colonel Charles Somers (1786–1812). Highly regarded by Wellington as one of the most promising officers in the British army, Cocks was killed during the first siege of Burgos, 19 September — 22 October 1812. He arrived in Portugal in 1809. In December he was attached to the Spanish army as an intelligence officer, and in 1810 he began a series of special missions for Wellington which earned the great soldier's high esteem.

Colborne, Colonel Sir John, Baron Seaton (1778–1863). During the Peninsular campaign Colborne commanded a brigade at Bussaco (1810) and at Albuera (1811). He lived to be a commander-in-chief, a field marshal and a peer. However the great days of his career were those in which he commanded the 52nd Foot with great distinction in the Peninsula and at Waterloo. After the war he served as Lieutenant Governor of Upper Canada and crushed a revolt there in 1838.

Cole, General Sir Galbraith Lowry (1772–1842). Promoted to Major-General in 1808, he commanded the 4th Division in the Peninsula from 1809 to 1814. His role determined the successful outcome of the battle of Albuera, 16 May 1811.

Colville, Sir Charles (1770–1843). He entered the army as an ensign in the 28th Foot in 1781, but did not join until 1787. A distinguished officer, he served in the West Indies (1791–1799), Egypt (1801), and Martinique (1809) before being posted to the Peninsula in 1810. He was present at Fuentes de Oñoro (1811), Badajoz (1811, 1812), Ciudad Rodrigo (1812), the Nivelle and the

Nive (1813), and Bayonne (1814). He also served at Waterloo (1815). He was promoted General in 1837.

Congreve, Sir William, Baronet (1772–1828). Congreve developed the explosive rocket which was used against the French at Boulogne in 1806, and against the Danes at the siege of Copenhagen in 1807. Because rockets offered erratic assistance, Wellington was not impressed with the weapon. Nonetheless British rocket troops served under Wellington's command in southern France. Congreve served as Controller of the Royal Laboratory at Woolwich from 1814 to 1828.

Constant, Baron (See Rebecque).

Corfield, Lieutenant Samuel (d. 1809). He entered the army on 1 December 1804 without purchase as a second lieutenant in the 23rd Foot. He died in Barbados in 1809.

Cotton, General Sir Stapleton, Viscount Combermere (1773–1865). Cotton entered the army in 1790, and four years later was a lieutenant-colonel of cavalry. In 1805 he was promoted to the rank of Major-General. From 1808 to 1812 he commanded British cavalry in the Peninsula. Because of wounds he was invalided to Britain. However he returned to fight in the Pyrenees, from 1813 to 1814. In 1815 Cotton commanded the Allied cavalry in France. After Waterloo he served in Barbados (1817–1820), Ireland (1822–1825), and in India (1825–1830). He was made a field marshal in 1855.

Craufurd, Major General Robert (1764–1812). A legendary commander of light troops, Craufurd, nicknamed "Black Bob", was the original commander of the famous Light Division. Loved by his men despite his reputation as a strict disciplinarian, Craufurd was mortally wounded in the breach at Ciudad Rodrigo (19 January 1812), and was buried at the foot of the breach which the Light Division stormed.

Dalhousie, General Sir George Ramsay, Earl of (1770–1838). He commanded the 7th Division in the Peninsula and in southern France. Wellington was sometimes critical of his generalship as, for example, when he arrived late on the battlefield of Vitoria in 1813. Towards the end of his career he became Governor of Canada and Commander-in-Chief in India.

Decaen, Général Charles, Comte (1769–1832). He served as Commander-in-Chief of the French Army of Catalonia, from 1811 to 1814.

Dick, Major-General Sir Robert (1785?–1846). He began his military service in 1800 as ensign in the 75th Foot. He served in Sicily (1806) and Egypt (1807) before being posted to the Peninsula (1809) where he served with distinction until 1814. He was present at Waterloo (1815) and was later killed at Sobraon (1846) during the First Sikh War (1845–1846).

Dickson, Major-General Sir Alexander (1777–1840). Commissioned into the Royal Artillery in 1794, he was attached to Portuguese forces under General Beresford. From 1811 he served as superintendent of Wellington's artillery in the Peninsula. After serving at Waterloo, he was appointed Inspector of Artillery in 1822. In 1833 he became Director-General of the field-train department.

Drouet, Maréchal Jean-Baptiste, Comte d'Erlon (1765–1844). Joining the Bourbon army in 1782, he saw considerable service during the revolutionary wars, rising rapidly in rank to *général de brigade* in 1799. After serving at Austerlitz (1805) and Friedland (1807), where he was wounded, he was posted to Spain in 1810. He served at many of the principal battles in Spain and southern France. He fought at Waterloo and was created a Marshal of France a year before his death.

Dubreton, Général Jean Louis, Baron (1773–1855). Commissioned in 1790, he was posted to Saint Domingue (Haiti) in 1802 where he was captured by the British during the following year. After his release he served in Poland and Spain. While in Spain he distinguished himself by successfully defending Burgos against Wellington in 1812.

Dumaresq, Captain H. Dumaresq served on Wellington's staff in the Peninsula as Deputy Assistant Quartermaster-General, beginning 25 April 1813, and was attached in this capacity to the 4th Division, until struck off on 25 May 1814.

"El Empecinado", Don Juan-Martin Diaz. A former soldier, he became one of the most famous Spanish guerrilla leaders. Celebrated for his exploits, he operated in Castile.

"El Pastor" ("The Shepherd"). One of the principal guerrilla leaders of the war.

Ellis, Lieutenant-Colonel Henry Watson. Commanded the 1st/23rd Foot at Nova Scotia (1808), Martinique (1809) and the Peninsula, beginning in 1810. He was wounded at Badajoz (1812) and again at Salamanca (1812).

España, General Carlos José d'Espignac (1775–1839). He entered Spanish service in 1792 and fought the French with varied success in the Peninsula. Wellington bitterly criticized him for abandoning the bridge at Alba de Tormes (July 1812), a serious mistake that enabled the French army to escape from the defeat of Salamanca (1812). A resolute absolutist, he was murdered by a member of his own party.

Evans, Sir George DeLacy (1787–1870). He began his distinguished career by joining the army in India as a volunteer in 1806. After service in India, he was posted to the Peninsula where he served from 1812 to 1814. He was twice severely wounded in the operations before New Orleans (1814–1815). He returned to Europe in time to serve at Waterloo (1815). He later commanded the British Legion in Spain (1835–1837) and a division during the Crimean War (1853–1856).

Fane, General Sir Henry (1778–1840). He entered the army in 1792 as cornet in the 6th Dragoon Guards. His distinguished service as a commander of cavalry was limited to the Peninsula, where he led a brigade and subsequently all the cavalry attached to Sir Rowland Hill's corps. The securing of the safe passage of the fords of the Tormes was one of many victories and earned him the reputation as being one of the best commanders of cavalry in the army.

Farmer, Lieutenant Thomas. He entered the army on 14 November 1804 by purchase as a second lieutenant in the 23rd Foot.

Fletcher, Lieutenant-Colonel Sir Richard (1768–1813). A distinguished commander of the Royal Engineers, his greatest achievement was the construction of the Lines of Torres Vedras near Lisbon, from 1809 to 1810. He conducted the sieges of Ciudad Rodrigo and Badajoz. He was killed during the first assault on San Sebastian, in July 1813.

Forrest, Captain C. R. He was appointed to Wellington's staff in the Peninsula as D.A.Q.M.G. on 6 August 1813 and retained this appointment in the Department to 25 June 1814.

Foy, Général Maximilien Sebastien, Comte de (1775–1825). A distinguished soldier, Foy was one of Napoleon's ablest divisional commanders. Thrice wounded at Vimiero (1808), Bussaco (1810) and at Waterloo (1815), Foy served in the Peninsula and southern France from 1807 to 1814. Retiring from active service in August 1815, he wrote a celebrated history of the Peninsular War (*Histoire de la guerre de la Péninsule*, 4 vols.; Paris: 1827).

Freire (Freyre), General Manuel (1765–1834). Spanish officer who was active in Murcia and Granada, 1810 to 1812. He is given credit for defeating the French at San Marcial (1813).

Gambier, James, first Baron Gambier (1756–1833). Gambier took part in the capture of Charlestown (1780) during the American Revolution. He led the British fleet at the bombardment of Copenhagen (1807). He later commanded the Channel fleet and was a commissioner for peace negotiations with the United States in 1814.

Gazan, Général Honoré Theodore Maxime, Comte de la Peyrière (1765–1845). Originally a coastal gunner, Gazan saw considerable service during the Revolutionary Wars. In 1808 he was posted to Spain where he served at Saragossa (1808–1809), Badajoz (1811), where he was wounded, and Albuera (1811). In 1813 he assumed command of the Army of Andalusia and briefly that of the Army of the Centre. From 1813 to 1814 he served as chief of staff of the Army of the Pyrenees. He held various inspectorships between 1815 and 1831 before finally retiring in 1832.

Girard, Général Jean-Baptiste, Baron de (1775–1815). Soon after he joined the army in 1793 as a volunteer he held several staff appointments. He fought at Austerlitz (1805) and Jena (1806) before transferring to Spain. As a general of division, he had a series of successes in 1809, 1810 and 1811. Defeated at Arroyo dos Molinos (1811), Girard was recalled to France in disgrace. Despite this setback, he served in Russia. Wounded on a number of occasions, he was mortally wounded at the battle of Ligny (1815).

Goodman, Major-General Sir Stephen (d. 1844). He entered the army in 1794 as ensign in the 48th Foot. He served with his regiment at Minorca (1800) and in the Peninsula (1809), where he was appointed Deputy Judge-Advocate in 1810. In 1814 he accepted a like post in the army left in Holland. He served in this capacity under Wellington during the Waterloo Campaign (1815). In 1819 he began his colonial service in Berbice (now Guyana) which extended over a period of twenty-four years.

Graham, General Sir Thomas, Baron Lynedoch (1748–1843). A fanatical Francophobe, he raised the 90th Foot at his own expense in 1794 and was appointed its unpaid lieutenant-colonel. He served as an aide-de-camp to Sir John Moore in the Corunna campaign, 1808 to 1809. Graham defeated Marshal Victor at Barrosa in 1811. He commanded the First Division and left wing of Wellington's army from 1811 to 1813. He was the chief founder of the United Services Club.

Green, John. A common soldier in the 68th Foot, he wrote *The Vicissitudes of a Soldier's Life* (1827), which was largely an account of his service in the Peninsula.

Grosvenor, Field Marshal Sir Thomas (1764–1851). He began his military career as an ensign in the 1st Foot Guards. In addition to his service in Flanders (1793) and the Helder (1799), he commanded a brigade at Copenhagen (1807) and at Walcheren (1809). In 1846 he and Sir George Nugent, the two senior generals in the army, and the Marquis of Anglesey, were created field marshals.

Hall, Lieutenant Robert West. Hall entered the army on 15 January 1806 as a second lieutenant in the 23rd Foot.

Hamilton, Lieutenant-General Sir John (1755–1835). After his appointment in 1771 to a Bengal cadetship, he served in operations against the Mahrattas in 1778. He also saw service in Saint Domingue (1796–1797) and the Kaffir War (1800) before being appointed Inspector-General of the Portuguese army under Marshal Beresford in 1809. He also commanded a Portuguese division at Albuera (1811) and on the Nivelle (1813), where he received special commendation (1813).

Hill, General Sir Rowland, Viscount (1772–1842). Commissioned in 1790, he fought in Egypt in 1801 and was wounded before Alexandria. After service in Ireland and Hanover, he was posted to the Peninsula. He fought at Corunna (1809), commanded the 2nd Division (1809–1814) and the right wing of the army (1813–1814). During his Peninsula campaign, he served with distinction at the Nivelle (1813) and Nive (1813), as well as at Bayonne (1814) and Toulouse (1814). He was Commander-in-Chief of the British army from 1828 to 1829.

Hoghton (Houghton), Major-General Daniel (d. 1811). This officer served in India and later at the siege of Copenhagen (1807) and the capture of

Martinique (1809). He commanded a brigade in Sir Rowland Hill's 2nd Division in the Peninsula and was killed at the head of the Fusilier Brigade at Albuera (1811).

Hood, Admiral Sir Samuel (1762–1814). Hood was a member of an illustrious seafaring family that produced several famous officers, four serving at roughly the same time, at the end of the eighteenth century. One of the "Band of Brothers", he served with Nelson at Santa Cruz (1797) and the Nile (1798), with Gambier at Copenhagen (1807) and with Saumarez in the Baltic (1808).

Hope, General, Earl of Hopetoun (1765–1823). Commissioned in 1784, he was second-in-command to Sir John Moore during the Corunna campaign (1809). He succeeded Graham as commander of the left wing of the army in the Peninsula (1813), and was wounded during the blockade of Bayonne (1814).

Houston, Sir William (1766–1842). He entered the army in 1781 as an ensign in the 31st Foot. He served in Egypt (1801) and during the Walcheren expedition (1809). He reached the rank of Major-General by 1811, when he was sent to the Peninsula. There he was given command of the 7th Division from January until August 1811, when he was sent home because of poor health. He was present at the battle of Fuentes de Oñoro (1811) and the attack on Fort Christoval, Badajoz (1811).

Howe, Richard, Earl Howe (1726–1799). An admiral in the Royal Navy, he held the North American command during the American Revolution. His greatest success was his victory over Admiral Villaret de Joyeuse of the Glorious First of June (1794). He was appointed First Lord of the Admiralty in 1783 and pacified naval mutineers at Portsmouth in 1797.

Hunter, General Sir Martin (1757–1846). A veteran of the American Revolution (1775–1783) and the campaigns against Tippoo Sahib (1790–1792), he began his military career in 1771 as an ensign in the 52nd Foot. After serving in the West Indies in 1797, he was given the command of the troops in Nova Scotia in 1803 and acted for some time as Lieutenant-Governor of New Brunswick.

Jackson, Lieutenant-Colonel Richard. An officer in the Coldstream Guards, he was appointed to Wellington's staff in the Peninsula in March 1811 as Assistant Quartermaster-General. He acted as A.Q.M.G. to the 1st Division until December 1812, and was struck off in May 1814. He later joined Wellington's staff during the Waterloo campaign (1815).

Jennings, Lieutenant G. (d. 1807). Jennings transferred to the 23rd Foot from the 34th Regiment. He was killed before Copenhagen on 4 September 1807.

Jourdan, Maréchal Jean-Baptiste, later Comte de (1762–1833). The son of a surgeon, he served with the French army in the American War of Independence. Promoted to divisional commander in 1793, he led the Army of the Sambre and Meuse to a decisive victory at Fleurus in 1794. He was created a Marshal of the Empire in 1804. He served as chief of staff to King Joseph in 1809 and from 1812 to 1813. Jourdan shared in the decisive defeat at Vitoria (1813), was later blamed by Napoleon for the debacle, recalled to France, and eventually retired from service.

Junot, Général Jean Andoche, Duc d'Abrantes (1771–1813). He served in Egypt, Syria and at Austerlitz before his appointment to head a force that entered Spain and invaded Portugal in 1807. He was defeated by Wellington at Vimiero (1808). In 1810 he served under Masséna's Army of Portugal, covering the siege of Ciudad Rodrigo (1810) and commanding the centre at Bussaco (1810). He also fought at Fuentes de Oñoro (1811).

Keane, Lieutenant-General, Lord Keane (1781–1844). He entered the army in 1794 with an appointment as Captain in the 24th Foot(?). He served in Egypt (1801) and at the reduction of Martinique (1809). In 1813 he joined the army in the Peninsula as a brigade commander and was present at Vitoria, the Pyrenees, the Nive (1813), and Toulouse (1814). He was present at New Orleans (1815) where he was severely wounded. In 1833 he was appointed commander-in-chief at Bombay.

Kellerman, Général François Etienne, Comte de (1770–1835). Commissioned into the cavalry in 1785, he commanded Junot's cavalry in the invasion of Portugal in 1807. He was responsible for negotiating the Convention of Cintra in 1808. His service in Spain included the pursuit of Moore's army and the battle of Corunna (1809). He was appointed to a cavalry command in Napoleon's Grand Army of Russia. In 1815 he fought with great distinction during the Waterloo campaign.

Kempt, General Sir James (1764–1854). After service in the Netherlands, the Mediterranean and Egypt, he was posted to the Peninsula where he was severely wounded at Badajoz (1812), but recovered to command the 1st Brigade of the Light Division through 1813 and 1814. At Waterloo he was given command of the 3rd Division on the death of Sir Thomas Picton.

La Martinière, Général Thomas (d. 1813). A French divisional commander, he was present at the decisive defeat of King Joseph's army at Vitoria (1813). He was killed a few months later during Soult's attempt to raise the British siege of San Sebastian (1813).

Larpent, Mr Francis Seymour (1776–1845). Called to the bar, he served in the Peninsula as Deputy Judge-Advocate-General from 1812 to 1814.

Leith, Lieutenant-General Sir James (1763–1816). His military career began in 1793 at Toulon under Lord Hood. He served under Sir John Moore at Corunna (1809) and commanded the 5th Division from 1810 to 1812 under Wellington. Knighted in 1813, he was made Commander-in-Chief of British forces in the West Indies in 1814.

Le Marchant, Major-General John Gaspard (1766–1812). An experienced soldier, his concern for the formal military training for officers led to his appointment as the first Commandant of the Military College at High Wycombe. A promising commander of heavy cavalry, he was killed at Salamanca (1812).

Loison, Général Louis Henri, Comte de (1771–1816). After holding various line and staff appointments, he served in Junot's army that invaded Portugal in 1807. He served in the sieges of Ciudad Rodrigo (1810, 1812) and shared the defeat at Bussaco (1810).

Louis XVIII, King of France (1755–1824). Brother of Louis XVI and uncle of the tragic Louis XVII who in fact never reigned, he succeeded in escaping from France in 1791. The Bourbons were restored when he became king in 1814. His reign was interrupted briefly on Napoleon's arrival from Elba in February 1815.

Lumley, General Sir William (1769–1850). He served in the Peninsula from 1810 to 1814. After the Napoleonic wars he served as Governor and Commander-in-Chief in Bermuda from 1819 to 1825.

MacKinnon, Major-General Henry (d. 1812). He commanded a brigade in Sir Thomas Picton's 3rd Division at Bussaco (1810). He was later killed in the breach at Ciudad Rodrigo (1812).

Maitland, General Sir Frederick (1763–1848). After joining the 14th Foot in 1779 as ensign, he saw considerable service in the West Indies during much of the period from 1783 to 1811. In 1812 he was appointed second in command in the Mediterranean under Lord William Bentinck.

Marmont, Maréchal Auguste Frédéric Louis Viesse de, Duc de Raguse (1774–1852). The son of a royalist officer, he came to Napoleon's attention during the siege of Toulon (1793). He commanded the Army of Portugal in 1811 until severely wounded at Salamanca (1812). An officer of considerable talents, his betrayal of Napoleon in 1814 permanently damaged his reputation.

Masséna, Maréchal André, Duc de Rivoli, Prince d'Essling (1758–1817). One of the best of Napoleon's marshals, Masséna began his military career by serving fourteen years in the army of Louis XVI. He was a commander of inexhaustible determination and rendered outstanding service to Napoleon by his extraordinary defence of Switzerland against Russian and Austrian armies in 1799. In April 1810 he was given the command of the Army of Portugal. His subsequent defeats at Bussaco (1810), Torres Vedras (1810–1811) and Fuentes de Oñoro (1811) virtually ended his active military service.

McGrigor, Sir James, Baronet (1771–1858). His long and distinguished medical career commenced when he began medical studies at Aberdeen and Edinburgh Universities. He became surgeon to the Connaught Rangers in 1793. In 1809 he was appointed Inspector-General of Hospitals, and in 1811 he was made Wellington's head of medical services in the Peninsula. From 1815 to 1851 he served brilliantly as Director-General of the British Army

Medical Services. Wellington gave credit to McGrigor for helping to win the great battle of Vitoria (1813) because thousands of soldiers had been returned from hospitals to their regiments after the disastrous retreat from Burgos (1812).

Mina, Francisco Espoz y. Considered to be one of the most cunning of the Spanish guerrilla leaders, he was active in Navarre. He won two major successes against strongly escorted French convoys. His campaigns against the French were noted for their atrocities.

Montbrun, Général Louis-Pierre, Comte de (1770–1812). An officer with much service experience, he was given command of the cavalry in Masséna's Army of Portugal in 1810. He is credited with having won the action of El Bodon (25 September 1811). He later served in eastern Spain and was killed at Borodino, Russia in 1812.

Montgomery, Major H. He was appointed to Wellington's staff in the Peninsula as Deputy Assistant Quartermaster-General on 28 October 1812, and was attached in this capacity to Sir Rowland Hill's corps. On 6 January 1814 he was appointed A.Q.M.G.

Moore, Lieutenant-General Sir John (1761–1809). Although a courageous officer who demonstrated tactical brilliance during his career, Moore's special gifts were the personal powers of leadership and as a great trainer of troops. He shares credit for creating the famous light troops of the Peninsular War when he was appointed to train select soldiers at Shorncliffe Camp in 1802. Given command of the British army in Portugal in 1808, he was forced to retreat to Corunna in Spain where he was killed.

Morillo, General Pablo. A Spanish divisional commander, he served at Vitoria (1813) and in the campaigns in northern Spain and south-western France (1813–1814). His troops were regarded as the best disciplined in the Spanish army.

Murray, General Sir George (1772–1846). He entered the army in 1789 as ensign in the 71st Foot. After serving in Flanders (1794), the West Indies (1796), Egypt (1801) and Copenhagen (1807), he served twice in the Peninsula, from 1809 to 1811 and 1813 to 1814. During this time he served as Wellington's Quartermaster-General. From 1819 to 1824 he held the post of Governor of the Royal Military College, Sandhurst.

Ney, Maréchal Michel, Prince de la Moskowa, Duc d'Elchingen (1769–1815). Ney was one of Napoleon's most celebrated generals; courageous, dashing and much admired by the ordinary soldier, he was fittingly nicknamed "the bravest of the brave". Created a marshal of the empire in 1804, Ney distinguished himself at the battle of Friedland (1807). In 1808 he was sent to Spain where he served with distinction as commander of the 6th Corps. He captured Ciudad Rodrigo (1810) and fought at Bussaco (1810). He also took a leading part in the invasion of and retreat from Russia (1812–1813). His actions during the Waterloo campaign earned criticism for his slowness and relative passivity. After Napoleon's final defeat, Ney was arrested by vengeful Bourbons, tried and shot.

O'Callaghan, General Sir Robert (1777–1840). After entering the army in 1794 as ensign in the 128th Foot, he served at Maida (1806). In 1811 he joined the army in the Peninsula, where he distinguished himself and was consequently mentioned in Wellington's despatches. He later commanded troops in north Britain (1825–1830) and India (1835).

O'Donnell, General Joseph Henry (1769–1834). A Spanish officer of Irish descent, he played an important role in the resistance to the French invasion during the Peninsular War. Although he won a minor victory at La Bispal in Catalonia, he suffered defeats at Lerida (1810) and Castalla (1812).

Offley, Major F. Needham (d. 1812). An officer in the 23rd Foot, he was killed at Salamanca on 22 July 1812.

Orange, Lieutenant-Colonel William, Hereditary Prince of (1792–1849). An aide-de-camp to Wellington in Spain from 1811 to 1813, he was promoted to British general in 1814. Commander-in-Chief of the Netherlands troops and of the 1st Netherlands Army Corps, he was wounded at Waterloo (1815). He succeeded his father as King (William II) of Holland in 1840.

Pack, Major-General Sir (1772?–1823). In 1791 he was gazetted a cornet in the 14th Light Dragoons. He served in Flanders (1794–1795), Ireland (1798), Cape of Good Hope (1806) and South America (1806–1807) before serving in the Peninsula. He commanded a brigade under Wellington and distinguished himself at Salamanca (1812) and Toulouse (1814). Wounded eight times in the Peninsula, he was again wounded at Waterloo (1815).

Pakenham, Sir Edward (1778–1815). He entered the army as a lieutenant in the 92nd Foot. Prior to the Peninsula campaign he served in the West Indies (1801, 1803), Copenhagen (1807) and Martinique (1809). He served as Deputy Adjutant-General in the Peninsula, 1810 to 1812. He commanded the 3rd Division (1812) and the 6th Division (1813). He was later killed at New Orleans (1815).

Pearson, Lieutenant-Colonel Thomas. He joined the Royal Welch Fusiliers as a second lieutenant in 1796. After various services, he saw action at Copenhagen (1807) and Martinique (1809). In October 1810 he embarked for the Peninsula, where he remained until 1812. During that time he was in the Lines of Torres Vedras, at Badajoz (1811), Albuera (1811) and Fuentes Guinaldo (1812), where he was severely wounded. In 1812 he was appointed on the staff in Canada and served with distinction during the war of 1812.

Peymann (Peyman, Peimann, Pyman), Major-General. Seventy-two year old commander of Danish forces during the British siege of Copenhagen in 1807. As a result of the loss of the Danish fleet to Britain, Peymann and two other generals were court martialled and sentenced to death, but were subsequently pardoned.

Phillimore, Captain Sir John (1781–1840). He entered the Royal Navy in 1795 on board the frigate *Nymphe*, Captain George Murray. He served under Sir Hyde Parker at Copenhagen (1801) and made the celebrated signal to Nelson to discontinue the action. After serving under Gambier at Copenhagen (1807), in 1810 he was appointed to the *Diadem*, a 64-gun ship, employed as a trooper. For the next three years the *Diadem* was engaged in carrying troops or prisoners to or from the Peninsula. In 1813 he was appointed to the *Eurotas*, a 46-gun frigate, on which he fought the French frigate *Clorinde* in a famous action (1814).

Phillipon, Général Armand, Baron (1761–1836). He began his career in 1778 by enlisting in a Bourbon regiment as an ordinary soldier. After a series of promotions from the ranks he became a brigade commander at the battle of Eylau (1807). Governor of Badajoz, he successfully defended the town against British siege attempts in 1811 and 1812. Phillipon was captured when Badajoz was stormed by Wellington's troops in April 1812. Subsequently imprisoned in England he escaped and fought at Kulm (1813). He retired from active service later that year.

Picton, Lieutenant-General Sir Thomas (1758–1815). Commissioned in 1772, he was promoted to Major-General in 1808. He served in the West Indies (1796–1797) and at Walcheren (1809). In 1810 he joined the army in Portugal and commanded the 3rd Division from 1810 to 1812 and again from 1813 to 1814. He played a prominent role at Fuentes de Oñoro (1811) and Vitoria (1813). He was killed leading his troops in the charge at Waterloo.

Platov (Platoff), General Matvei Ivanovich (1751–1818). Hetman of the Don Cossacks, he and his unruly horsemen played a significant role during Napoleon's invasion of Russia in 1812. A legendary figure, he served at Leipzig (1813) and took part in the Allied occupation of Paris in 1814.

Popham, Rear-Admiral Sir Home Riggs (1762–1820). He served at the Cape of Good Hope (1806) and Copenhagen (1807). In 1812 he led a raiding squadron along the north coast of Spain in conjunction with the guerrillas during the Salamanca campaign. His greatest service to the Royal Navy was his development of a new code of signalling (*Telegraphic Signals, or Marine Vocabulary*, 1800).

Power, Lieutenant-General Sir Manley (1773–1826). Power saw much active service following his commission as ensign in the 20th Foot in 1783. After serving in Holland (1799) and Egypt (1801), he took part in the Peninsular War. He commanded a Portuguese brigade and was present at Salamanca (1812), Vitoria and the Nivelle (1813), and Orthez (1814).

Prevost, Lieutenant-General Sir George. Appointed ensign in the 60th Foot in 1779, Prevost saw considerable service in the West Indies from 1791–1796,

1797–1802, and 1803–1805. In 1809 he again served in the West Indies, this time as a member of the expedition against Martinique. After this service he was appointed Commander-in-Chief in Canada.

Rapp, Général Jean, Comte de (1771–1821). A much-wounded aide-de-camp of Napoleon, he served in Egypt, at Austerlitz (1805) and Russia. He rallied to Napoleon's side in 1815 and won the action of La Suffel near Strasbourg ten days after Waterloo had been fought.

Rebecque, Baron J. V. de Constant (1794–1850). He served at Waterloo as chief of staff of Dutch-Belgian troops.

Reille, Général Honoré Charles Michel Joseph, Comte de (1775–1860). Present at many battles during his career which began in 1791, he transferred to Spain in 1808. In 1811 he returned to serve under Suchet before taking command of the army of Portugal. He fought against Wellington at many of the major battles from 1813 to 1814. In 1847 he was created a marshal.

Reynier, Général Jean Louis Ebénézer (1771–1814). Beginning as a volunteer gunner in 1792, he rose rapidly in rank. In 1810 he was posted to Spain under Masséna's command. He won the action of Sabugal (3 April 1811) during Masséna's retreat from the Lines of Torres Vedras. In 1812 he followed Napoleon into Russia.

Robinson, General Sir Frederick (1763–1852). He entered the service in 1777 as ensign in his father's regiment, the Loyal American Regiment. After his service during the American Revolution, he took part in Sir Charles Grey's expedition to the West Indies in 1793. His next active service was in the Peninsula, beginning in 1812, where he commanded a brigade. At the close of the French war in 1814 he was posted to Canada.

Ross, Major-General Robert (1766–1814). This brave and often wounded officer began his career in 1789 as ensign in the 25th Foot. He served with distinction in Holland (1799), Egypt (1801), Sicily (1806) and Corunna (1809). He served under Wellington as the commander of the fusilier brigade. During the war against the United States, he captured Washington (1814), but was killed during the abortive attack against Baltimore (1814).

Sainte-Croix, Général Charles de (1782–1810). A brilliant and energetic cavalry officer, he was first attached to Talleyrand's ministry, but in 1805 volunteered for service with Masséna's army. After fighting at Lobau and Wagram (1809) he was promoted to General of Brigade. Sent to Spain in 1810, he was killed before the Lines of Torres Vedras.

Sanchez, Don Julian. The son of a wealthy Spanish landowner, he waged a private guerrilla war against the French to avenge the honour of his family. His small army consisted of approximately 300 cavalry and some 500 infantry.

Santocildes, General José. The stubborn Spanish defender of Astorga, he surrendered the town to the French on 10 April 1810. He subsequently commanded Spanish forces in Galicia.

Schwarzenberg, Field Marshal Karl Philip, Prince (1771–1820). An Austrian soldier, he fought both against and alongside French armies. Defeated at Dresden (1813) by Napoleon, he was victorious at the battle of Leipzig (1813). In 1814 he led the Army of Bohemia in the invasion of France. Upon Napoleon's return from Elba in 1815, he set out from Austria for the Rhine, but Waterloo (1815) forestalled his arrival in force.

Smith (Smyth), Sir Henry (1787–1860). This distinguished soldier, the victor at Aliwal (1846) and governor of the Cape of Good Hope (1847–1852), entered the army as an ensign in the 95th Foot. He served in the Peninsula (1809–1814), New Orleans and Waterloo (1815). He later served in Jamaica (1826–1828) and in Cape Colony during the Sixth Kaffir War (1835).

Somerset, General Lord Fitzroy James, Baron Raglan (1788–1855). From 1808 to 1810 he served Wellington as an aide-de-camp and subsequently as his Military Secretary. He was wounded at Waterloo (1815). As Field Marshal Lord Raglan he commanded the British army in the Crimea from 1854 to 1855, where he died.

Souham, Général Joseph (1760–1837). He was promoted from the ranks of Bourbon cavalry. He commanded the Army of Portugal late in 1812 and inflicted a rare defeat upon Wellington at Burgos (1812). Later he was seriously wounded at the battle of Leipzig (1813).

Soult, Maréchal Nicolas Jean de Dieu, Duke of Dalmatia (1769–1851). He enlisted in the Bourbon army in 1785. As one of Napoleon's ablest commanders, who was greatly revered by the French people, he served with distinction at Austerlitz (1805). He saw considerable service in the Peninsula from 1808 to 1814. He served as a corps commander from 1808 to 1809, and led the Army of the South from 1810 to 1812 and the Army of Spain from 1813 to 1814. He also served as Napoleon's chief of staff at Waterloo.

Spencer, General Sir Brent (1760–1828). After seeing considerable service in the West Indies (1772–1782, 1790–1794, 1797), he fought in the Netherlands, Egypt, Copenhagen and Cadiz. He served in the Peninsula from 1808 to 1811. In 1810 he commanded the 1st Division only to be relieved of this command by Graham in 1811 because of Wellington's lack of confidence in him.

Stewart, Lieutenant-General Sir Charles (1778–1854). Half-brother to Lord Castlereagh, he served as Wellington's Adjutant-General in the Peninsula from 1809 to 1812. He led a mission to the Prussian army from 1813 to 1814. Created Lord Stewart in 1814, he succeeded as 3rd Marquess of Londonderry in 1822.

Stovin, General Sir Frederick (1783–1865). Following his commission as ensign in the 52nd Foot in 1800, he served at Ferrol (1800), Bremen (1805), Copenhagen (1807), Sweden (1808), Corunna (1809) and Walcheren (1809). He returned to the Peninsula in 1811 and was present at Ciudad

Rodrigo and Badajoz (1812), Salamanca (1812), Vitoria, the Pyrenees and the Nivelle (1813), and Orthez and Toulouse (1814). In 1814 he was appointed Deputy Adjutant-General to the expeditionary force against the United States and was wounded at New Orleans (1815).

Suchet, Maréchal Louis Gabriel, Duc d'Albufera (1770–1826). He was commissioned in the National Guard cavalry in 1791. A talented officer, he served in Spain for six years, beginning in 1808, during which time he gained an unmatched reputation among Napoleon's marshals who served there. From 1811 to 1814 he commanded armies in Catalonia where he gained great repute as a fair administrator. He was ably assisted in this effort by his wife. French defeats in other parts of Spain led to his evacuation of eastern Spain in 1814.

Thouvenot, Général Pierre, Baron (1757–1817). He was commissioned into the colonial artillery and served in the West Indies from 1780 to 1788. He served again in the West Indies (Haiti) from 1802 to 1803. Service in Spain followed soon thereafter and for a period he was governor of San Sebastian. Eventually he was made Governor of Bayonne. He remained there until he retired in 1815.

Torrens, Major-General Sir Henry (1779–1828). Commissioned in 1793, he saw service in the West Indies, Netherlands, Nova Scotia and India. From 1808 to 1809 he served Wellington as his Military Secretary. In 1809 he was appointed Military Secretary to the Duke of York and in 1812 became an aide-de-camp to the Prince Regent. In 1820 he became Adjutant-General and spent considerable time revising infantry regulations.

D'Urban, Lieutenant-General Sir Benjamin (1777–1849). A distinguished cavalry commander, D'Urban fought in numerous Peninsular battles. At Salamanca (1812) and Vitoria (1813) D'Urban led Portuguese dragoons.

Van der Maessen, Général Louis (d. 1813). A French divisional commander, he was killed in August 1813 during Soult's attempt to raise the British siege of San Sebastian.

Vauban, Sébastien Le Prestre, Marquis de (1633–1707). A brilliant military engineer who directed fifty-three sieges for Louis XIV, he also strengthened the French frontiers, constructed thirty-three fortresses and fortified 300 additional cities.

Victor, Maréchal Claude Victor-Perrin, Duc de Bellune (1764–1841). Enlisted in the Bourbon army in 1781 as a humble drummer boy, he distinguished himself and was awarded a coveted marshal's baton in 1807. In Spain he was victorious at Medellin (1809) and Ucles (1809), but trounced by Wellington at Talavera (1809) and by Graham at Barrosa (1811). He returned to France in 1812 in time to serve in Russia.

Villaret de Joyeuse, Vice Admiral Louis Thomas, Comte (1748–1812). An experienced naval officer, he became a Rear-Admiral in 1793 after successfully escorting to France a huge convoy of American grain ships. He was defeated by Lord Howe at the battle of the First of June (1794), the first major naval engagement of the Revolutionary Wars. In 1802 he was appointed Captain-General of Martinique and St Lucia, a command he held until 1809 when he was forced to capitulate to a British expedition led by Sir George Beckwith.

Warde, Sir Henry (1766–1834). He entered the army as an ensign in the 1st Foot Guards in 1783. In 1807 he took part in the expedition to Copenhagen. Afterwards he served in Spain (1808–1809) and in the capture of Mauritius (1810). He served as Governor of Barbados from 1821 to 1827. In 1830 he attained the rank of General.

Warren, Sir John (1753–1822). He was commissioned a lieutenant in the Royal Navy in 1778. He twice defeated French squadrons in 1794, and in 1798 intercepted and defeated a French fleet on its way to Ireland. He ended his service with the rank of Admiral.

Wellesley, Field Marshal Sir Arthur, Duke of Wellington, Viscount Douro (1769–1852). This master tactician, strategist and logistical expert entered military service in 1787. After serving in the Netherlands, India, Germany, Ireland and Copenhagen, he was sent to the Peninsula (in 1808) where he would establish his reputation as one of Britain's finest soldiers. For his victory at Talavera (1809) he was created viscount. His subsequent victories were to win him additional titles: Marquis of Torres Vedras, Duke of Ciudad Rodrigo, Duke of Vitoria, and Grandee of the First Class in Spain. His defeat of Napoleon at Waterloo (1815) was his final and most famous triumph. A political career followed and in 1828 he became Prime Minister.

Wentworth, Sir John (1737–1820). He served as Governor of New Hampshire (1766–1776) and Nova Scotia (1792–1808). He married Frances (Lady) Wentworth in 1769.

Wimpffen (Wimpfen), Don Luis. A Spanish general, although Swiss by birth, he was appointed Spanish Quartermaster-General at Wellington's headquarters.

Wrede, Field Marshal Carl Philipp, Prince of (1767–1838). A Bavarian, he served both Austria and France. He fought against Napoleon at Leipzig (1813). In 1815 he attended the Congress of Vienna and seven years later was appointed Generalissimo of the Bavarian army.

Wylly, Captain A. C. In 1813 Wylly served with Wellington's headquarters in Spain as aide-de-camp to the Adjutant-General, Major-General Sir Edward Pakenham.

Wynne, Lieutenant Watkin (d. 1811). He entered the army on 29 May 1806 without purchase as a second lieutenant in the 23rd Foot. He died of fever in Portugal in 1811.

York, Frederick Augustus, Duke of York and Albany (1763–1827). Although his conduct on the battlefield demonstrated that he lacked the qualities of greatness as a field commander, the Duke of York nonetheless distinguished himself as a first-class administrator of the British army. His many reforms of the army included serious efforts to curb the corrupt system of purchasing commissions and promotions and to get officers promoted on merit only. He served as Commander-in-Chief of the army from 1795 to 1809, and again from 1811 to his death in 1827.

Appendix B

ARTICLES OF CAPITULATION FOR THE TOWN AND CITADEL OF COPENHAGEN, 7 SEPTEMBER 1807

Articles of Capitulation for the Town and Citadel of Copenhagen, agreed upon between Major General the Right Honorable Sir Arthur Wellesley, Knight of the Bath, Sir Home Popham, Knight of Malta and Captain of the Fleet, and Lieutent. Colonel George Murray, Deputy Quarter Master General of the British Forces, being thereto duly authorized by James Gambier, Esquire, Admiral of the Blue and Commander in Chief of His Britannic Majesty's Ships and Vessels in the Baltic, and by Lieutenant General the Right Honorable Lord Cathcart, Knight of the Thistle, Commander in Chief of His Britannic Majesty's forces in Zealand and the North of the Continent of Europe on the one part; and Major General Waltersdorff, Knight of the Order of Danebroge, Chamberlain to the King and Colonel of the North Zealand Regiment of Infantry, Rear Admiral Lutken, and J. H. Kirchhoff, Aide de Camp to His Danish Majesty; being duly authorised by His Excellency Major General Peymann, Knight of the Order of Danebroge and Commander in Chief of His Danish Majesty's Forces in the Island of Zealand, on the other part.

Article 1st

When this Capitulation shall be signed and ratified the Troops of His Britannic Majesty are to be put in possession of the Citadel.

Article 2nd

A Guard of His Britannic Majestys Troops shall likewise be placed in the Dock Yard.

Article 3rd

The Ships and Vessels of War of every description, with all the Naval Stores belonging to His Danish Majesty, shall be delivered unto the charge of such persons as may be appointed by the Commanders in Chief of His Britannic Majestys Forces, and they are to be put in immediate possession of the Dock Yards, and all the Buildings and Storehouses belonging thereto.

Article 4th

The Storeships and Transports in the Service of His Britannic Majesty are to be allowed, if necessary, to come into the harbour, for the purpose of embarking such Stores and Troops as they have brought into this Island.

Article 5th

As soon as the Ships shall have been removed from the Dock Yards, or within six weeks from the date of this Capitulation, or sooner if possible, the Troops of His Britannic Majesty shall deliver up the Citadel to the Troops of His Danish Majesty, in the state in which it shall be found when they shall occupy it. His Britannic Majesty's Troops shall likewise within the before mentioned time, or sooner if possible, be embarked from the Island of Zealand.

Article 6th

From the date of this capitulation hostilities shall cease throughout the Island of Zealand.

Article 7th

No Person whatsoever shall be molested, and all Property public or private, with the exception of the Ships and Vessels of War and the Naval Stores beforementioned belonging to His Danish Majesty, shall be respected; and all civil and military Officers, in the service of His Danish Majesty, shall continue in the full exercise of their authority throughout the Island of Zealand; and every thing shall be done which can tend to produce union and harmony between the two Nations.

Article 8th

All Prisoners taken on both sides shall be unconditionally restored; and those Officers who are prisoners on parole shall be released from its effects.

Article 9th

Any English property that may have been sequestered in consequence of the existing hostilities, shall be restored to the owners.

This Capitulation shall be ratified by the respective Commanders in Chief, and the ratifications shall be exchanged before twelve o'clock at noon this day.

Done at Copenhagen this 7th day of September 1807.

(signed)   (signed)
Ernst Frederick Waltersdorff   Arthur Wellesley

(signed)
O. Lutken

(signed)
Home Popham

(signed)
J. H. Kirchhoff

(signed)
George Murray

Ratified by me

signed

Peimann

Source: W.O. 1/187, enclosure in Gambier to Castlereagh, 7 September 1807. The capitulation was also recorded in French.

Appendix C
EVIDENCE OF THE ABANDONMENT OF BRITISH ARMY WOMEN

No. 1—Petition of Elezabeth McLane, 14 May 1800

To His Royal Highness Duke of York
the Pitition of Elezabeth McLane Humbly showeth that your Pititioner is the Widow of the Late sergant John McLane Whom served in the 21th Redgt, 23 years sergant and 6 years private in the Above Redgt. your Pititioner submits the following to your Royal Highness consideration. Leutenant Colpeper Left the 21th Redgt Letly to go to the sevent Wast indian Redgt. Mr Colpeper owed My Late husband one pound three shillings and four pence as apears by the Books of the Redgt. I wrote to Mr Colpeper and to Mr Campbell Agand for the sevent Wast india Redgt but got No answer. I hade A son in the 21st Redgt whom dyed in the Wast indias and both My Husband and son being dead I have No person to asist Me and the paymaster capt McKay ordred all My Husbands Effects to be sold to pay his funeral charge and Left Me destitute. on hearing of your Royal Highness goodness for Which you are so Justly seleberated inboldned Me to adress your knowing Humanity, houping from your goodness of hart that your Royal Highness Will order this smal sume to be Remited to Me at Mr Hird Mans Dunfermilin, and your pititioner is in duly Bound and Will Ever pray
May 14th 1800   Elezabeth McLane

Source: Edinburgh, Scottish Record Office, "Public Office Letters 1800", NRA [SCOT], McLane to the Duke of York, 14 May 1800, enclosed in Brownrigg to Campbell, 19 May 1800

No. 2—Petition of Elinor Quinn, 3 July 1808

To His Excellency Sir James Henry Craig Governor and Commander in Chief—etc.—etc.—etc.
The Petition of Elinor Quinn, wife of Michl. Quinn late of the 100th Regiment Deceased.
Humbly Shewith.
That your Excellency's Petitioner's husband died of a lingering disease (the 18th of June last) in Quebec & left Petitioner in a very distressed Situation with two small Children totally depending to the humanity of the Gentleman of

the Garrison, Petitioner being rendered incapable of going to service by means of her small orphans humbly implores the charity of your Excellency as she has not means of support in Consequence of no Rations being allowed her since the death of her Husband. Petitioner having no other Gentlemen who knows her here but Major Lloyd of the 98th Regt. and Lieutenant Dixon of the 100th Regimt. who can certify to your Excellency her Character, as also Colonel Bruyeres as to her deceased Husband, totally depends on your Excellency's humanity, to assist her as she wishes to return home to Ireland, and having not the least means at present to support herself & helpless Orphans unless through the humanity of your Excellency whose assistance Petitioner implores by allowing her Rations untill she may be enabled to procure a passage home. & Petitioner and Orphans shall as in Duty bound ever pray for the prosperity of your Excellency.

Quebec 3rd July 1808   (signed) Elinor Quinn

and

No. 3 — Petition of Margaret Fraser, 22 December 1808

To Lieutenant General Sir James Henry Craig Commander in Chief— etc.—etc.—etc.—

The humble Petition of Margaret Fraser widow of Angus Mcleod, late a private in His Majesty's 10th Royal Veteran Battalion, humbly begs leave to represent to your Excellency that a short time ago, having had the Misfortune of losing her Husband in this place, and being left with an infant Child not yet three months old, and at present in the greatest distress being unable to go to Service with her child so young, ortherwise is capable of industring for her livilihood, humbly begs your Excellency would pity her distressed situation and be graciously pleased to allow her, One Ration, or any kind of assistance that your Excellency may be pleased to think fitt until she can procure a Passage to Scotland her native Country. your Petitioner begs to inform your Excellency that her late husband was upwards of thirty One years in His Majesty's Service, Nineteen of which he served in India in His Majesty's 71st Regiment, when upon his return to England he was invalided. Your Petitioner begs your Excellency will pardon this liberty but from having heard off your humanity to the distressed, prays your Excellency will be pleased to assist her.

Your Petitioner begs to inform Your Excellency that her late husband had two Brothers in His Majesty's Service one who fell in Battle by the side of her late husband, and the other drowned upon the Passage to England.

Quebec 22nd December 1808.

Source: Ottawa, Public Archives of Canada, British Military and Naval Records, RG8, I, "C Series", vol. 1334: Military Correspondence, Nova Scotia Command, 21 March 1806 to 3 April 1809.

Appendix D
INSTRUCTIONS FOR OFFICERS IN OBSERVATION ON THE LA RHUNE MOUNTAINS, 9 NOVEMBER 1813

Vera [St. Jean de Luz?] November 9th 1813

Instructions for the Officers stationed in observation upon the Mountains of La Rhune

Captain Stavely—D.A.Q. Mr. Gl

Captain Browne—D:A:A: Gl

1. To be upon the Top of the Mountains at Day-Break tomorrow.
2. To observe and note down as exactly as they can, the position of the enemy's Force, when it can be first observed; specifying the situation in which their Troops are stationed, and their numbers which they estimate to be in each place—mentioning either the number of Men or the number of Battalions, Companies, or other separate Bodies observed in each place—also what Artilery is observed, & what Cavalry, if any, is seen.
3. To note the several movements which are made by any part of the Enemy's Force in the course of the Day, & to express in the most distinct manner the seeming amount of the Force moved, the time of the movement, specifying whether the movement is towards the *enemys* right or his left, towards his front, or his rear. Also to state (if they are known) the name of the place, where the movement is made, and that towards which it appears to be directed.
4. The Line of Direction of the Enemy's present positions, seen from the Mountains of La Rhune is—the Works which cover *Socoa & Ciboure*—*The Camp overlooking Urrugne*—The Detached Works on *The Enemy's left of the Camp overlooking Urrugne*—*A Camp* on the left of the *Nivelle* river a little below Ascain, and which covers a Pontoon Bridge on that part of the River—The Village of *Ascain* and its *Stone Bridge*—The Village of *Serres* (opposite Ascain, and the camps & works in its Vicinity—on the right bank of the Nivelle=*A white House* on the right bank of the Nivelle, about an English Mile *above the Bridge of Ascain*, below which there is a Ford, and near

which a Work has been constructed on the right Bank of the river — *The Petite La Rhune* against which the first attack of the Light Divisions is to be directed — *The Heathy Heighths* behind it, between the village of Ascain & the Village of Sare. *The Village of Sare* & the position behind it, & two Works in front of it — the *Village of St. Pe* — The position occupied by the enemy on the long Hill behing *Ainhoa. The Village of Ainhoa — The Village of Espelette — Cambo Ustaritz — Bayonne* =

5. The most important observations respecting the movements, which the enemy may make, are: *Movements* to his *right* or *left*, to *reinforce* any part of his line — *Movements* which might indicate his acting offensively against any part of our Line =

   Appearances which might indicate his retiring to a new position — or his withdrawing altogether — either towards Bayonne, or beyond the River Nive, which runs by Cambo, and Ustaritz, towards Bayonne.

6. The Observations made, are to be sent down, from time to time, addressed to Lord Wellington — each report is to be numbered, and the hour at which it is dispatched is to be noted upon it.

   Major General Alten will be directed to leave a Non-Commissioned Officer & Party of the Light Division, at the Chapel on the Mountain, to be at the Disposal of the Officers in observation — and Lieut-Gnl Sir Lowry Cole will be directed to station a few small parties, in such a manner as to convey the reports expeditiously, in the direction of General Givons present encampment, where a party of the Mounted Staff Corps will be stationed to receive them —.

7. Copy of a memorandum given to Mr. Hooke is inclosed, that the Officers in Observation may act upon it, should circumstances seem to render it necessary.

> Signed
> Geo. Murray.
> Q.M.Gl.

Memorandum for Mr. Hooke

Should any circumstances occur in the course of tomorrow to render it necessary for the Baggage of Head Quarters to move further to the Rear, Mr. Hooke will order it to proceed to Lesaca — Mr. Hook will be apprized of the necessity of such an order, either from the Staff with the Commander of the Forces, or from the Officers stationed in Observation upon the Mountain of La Rhune, who will apprize Mr. Hook *in writing* should any thing occur upon the left of the Army to render it expedient to move the Baggage of Head Quarters from Vera.

signed
Geo. Murray
Q. M. Gl.

Lt Hooke
Mounted Staff Corps.

Source: Browne Family Papers.

Notes

1. Wellington constantly reminded his officers of their many faults. He wrote for instance: "The Commander of the Forces is always concerned to be observing upon the conduct of officers who have invariably conducted themselves well in the field: but the officers of the army must recollect that to perform their duty with gallantry in the field is but a small part of what is required of them; and that obedience to orders, accuracy in the performance, and discipline are necessary to keep any military body together and to perform any military operation with advantage to their country or service to themselves." Quoted in Michael Glover, *Wellington's Army in the Peninsula, 1808–1814* (New York: Hippocrene Books, Inc., 1977), p. 75.

2. This concept of military professionalism, the three distinguishing characteristics of which are skill, responsibility and corporateness, is taken from Samuel P. Huntington, *The Soldier and the State: The Theory and Politics of Civil-Military Relations* (New York: Random House/Vintage Books, 1957), pp. 7–18.

3. "Officer corps" and "officer class", more commonly used terms, have been avoided since both are now viewed as something of a fiction. As J. A. Houlding has demonstrated the so-called British officer corps, after 1715, was in fact a social mixture. It had neither the caste exclusiveness of the Prussian officer corps, nor the cosmopolitan and frequently professional character of the Austrian officer corps, nor even the increasing élitism which was descriptive of the French officer corps. Instead, British officers were recruited from four social groups: the landed gentry and nobility; the lesser gentry, distinguished families now involved in trade or professions, the clergy and surviving yeomen farmers; sweepings from a wide distribution across the first two groups and a significant minority of foreigners, primarily Huguenots; and subaltern officers of advanced age who were promoted from the ranks, sometimes for good conduct, sometimes for conspicuous bravery. See Houlding's *Fit for Service: The Training of the British Army, 1715–1795* (Oxford: Clarendon Press, 1981), pp. 104–116.

4. Huntingdon, *The Soldier and the State*, pp. 22–28, 36.

5. In 1808 a British expeditionary force under the command of Lieutenant-General Sir Arthur Wellesley (1769–1852), the future Duke of Wellington, was sent to the Peninsula to support the Portuguese against

France. Wellesley was subsequently superseded in command and recalled home. Command of the army was finally given to Lieutenant-General Sir John Moore (1761–1809). Mounting dangers and difficulties led to Moore's precipitate retreat in 1809 to Corunna, Spain, where he was killed and from which point the British army was evacuated. In the spring of 1809 the army returned to the Peninsula with Wellesley once again in command.

6. If, according to Samuel Huntington, it were necessary to cite a precise date for the origin of the military profession, 6 August 1808 would be selected. On that day the government of Prussia issued its decree on the commission of officers which established the basic standard of military professionalism. This edict, along with the great reforms of Grolman, Scharnhorst, Gneisenau and the Prussian Military Commission, signal the actual beginnings of the military profession in the Western world. For all of this, see Huntington, *The Soldier and the State*, pp. 30–31.

7. Browne Family Papers. Also see Frederic Boase, *Modern English Biography* (London: Frank Cass & Co. Ltd., 1965), 1:446; Henry F. Chorley, *Memorials of Mrs. Hemans, With Illustrations of Her Literary Character from her Private Correspondence*, 2 vols. (New York: Saunders and Otley, 1836), 1:8–9, 13; and [Harriet Browne-Owen,] *The Works of Mrs. Hemans; With a Memoir of Her Life*, 7 vols. (London: William Blackwood and Sons, 1857), 1:4, 13. The latter work is dedicated to "Colonel Sir Henry Browne, K.C.H." The dedication continues: "THESE PAGES, WRITTEN UNDER HIS ROOF, WHICH HAS ALWAYS BEEN A REFUGE FOR THE SORROWFUL, ARE DEDICATED, BY HIS SURVIVING SISTER, IN REMEMBRANCE OF HER WHO, DURING MANY YEARS OF TRIAL, FOUND HER BEST EARTHLY SOLACE IN HIS CARE AND AFFECTION." "IN REMEMBRANCE OF HER" is a reference to Felicia Hemans (née Felicia Dorothea Browne, 1793–1835), Thomas Browne's next to eldest sister. For more about her, see below.

8. *The Royal Military Calendar, or Army Service and Commission Book*, 3rd ed., 5 vols. (London: A. J. Valpy, 1820), 5:154. Hereafter referred to as the *Royal Military Calendar*. Also *The London Gazette*, 2 November 1805 and *A List of All the Officers of the Army and Royal Marines on Full and Half-Pay*, (War Office, 14 February 1806), p. 157. The latter is hereafter cited simply as the *Army List*. The 23rd Foot was a two-battalion regiment. Typically, one battalion served abroad while its pair remained in Britain, at the depot, as a training and reinforcement unit. The present spelling "Welch" was adopted for the regiment in 1920 as a result of Army Order 56. "Welsh" is employed for regular usage.

9. Robert Southey provides the reader of his *Letters from England* with a glimpse of the hazards of Liverpool's hurried economic development.

"Fortunes are made here", he wrote between 1803 and 1807, "with a rapidity unexampled in any other part of England. It is true that many adventurers fail; yet with all the ups and downs of commercial speculation Liverpool prospers beyond all other ports." Jack Simmons, ed. (Gloucester, England: Alan Sutton Pub. Ltd., 1984), p. 223.

10. George, the next to eldest, and Claude were Thomas' two brothers. The former followed his older brother into the 23rd Foot. The date of his non-purchased commission is given as 10 July 1806. He achieved lieutenant-colonel and commanded a company in the Peninsula, where he was twice wounded. He received his first wound during the siege and assault of Badajoz, 6–7 April 1812. The latter, born in 1794, served as a deputy-assistant commissary general at Kingston, Upper Canada, where he died in 1821. For all this see *Army List*, 1807; A. D. L. Cary and Stouppe McCance, comps., *Regimental Records of the Royal Welch Fusiliers*, 4 vols. (London: Forster Groom & Co. Ltd., 1921–29), 1:239, 248, 260; and *The Works of Mrs. Hemans*, 1:8.

11. The sailor's contempt of the soldier doubtless stemmed in part from an inter-service rivalry, which was as old as the Royal Navy and British army. However, the use of the Royal Navy as the first and main line of defence against a French invasion of Britain, particularly during the period 1803 to 1805, combined with the popular view that the regular army was not an effective fighting force and, thus, was not bearing its rightful burden, exacerbated the sailor's open disrespect of the soldier. It must be noted, too, that Southey had very little personal knowledge of naval matters. He compensated for this insufficiency by appealing to his brother for information. See *Letters From England*, xix–xx, p. 486.

12. Michael Glover, *Wellington's Army*, p. 36.

13. Quoted in *ibid*.

14. *Ibid*.

15. Richard Glover, *Peninsular Preparation*, pp. 146–7; and Michael Glover, *Wellington's Army*, p. 43. The incentive to purchase a commission was financial. If an officer who had purchased his commission sold out entirely, he received the value of his commission as a retirement fund. Since most officers obtained at least one promotion without purchase, they not only got their money back but in this way made a handsome profit. Free commissions, on the other hand, could not normally be sold. See Houlding, *Fit for Service*, pp. 100–104.

16. London, British Museum, Moore MSS, No. 57321, Moore to Brownrigg, 4 September 1796.

17. French military dress was equally seductive. "View of the Gardens of Tivoli", a contemporary engraving, shows soldiers achieving success with the ladies. A copy of this appears in J. Christopher Herold, *The Horizon*

Book of the Age of Napoleon (New York: American Heritage Pub. Co., Inc./ Bonanza Books, 1983), p. 100.

18. *Pride and Prejudice* (1813; New York: Harper and Row, 1965), p. 61.

19. Two of Mrs Bennet's daughters, Catherine and Lydia, were similarly afflicted. "They", according to Austen, "could talk of nothing but officers; and Mr Bingley's large fortune, the mention of which gave animation to their mother, was worthless in their eyes when opposed to the regimentals of an ensign." *Ibid.*, pp. 24–25.

20. A number of circumstances induced the British government of Henry Addington (1801–1804) to seek a general pacification with France in 1801. Peace between the two nations was reached at Amiens on 25 March 1802. Napoleon apparently never regarded the peace as anything more than a breathing space, however. As a result, war resumed on 17 May 1803.

21. For all of this see Clive Emsley, *British Society and the French Wars, 1793–1815* (Totowa, New Jersey: Rowman and Littlefield, 1979), pp. 112–114. Compare Wordsworth's call for patriotic death with a similar demand in revolutionary France, where soldiers and civilians apparently resolved to die for the Patrie and the République. Judge the "Chant du départ" which was second only in popularity to the "Marseillaise" as a hymn of the French Revolution.

> The Republic calls us,
> We know how to vanquish, we know how to perish!
> The French ought to live for her,
> And for her the French ought to die!

See John A. Lynn, *The Bayonets of the Republic: Motivation and Tactics in the Army of Revolutionary France, 1791–1794* (Chicago: University of Illinois Press, 1984) pp. 173–177.

22. See Austen, *Pride and Prejudice*, p. 24.

23. The news of Nelson's victory and death reached London on 5 November. Nelson's victory did not prevent a French invasion of England, which had been abandoned by early September when the French army left its staging camp at Boulogne and marched against Austria. Rather, the victory of Trafalgar made any revival of invasion impossible. See J. Steven Watson, *The Reign of George III, 1760–1815* (Oxford: Clarendon Press, 1960), pp. 421–434.

24. Emsley, *British Society and the French Wars*, p. 113.

25. *Ibid.*

26. See London, Public Record Office, War Office Papers 12/4036. Hereafter War Office Papers cited as W.O. The functions of the regimental agent were briefly stated in 1798 to the Committee of Finance by the then Deputy Secretary at War. They were: "To apply for, receive, disburse

and account for public money advanced to him under general regulations or by particular orders. He is the ordinary channel of communication between the Regiment and the Public Departments and is resorted to not only for providing and forwarding of arms, clothing and other regimental supplies but also in the business, public or private, of the individual officers." Quoted in J. D. Turner, "Army Agency," *Journal of the Society for Army Historical Research* vol. 13 (1934):30.

27. The information concerning the agency of Greenwood and Cox is taken from K. R. Jones, "Cox and Co.: Army Agents, Craig's Court: The Nineteenth Century," *Journal of the Society for Army Historical Research* vol. 40 (1962): 178, 180; K. R. Jones, "Richard Cox, Army Agent and Banker," *Journal of the Society for Army Historical Research* vol. 34 (1956): 180–181; and Turner, "Army Agency," *Journal of the Society for Army Historical Research:* 30. Officers customarily visited their agents when gazetted. Ensign John Moore, the future Sir John Moore, called upon Mr Mair, agent to the 51st Foot. Moore's request to see his mother before joining his regiment is testimony to the authority of the regimental agent. See Carola Oman, *Sir John Moore* (London: Hodder and Stoughton, 1953), p. 37. The agency was thus a place where officers could routinely expect to meet brother officers. In Thackeray's *Vanity Fair*, Captain Dobbin communicates some information to Ensign Stubble "whom he met at the agent's". *Vanity Fair* (New York: Penguin Books Ltd., 1984), p. 285.

28. The unlawful absence of officers was a serious problem in the British army at the close of the eighteenth century. In January 1795, William Windham, then Secretary at War, concerted his efforts with those of the Duke of York to ensure the attendance of officers unlawfully away from their duties. This joint effort resulted in a number of important reforms initiated by the Duke. Much use was made of dismissing or superseding those officers found guilty of absence from their regiments without official approval. Beginning in the summer of 1795, regimental agents were instructed repeatedly to direct absent officers to join their units at once. Information on these officers was provided by periodic returns, and commanding officers were reminded of these regulations. The Duke of York demanded a special fortnightly return which was to be forwarded from June to September. It was to show, among other things, the number of officers present with each unit. Furthermore, towards the end of 1795 and early in 1796, colonels were notified through their agents of the conditions under which officers could be lawfully absent and the date by which those without approved leave had to rejoin their regiments on pain of being superseded. Grounds justifying an officer's absence were attendance in Parliament, if he were a Member; recruiting; urgent private

business which demanded the officer's immediate personal attendance; and, of course, ill health duly certified by a qualified physician. The Duke of York also personally reviewed and approved or rejected all applications for leaves of absence. These decisions were then forwarded to the Secretary at War, who in turn informed the applicant's commanding officer. According to Richard Glover, the Duke of York's efforts against recalcitrant absentee officers were "clearly successful". This assessment is misleading for it suggests that the Duke's efforts eliminated absenteeism, when in fact they did not. The abuse continued in European regiments serving in the West Indies. It was also a problem in Britain's West India Regiments. Glover came to this conclusion because he apparently did not extend his study of unlawful officer absenteeism past 1800. An examination of the various periodic returns, particularly those for the army in the West Indies, shows that the Duke's reforms had little effect on those determined not to join their regiments. For all this see Richard Glover, *Peninsular Preparation*, pp. 167–169; and Roger N. Buckley, *Slaves in Red Coats: The British West India Regiments, 1795–1815* (New Haven: Yale University Press, 1979), pp. 32–34.

29. The premises of at least one military tailor and outfitter were located on Leadenhall Street, between Cheapside and Whitechapel, that being Messrs Welch and Stalker at number 134. For an illustrated glimpse into the world of the military tailor, see James Laver, *British Military Uniforms* (London: Penguin Books, 1948), pp. 23–26, 29 and plates 6 and 7.

30. William Thackeray, *Vanity Fair*, pp. 348–9.

31. For Browne's uniform see the following: R. Money Barnes, *A History of the Regiments & Uniforms of the British Army* (London: Seeley Service & Co. Ltd., 1957), pp. 28, 51, 105–6; and R. G. Harris, "Two Military Miniatures," *Journal of the Society for Army Historical Research*, LXIII, No. 254 (Summer 1985): 100–101.

32. See pp. 113–16.

33. R. G. Harris, "Six Portrait Miniatures," *Journal of the Society for Army Historical Research* LXI, No. 245 (Spring 1983): 1. Many miniature painters went to India to paint, where they sought the patronage of distinguished clients. For a glimpse of the career of Charles Shirreff, see Pamela P. Bardo, *English and Continental Portrait Miniatures: The Latter–Schlesinger Collection* (New Orleans: New Orleans Museum of Art, 1978), p. 24.

34. William Grimaldi, of Genoese descent and English birth, who was widely known for his ability to paint dazzling portrait miniatures featuring, for instance, opaque white in the hair and on the face and colourful backgrounds, was First Miniature Painter to the Duke of York. For all this see Daphne Foskett, *British Portrait Miniatures: A History* (London:

Methuen and Co. Ltd., 1963), p. 144; and Bardo, *English and Continental Portrait Miniatures*, pp. 23–24.

35. The episode surrounding the portmanteau is a reconstruction based partially on plate I ("Fitting Out") of an 1820 satirical comic strip by George Cruikshank entitled "Progress of a Midshipman". A reproduction of this drawing appears in David Kunzle, *The Early Comic Strip: Narrative Strips and Picture Stories in the European Broadsheet from c. 1450 to 1825* (Berkeley: University of California, 1973), p. 387.

36. Portions of the above sections are fictive, as indicated. The documentation, however, demonstrates that the several reconstructions all have some basis in fact.

37. In their collective efforts to contain and then to destroy the military and political menace of revolutionary and Napoleonic France, the established monarchies of Europe entered into seven alliances or coalitions. The First Coalition was formed in June 1792 and the Seventh and last in March 1815.

38. See John M. Sherwig, *Guineas & Gunpowder: British Foreign Aid in the Wars with France, 1793–1815* (Cambridge: Harvard University Press, 1969), pp. 166–183.

39. Cary and McCance, *Regimental Records of the Royal Welch Fusiliers*, 1:211.

40. David G. Chandler, *Dictionary of the Napoleonic Wars: The Soldiers, Strategies, Armaments, Movements, and Battles That Shaped Events During Napoleon's Reign* (London: Arms and Armour Press, 1979), p. 348.

41. Cary and McCance, *Regimental Records of the Royal Welch Fusiliers*, 1:212.

42. Richard Glover, *Peninsular Preparation*, pp. 193–201.

43. George Bell, *Soldier's Glory: Being 'Rough Notes of an Old Soldier'* (London: G. Bell & Sons, Ltd., 1956), p. 2.

44. Houlding, *Fit for Service*, pp. 160–1.

45. Quoted in Michael Glover, *Wellington's Army*, p. 42.

46. Denis Winter, *Death's Men: Soldiers of the Great War* (New York: Penguin Books Ltd., 1985), pp. 37–49.

47. *Ibid.*, p. 44; and Michael Glover, *Wellington's Army*, p. 38.

48. Michael Glover, *Wellington's Army*, p. 65.

49. Michael Grant, *The Army of the Caesars* (New York: Charles Scribner's Sons, 1974), xxvii.

50. George Pinckard, *Notes on the West Indies: Written during the Expeditions under the Command of the Late General Sir Ralph Abercromby*, 3 vols. (London: Longman, Hurst, Rees and Orme, 1806), 3:188–192.

51. Quoted in Richard Glover, *Peninsular Preparation*, p. 175.

52. *The Military Adventures of Johnny Newcome: With an Account of His Campaign on the Peninsula and in Pall Mall and Notes* (1816; reprint ed.,

London: Methuen and Co., 1904), p. 146. The author of this volume has been identified as Lieutenant-Colonel David Roberts. See Kunzle, *The Early Comic Strip*, p. 386.

53. See W. O. 90/1.
54. W. O. 27/113.
55. Bell, *Soldier's Glory*, p.. 2.
56. W. O. 25/652.
57. Houlding, *Fit for Service*, p. 168.
58. W. O. 27/113, Major General Edward Stehelin's Report of 28 October 1812.
59. W. O. 27/113, M. A. Bozon's Report of 10 November 1812.
60. Reginald Hargreaves, *This Happy Breed: Sidelights on Soldiers and Soldiering* (London: Skeffington and Son Ltd., 1951), p. 12.
61. Cary and McCance, *Regimental Records of the Royal Welch Fusiliers*, 1:213–214.
62. *Ibid.*, 1:212, 217, and W. O. 12/3970, 3971, 4036, 4037. The most famous method of recruiting was "beating up" for volunteers, that is, regiments were authorized by "beating orders" from the War Office to raise men in a particular area. The recruiting party was announced by the beat of the drum.
63. Houlding, *Fit for Service*, pp. 120–125.
64. Cyril Ray, *The Lancashire Fusiliers* (London: Leo Cooper Ltd., 1971), p. 63.
65. Barnes, *A History of the Regiments and Uniforms of the British Army*, pp. 75, 319.
66. *Ibid.*, p. 58.
67. *Ibid.*, p. 8.
68. "Replies" [Regimental Pets,] *Journal of the Society for Army Historical Research* 13:187.
69. For all this see Barnes, *History of the Regiments and Uniforms of the British Army*, plate xviii, p. 229; H. L. Wickes, *Regiments of Foot: A Historical Record of all the Foot Regiments of the British Army* (Reading, U.K.: Osprey Pub. Ltd., 1974), pp. 10–11; R. Money Barnes, *Military Uniforms of Britain and the Empire* (London: Seeley Service and Co. Ltd., 1960), p. 161; and "Replies," *Journal of the Society for Army Historical Research*, pp. 186–7.
70. The flash is composed of five pieces of black ribbon, each about nine inches long and $2\frac{1}{2}$ inches wide, with a triangular cut-out at the base of each. The ribbons are placed together, overlapping one another, in a fan-like fashion resembling the tail of a bird. At the collar, the middle ribbon overlaps the others almost completely, making the flash about three inches wide at this point, while the maximum width near the bottom is

about seven inches. A narrow separate length of ribbon, placed horizontally at the collar, holds the flash together.

71. "Replies," *Journal of the Society for Army Historical Research*, p. 186; and Barnes, *Military Uniforms of Britain and The Empire*, pp. 160–1 and *History of the Regiments and Uniforms of the British Army*, pp. 227–8.

72. The idea for this passage is taken from Barnes, *History of the Regiments and Uniforms of the British Army*, pp. 314–15. Robert Graves, the poet, was well informed of the proud traditions of the 23rd, in which he served as an officer during World War One. See his autobiography, *Good-bye to All That* (Doubleday, 1957, pp. 82–90).

73. Stendhal, *The Red and the Black* (New York: Bantam Books, 1959), p. 331.

74. Henry Lachouque, *The Anatomy of Glory: Napoleon and His Guard, A Study in Leadership*, trans. Anne S. K. Brown (Providence, Rhode Island: Brown University Press, 1961), p. 516.

75. See Michael Glover, "Purchase, Patronage and Promotion in the Army at the Time of the Peninsular War," parts I and II, *The Army Quarterly* 1 and 2 (1973), 211–215, 355–362.

76. Glover, unfortunately, does not say how long an officer would remain in the rank of major before promotion to lieutenant-colonel. A clue to this question may be provided by looking at the rate of promotion at the beginning of the 1793–1815 war, when the expansion of the army began. According to Houlding, in 1793 majors in foot regiments were accustomed to waiting an average of six years before promotion to lieutenant-colonel; majors in cavalry regiments waited an average of five years. See *Fit for Service*, p. 109.

77. The following works were used to construct Browne's service records: *The London Gazette*, 29 October–2 November 1805; *Army Lists*, 1805, 1806, 1807, 1813, 1816 and 1840; and the *Royal Military Calendar*, 5:154.

78. *Journal*, p. 77.

79. Browne is unclear concerning the date of his appointment to Wellington's staff. He gives two dates: March and September 1811. See *Journal*, pp. 125, 136. According to Ward, however, Browne had a staff appointment on 9 August 1811, when he served as commandant of the Depot of Belém, Portugal. On 12 April 1812 Browne was appointed D.A.A.G. and afterwards served in the field in the Adjutant-General's office. See *Wellington's Headquarters*, pp. 170–1.

80. Ward, *Wellington's Headquarters*, pp. 46–9.

81. Robert Stewart, Viscount Castlereagh, Marquis of Londonderry; best known as Viscount Castlereagh (1769–1822). He served as, among other duties, foreign secretary, 1812–1822. Watson, *Reign of George III*, p. 399.

82. *Journal*, p. 281.

83. John W. Fortescue, *A History of the British Army*, 13 vols. (London: Macmillan and Co., Ltd., 1899–1930), 7:424–5.

84. Boase, *Modern English Biography*, 1:446.

85. Browne Family Papers.

86. A. A. Payne, *A Handbook of British and Foreign Orders, War Medals and Decorations, Awarded to the Army and Navy* (Sheffield, U.K.: Northend, 1911), p. 15.

87. Browne Family Papers.

88. I am grateful to W. D. Cribbs (Ministry of Defence), Surrey, for this information. See, also, John Burke and John B. Burke, *Genealogical and Heraldic Dictionary of the Landed Gentry of Great Britain & Ireland*, 2 vols. (London: Henry Colburn Pub., 1846), 1:149.

89. N. B. Leslie, *The Succession of Colonels of the British Army From 1660 to the Present Day* (London: Gale and Polden Ltd., 1974), p. 108.

90. A note in the handwriting of Henry Ralph Browne, Sir Thomas' eldest son, is appended to the end of the Journal. It reads: "commands were more than once offered to my father as a General Officer, but he declined them." Another reference to Sir Thomas' apparent disinterest in obtaining a major command for himself appears in a document written by Sir Thomas' great-granddaughter and is part of the Browne Family Papers. It reads: "On one document my grandfather [Henry Ralph Browne] pencilled a note that Sir [Thomas] Henry had in later years been offered commands but refused them. This is borne out by a letter from Sir [Thomas] Henry to his brother George in 1852 in which he [Thomas] referred to a General 'an excellent officer' who 'has been appointed to the command in Australia, since my refusal of it'."

91. Richard Glover, *Peninsular Preparation*, pp. 32–3.

92. Christopher Hibbert, ed., *The Wheatley Diary: A Journal and Sketch-Book kept during the Peninsular War and the Waterloo Campaign* (London: Longman, Green and Co. Ltd., 1964), p. 2.

93. Stendhal, *The Red and the Black*, p. 102.

94. *Journal*, p. 68.

95. Pages 9–10.

96. John Augustine Waller, a surgeon in the Royal Navy, was struck by the rapid onset of night at Barbados, where he served from 1807 to 1808: "I have noticed the circumstance of the uniform length of the days, from six in the morning to six in the evening, but it may not be amiss to observe, that the new comer to these islands will feel himself surprised at the sudden disappearance of light on the setting of the sun, there being little or no twilight, and in less than a quarter of an hour it becomes quite dark." See Waller's *A Voyage in the West Indies* (London: 1820), p. 24. The interplay of sunlight and colourful vegetation drove an anonymous soldier

of the 21st Royal North British Fusiliers to include this rhapsodic passage among his first impression of Barbados in 1794: ". . . the increasing brilliance of the Sun, as his beams fell in broad flakes between the great cabbage-trees, lit up the leaves, stalks & petals of the flower-beds, seeming to gem them round with emeralds & diamonds, for yet the dew lay deep on every Shrub & tree." See St Ann's Garrison, Barbados, The Barbados Museum and Historical Society, "An English Soldier of 21st Fuziliers first impression of Barbados in 1794." This phenomenon similarly attracted the attention of European artists and scientists. For this, see Bernard Smith, *European Vision and the South Pacific, 1768–1850: A Study in the History of Art and Ideas* (New York: Oxford University Press, 1969), passim.

97. Fortescue, *A History of the British Army*, 8:404–5.

98. See Edinburgh, Scottish Record Office, "Public Office Letters 1800", General Orders of 29 October 1800, enclosed in Circular to Regimental Agencies from the Adjutant General's Office, 29 October 1800. In 1807 this order was still in effect. See Richard Glover, *Peninsular Preparation*, p. 221.

99. André Corvisier, *Armies and Societies in Europe, 1494–1789*, trans. Abigail T. Siddall (Bloomington: Indiana University Press, 1979), pp. 174–75.

100. *Journal*, p. 220.

101. Henry Browne's military service began on 3 April 1846, the date of his commission as an ensign in the 9th or East Norfolk Regiment. Before his retirement from the service in 1885, he served in the Crimea, India, Canada, West Indies, South Africa, Hong Kong and Japan. In 1852 he married Frances Mary Ann Parsons, the only daughter of Admiral Robert White Parsons, by whom he had a son, Thomas Henry Browne, who was born in 1857. See London, National Army Museum, Journal of General Henry Ralph Browne, which is appended to the Journal of Sir Thomas Henry Browne. I am again indebted to W. D. Cribbs, this time for information pertaining to the life of Henry Ralph Browne.

102. Death Certificate of Thomas Henry Browne, registered 12 March 1855, St. Pancras, Kentish Town, Middlesex; and Browne Family Papers.

103. Denmark, Russia and Sweden were the original signatories. On 18 December 1800, the adherence of Prussia to the Northern Convention completed the alliance.

104. For all this see Chandler, *Dictionary of the Napoleonic Wars*, 16–17, 103–5; Cary and McCance, *Regimental Records of the Royal Welch Fusiliers*, 1:214–6; C. T. Atkinson, "Gleanings from the Cathcart MSS.: Part VI—The 'Conjoint' Expedition to Copenhagen, 1807," *Journal of the Society for Army Historical Research* 30 (1952): 80–87; Grant Uden and Richard Cooper, *A Dictionary of British Ships and Seamen* (New York: St Martin's

Press, 1980), pp. 175–6; and London, The British Library, Jellicoe Papers, Diary of Field Marshal Lord Grosvenor, p. 40. Hereafter Grosvenor Diary. For a Danish version of the siege, see Anon., *An Authentic Account of the Siege of Copenhagen by the British, in the Year 1807. Containing the Danish Description of the Attack and Bombardment, with the most Remarkable Proclamations and Bulletins of the Danes* (London: Faden/ Bulmer, 1807).

105. Herald, *The Horizon Book of the Age of Napoleon*, p. 218.

106. Mary D. George, *Catalogue of Political and Personal Satire*, 11 vols. (London: British Museum, 1947) 8:562. For a convincing defence of the expedition and siege, see Atkinson, "Gleanings from the Cathcart MSS . . . The 'Conjoint' Expedition to Copenhagen," pp. 80–87, and Watson, *The Reign of George III*, pp. 455–8. There is evidence which suggests that the siege could have ended earlier had it not been for Danish intransigence. See Preston, U.K., Lancashire Record Office, Hoghton Papers (Copenhagen Journal).

107. Browne is apparently referring to the secret articles agreed to at Tilsit, 7 July 1807, between France and Russia, whereby both signatories agreed to force Denmark and Sweden to join their condominium of Europe against Britain. This coercion of Denmark meant, for instance, the commandeering of the Danish fleet by Napoleon.

108. Christian VII (1766–1808).

109. The following old proverb captures the low regard with which the army cook was held by the soldier: "The good God sends the food and the devil sends the cooks." See Hargreaves, *This Happy Breed*, p. 27.

110. Hostilities evidently had not yet begun between the two nations. From 6 August to about 10 August, a British envoy, Francis Jackson, conducted talks with the Prince Regent of Denmark for the "temporary deposit" of the Danish fleet in British ports. The failure of these discussions on 10 August led to British landings, beginning on 16 August. Until that time, according to an anonymous Danish writer, "The English Troops being yet regarded as friends, were provided with necessaries at Elsinor till the 14th of August." See *An Authentic Account of the Siege of Copenhagen*, pp. 2–10. A copy of the British proclamation of hostilities of 16 August appears on pages 7–10.

111. In 1772 a young Gustavus III executed a monarchist coup d'état, which supplanted fifty years of domination by Sweden's aristocracy with an enlightened absolutism. At one point during his coup, Gustavus appeared in the streets of Stockholm with a white armband, which was enthusiastically adopted by thousands of his supporters. Items of apparel had become important political symbols, and white was selected since it was apparently (as in France before the Revolution of 1789) the colour

associated with the monarchy. Almost exactly twenty years later, on 16 March 1792, Gustavus III was assassinated at the opera in Stockholm by disgruntled noblemen. See R. R. Palmer, *The Age of the Democratic Revolution: A Political History of Europe and America, 1760–1800*, 2 vols. (Princeton: Princeton University Press, 1959) 1:99–100, 102, and 398–402. At the time of Browne's brief visit to Sweden, that country was moving closer to an alliance with Britain as a result of menacing moves against Sweden by Denmark, Russia and France. On 8 February 1808, Sweden and Britain signed a subsidy treaty. A few days later, Russian troops entered Finland, a Swedish possession, and soon thereafter, Denmark declared war against Sweden. See Sherwig, *Guineas and Gunpowder*, pp. 192–193.

112. In an effort to support Sweden, the bulk of the King's German Legion was sent to Swedish Pomerania (now East Germany), arriving on 7 July 1807. Some of these troops were placed in garrisons on the island of Ruegen, others at Stralsund. Upon their arrival, however, news was received of the Tilsit agreement which led, consequently, to the withdrawal of the K.G.L. and its attachment to the Copenhagen expeditionary force. These troops began arriving off Copenhagen on 14 August 1807. Cathcart had gone to Swedish Pomerania earlier, to supervise the activities of the K.G.L. He arrived at Stralsund on 16 July only to find the unit in an untenable position, whereupon he ordered them to join British operations against Copenhagen.

113. "Askers" were apparently a variety of parasitic flea that infested the area.

114. A Danish deserter informed Major-General Grosvenor that the cutting off of Copenhagen's water supply caused considerable distress among the inhabitants. See Grosvenor Diary, p. 19.

115. Major-General Grosvenor provides a different account of this episode. Grosvenor claims that the fleeing royal princesses and their entourage were given permission to leave Copenhagen with nine wagons. When thirty wagons appeared, all but nine were sent back. Grosvenor records this amusing event as occurring on 18 August. See Grosvenor Diary, pp. 7–8.

116. The war rocket, an explosively propelled projectile, was first used in Asia in the thirteenth century. It was used against the British during the siege of Seringapatam, India, in 1799, which attracted the attention of Colonel Sir William Congreve (1771–1828), a British gunnery expert. Congreve, who later became Controller of the Royal Laboratory in 1814, took the Indian rocket as his model and developed the first practicable rocket in 1805. A Congreve rocket weighed as much as forty-two pounds and carried a missile of approximately eighteen pounds in the form of a thin perforated case packed with explosives. The Congreve rocket was first

used in the field in 1806, at the siege of Boulogne. See John F. C. Fuller, *The Conduct of War, 1789–1961: A Study of the Impact of the French, Industrial, and Russian Revolutions on War and its Conduct* (New Brunswick, N.J.: Rutgers University Press, 1962), pp. 89–90; and Barnes, *A History of the Regiments and Uniforms of the British Army*, p. 70.

117.   Wellesley, the future Duke of Wellington, reported Danish losses as ". . . many have fallen, & there are nearly 60 Officers & 1100 men prisoners." For his description of the Danish defeat at Kiöge, see W.O. 1/188, Wellesley to Cathcart, 29 August 1807.

118.   All the houses were evidently numbered. During the early part of the eighteenth century, it was recommended that London houses be similarly numbered. This was a new idea at the time. See R. J. Mitchell and M. D. R. Leys, *A History of London Life* (Baltimore: Penguin Books, 1963), p. 216. A century later, few houses, anywhere in England, were numbered, which may explain Browne's apparent surprise at this custom.

119.   Browne's evident astonishment with the great skill of Copenhagen's firefighters is understandable since most British cities at the time were apparently without a municipal fire brigade. London, for instance, was without one until 1833. See Mitchell and Leys, *A History of London Life*, p. 228. The fires were largely, apparently, the result of Congreve's rocket attack. Certainly, one of the principal objectives of a coordinated rocket barrage was the ensuing destruction of property by fire. Congreve drew attention to this capability of the rocket when he wrote in defence of the weapon. "For a hundred fires breaking out at once, must necessarily produce more destruction than when they happen in succession, and may therefore be extinguished as fast as they occur." See William Congreve, *The Details of the Rocket System* (London: J. Whiting, 1814; reprint ed., Ottawa, Ontario: Museum Restoration Service, 1970), p. 46.

120.   John Harris of the 95th Rifles provides us with this additional view of the rocket attack: ". . . as they rushed through the air in the dark, they appeared like so many fiery serpents, creating, I should think, terrible dismay among the besieged." See Christopher Hibbert, ed., *Recollections of Rifleman Harris* (London: Leo Cooper, 1970), p. 8.

121.   Browne never sent these pitiful remains of Lieutenant Jennings to the latter's friends. Perhaps he thought it both wise and humane not to do so. Whatever the reason, Browne kept the remains among his personal effects. There it remained until discovered by Browne's eldest son, Henry Ralph Browne, some time, apparently, after the death of his father in March 1855. In a postscript written across the appropriate page in his father's Journal, Henry Browne acknowledged his discovery of the grisly memento and identified its final destination: "I found the packet with the lock of hair amongst my Father's papers—and sent it to the Regiment

[presumably the Royal Welch Fusiliers] a few years ago.—[signed] Henry Ralph Browne."

122. The church identified by Browne was the magnificent Fruekirke. The violence of the British siege may be judged from the bombardment of the second night, 4 September, which a British observer described as "much slackened". The same eyewitness concluded that "only" one thousand shells were thrown into the city. See anon., *Authentic Account of the Siege of Copenhagen*, pp. 25–8.

123. The capitulation was agreed to on 7 September 1807. The articles of capitulation for the city of Copenhagen and its citadel appear as Appendix B.

124. Traiteurs: shopkeepers.

125. Browne's reservations about Danish female beauty were not shared by all, particularly by some of the riflemen of the old 95th Regiment. Rifleman John Harris has left us this account of an incident when Danish good looks got the better of his coarse comrades.

"Occasionally, also, we had some pleasant adventures among the blue-eyed Danish lasses, for the Rifles were always terrible fellows in that way.

One night, I remember, a party of us had possession of a gentlemen's house, in which his family were residing. The family consisted of the owner of the mansion, his wife, and five very handsome daughters, besides their servants.

The first night of our occupation of the premises the party was treated with the utmost civility, and everything was set before us as if we had been their equals; for although it was not very pleasant to have a company of foreign soldiers in the house, it was doubtless thought best to do everything possible to conciliate such guests. Accordingly, on this night, a large party of the green-jackets unceremoniously sat down to tea with the family.

Five beautiful girls in a drawingroom were rather awkward companions for a set of rough and ready Riflemen, unscrupulous and bold, and I cannot say I felt easy. All went on very comfortably for sometime; our fellows drank their tea very genteelly, whilst one young lady presided at the urn to serve it out, and the others sat on each side of their father and mother, chatting to us, and endeavouring to make themselves as agreeable as they could.

By and bye, however, some of our men expressed themselves dissatisfied with tea and toast, and demanded something stronger; and liquors were accordingly served to them. This was followed by more familiarity, and, the ice once broken, all respect for the host and hostess was quickly lost. I had feared this would prove the case, and on seeing several of the men commence pulling the young ladies about, kissing them, and proceeding to other acts of rudeness, I saw that matters would quickly get worse, unless I interfered. Jumping up, therefore, I endeavoured to restore order, and upbraided them with the black-guardism of their behaviour after the kindness with which we had been used.

This remonstrance had some effect; and when I added that I would immediately go in quest of an officer, and report the first man I saw ill-use the ladies, I at length succeeded in extricating them from their persecutors.

The father and mother were extremely grateful to me for my interference, and I kept careful guard over the family whilst we remained in that house, which luckily was not long." *Recollections of Rifleman Harris*, pp. 10–11.

126. Gustavus Adolphus IV (1792–1809). The eccentric Gustavus had yet another reason to review the powerful British armament as it slipped through the northern neck of the Ore Sound and into the Kattegat. The manifest strength of the armada undoubtedly reassured Gustavus since Sweden's independence depended to a large degree on British assistance, particularly in the form of subsidies. In 1807, for instance, Gustavus received £248,128 in subsidy payments. The following year the amount was significantly increased to £1,094,023. For a sketch of British subsidy payments to Gustavus, see Sherwig, *Guineas and Gunpowder*, pp. 162–4, 188, 192, 206–7, and 366–7.

127. The cockpit was a dark and stuffy apartment in old sailing ships below the water-line. There were two cockpits, one fore and one aft. The fore cockpit was located in the bows and served as the quarters of the carpenter and boatswain. The after cockpit was on the lowest deck and was the quarters of the midshipmen. Of the two, the after cockpit was the more unattractive. Uden and Cooper, *A Dictionary of British Ships and Seamen*, pp. 90–1. In H.M.S. *Victory*, which was launched at Chatham in 1765, the cockpit was located amidship on the lowest deck. See C. Nepean Longridge, *The Anatomy of Nelson's Ships* (Watford, U.K.: Model and Allied Publications, Argus Books Ltd., 1981), plan No. 1 — "H.M.S. Victory-Inboard Works", facing p. 20.

128. Bowsprit: a spar extending forward from the bows of a ship, which serves a subsidiary mast carrying its own sail.

129. A reef is that part of the sail that can be taken in, rolled up and secured by reef-points, or short lines attached directly to the sail or to reef-bands, which are extra strips of canvas running horizontally along a square sail for bracing the hold of the reef-points. Close-reefed is when the sails are shortened or taken in to the full extent. Topsails are the *square sails* set

above the lowest sail on the mast. See Uden and Cooper, *A Dictionary of British Ships and Seamen*, pp. 88, 415 and 445.

130. Prize money was the money derived from the sale of a ship and its contents captured in wartime. This loot was distributed among those who participated in the capture. The money was handed over to a general fund and then distributed in shares to the captors according to rank. There were frequently long delays in settling the proportions of the distributions and making payment. On some occasions the charges made by prize agents significantly reduced the amount finally paid to the captors. Prize money was one, and in numerous cases the sole, means by which officers in both the army and navy could hope to acquire wealth. Some earned a fortune in a single day, as, for instance, in the case of four British frigate captains who each earned more than £40,000 in 1799, after their ships captured two Spanish vessels whose combined freights were valued at £600,000. See Turner, *Gallant Gentlemen*, p. 107. Browne's share, which was minuscule when compared to the sums awarded to the navy and army commanders of the Copenhagen expedition, was, nonetheless, a tidy sum for those days. The purpose of prize money was to inspire greater effort by the armed forces. The offer of private gain for public service, however, entailed the inherent gamble that the pursuit of gain would encourage rapacity and distract from duty. To see how prize money affected British military operations during the long 1793–1815 war, see, for instance, J. M. Fewster, "Prize-Money and the British Expedition to the West Indies of 1793–4," *Journal of Imperial and Commonwealth History* XII (October 1983) 1:1–28.

131. J. Leitch Wright, Jr, *Britain and the American Frontier, 1783–1815* (Athens: University of Georgia Press, 1975), p. 143.

132. Brian C. Cuthbertson, *The Loyalist Governor: Biography of Sir John Wentworth* (Halifax: Petheric Press, 1983), pp. 134–5.

133. This was the 23rd's second tour of duty in North America. The first tour largely coincided with the American Revolution. The regiment arrived in New York on 14 June 1773. It later served at Lexington, Concord, Bunker Hill, Long Island, Brooklyn, White Plains, Fort Washington, Danbury, Ridgefield, Brandywine, Philadelphia, Germantown, Monmouth Court House, Fort Lafayette, Charleston, Camden, Guildford Court House and Yorktown where the regiment was captured. The 23rd returned to England in January 1784. See Department of National Defence Library, "The Service of British Regiments in Canada and North America," p. 145, Ottawa, 1962. (Mimeographed.)

134. Lady Frances Wentworth, the flamboyant wife of Sir John Wentworth, gave a magnificent ball in honour of Captains Alexander Cochrane's and John Beresford's brilliant action in 1795, when they captured two French

warships which they brought into Halifax. All the ladies wore navy blue cockades, and ornaments of blue on which the captains' names were inscribed in gold. See Cuthbertson, *The Loyalist Governor*, p. 92. In 1809, an expedition to Martinique was organized in Halifax. The 23rd Royal Welch Fusiliers participated in this successful operation. (See below.) The leading citizens of Halifax gave a ball at the Masonic Hall in honour of the capture of the island. See T. B. Akins, *History of Halifax* (Belleville, Canada: Mika Publishing, 1973), p. 144.

135. Cuthbertson, *The Loyalist Governor*, p. 133.

136. Public Record Office, London, MPH/490 (1). I am grateful to Carol M. Whitfield, Operations Manager, Halifax Defence Complex, Nova Scotia, for the information regarding the current state of the old Eastern Battery/ Fort Clarence site.

137. All officers were, in theory, socially equal off parade. There was, however, the tendency of some senior officers to use their rank in the mess, with the result that the messes of some regiments were carefully regulated by written rules. This may explain why the mess of the 23rd was governed by some forty-five written rules by 1 June 1795. Additional rules were added, for instance, between 1797 and 1805. See Cary and McCance, *Regimental Records of the Royal Welch Fusiliers*, vol. I, Appendix II.

138. Browne was not aware at this time of the precise location of this overseas service, which, apparently, was a practice in the army. Under these circumstances troops prepared as best they could, as in the case of William Surtees who left us this account of troops ignorant of their destination: ". . . we received an order to prepare again for foreign service, and the nature of that service being kept a profound secret, we scarcely knew what necessary articles of equipment to prepare. The general opinion, however, was that our destination was some part of America, consequently we endeavoured to meet all contingencies by preparing both for a warm and cold climate." See Surtees' *Twenty-Five Years in the Rifle Brigade* (London: Frederick Muller Ltd., 1973), p. 324.

139. All officers on foreign service were paid sixpence each day for the forage rations of bât animals to carry their baggage in the field. A lieutenant-colonel, for instance, was allowed ten rations. Subaltern officers were each granted one ration. When a regiment was ordered on overseas service in 1809, each officer was given an advance of two hundred days bât and forage money and a further grant known as baggage money. See Michael Glover, ed., *A Gentleman Volunteer: The Letters of George Hennell from the Peninsular War, 1812–1813* (London: Heinemann, 1979), p. 33, note 1.

140. The battle of Albuera (Spain), 16 May 1811, where British troops and

allies under Marshal [in the Portuguese army] William Beresford defeated a French army led by Marshal Nicolas Soult in a hard-fought action. A much celebrated charge by the Fusilier Brigade, which included the 23rd Regiment, routed the French.

141. Grampus: a marine mammal related to and resembling the dolphin, but lacking a bearlike snout.

142. Mother Carey's chicken: any of numerous petrels, especially the storm petrel.

143. Bermuda's naval facilities were of some concern to the United States. During the American Revolution, for example, Marquis de Lafayette had recommended that the Continental Congress order the capture of Bermuda because of its strategic position astride the important sea lanes. It was, however, the use of Bermuda as a base for British privateers that greatly alarmed the United States. For instance, throughout 1795 and into 1796, British privateers based in the Caribbean, but particularly those sailing out of Bermuda, almost daily captured American merchant ships. An angry Boston mob reacted to British commerce raiding by burning to the water line a suspected privateer that had docked in Boston in June 1795. By 1797, British captures of American ships had declined significantly. Nonetheless, the challenge of privateering to commerce, as well as to national honour, led some merchants to press the United States for action against Bermuda and other bases of British privateers. See Gerard H. Clarfield, *Timothy Pickering and American Diplomacy, 1795–1800* (Columbia: University of Missouri Press, 1969), pp. 74–6.

144. The total strength of the Nova Scotia command around this time, 1 June 1808, excluding officers and staff, was 5,245. See W.O. 17/5245.

145. Shrub: a beverage made from fruit juice, sugar and a liquor such as rum or brandy.

146. For reasons unexplained, Browne apparently did not enquire as to Tom's real name, which would have been a relatively easy matter, given the evident ease with which both men communicated with each other.

147. The reason for the 23rd's dislike of service in the West Indies was the well-deserved evil reputation of the region as the graveyard of white men. The source of this notoriety was malaria and yellow fever, which were particularly lethal to newcomers to the islands. In time the ominousness of the region became common knowledge in Britain. For example, Thackeray's Captain William Dobbin miraculously "returned from yellow fever, in the West Indies". And the redoubtable Major Monsoon darkly advised a listener: "It's very hard to leave the West Indies if once you've been quartered there, what with the seductions of the coffee plantations, the sugar-canes, the monsoons, the brown skins, the rainy season, and the yellow fever, most of us settled there." British soldiers

ordered to the West Indies were fully aware of the enormous danger of that service, according to Dr Pinchard, who writes on the eve of his departure to the region in 1795: "A degree of horror seems to have overspread the nation from the late destructive effects of yellow-fever, or, what the multitude denominates, the West India plague; insomuch that a sense of terror attaches to the very name of the West Indies — many, even, considering it synonymous with the grave; and, perhaps, it were not too much to say, that all, who have friends in the expedition [of 1795–1796], apprehend more from disease than the sword. Such discouraging sentiments I am sorry to find have not been concealed from the troops. The Fearful farewell of desponding friends is every day, and hour, either heedlessly, or artfully sounded in their ears. People walking about the camp, attending at a review, or a parade, or merely upon seeing parties of soldiers in the streets, are heard to exclaim, — 'Ah, poor fellows! You are going to your last home! What pity such brave men should go to that West India grave! — to that hateful climate to be killed by the plague! Poor fellows, good bye, farewell! we shall never see you back again!' With such like accents are the ears of the soldiers incessantly saluted; and the hopeless predictions are loudly echoed, for the worst of purposes, by the designing, whose turbulent spirits would feast in exciting discontentment among the troops." Another doctor, Royal Navy surgeon John Augustine Waller, writing just before Browne served at Martinique, noted the fear which overcame his shipmates as they approached the West Indies. "We had in the convoy a considerable reinforcement for the regiments in the country, as well as a number of young persons destined to fill various civil situations, public and private; their sanguine hopes of fortune and promotion, could not fail to be mingled with dread, at approaching shores so notified for their pestiferous atmosphere. These combined sensations must, in spite of philosophy and hardihood, find their way into the heart of all new comers." For all this see Thackeray, *Vanity Fair*, p. 86; Philip Guedalla, *Wellington* (New York: The Literary Guild, 1931), p. 53; Pinchard, *Notes on the West Indies*, 1:15–16; and Waller, *A Voyage in the West Indies*, p. 2.

148. Villaret de Joyeuse served as Governor of Martinique from 1802 to 1809.

149. Alfred B. Ellis, *The History of the First West India Regiment* (London: Chapman and Hall, Ltd., 1885), p. 125.; and M. E. S. Laws, "The Royal Artillery at Martinique 1809," *Royal Artillery Journal* LXXVII, No. 1, pp. 70, 73.

150. Laws, "The Royal Artillery at Martinique 1809," p. 80.

151. *Ibid.*, p. 78.

152. W.O. 78/812, map of Ville du Fort Royal and environs.

153. Laws, "The Royal Artillery at Martinique 1809," p. 71.

154. *Ibid.*, pp. 78–79.

155. *Ibid.*, p. 79.

156. *Ibid.*, p. 81. See, also, Appendix K ("British Regiments Which Have Been Awarded Battle Honours For Service In The West Indies"), pp. 758–760, in Allan C. Burns, *History of the British West Indies* (London: George Allen and Unwin, Ltd., 1954).

157. Laws, "The Royal Artillery at Martinique 1809," p. 81.

158. Shrouds: standing rigging or a set of ropes stretched from the masthead to a vessel's sides to support the mast.

159. This mock ceremony was often held on ships to initiate those who were crossing the Equator (or crossing the line) for the first time. This event occasioned dressing up amid much high spirits and fooling as King Neptune and his attendants supposedly came aboard to receive the initiates into his court. The ceremony may well have a pagan ancestry; it dates from ancient times when rites were performed prior to a voyage in order to propitiate the sea-gods. Uden and Cooper, *A Dictionary of British Ships and Seamen*, p. 105,

160. The British landing at Corunna, Spain was a reference to the operations of a British expeditionary force under the command of Sir John Moore.

161. "Johnny New-Come" was a title universally applied throughout the British colonies to European males, civilians as well as military, who had come to the West Indies for the first time. The imprudent lifestyle of this newcomer to the region, which was both comic and frequently tragic, led to the creation of a popular cartoon of the same title. Browne's own escapades, described below, match those of the stereotypical "Johnny New-Come".

162. The tavern, a popular rendezvous for British naval and military personnel, was formerly owned by the well-known freedwoman, Rachel Pringle, who died in 1791. The celebrated "Royal Naval Hotel" was acquired in the 1790s by Nancy Clarke, herself a freedwoman. At the time of Browne's visit, the tavern still, apparently, retained its notoriety. Browne failed to mention, and with good reason, that prostitution was a major attraction of the taverns. See Jerome S. Handler, *The Unappropriated People: Freedmen in the Slave Society of Barbados* (Baltimore: Johns Hopkins University Press, 1974), pp. 133–138.

163. Browne is here describing the permanent European population of Barbados.

164. Despite Browne's critical remarks about the movements and interior economy of the West India Regiments, the First was awarded the battle honour "Dominica" in 1805; and the First and the Fourth West India Regiments would soon be accorded battle honours for their efforts during the reduction of Martinique in 1809 and Guadeloupe in 1810. The

stench Browne alluded to resulted from inferior (and at times even scandalously inadequate) housing for West India soldiers. These troops were frequently "hutted", some, according to official reports, under "miserable" conditions. The appearance as well as the health of the troops were thus affected by this situation. The "vapour" may have stemmed from continuous clothing shortages; and it was not uncommon for black troops to be issued discarded clothing, and even weapons! Such conditions made it exceedingly difficult, if not impossible, to maintain the good appearance of uniforms and accoutrements. For all this, see Buckley, *Slaves in Red Coats: The British West India Regiments, 1795–1815,* pp. 94, 121–123, 156.

165. Browne's concise description of the recruitment of the West India Regiments points at what was probably the worst kept secret in the Caribbean, that the slave trade was used to maintain these corps. From 1795 to 1808, the British government bought approximately 13,400 slaves for its West India Regiments at the considerable cost of about £925,000. William Pitt was the prime minister when most of these purchases were made. Evidently, Browne was unaware in January 1809 that the British slave trade had been abolished in March 1807. Under the act, British subjects could still legally purchase slaves up to 1 March 1808, the final date ships leaving England by 1 May 1807 were permitted to arrive in the West Indies. Nonetheless, Browne's description of the purchase and induction of African slaves into military service in January 1809 would indicate that the government of the Duke of Portland was then in violation of British law. Major Richard Augustus Wyvill, an inspector of African recruits for the West India Regiments from 1805 to 1807, corroborates Browne's account. Arriving in Trinidad in September 1805, Wyvill recorded the following: "On the 3d of October, I was on quite a new Duty to me, that, of approving of 80 African Negroes as Recruits, for the 8th West India Regiment, out of which number I rejetted 15. A great number of these had been wounded in their own Country; and some had balls still in their bodies. They seemed quite delighted at the Idea, of becoming Soldiers, and being dressed in such fine Regimentals, as they observed, on their Brother Negroes." Reassigned to Barbados, Wyvill made this entry into his journal on 22 March 1807: "On the arrival of Negroes as recruits for Black Regiments a peice of paper is suspended round their necks with the name that has been given them by their Captains. This they are taught to understand, also the different words of Command, as they are drilled." For all this, see Buckley, *Slaves in Red Coats,* pp. 52–62; and Wyvill Memoirs, Peter Force Papers, Series 8D, Library of Congress, Washington, D.C. The Barbados portion of Wyvill's journal has been edited and published by

Jerome S. Handler, "Memoir of an Old Army Officer: Richard A. Wyvill's Visits to Barbados in 1796 and 1806–7," *Journal of the Barbados Museum and Historical Society* 35 (March 1975)) No. 1, pp. 21–30.

166. Susan Austin or Austen was one of two free coloured women who owned hotel-taverns in Bridgetown around this period; the other proprietress-hostess was Nancy Clark. Apparently, these women had been the favoured *innamorata* of local white proprietors, from whom they had gained their freedom and, perhaps, several slaves to assist them in their business. Both Clark's and Austen's establishments were celebrated in the following song, which was popular in Barbados at the time:

> If you go to Nancy Clark,
> She will take you in the dark;
> When she get you in the dark,
> She will give you aquafortis.

> If you go to Susy Austin,
> She will take you in the parlour;
> When she take you in the parlour,
> She will give you wine and water.

See Neville Connel, "Hotel Keepers and Hotels in Barbados," *Journal of the Barbados Museum and Historical Society* 32 (November 1970) no. 4: 162–168.

167. This was a reference to General Moore's retreat in Spain, a disastrous operation that commenced in the bitter cold of December 1808 and involved a march over 250 miles of mountainous country. It ended with Moore's death on 16 January 1809 and British evacuation from Corunna on 17 January.

168. Browne's troop strengths are not entirely correct. According to the official return of 27 January 1809, the total strength of the First Division (Prevost's) was 7,071; and that for the Second Division (Maitland's) was given as 3,710, for a combined total of 10,781. Furthermore, Browne's order of battle does not conform entirely to the official one. According to the latter, a Royal Artillery detachment and artificers were also attached to the First Brigade, First Division. A field artillery unit was similarly attached to the "Light Corps", First Division. With regard to the Second Division, the flank companies of the 15th and 46th Regiments were attached to the Fourth Brigade, and not the Third Brigade. W.O. 1/95, enclosure No. 1 in Beckwith's despatch of 8 March 1809.

169. Yellow fever, malaria and a host of other diseases collectively took their well-known toll of life in British garrisons in the West Indies. Troops, particularly those arriving in the West Indies from Europe and North

America, were also progressively worn down by their heavy uniform which prevented proper thermo-regulation. Browne's reference to flannel underclothing is corroborated by Dr William Ferguson, Inspector of Military Hospitals in the West Indies from 1815 to 1817. The flannel described by Ferguson, in his inspection of the medical facilities at Prince Rupert's Head, Dominica, in January 1816, was evidently made from wool, which was completely unsuitable for tropical service since it is heavier than cotton and retains moisture. Lieutenant-Colonel Alexander Whalley Light similarly depicts British troops in a uniform obviously issued for European winter service, in his remarkable and unique *Views in the West Indies*. Executed in the West Indies between 1811 and 1814, one pen and pencil drawing clearly shows an officer in European dress, which included the densely textured dark-coloured woollen-cloth knee-length frock coat. Kitted out in this fashion, officers and men became exhausted quickly and subject to heat stress. This sartorial lunacy continued long after the 1793–1815 war. Robert H. Schomburgk, the historian of Barbados, who spent some time in the West Indies between 1830 and 1835 and, again, from 1841 and 1843, noted that: "The English troops in their military coats, made of broad-cloths, and, as it has been the case with fusileer regiments, their head covered with a heavy fur cap, must of course be much more subject to the influence of the heat under the Tropics, than the French and Spanish soldier in the West India colonies, who is attired in a light linen dress and his head covered with a light tzshako of felt." For all this see Ferguson Letterbooks, Royal Army Medical Corps Historical Museum, Aldershot, U.K.; Alexander Whalley Light's *Views in the West Indies 1811–1814* (MPH/111), Public Record Office, London; and Robert H. Schomburgk, *The History of Barbados* (London: Longman, Brown and Green, 1848; reprint ed., London: Frank Cass & Co. Ltd., 1971), p. 77.

170. Cholera morbus: acute gastro-enteritis occurring in summer and autumn, and distinguished by severe cramps, diarrhoea and vomiting.

171. Sir George Beckwith's plan of operations was apparently not completed until 27 January 1809, just two days before the expedition sailed to Martinique. This would confirm Brown's suspicions of indecision in Beckwith's war council. Terse and confident in tone, the plan does suggest, nonetheless, the difficulties of the operation and the strength of the French position.

It is intended in the attack of Martinique to limit the debarkation to two points.

The Army will therefore land in two Divisions.

It is proposed that the 2d Division, under the Command of Major General Maitland, shall disembark to Leeward between Point

Solomon and St Luce according to circumstances, preceding the landing of the 1st Division and other Corps which compose the Body of the Army intended to be landed in Robert Bay by twenty four Hours.

The object of the Corps to Windward [Browne's division], with which the Commander of the Forces means to land, is to move towards the height of Surirey, and by preserving the heights to turn the Enemy's Left, and to obtain possession of the heights as circumstances shall admit.

The object of the Corps to Leeward is, after turning the Batteries to secure Anchorage for the shipping, to push forward to the River Sallée, to take possession of the heights near Pigeon Island, and with the Admiral's cooperation to land such Ordnance and Stores as Brigadier General Sir Charles Shipley, Commanding Royal Engineer[s] and Brigadier General Stehelin, Commanding the Royal Artillery, shall judge necessary for the attack of that important Post. The Admiral having given assurances that even prior to the fall of Pigeon Island, he will be enabled on our possessing the South Side of Fort Royal Bay to feed the Army at Lamentin or Cohe Bay. This point ascertained, Major General Maitland will leave such a Corps for carrying on the attack of Pigeon Island as he shall judge proper, and on finding the Body of the Army upon the heights, he will pass the River Salée and place himself upon the Left of it, provided no unforeseen circumstance should arise, which in his judgment shall render this measure too hazardous.

Barbados   Geo Beckwith
27th January 1809.   Comr. Forces

See W.O. 1/95, enclosure no. 2 in Beckwith's despatch of 8 March 1809. French troop strength on the island was considerably less than that of the British, and for that reason the French commander chose not to contest the landing. As Browne recorded in his Journal, enemy resistance stiffened in the mountainous interior of the island since this high ground commanded their principal defensive works in and around Fort Royal.

172. This was a reference to the "Battle of the First of June" or the "Glorious First of June" 1794, an action fought in the Atlantic, approximately 400 miles west of Ushant (Brittany, France), between Lord Howe, who commanded the Channel Fleet, and Villaret-Joyeuse, who was attempting to bring home a large convoy of over 100 vessels loaded with grain from the United States. Villaret-Joyeuse succeeded in his mission, although several French ships were captured and one sunk. Uden and Cooper, *A Dictionary of British Ships and Seamen*, p. 155.

173. Laudanum was a tincture of opium. Its general use in the Army as a medicine, particularly as a curative for yellow fever, suggests that the

Army was faced with a dual addiction problem: that of alcohol as well as drug addiction.

174. For a full description of Pearson's service record, as well as a silhouetted portrait miniature of Pearson, executed between 1803–1804, see Harris, "Two Military Miniatures," pp. 100–103 and illustration facing page 94.

175. An eagle was the French regimental standard or colour, so named because a gilded copper eagle with wings displayed was fixed on the top of the staff. Napoleon selected the eagle as the Imperial emblem soon after the establishment of the Empire in 1804. This change in the colours and standards of the French army was inspired by the legionary eagles of the Roman army. The flag was attached to the staff some distance below the eagle as was the Roman labarum. The Napoleonic eagle stood on a brass tablet bearing in raised figures the regimental number. As a result of this design, the flag was no longer the regimental standard, but an ornamental ancillary to the eagle. Each eagle was presented personally by Napoleon with the inevitable result that they became highly prized as war trophies among enemy soldiers. Because a number of eagles had been captured in battle, a decree of 18 February 1808 restricted them to line regiments. See H. C. B. Rogers, *Napoleon's Army* (New York: Hippocrene Books, 1982), pp. 66–68. Four eagles, including those belonging to the 28th and 82nd Demi-brigades, were surrendered at Martinique. The eagle of the 82nd is part of the collection of the National Army Museum, London. I am grateful to Mrs D. B. Wilcox, Assistant Director and Keeper of Uniforms at the National Army Museum, for this information.

176. In order to obtain more cohesion and even quality in the French army, a law of 21 February 1793 established three-battalion regiments or demi-brigades. A typical demi-brigade then consisted of a 2nd battalion, which was a regular unit, and a 1st and a 3rd battalion, both of which were volunteers. The demi-brigade organization was retained until September 1803, when all permanent demi-brigades became regiments. The term demi-brigade remained in use for provisional groupings of battalions. After 1803, some line regiments had four battalions, others three. In February 1808, Napoleon decreed that line and light infantry regiments would be composed of five battalions. The same decree fixed the strength of each regiment at 3,970, all ranks, of which 3,862 were non-commissioned officers and men, 108 officers. See H. C. B. Rogers, *Napoleon's Army*, pp. 60–62.

177. According to the official returns, total casualties for all ranks, from 1 to 25 February, amounted to 561. That for both the 7th and 23rd Regiments, all ranks, was 310. These figures are incomplete, however. Browne's name, for example, does not appear on the list of wounded officers. See W.O., 1/95, enclosure No. 7 in Beckwith's despatch of 8 March 1809.

178. Small rocky islets between Guadeloupe and Dominica, the scene of Admiral Rodney's defeat of Admiral de Grasse in April 1782.

179. Quite possibly the most impressive British fortification in the West Indies, the Brimstone Hill Fortress covers the top of a steep volcanic hill 800 feet high and approximately 600 feet from the eastern shore of St Kitts. First fortified by the French in 1690, the British gained possession of the fort and completed the present series of defences between 1793 and 1794. One of the principal architectural features of the fortification complex is the arcade, which is an ubiquitous mark of military architecture throughout the West Indies. Henri Christophe, the King of Haiti (1811–1820) whose birthplace was St Kitts, is said to have been inspired by Brimstone Hill when he built Citadelle la Ferrière, unquestionably the greatest military structure in the West Indies. See D. Lloyd Matheson, *The Brimstone Hill Fortress* (Basseterre, St Kitts: Society for the Restoration of Brimstone Hill, n.d.) passim; and Pamela Gosner, *Caribbean Georgian: The Great and Small Houses of the West Indies* (Washington, D.C.: Three Continents Press, 1982), pp. 31–3.

180. The south-eastern corner of the fortifications complex on top of Brimstone Hill was apparently the abode of this colony of primates, since an eminence there bears their name. It follows, then, that the structures built there were designated the "Monkey Hill Barracks and Officers Quarters" and "Monkey Hill Battery". See Light's "Views in the West Indies, 1811–1814", Plate No. 1, "Plan of Brimstone Hill Island of St Kitts", and legend for Plate No. 1. Primates still inhabit the fortress which was abandoned as a place of defence in 1853. On a visit to Brimstone Hill in June 1984, the editor encountered a troop of unflappable monkeys along the access road which winds its way along the northern face of the Hill to the crest.

181. "Few come out, though many go in", a poignant phrase attributed to Sir John W. Fortescue, is an appropriate description of military service in the West Indies during the French Revolutionary and Napoleonic Wars, 1793–1815. (In fact, it is equally correct for virtually all wars waged in the region during the colonial period.) This is an oblique reference to the more than 60,000 British soldiers who died in the area, the vast majority of whom died of diseases unrelated to the battlefield. In an earlier work ("The Destruction of the British Army in the West Indies, 1793–1815: A Medical History", *Journal of the Society for Army Historical Research*, 56, No. 226, Summer 1978, pp. 79–82), the editor argued that 75,000 deaths occurred in British garrisons in the West Indies during the 1793–1815 period. This estimate was based on official returns. The tally also utilized, however, Fortescue's famous computation of British casualties which requires re-evaluation. At this time, the editor has obtained additional

verifiable official returns which puts British army deaths during the war, for both black and white troops, at about 60,000. This number is expected to go even higher since the editor has been directed to previously untabulated returns located at several archives in the United Kingdom and the West Indies. The editor plans to publish the results of this re-examination of mortality and morbidity in the British garrison in the West Indies during the 1793–1815 war.

182. The battle of Corunna occurred on 16 January 1809. The embarkation of some 27,000 Brititish troops was completed on the 18th. Among the evacuated army was Browne's brother, George Baxter Browne, an officer serving in the 2nd Battalion/23rd Foot.

183. Nankeen: a sturdy yellow or buff cotton cloth.

184. The folly of powdered hair and pigtails was abolished in August 1808. For an amusing description of "military friseurship" in the British army, see Reginald J. Macdonald, *The History of the Dress of the Royal Regiment of Artillery, 1625–1897* (London: Henry Sotheran & Co., 1899), pp. 50–52. Pigtails were similarly worn in the French army. In August 1806, however, French troops were ordered to cut off their queues. See Rogers, *Napoleon's Army*, p. 45.

185. Browne was apparently suffering from an attack of intermittent malaria.

186. Eleven regiments, among them the Royal Welch Fusiliers, were awarded battle honours for their services in the capture of Martinique.

187. The prize records for the capture of Martinique are located in W. O. 164/182, 189.

188. For all this see Henry Lachouque, Jean Tranie, and J.-C. Carmigniani, *Napoleon's War in Spain: The French Peninsular Campaigns, 1807–1814*, trans. Janet S. Mallender and John R. Clements (London: Arms and Armour Press, 1982), pp. 9–144; Chandler, *Dictionary of the Napoleonic Wars*, pp. 329–338, 443–444, 466–467; and Watson, *The Reign of George III*, pp. 457–462, 479–496.

189. Lieutenant Clotworthy Gillmor, a Royal Navy officer attached to the Naval Brigade serving with the army in the lines of Torres Vedras, confirms Browne's desolate description of Alhandra with the following entry in his diary of 29 October 1810: "This deserted Town a picture of the miseries of war, the houses gutted: soldiers and sailors boiling their kettles in the streets with broken mahogany furniture; two Churches: one for Soldiers, one for Sailors; the latter nearly despoiled of all its graven images." See H. N. Edwards, "The Diary of Lieutenant C. Gillmor, R.N.—Portugal—1810," *Journal of the Society for Army Historical Research* 3 (1924): 149.

190. Soon after the 23rd arrived in Portugal in November 1810, both hostile armies went into cantonments, which explains the absence of any

significant activity in Browne's Journal until 3 March 1811, when Masséna acknowledged his strategic defeat before Torres Vedras and began to retreat to the Portuguese frontier. During the winter of 1811, Browne was in command at Belem. His tiny force included five sergeants, three drummers and thirty-one rank and file. See Cary and McCance, *Regimental Records of the Royal Welch Fusiliers*, 1:235.

191. The huge monastery of Montserrat in Catalonia, Spain, was a case in point. It commanded roads in the area and was subsequently transformed by Spanish regulars and irregulars into a formidable edifice, bristling with embrasures and redoubts. On 24 July 1811, it was stormed by a French force under Marshal Louis Suchet. The paintings of Delaroche, Alvarez Dumont and Baron Lejeune depict French troops assaulting convents and churches defended by Spanish insurgents, regulars, and, in some cases, monks. See Lachouque et al, pp. 37, 59, 73, illustration facing p. 84, and 133–4.

192. Badajoz, a fortified town astride the Guadiana River, which guarded the Spanish side of the southern corridor connecting Spain and Portugal, was besieged four times during the war. The first was from 26 January to 9 March 1811, when the French tricked the Spanish garrison into surrender. Wellington subsequently ordered Marshal William Beresford to recapture the strategic fortress. These operations began on 8 May 1811. The siege was lifted after only five days, on 12 May, on the approach of a relieving army under Marshal Nicolas Soult. The relief never arrived, but the French garrison sallied from the town to destroy the siegeworks as Beresford disengaged his army in order to fight the battle of Albuera on 16 May 1811. Thus ended the second siege.

193. Marshal André Masséna's defeat in Portugal (see note 190) cost him 25,000 men, 9,000 horses and virtually his entire waggon train. By 5 April 1811, the only French troops remaining in Portugal were a small garrison at Almeida, which guarded the Northern Corridor or invasion route into Portugal. (Ciudad Rodrigo and Fort San Concepcion protected the Northern Corridor on the Spanish side of the frontier.) This defeat, however, did not discourage Masséna from making a second attempt to conquer Portugal. Retiring behind Ciudad Rodrigo, he quickly reorganized and replenished his defeated army and attacked again, this time in an effort to relieve the British and Portuguese siege of Almeida. Once again he was defeated, at the hard-fought two-day battle of Fuentes de Oñoro, 3 and 5 May 1811. French losses were 2,192 casualties to the Allies 1,545. Masséna ordered a retreat on 10 May and once again retired behind Ciudad Rodrigo. A few days later, he was replaced as the commander of the Army of Portugal by Marshal Auguste Marmont. See Michael Glover, *Wellington's Peninsular Victories* (New York: Macmillan

Co., 1963), pp. 50–53; and Chandler, *Dictionary of Napoleonic Wars*, pp. 164–5.

194. Within a few minutes of the attack by the 1st Lancers of the Vistula and the 2nd Hussars, three of the battalions of Colborne's brigade had lost two-thirds of their effective strength.

195. Michael Glover correctly describes Albuera (16 May 1811) as the "worst of the pounding matches". Of the 7,640 British infantry present, 3,933 were casualties, according to Glover. Hoghton's Fusilier brigade was nearly annihilated. The unit, which arrived during the battle after a forced march from Badajoz, and went immediately into action, sustained eighty per cent casualties. Several British colours (six according to General Regnault) were captured by French troops during the battle. (According to a French source, Napoleon's troops captured twenty-two British colours in the Peninsula. By comparison, the French army lost only eleven eagles, eight of which had been captured by British troops.) For all this, see Glover, *Wellington's Army in the Peninsula, 1808–1814*, p. 163; and Lachouque et al, *Napoleon's War in Spain*, pp. 125, 127.

196. This was the third siege of Badajoz. The town was blockaded on 19 May and a full Allied siege commenced on the 24th/25th May. Once again Wellington was forced to raise the siege when a numerically superior force of 60,000 French troops under Marshal Auguste Marmont converged on Badajoz. The siege was abandoned on 19 June 1811.

197. The "treaty of Cintra" was the controversial Convention of Cintra, of 22 August 1808.

198. The capture of Ciudad Rodrigo secured the northern invasion route which permitted Wellington to attack Badajoz once again. Wellington had 32,000 troops at his disposal. Four divisions were to cover the operation and four more were placed in the siege lines. Although a costly siege, the capture of Badajoz on 6 April 1812 (the fourth and final siege) was a strategic victory for it gave Wellington control of both corridors which enabled him to prepare for the invasion of Spain.

199. The French garrison consisted of 5,000 troops and over 600 sick.

200. The high price in blood Wellington paid in all of his sieges was due to the want of an effective engineering branch. Although the Ordnance Department supplied him with trained officers, Wellington enjoyed none of the lavish establishment of trained sappers and miners and sundry equipment that every French *corps d'armée* enjoyed. The pitiful state of Wellington's corps of engineers can be judged by a comparison between Wellington's engineer transport with that of the French. By 1813, the British army's entire engineer transport in the Peninsula consisted of a total of 120 pack mules against 230 draught horses hauling thirty-five waggons in each *corps d'armée*. Given this, French sapper and miner units

carried far more tools than their British counterparts. Since Wellington's army was not equipped, therefore, for siege warfare, assaulting columns routinely had to go over the top of the sap or trench at a great and dangerous distance from the breach. At Badajoz, the need to enlist infantrymen part-trained as engineers undoubtedly explains why some scaling ladders were constructed of green wood which opened and separated, or were not of sufficient length. The horror of Badajoz is conveyed in the following letter to George Hennell, a volunteer originally attached to the old 94th Foot. "The dead bodies lay in every form, some dashed to pieces by bombs, many naked, and you saw where the balls went—many rolled in the dust & blood & dust sticking all over them. When I came to the spot where the grape shot came, the blood lay very thick but bore no comparison to the breach. There they lay, one upon the other, two or three deep, many in the ditch half in and half out of the water. In coming out you were obliged to tread on many. I went two or three times to the town, the last time the smell was horrible. You were continually treading upon feet or heads." The main breach described by Hennell was crammed with the dead and wounded bodies of some 1,300 to 1,500 British soldiers. Those who survived the breach subjected the town to what Philip Guedalla described as three full days of "unprecedented riot" in the annals of the British army. As discreditable as this affair was, to condemn the soldiers' action as inexcusable, as Michael Glover has, is to blame the victim. This undeserved criticism suggests that human beings have an inexhaustible capacity for self-restraint in the face of any horror. It also infers that the extraordinary human emotions and powers which miraculously drove British troops to mount no less than forty assaults into the breach, were suddenly to be turned off like an electric light switch once the town had fallen. Glover's wrongful condemnation of the British soldier at Badajoz is painfully reminiscent of the insensitivity and inhumanity of the First World War senior British commanders, who, refusing to believe that some of their troops were suffering from severe emotional shock and nervous exhaustion associated with trench warefare, ordered the execution of several hundred traumatized men and officers. Blame for the outrages at Badajoz resides ultimately with the British army's high command for failing to provide the army in the Peninsula with an efficient corps of engineers. Wellington, too, must be severely censored for failing to appreciate the limitations of human endurance when he ordered his brave soldiers to do the impossible at Badajoz. He had every reason to weep bitterly when he saw the casualty returns. For all this see Richard Glover, *Peninsular Preparation*, pp. 105–109; Michael Glover, *A Gentleman Volunteer*, p. 18 and *Wellington's Peninsular Victories*, p. 62; and Anthony Babington, *For the Sake of*

Example: Capital Courts Martial, 1914–1920 (New York: St. Martin's Press, 1983), *passim*.

201. From about mid-1808 to 1814, a sizeable portion of the French army was absorbed in a viciously fought struggle against Spanish guerrillas. By 1812, it is estimated that guerrilla forces numbered 7,000 men and women, divided into numerous bands, the largest of which was about 150 strong. It is also estimated that of the 200,000 casualties sustained by the French army during the Peninsular War, at least 50,000 are attributed to actions against the guerrillas. Guerrillas were particularly adept at cutting French communications. The Gendarmerie of Spain was established to assure communications. It was composed of twenty squadrons. Sixteen of these guarded the main road from Bayonne, in south-eastern France, to Madrid, in central Spain. The remaining four were held in reserve. Another measure against the guerrillas was the construction of huge block houses at strategic intervals along key highways. Built of wood, they were manned with infantry who were to escort couriers and guard convoys. Wellington received valuable intelligence from the guerrillas and rewarded them with money and arms. In the long run, the various guerrilla bands demoralized the French army which was unaccustomed to fighting an entire nation in arms. The ferocity of the guerrilla war in Spain was brilliantly if gruesomely captured by Francisco de Goya in his "The Disasters of War", a series of etchings and aquatints printed from 1810 to 1820.

202. The high-living Commissary General was Sir Robert Kennedy.

203. See Watson, *The Reign of George III*, pp. 493–497, 550–561; Chandler, *Dictionary of the Napoleonic Wars*, pp. 338–340.

204. The 11th and 12th Cavalry Regiments of the Portuguese army wore dark blue tunics with red hackles attached to their helmets, as did, for instance, lancer-gendarmes in the French army.

205. The battle of Salamanca, which began piecemeal, ended with the decisive defeat of Marshal Auguste Marmont's army. French losses were twenty guns and 14,000 men, including Marmont who was badly wounded. But for the failure of a Spanish force to block the bridge at Alba de Tormes, the defeat of the French would have been complete. The remnants of Marmont's eight battered divisions straggled back to Burgos and the French frontier, while Spanish guerrillas relentlessly harassed the retreating army. The great victory of Salamanca shattered French control of central and north Spain. The victory also opened the road to Madrid, which Wellington entered triumphantly on 12 August 1812. (He subsequently evacuated the city on 20 October 1812, at the approach of a large combined French army.) The losses for the Allies were about 5,200.

206. This action, which occurred at Garcia Hernandez on 23 July 1812, was

the greatest victory of Wellington's cavalry during the war. Two regiments of dragoons of the King's German Legion, led by General von Bock, charged and broke two formed squares belonging to the French 66th and 22nd Regiments. During the action, the eagle of the 22nd was captured. This was a feat virtually unequalled against well trained troops. The dragoons suffered 127 casualties out of 770 men who charged, but inflicted a loss of 1,100 men on the French army. George Hennell, who somehow confused the dragoons with hussars, described the chaos of the battlefield. "We halted and slept about 10 o'clock till sun rise [on the 23rd of July], then we advanced & crossed the river 1½ leagues above Salamanca & about 11 o'clock we came to a plain surrounded by hills where the German Hussars came up with the enemy. They (the enemy) formed a square but soon retired in the greatest disorder, throwing away everything that impeded their running. We took a great many prisoners. It was about two hours before we came up. You have frequently seen paintings of a field of battle with a hussar & his horse lying just as they fell & weltering in their gore: another with his head cleft in two: many in all positions, some dead, some wounded. This was one of those scenes for a mile. Every step was over cartridge boxes, belts, arms & ammunition of every kind and their cooking utensils, but when we came to the hill their arms lay in columns and bodies very thick. They had made a slight stand there and our Germans rode into the midst of them. There was a great number killed upon the spot but they put them entirely to rout. Everybody said how well the Germans fought." See Glover, *A Gentleman Volunteer*, pp. 31–32.

207. French prisoners numbered 7,000.

208. If, as Browne indicates, British army women were indeed reprehensible characters, given to marauding and licentiousness, the behaviour resulted directly from the bitterly harsh conditions and uncertainty of military life, particularly when on active service. More research is necessary to determine a pattern or policy. However, a review of available records indicates that upon the death of a soldier, his wife or consort was immediately abandoned by the army; no longer was she entitled to rations or living accommodations. The fact that an army woman had dependent children neither delayed nor prevented her prompt dismissal from the service and the resulting official cessation of benefits. (See Appendix C.) In an effort to survive under a callous system in which they were virtually powerless, army women were routinely driven to marauding and "engaging themselves . . . to future husbands." The system was at fault, not the army woman, who, despite her great value to the army, endured the great hardships of eighteenth-century warfare and who, when in breach of the Article of Wars, was brutally punished. Distressed army women were to

be found in Britain as well as with the army overseas. So common was the poverty of servicemen's families that they became a subject for poets. In *Margaret; or, the Ruined Cottage*, Wordsworth depicted the mounting suffering of an army woman and her two young children, after her soldier-husband enlisted leaving his family his bounty money only. In 1798, an anonymous poet captured the plight of the army woman when he penned in the *Cambridge Intelligencer*:

> She told us that her husband serv'd
> A soldier far away
> And therefore to her parish she
> Was begging back her way.

George Bell has left a wonderfully evocative description of Mrs Skiddy, a tough-as-nails and determined army woman, who had this to say when Wellington's Provost Marshal gave orders to shoot the donkeys of two women as a way of deterring them from impeding the progress of the army during the retreat from Burgos: 'We must risk something to be in [camp] before the men, to have the fire and a dhrop of tay ready for them after their load and their labour: and sure if we went in the *rare* the French, bad luck to them, would pick me up, me and my donkey, and then Dan Skiddy would be lost entirely without me.' Army women were spared none of the slaughter of the battlefield. Witness the violent death of Mrs Maibee, as described by Private William Wheeler of the 51st Foot. "On the morning of the 28th October [1812, near Valladolid] the enemy brought some guns and fired into the camp. The first round they fired killed Serjeant Maibee's wife, her husband had just gone to the bridge on duty and had left her to prepare his breakfast, she was in the act of taking some choclate off the fire when the shot carried away her right arm and breast." For all this see W. O. 71/86, the Court Martial Proceedings of Mary Colethrate and Elizabeth Clarke, pp. 156–158; Sylvia R. Frey, *The British Soldier in America: A Social History of Military Life in the Revolutionary Period* (Austin: University of Texas Press, 1981), pp. 20, 36, 61, 64, 76–77; Emsley, *British Society and the French Wars, 1793–1815*, p. 75; George Bell quoted in Charles Oman, *Wellington's Army, 1809–1814* (London: Edward Arnold, 1912), p. 275; and B. H. Liddell Hart, ed., *The Letters of Private Wheeler, 1809–1828* (London: Michael Joseph, 1952), pp. 99–100.

209. Wellington was warmly received by the citizenry of Madrid. Quickly, however, Wellington's distant and haughty demeanour earned him the unpopularity of the inhabitants.

210. The Retiro was a park which contained a fort. Before he left Madrid, Joseph put a garrison into the fort. Hennell described these troops as

"very fine French soldiers". Their precipitate surrender was due apparently to an inadequate water supply. Wellington reported that among the vast equipment found in the Retiro were the eagles belonging to the 12th and 51st Regiments. See Michael Glover, *A Gentleman Volunteer*, p. 37.

211. Despite the difficulty of checking Spanish hatred of the French, as evident in this episode, the guerrillas played a decisive role in Wellington's victory in the Peninsula. According to a French source, more than half of the total casualties sustained by Napoleon's troops were caused by the guerrilla struggle. See Lachouque et al, *Napoleon's War in Spain*, p. 10.

212. The "Revolution" Browne refers to was the rising in the Hague on 17 November 1814 against the French, who had invaded the Dutch Republic in 1795 and established the puppet Batavian Republic, which replaced the old Dutch provinces. The first concern of the Dutch nationalists was to seek British help and to recall the Prince of Orange, who answered the call immediately. The old Dutch Republic was revived as the kingdom of the Netherlands with the house of Orange as a hereditary monarchy. To this was added Belgium, the old Austrian Netherlands. It was hoped in Europe that the combined Dutch-Belgian kingdom would prove a strong barrier against historic French ambitions in the Low Countries. See George Lefebvre, *Napoleon*, 2 vols., trans. J. E. Anderson (New York: Columbia University Press, 1969): 2: 338–341.

213. George Hennell also attended the grand bull-fight given in honour of Wellington. Unlike Browne, he was unrestrained in his criticism of the ritualistic and bloody slaughter of bulls as public amusement in his letter to his brothers dated Madrid, 1 September 1812. Those whose function it was to kill or tease the animal were the real "brutes". Bull fighting was reduced to nothing more than a "scene of blood". Hennell closed his letter with these bitter words: "I have given a full description of this, for I shall see no more I assure you. Remember I was an eye-witness, therefore you may believe what I write. *The half of the audience were ladies and they applauded it.*" See Glover, *A Gentleman Volunteer*, pp. 44–48.

214. The Palace of El Escorial was dedicated to St Lawrence, a native of Huesca, Spain, who, because of his Christian beliefs, was slow-roasted on a gridiron in A.D. 261. The Palace was built by Philip II between 1559 and 1584 and combines a monastery, royal palace and mausoleum, the whole appropriately in the shape of a gridiron. The Pantheon or *Panteon de los Reyes* was the royal mausoleum where various kings of Spain and their mothers were interred.

215. According to Lachouque et al, Clausel handed over his command to

Souham in early September because Clausel was still suffering from a wound received at Salamanca. Rather than risk battle with Wellington whose army outnumbered his, Souham avoided this clash until the junction of his troops with those of other armies, which would give the French an important numerical superiority. The French achieved this advantage on 7 November 1812, at Medina de Campo, when several of their armies united. This gave them a combined strength of 80,000 troops against Wellington's 68,000 men. See *Napoleon's War in Spain*, pp. 150, 152.

216. Before he took the offensive against Wellington, Souham left a garrison of 1,800 troops under General Dubreton in the imposing castle at Burgos. Recognizing the strategic importance of Burgos, which controlled a vital section of the main highway linking Madrid with France, Wellington hurried from Madrid to capture the Castillian city. As is evident in Browne's description of the siege, the reckless bravery of the British soldier could not make up for the want of equipment, organization and leadership. The siege of Burgos was undoubtedly Wellington's worst operation during the war. Wellington had virtually no siege train, whereas the French had the reserve artillery of an entire army. The Duke's mistake, according to Fortescue, was that he failed to provide a single assault with enough troops to be successful. The result was the sacrifice of almost 2,000 brave men in petty attacks, all of which failed to achieve their ultimate objective. Wellington's miserable handling of the operation temporarily, at least, undermined confidence in his generalship. Captain George Bowles, of the Coldstream Guards, spoke for those who were critical of Wellington, when he wrote while in front of Burgos: "This is one of the longest jobs the noble Marquis has had in hand for some time, and, much as I *revere* him, I must say that in this case he has shown rather more of a quality nearly allied to obstinacy than is to be wished. The fact is that he was repeatedly told by those whom he consulted previous to commencing operations, his means (three eighteen-pounders, four howitzers) were totally insufficient." Of all the casualties sustained by the British during the siege, Wellington was noticeably shaken by the death of Major Edward Cocks, who, had he survived the war, would have become, in Wellington's opinion, "one of the first Generals of England". While Wellington was "frittering away his strength" before Burgos, the French were regrouping theirs, which quickly led to the nearly precipitous retreat of the British army to the Portuguese frontier. The following year, from 10 to 12 June 1813, the Allies renewed the attack on Burgos, which proved successful. Unlike the first siege, the French garrison held out for two days only. See John W. Fortescue, *Wellington* (London: Ernest Benn Ltd., 1960), p. 145; Anthony Brett-James, *Wellington at War, 1794–1815*

(New York: St Martin's Press, 1961), pp. 244–246; and Chandler, *Dictionary of the Napoleonic Wars*, p. 72.

217. The "disorder" was probably the rout of General George Anson's dragoons by French cavalry at Villadrigo. British losses were put at more than 300 during the action which lasted less than ten minutes. French losses were 179. Lachouque et al, *Napoleon's War in Spain*, p. 151.

218. This was the minor action at the Tordesillas bridge on 27 October 1812, which was distinguished by the French fighting naked after their swim. In this state of undress, except for their cross belts and ammunition pouches, they stormed the tower of the destroyed bridge and took several prisoners. *Ibid.*

219. The year 1812 was indeed a difficult year for Wellington, for, after his early successes at Ciudad Rodrigo (19 January), Badajoz (6 April) and Salamanca (22 July), he was forced to return to Freneda, Portugal, where he had spent the autumn of 1811 and portions of the lulls between the sieges of Ciudad Rodrigo and Badajoz. As Fortescue correctly argued, however, a victory at Burgos would not have necessarily served to protect his early victories. In 1812 Wellington did not have the manpower to hold Madrid and Burgos, which was on the main French line of communications with Spain. Wellington's capture of Madrid, although of great symbolic value, was actually premature. A few months after his march to Madrid, Wellington had to face greatly superior forces, which necessitated his embarrassing retreat to the Portuguese frontier. His capture of Madrid in August 1812 was altogether too risky, and he paid penalty for this strategic error. What eluded Wellington in 1812 he gained in 1813. During the relative quiet of the winter of 1812–1813, Wellington reformed his army with numerous reinforcements which put some 80,000 men at his immediate disposal. In addition to this force, some 50,000 Spanish troops were available in Galicia and New Castile. There was also the active presence of British-Sicilian troops at Alicante on Spain's south-eastern coast, which threatened additional lines of communication with France. Against this array of forces, the French situation was steadily weakened to support Napoleon's attack against Russia in June 1812 and his subsequent campaigns in central Europe throughout 1813, following his disastrous defeat in eastern Europe. See Fortescue, *Wellington*, p. 147.

220. Sir Neil Cantlie's massive history of the British army's Medical Department provides us with a clear picture of mortality and morbidity among Wellington's soldiers in Spain and Portugal. Voluminous official statistical information indicates that few if any escaped unscathed the inherent dangers of the battlefield or the ravages of disease. Army returns also

show that nearly three times as many soldiers died from disease as died from wounds received on the *champ d'honneur*. The mean strength of the army in the Peninsula, from January 1811 to May 1814, a period of forty-one months, was 66,772. During the same time there were a total of 35,525 deaths, of whom only 9,948 died in battle or from related wounds. The chief causes of death from disease for the period 1812–1814 were dysentery, continued fever, typhus and hospital gangrene. See Neil Cantlie, *A History of the Army Medical Department* (London: Churchill Livingstone, 1974):1:373.

221. This evident scarcity of food resulted from the failure of the transport and supply system during the retreat. Because of mismanagement, the commissary stores were sent ahead with the baggage to Ciudad Rodrigo. The troops, rank and file as well as officers, were forced to seek other sources of food. A General Order of 16 November 1812 prohibited the shooting of pigs. The same Order warned hungry and worn-out British soldiers that two men were already sentenced to be hanged for failure to comply with Wellington's instructions. A copy of this General Order appears in Brett-James, *Wellington at War*, pp. 247–248.

222. The most difficult part of the retreat occurred from 16 to 18 November, a period of heavy rain and cold weather. Perhaps the most miserable aspect of the retreat was failure of the Commissary-General to replenish the food magazines along the line of retirement. This occasioned considerable indiscipline among the troops. There was also one signal incident of extraordinary disobedience by three divisional generals, who disregarded the route Wellington instructed them to follow. Fortunately for the British, who left 6,000 men along the road, Soult's army did not press the pursuit. On 19 November 1812, the last British soldier had reached the haven of Ciudad Rodrigo. By December the army was dispersed in cantonments, where it remained inactive for several months. This was a most welcome rest for the army, which had just ended eleven months' hard campaigning and a gruelling and demoralizing retreat. The army also refitted in preparation for the advance to the Spanish-Portuguese frontier, which was crossed in May 1813. See Fortescue, *Wellington*, pp. 145–150; and Brett-James, *Wellington at War*, p. 220.

223. Browne's summary expulsion of the unfortunate priest from his bed, and Browne's prompt occupation of same, makes one question the magnanimity of British officers here alleged.

224. Antonia was probably one of the three women attached to Wellington's staff. See Ward, *Wellington's Headquarters*, p. 194.

225. Winter cantonments were evidently a happy period for Wellington's army. Officers engaged in shooting, hunting and, of course, fishing.

Others, like George Hennell, satisfied not-so latent theatrical aspirations by organizing and participating in plays. As for the rank and file, some undoubtedly hunted hares and rabbits, while the Irish soldiery played handball. Several continuous months of this suspension of the fear, exhaustion and death from campaigning had predictable effects on the deportment of the troops. As Fortescue put it: "All traces of Frederick the Great's influence upon them had vanished." Slovenliness generally replaced the once smart bearing of the men. Even Wellington's own sentries caught the contagion, which frequently embarrassed the commander. Browne's positive description of the army was thus a view of the troops on the eve of the forthcoming campaign, well after corrective disciplinary measures had been implemented. See Glover, *A Gentleman Volunteer*, pp. 64–65; and Fortescue, *History of the British Army*, 9: 107–110.

226.　This figure, as well as the preceding strength for Portuguese cavalry are obviously in error and should read 1,400 and 2,800.

227.　At the start of the campaign some 12,000 Spanish troops were given to Wellington.

228.　News of Napoleon's disastrous defeat in Russia, which reached Wellington on 18 January 1813, had a decisive influence on the Duke's plan for the defeat of the French in Spain. Realizing that the French debacle in Russia would prevent reinforcements being sent to Spain, Wellington hoped to manoeuvre King Joseph quickly into a decisive battle, the outcome of which would compel the French to evacuate Spain. Wellington was also encouraged to proceed in this manner when Napoleon ordered his brother to dispatch a considerable portion of his command to assist French efforts in crushing the guerrillas in Biscay and Navarra. This meant that Joseph's army watching the Spanish-Portuguese frontier was numerically inferior to Wellington's army. The need to destroy Joseph's army quickly was therefore great since failure to do so would merely succeed in driving Joseph back on his reserves of 60,000 troops, which would then give the advantage of numbers to the French. A series of outflanking movements begun in Portugal forced the French to retreat daily, until by 20 June Joseph's army, without its reserves, had retreated to Vitoria, a scant sixty-five miles from the French border. Since the start of the campaign on 21 May, Wellington had advanced 300 miles in twenty-nine days. Everything was set for a major battle. See Glover, *A Gentleman Volunteer*, pp. 69–70.

229.　The 3rd Hussars were one of eleven hussar regiments. All the garments of this showy regiment were silver grey with white braid. See Liliane and Fred Funcken, *L'Uniforme et les Armes des Soldats du Premier Empire* (Tournai, Belgium: Casterman, 1979) 1: 64–68.

230. George Baxter Browne, at the time a first lieutenant in the 23rd Royal Welch Fusiliers.

231. Wellington later denounced the plundering of the 18th Hussars with these words: They "are a disgrace to the name of a soldier in action as well as elsewhere; & I propose to draft their Horses from them & to send the men to England, if I cannot get the better of them in any other manner." The 18th also earned Wellington's displeasure when a detachment failed to guard a carriage containing papers of consequence belonging to the French army, which were subsequently lost. See Brett-James, *Wellington at War*, pp. 267–268.

232. Bleeding, a practice employed by ancient physicians, was resorted to in virtually all illnesses. In his important study of febrile diseases, Dr Robert Jackson, a distinguished army doctor and contemporary of Browne, explains what was considered in the eighteenth century to be the therapeutic power of what was termed "subtraction of blood". "It is a fact", Jackson argued, "if any thing is to be regarded as fact in medical science, that febrile action consists in actions subverted, changed or modified in some shape or other from the action of health. If this be admitted as preliminary, it follows by consequence that the first just step in the process of cure consists in arresting changed or perverted action; the second, in soliciting or moving action that is analagous to that of health. This is self-evident, and it is farther evident, — in so far as we dare venture to reckon on the certainty of medical evidence, that animal action is moved through the whole extent of the system by the impulse of the circulating blood. If that be granted, it follows by consequence that the withholding the application of the impulse, disturbs the order, even necessarily arrests the very action itself, whether healthy or diseased. The subtraction of the impulse is effected through the subduction of blood from the veins: hence bleeding presents itself as the first remedy in point of time, as it is the most important in point of power for the cure of febrile diseases of any of which we have knowledge. It is demonstrable that subduction of blood from the veins may be so managed as to arrest the existing action at the time; it is thus preliminary of cure, if not absolutely and finally curative in itself . . ." If the patient was subject to violent febrile action, Jackson proffered the following surgical procedure: ". . . The Patient is to be laid in a recumbent posture, the head somewhat elevated, a large vein or two large veins to be selected, and a large opening made in the veins, so that the subduction be sudden as it can possibly be made." The febrifuge method of bloodletting was not without its dangers. The renowned eighteenth-century Virgin Island physician, John Lettsom, evidently lost not a few unlucky patients to this procedure. A wag wrote of him:

I, John Lettsom,
Blisters, bleeds and sweats 'em.
If after that, they please to die,
I, John Lettsom.

For this see Robert Jackson, *A Sketch of the History and Cure of Febrile Diseases* (Stockton, England: T. and H. Eeles, 1817), 182, 190; and David Clyde, *Two Centuries of Health Care in Dominica* (New Delhi: Sushima Gopal, 1980), p. 2.

233. Wellington commanded 70,000 men at Vitoria, of whom 35,500 were British, 27,500 Portuguese, and 7,000 Spanish. Allied losses were 3,300 British and 1,600 Spanish and Portuguese combined. See Henry Newbolt, *The Story of the Oxfordshire and Buckinghamshire Light Infantry* (London: Country Life, 1915), p. 117.

234. Although much hard fighting remained in the north-eastern corner of Spain and southern France, Vitoria was a climactic battle for it signified the strategic defeat of Napoleon in the Peninsula. Amid the chaos of the battlefield, some 400 pieces of artillery and a fabulous booty made Vitoria a brilliant victory for Wellington, who was promptly promoted to the rank of field marshal. The remnants of several French armies streamed through the Pyrenean passes into France. By early July 1813, the French presence in Spain was reduced to garrisons in San Sebastian, an important port in the vicinity of several roads leading into France on the western end of the Pyrenees, and Pamplona, which guarded two key passes through the same mountains. A small French army under Marshal Suchet also clung tenaciously to a section of northern Catalonia. An ambitious plan of Marshal Soult, whom Napoleon had ordered to Bayonne after the debacle at Vitoria to reorganize French forces, failed to relieve the besieged garrisons in a series of actions collectively known as the battle of the Pyrenees, 25 July to 2 August 1813. Both strongholds fell subsequently to Wellington's troops on 8 September and 31 October, respectively.

235. In his effort to keep the Bayonne road open as a line of retreat, King Joseph detached General Bertrand Clausel with an army of four divisions, some 10,000 troops, on the road from Logroño. Too far off to intervene in the rout of Joseph's army at Vitoria, Clausel took the road to Saragossa and retreated into France via the Pyrenean passes at Jaca and Canfran. The British 6th Division was ordered to intercept Clausel which it was unable to do. The pursuit was broken off and the 6th Division marched instead to participate in the investment of Pamplona. Mina y Epoz, the guerrilla leader, did manage, however, to harass Clausel's rear guard.

236. This was the first attempted storming of San Sebastian, which occurred on 25 July 1813. The failure of this attack resulted in the siege being conducted at a reduced level, during which time a French attempt to relieve the garrison was beaten back at Sorauren on 28 and 30 July. On 8 August a full siege was reimposed.

237. The siege was entrusted to General Oswald and the 5th Division.

238. With a force of 88,000 troops, Soult launched one corps commanded by Count d'Erlon to secure the Maya Pass, and two additional corps under General Reille to occupy the Roncesvalles Pass. Soult's objectives were first to relieve Pamplona and then San Sebastian. The initial French attacks succeeded in driving back weak British covering forces. Nonetheless, the Anglo-Portuguese army rallied in the hills above the village of Sorauren, where on 28 July and again on 30 July Soult was beaten. Three days later Soult admitted defeat and retreated back towards France.

239. George Baxter Browne was wounded on 25 July 1813, at Roncesvalles. At the time Browne commanded the left company of the 23rd Royal Welch Fusiliers, which had been detached from the regiment in order to support the 28th Foot. Because of the severity of the wound, Browne was awarded a pension. Browne's sister, Felicia Hemans, commemorated the battle in a poem entitled "English Soldier's Song of Memory", which was sung to the air "Am Rhein, Am Rhein!". The fifth stanza of this brief piece reads:

> They that upheld the banners, proudly waving,
> In Roncesvalles' dell,
> With England's blood the southern vineyards laving—
> Forget not how they fell!

For this see Cary and McCance, *Regimental Records of the Royal Welch Fusiliers*, 1: 248, 254; [Hemans], *The Poems of Felicia Hemans*, p. 358.

240. The action fought on 31 August 1813, including the combat at the Vera bridge over the Bidassoa River, is known as the battle of San Marcial. Soult's failure at San Marcial sealed the fate of the French garrison at San Sebastian.

241. The infantry of the French army was divided into light and line battalions. Light troops were primarily intended to conduct open order fighting. Line battalions, on the other hand, performed the more mechanical and rigid functions of the infantry. The latter was originally organized into one grenadier and eight fusilier companies. Fusiliers constituted the main body of a line battalion; the grenadiers were elite troops. In order to provide line units with greater tactical versatility, one of the fusilier companies was converted into *voltigeurs* during the 1793–1815 war. The equivalent of light troops, this new branch of elites was intended primarily

for open order fighting and skirmishing. See Richard K. Riehn, *The French Infantry and Artillery, 1795–1812* (New York: Helenic Publications, 1960), p. 1.

242. At noon on 9 September, the survivors marched out of the citadel with the honours of war. The determined defence of San Sebastian, which lasted from 27 June to 9 September, was directed by General Baron Rey.

243. Pamplona surrendered on 31 October 1813.

244. French efforts to lure Allied troops into deserting is reminiscent of Mexican activities during the 1846–1848 war against the United States. The Tercio San Patricio (St Patrick's Battalion), a unit composed entirely of regular army American soldiers, most of whom were Irish Catholics, were enticed from their allegiance by unceasing and cunningly-worded Mexican appeals to their religion. See Ernest Dupuy, *The Compact History of the United States Army* (New York: Hawthorn Books, Inc., 1956), pp. 100–101.

245. The multi-battalion 60th Regiment, which began life in 1755 in the Thirteen Colonies with the appropriate title of Royal Americans, was recruited throughout the eighteenth century with large numbers of foreigners, particularly German, Dutch and French. The 5th Battalion of the 60th Foot, whose distinguished record in the Peninsular War stands comparison with any regiment in the army, was largely composed of German riflemen. Raised in 1797, its first commanding officer was a Bavarian, Lieutenant-Colonel Baron de Rottenburg. See Lewis Butler, William George and Steuart Hare, *The Annals of the Kings Royal Rifle Corps* (London: Smith, Elder & Co., and John Murray, 1913–1932), 1: 2–3, 261, 269; and Barnes, *Military Uniforms of Britain and the Empire*, pp. 58–59.

246. On 10 November 1813, the battle of Nivelle, Wellington launched his invasion of France. Attacking inland, which surprised Soult who expected the assault to come from the British left resting on the coast, Wellington outflanked the French defence line. French losses were considerable: approximately 4,500 men and sixty-nine guns. By nightfall, allied troops were in possession of St Jean de Luz. Spanish troops engaged in this operation plundered so terribly, obviously in retaliation for French excesses in Spain, that they were ordered back to their country. This bold decision evidently sacrificed Wellington's numerical superiority, but it did win him the confidence of the French people. Soult retreated to the River Nive outside Bayonne. This new line was subsequently taken in the course of heavy fighting from 10–13 December, the battle of St Pierre d'Irube. These reverses compelled Soult to fall back further to the Adour river line.

247. For Browne's instructions at La Rhune, see Appendix "D".

248. Hennell provides this additional description of the Basque town. "St Jean de Luz", he wrote, "is a beautiful town about a league from the bottom of the mountains, with a river [Nivelle] running through it & a small harbour. There are innumerable single houses all round the country which seems beautiful." Glover, *A Gentleman Volunteer*, p. 137.

249. Louis-Antoine de Bourbon, Duc d'Angoulême, was the eldest son of the Comte d'Artois. His arrival at St Jean de Luz coincided with Napoleon's defeats in 1813 in Spain and Central Europe, and revived royalists' hopes for the restoration of the House of Bourbon. Wellington was of the opinion that the Bourbons could regain the throne of France if Britain supported a prince of the House of Bourbon who joined the allies in the field. Members of Wellington's staff were not entirely impressed with Angoulême, who, it seems, was similarly unpopular with the citizenry of Bordeaux. See Hibbert, *The Wheatley Diary*, p. 36.

250. The reference to Châtillon pertained to Castlereagh's efforts to get Russia, Prussia and Austria to present a common front to Napoleon. The major question dividing the allies in Mid-January 1814 was whether to enter into peace talks with the French. Castlereagh was temporarily able to close the rift between the four major powers when they agreed to meet at Châtillon. The conference began on 7 February 1814. Because the allied foreign ministers were not themselves to participate in the discussions, Britain was represented by the Earl of Cathcart, the Earl of Aberdeen and General Sir Charles Stewart. See Sherwig, *Guineas and Gunpowder*, pp. 317–322.

251. This was the start of Soult's St Pierre d'Irube operation which would end in French defeat and the establishment of a defence line on the River Adour.

252. The Adour River, a considerable obstacle west of Bayonne, was crossed on 23 February 1814. On the 24th, a bridge was completed over the Adour which enabled Wellington to both blockade Bayonne and attack Soult at Orthez on 27 February.

253. Apparently at no time during the long 1793–1815 war was the Army properly clothed. The inability to do so stemmed in large measure from an ancient system, which permitted colonels of regiments to profit from clothing their troops. This historic practice led to delay, inefficiency and abuse within the army's clothing system. The difficulties also resulted from the unexpected scale of the long war and the inability of Britain's still fledgling textile industry to keep pace with the army's need. Between 1793 and 1795, for example, army manpower estimates called for more than a threefold increase in troop strength, to a total of about 318,000 soldiers. In 1798, several proposals for reforming the existing clothing system were suggested by the Finance Committee of the House of

Commons. These, however, were found unacceptable and in 1801 the old system was continued with only a few minor changes. See Buckley, *Slaves in Red Coats*, pp. 121–123.

254. Worn army uniforms were not always discarded. An inspection of a detachment of the 4th West India Regiment at Surinam in August 1806 revealed that "the Regiment have received no Caps for their Augmentation, and the men are furnished partly with old Caps of different Corps." See W. O. 27/90, part 1, Brigadier General Hughes' Inspection Report, 26 August 1806.

255. According to Michael Glover, there was at least one occasion when British soldiers caught in the act of plundering by the Provost Marshal were hanged on the spot without the benefit of trial. Soldiers convicted of plundering were ordinarily flogged or executed. As Browne has admitted, officers routinely plundered houses in the Peninsula. Curiously, however, very few officers were brought before a court martial for this misdeed during the 1793–1815 war. Equally curious, those officers judged guilty of plundering were all given mild sentences, apparently. A lieutenant of the 15th Foot, for instance, charged and found guilty of breaking into a house of an inhabitant in Guadeloupe in 1810, was privately reprimanded only. It would appear that there were two distinct military codes in operation in the British army during the war: one for rankers which was harsh, and one for officers which was scandalously lenient. For this, see Glover, *A Gentleman Volunteer*, p. 147; and W. O. 90/1.

256. Private Wheeler has left us this harrowing account of an execution of three soldiers by a firing squad in a letter dated 5 September 1811. "The method of carrying the sentence into execution is as follows. The division is formed into a square having three faces, the prisoners are formed into line, in the square with their backs to the opening, the firing party composed of men from the regiment [of the condemned soldiers] are drawn up in front of the men only a few paces from them. After the Court Martial is read, and the men have received spiritual assistance from the Chaplain, or if he be a Roman Catholic from a priest, their eyes are bound and they kneel down. When they have made a signal, the firing party— who are ready loaded and firelocks cocked—watch the Provost Martial who stands with a handkerchief. At the first signal the firing party presents, and at the next they fire. The muzzles of the pieces are so close to the unfortunate culprits that it is impossible any one can miss the mark, but to make doubly sure the muzzle of a firelock afterwards is put close to the head of each as they lie on the ground and discharged. The division then march past the dead bodies in sections of three, as the men pass the dead bodies the word of command is given 'Eyes left'. I shall not attempt

to describe to you the frightful appearance of the mangled bodies. You can easily imagine that when you are informed that a party of one [condemned] man contains ten and for every additional culprit four or six are added." See Hart, *Letters of Private Wheeler*, p. 68.

257. A *chef de bataillon* was a battalion commander and equivalent to a British army major.

258. According to Fortescue, the two most remarkable accomplishments in engineering achieved during the Peninsular War were the suspension bridge at Alcantara and the boat bridge on the Adour. Both feats were the work of Major Sturgeon and Captain Todd. See Fortescue, *History of the British Army*, 10:204.

259. The French defeats "in the North" were a reference to the allied invasion of France, which lasted from January to 6 April 1814, when Napoleon signed his first abdication. The decisive defeat of Napoleon around Leipzig, 16–19 October 1813, precipitated a French withdrawal to the west bank of the Rhine followed by the invasion of France in January 1814.

260. A considerable portion of the French army was composed of troops from countries allied to Napoleon. These included Swiss, Dutch, Polish and Italian soldiers. There were also German units from the Confederation of the Rhine, among which were both infantry and cavalry regiments from the small duchy of Nassau. Several thousand Spanish soldiers similarly served with the French. Most of these troops apparently served in Joseph Napoleon's army about which little is known.

261. Having spanned the Adour estuary with a bridge of boats, General Sir John Hope successfully crossed some 15,000 troops to the northern bank, the purpose of which was to encircle Bayonne. However, before a proper siege could be implemented, it was considered necessary to get close to the Citadel which commanded Bayonne from the northern side of the Adour River. To accomplish this operation involved the storming of the outer works around the base of the Citadel hill in the suburbs of St Etienne. Ensign Edmund Wheatley of the 5th Line Battalion of the King's German Legion, who, it will be remembered, left us his first impressions of battle in the Peninsula, provides these glimpses of the battle of St Etienne. "Descending a hill we wound round a lake and ascending a hill went through an orchard. Presently a ball whizzed over us, then another. Running forward, we dashed on and soon saw crowds of enemies. They would not meet our bayonets but scampered off. Our battalion ran into a narrow bye road, the 1st Battalion [King's German Legion] before us, and soon gaining the end of the lane we found a Church before us, behind the walls of which were crowds of heads." "The men and officers", dressed in grey trousers and dark green tunics,

"fell thick and frequent. A pole firing across my face received a ball through his chest and fell upon me so heavily that my knees sank and I dropped on my back." Upon reaching the church of St Etienne, which stood a half mile north of Bayonne, "We all took shelter inside . . . until further orders and the smashing of the windows from the balls together with the thunder of the Cannon in a peaceable room like a church, quite bewildered me." Later: "The house we were ordered to defend faced all the batteries of Bayonne looking to the north and the Citadel stared it in the face." After several hours of firing at the French "I had sent two wounded away from the left [room] and had one more killed in the Centre [room]. Just at this time the French poured in grape [shot] at us and one or two forty-eight pounders which filled the rooms with mortar dust and we fired back at random. The top of my military cap was taken off by a cannon shot and smashed against the wall. Just then a violent scream from the next room, with a thundering noise announced the corners of the house being blown down." The situation was now desperate. "The two corners of the house were laid open and near one hundred and thirty cannons pointing at us. My men were reduced from fifteen to five and the Serjeant. And I was just making up my mind when a confusion as if heaven and earth were in contact suddenly came over me. The roof fell in and buried the whole of us." See Hibbert, *The Wheatley Diary*, pp. 40–43.

262. The battle of Orthez, 27 February 1814, was a defeat for the French, who retreated towards Toulouse. This setback for Napoleon encouraged royalist activity in the south of France.

263. Fighting on 5 March 1811, an Anglo-Spanish force under General Thomas Graham, Baron Lynedoch, successfully disrupted the French blockade of Cadiz outside that city at Barrosa.

264. On 27 April 1814, General Pierre Thouvenot surrendered Bayonne.

265. The battle of Toulouse, fought four days after the first abdication of Napoleon, on 6 April, was the last major engagement of the Peninsular War. Although a French defeat, the allies suffered 4,500–5,000 casualties.

266. Losses among Wellington's generals were high during the war. By the time the battle of Waterloo was won, twelve generals had been killed on the battlefield and two had died of disease. Two more were killed in falls from balconies in Lisbon. Glover, *Wellington's Army*, p. 150.

267. The Anglo-American war had begun in June 1812. It came to an official end in December 1814, several weeks before the battle of New Orleans, which was fought in early January 1815.

268. Apparently, Browne intended to insert the appropriate statistics in the blanks. For reasons unexplained, he never completed this work.

269. Calvert to Browne, 8 August 1814. Browne Family Papers.
270. According to Hart's *New Annual Army List* (1840), Browne was placed on half pay on 25 December 1814.

Bibliography

The Napoleonic era has spawned a vast printed literature. Significant additions will be made to this great corpus as students of the period continue to exploit more and more of the nearly inexhaustible manuscript collections. This modest list of printed and manuscript works, however, is limited solely to those items used as aids in the preparation of the Introduction and in editing the Journal. Although all the works listed were useful, the editor owes an immense debt to the following: David G. Chandler, *Dictionary of the Napoleonic Wars* (1979), Henry Lachouque et al, *Napoleon's War in Spain: The French Peninsular Campaigns, 1807–1814* (1982), Michael Glover, ed., *A Gentleman Volunteer: The Letters of George Hennell from the Peninsular War, 1812–1813* (1979), and, of course, John W. Fortescue, *A History of the British Army* (1899–1930). Other very useful titles include J. A. Houlding, *Fit for Service: The Training of the British Army, 1715–1795* (1981) and Richard Glover, *Peninsular Preparation: The Reform of the British Army, 1795–1809* (1963).

MANUSCRIPTS

Papers of Sir Thomas Henry Browne, K.C.H., and Family Papers, U.K.

Aldershot, U.K. Royal Army Medical Corps Historical Museum. Ferguson Letterbooks.

Edinburgh. Scottish Record Office. "Public Office Letters 1800". NRA [SCOT] 0473.

London. The British Library. Jellicoe Papers, Diary of Field Marshal Sir Thomas Grosvenor.

London. The British Library. Moore Papers.

London Public Record Office.

C.O. 318/35

MPH/111, Lieutenant-Colonel Alexander Whalley Light's *Views in the West Indies, 1811–1814.*

MPH 490 (1).

W.O. 1/ Correspondence: In-letters, Secretary at War and Secretary for War /95, 187, 188.

W.O. 12/ Returns: General /3970, 3971, 4036, 4037.

W.O. 17/ Returns: Monthly /2357, 5245.

W.O. 25/ Returns: Registers, Various /652.

W.O. 27/ Returns: Inspection
/90, 113.
W.O. 71/ Judge Advocate General's Office: Courts-Martial,
    Proceedings
/86.
W.O. 78/ Maps and Plans
/812
W.O. 90/ General Courts-Martial: Abroad
/1.
W.O. 164/
/182, 189.
Ottawa, Public Archives of Canada, British Military and Naval Records, RG8, I,
    "C Series."
Preston, U.K. Lancashire Record Office. Hoghton Papers.
St Ann's Garrison, Barbados. The Barbados Museum and Historical Society.
    "An English Soldier of 21st Fuziliers first impression of Barbados in 1794."
Washington, D.C. Library of Congress. Peter Force Papers, Wyvill Memoirs,
    Series 8D.

PRINTED MATERIALS
Books/Articles

Anon. *An Authentic Account of the Siege of Copenhagen by the British, in the Year
    1807*. London: Faden/Bulmer, 1807.
Atkins, T.B. *History of Halifax*. Belleville, Canada: Mika Publishing, 1973.
Atkinson, C.T. "Gleanings from the Cathcart MSS.: Part VI—The 'Conjoint'
    Expedition to Copenhagen, 1807." *Journal of the Society for Army Historical
    Research* 30 (1952):80–7.
Austen, Jane. *Pride and Prejudice*. 1813.
Babington, Anthony. *For the Sake of Example: Capital Courts Martial, 1914–1920*.
    London: Secker & Warburg, 1983.
Bardo, Pamela P. *English and Continental Portrait Miniatures: The Latter—
    Schlesinger Collection*. New Orleans: New Orleans Museum of Art, 1978.
Barnes, R. Money. *A History of the Regiments and Uniforms of the British Army*, 4th
    ed. London: Seeley Service and Co. Ltd., 1957.
———. *Military Uniforms of Britain and The Empire*. London: Seeley Service and
    Co. Ltd., 1960.
Bell, George. *Soldier's Glory: Being 'Rough Notes of an Old Soldier'*. London: G.
    Bell and Sons, Ltd., 1956.
Birch, J.H. *Denmark in History*. London: John Murray, 1938.
Boase, Frederic. *Modern English Biography*, 2 vols. London: Frank Cass and Co.,
    Ltd., 1965.

Brett-James, Anthony, ed. *Wellington at War, 1794–1815: A Selection of His Wartime Letters.* New York: St. Martin's Press, 1961.

[Browne-Owen, Harriet], *The Works of Mrs Hemans: With a Memoir of Her Life.* 7 vols. London: William Blackwood and Sons, 1857.

Buckley, Roger N. *Slaves in Red Coats: The British West India Regiments, 1795–1815.* New Haven: Yale University Press, 1979.

————. "The Destruction of the British Army in the West Indies 1793-1815. A Medical History." *Journal of the Society for Army Historical Research* 56, No. 226 (Summer 1978): 79–92.

Burke, John and Burke, John B. *Genealogical and Heraldic Dictionary of the Landed Gentry of Great Britain & Ireland.* 2 vols. London: Henry Colburn, 1846.

Burns, Allan C. *History of the British West Indies.* London: George Allen and Unwin, Ltd., 1954.

Butler, Lewis; George, William; and Hare, Steuart. *The Annals of the King's Royal Rifle Corps.* 5 vols. London: Smith, Elder & Co., and John Murray, 1913–1932.

Cantlie, Neil. *A History of the Army Medical Department.* 2 vols. London: Churchill Livingstone, 1974.

Cary, A.D.L., and McCance, Stouppe. *Regimental Records of the Royal Welch Fusiliers.* 4 vols. London: Forster Groom & Co. Ltd., 1921–1929.

Chandler, David G. *Dictionary of the Napoleonic Wars: The Soldiers, Strategies, Armaments, Movements, and Battles That Shaped Events During Napoleon's Reign.* London: Arms and Armour Press, 1979.

Chorley, Henry R. *Memorials of Mrs Hemans, With Illustrations of Her Literary Character from her Private Correspondence.* 2 vols. New York: Saunders and Otley, 1836.

Clarfield, Gerard. H. *Timothy Pickering and American Diplomacy, 1795–1800.* Columbia: University of Missouri Press, 1969.

Clyde, David. *Two Centuries of Health Care in Dominica.* New Delhi: Sushima Gopal, 1980.

Congreve, William. *The Details of the Rocket System.* London: J. Whiting, 1814; reprint ed., Ottawa, Ontario: Museum Restoration Service, 1970.

Connell, Neville. "Hotel Keepers and Hotels in Barbados." *Journal of the Barbados Museum and Historical Society* 32 (November 1970) No. 4, pp. 162–85.

Corvisier, André. *Armies and Societies in Europe, 1494–1789,* trans. Abigail T. Siddall. Bloomington: Indiana University Press, 1979.

Cuthbertson, Brian C. *The Loyalist Governor: Biography of Sir John Wentworth.* Halifax, Nova Scotia: Petheric Press, 1983.

Department of National Defence Library. "The Service of British Regiments in Canada and North America." Ottawa, 1962. (Mimeographed.)

Dictionary of National Biography.

Dupuy, Ernest. *The Compact History of the United States Army*. New York: Hawthorn Books, Inc., 1956.

Edwards, H.N. "The Diary of Lieutenant C. Gillmor, R.N.—Portugal—1810." *Journal of the Society for Army Historical Research* 3 (1924): 148–61.

Ellis, Alfred B. *The History of the First West India Regiment*. London: Chapman and Hall, Ltd., 1885.

Emsley, Clive. *British Society and the French War, 1793–1815*. London: Macmillan, 1979.

Fewster, J.M. "Prize-money and the British Expedition of 1793–4." *Journal of Imperial and Commonwealth History* XII (October 1983) 1: 1–28.

Fortescue, John W. *A History of the British Army*. 13 vols. London: Macmillan & Co. Ltd., 1899–1930.

———. *Wellington*. London: Ernest Benn Ltd., 1960.

Foskett, Daphne. *British Portrait Miniatures: A History*. London: Methuen and Co. Ltd., 1963.

Frey, Sylvia R. *The British Soldier in America: A Social History of Military Life in the Revolutionary Period*. Austin: University of Texas Press, 1981.

Fuller, John F. C. *The Conduct of War, 1789–1961: A Study of the Impact of the French, Industrial, and Russian Revolutions on War and its Conduct*. New Brunswick, N.J.: Rutgers University Press, 1962.

Funcken, Liliane and Fred. *L'Uniforme et les Armes des Soldats du Premier Empire*. 2 vols. Tournai, Belgium: Casterman, 1979.

George, Mary D. *Catalogue of Political and Personal Satire*. 11 vols. London: British Museum, 1947.

Glover, Michael, ed. *A Gentleman Volunteer: The Letters of George Hennell from the Peninsular War, 1812–1813*. London: Heinemann, 1979.

———. "Purchase, Patronage and Promotion in the Army at the Time of the Peninsular War." Parts I and II, *The Army Quarterly* 1 and 2 (1973): 211–5, 355–62.

———. *Wellington's Army in the Peninsula, 1808–1814*. Newton Abbot: David & Charles, 1977.

———. *Wellington's Peninsular Victories*. London & New York: Macmillan Co., 1963.

Glover, Richard. *Peninsular Preparation: The Reform of the British Army, 1795–1809*. Cambridge: Cambridge University Press, 1963.

Gosner, Pamela. *Caribbean Georgian: The Great and Small Houses of the West Indies*. Washington, D.C.: Three Continents Press, 1982.

Grant, Michael. *The Army of the Caesars*. London: Weidenfeld & Nicolson, 1974.

Graves, Robert. *Good-Bye to All That: An Autobiography*. London: Cassell & Co., 1957.

Great Britain, War Office. *Army Lists*, 1805–7, 1813, 1816 and 1840.

Green, John. *The Vicissitudes of a Soldier's Life*. Louth, U.K.: 1827; reprint ed., East Ardsley, U.K.: E.P. Pub., Ltd., 1973.

Guedalla, Philip. *Wellington*. New York: The Literary Guild, 1931.

Handler, Jerome S. *The Unappropriated People: Freedmen in the Slave Society of Barbados*. Baltimore: Johns Hopkins University Press, 1974.

Hargreaves, Reginald. *This Happy Breed: Sidelights on Soldiers and Soldiering*. London: Skeffington and Son Ltd., 1951.

Harris, R.G. "Six Portrait Miniatures." *Journal of the Society for Army Historical Research* 61, No. 245 (Spring 1983): 1–2.

———. "Two Military Miniatures." *Journal of the Society for Army Historical Research* 63, No. 254 (Summer 1985): 99–103 and illustration facing page 94.

Hart, B.H. Liddell, ed. *The Letters of Private Wheeler, 1809–1828*. London: Michael Joseph, 1952.

Hay, Douglas; Linebaugh, Peter; Rule, John G.; Thompson, E.P.; and Winslow, Cal. *Albion's Fatal Tree: Crime and Society In Eighteenth-Century England*. London: Allen Lane, 1975.

Herold, J. Christopher. *The Horizon Book of the Age of Napoleon*. New York: American Heritage Pub. Co., Inc./Bonanza Books, 1983.

Hibbert, Christopher, ed. *The Wheatley Diary: A Journal and Sketch-Book kept during the Peninsular War and the Waterloo Campaign*. London: Longmans, Green and Co. Ltd., 1964.

———. *Recollections of Rifleman Harris*. London: Leo Cooper, Ltd., 1970.

Houlding, J.A. *Fit for Service: The Training of the British Army, 1715–1795*. Oxford: Clarendon Press, 1981.

Huntington, Samuel P. *The Soldier and the State: The Theory and Politics of Civil-Military Relations*. New York: Random House/Vintage Books, 1957.

Jackson, Robert. *A Sketch of the History and Cure of Febrile Diseases: More Particularly as They Appear in the West Indies Among the Soldiers of the British Army*. Stockton, England: T. and H. Eeles, 1817.

Jones, K.R. "Cox and Co.: Army Agents, Craig's Court: The Nineteenth Century." *Journal of the Society for Army Historical Research* 40 (1962): 178–86.

———. "Richard Cox, Army Agent and Banker." *Journal of the Soceity for Army Historical Research* 34 (1956): 178–81.

Kunzle, David. *The Early Comic Strip: Narrative Strips and Picture Stories in the European Broadsheet from c. 1450 to 1825*. Berkeley: University of California Press, 1973.

Lachouque, Henry. *The Anatomy of Glory: Napoleon and His Guard, A Study in Leadership*, trans. Anne S.K. Brown. Providence, Rhode Island: Brown University Press, 1961.

Lachouque, Henry; Tranie, Jean; Carmigniani, C.J. *Napoleon's War in Spain: The French Peninsular Campaigns, 1807–1814*, trans. Janet S. Mallender and John R. Clements. London: Arms and Armour Press, 1982.

Laver, James. *British Military Uniforms*. London: Penguin Books, 1948.

Laws, M.E.S. "The Royal Artillery at Martinique 1809." *Royal Artillery Journal* LXXVII, No. 1: 70–81.

Lefebvre, Georges. *Napoleon*. 2 vols., trans. Henry F. Stockhold and J.E. Anderson. London: Routledge & Kegan Paul, 1969.

Leslie, N.B. *The Succession of Colonels of the British Army From 1660 to the Present Day*. London: Gale and Polden Ltd., 1974.

Lister, Raymond. *The British Miniature*. London: Isaac Pitman and Sons, Ltd., 1951.

Longford, Elizabeth. *Wellington: The Years of the Sword*. London: Weidenfeld & Nicolson, 1969.

Longridge, C. Nepean. *The Anatomy of Nelson's Ships*. Watford, U.K.: Model and Allied Publications, Argus Books Ltd., 1981.

Lynn, John A. *The Bayonets of the Republic: Motivation and Tactics in the Army of Revolutionary France, 1791–1794*. Chicago: University of Illinois Press, 1984.

McNeill, William H. *The Pursuit of Power: Technology, Armed Force, and Society since A.D. 1000*. Chicago: University of Chicago Press, 1982.

Macdonald, Reginald J. *The History of the Dress of the Royal Regiment of Artillery, 1625–1897*. London: Henry Sotheran & Co., 1899.

Matheson, D. Lloyd. *The Brimstone Hill Fortress*. Basseterre, St Kitts: Society for the Restoration of Brimstone Hill [N.D.].

Mitchell, R.J., and Leys, M.D.R. *A History of London Life*. London: Penguin Books, 1963.

Newbolt, Henry. *The Story of the Oxfordshire and Buckinghamshire Light Infantry*. London: Country Life, 1915.

Oman, Carola,. *Sir John Moore*. London: Hodder & Stoughton, 1953.

Oman, Charles. *Wellington's Army, 1809–1814*. London: Edward Arnold, 1912.

Palmer, R.R. *The Age of Democratic Revolution: A Political History of Europe and America, 1760–1800*. 2 vols. Princeton: Princeton University Press, 1959–1964.

Payne, A.A. *A Handbook of British and Foreign Orders, War Medals and Decorations, Awarded to the Army and Navy*. Sheffield, U.K.: Northend, 1911.

Pinckard, George. *Notes on the West Indies: Written during the Expeditions under the Command of the Late General Sir Ralph Abercromby*. 3 vols. London: Longman, Hurst, Rees and Orme, 1806.

Ray, Cyril. *The Lancashire Fusiliers*. London: Leo Cooper Ltd., 1971.

"Replies" [Regimental Pets.] *Journal of the Society for Army Historical Research* 13: 185–7.

Riehn, Richard K. *The French Infantry and Artillery, 1795–1812*. New York: Helenic Publications, 1960.

[Roberts, David.] *The Military Adventures of Johnny Newcome: With an Account of*

His Campaign on the Peninsula. 1816; reprint ed., London: Methuen and Co., 1904.

Rogers, H.C.B. *Napoleon's Army.* New York: Hippocrene Books, 1982.

Royal Military Calendar, or Army Service and Commission Book. 3rd ed., 5 vols. London: A.J. Valpy, 1820.

Schomburgk, Robert H. *The History of Barbados.* London: Longman, Brown and Green, 1848; reprint ed., London: Frank Cass & Co. Ltd., 1971.

Sherwig, John M. *Guineas & Gunpowder: British Foreign Aid in the Wars with France, 1793–1815.* Cambridge: Harvard University Press, 1969.

Smith, Bernard. *European Vision and the South Pacific, 1768–1850: A Study in the History of Art and Ideas.* Oxford University Press, 1969.

Southey, Robert. *Letters From England.* Gloucester, U.K.: Alan Sutton Pub. Ltd., 1984.

Stendhal. *The Red and the Black.*

Surtees, William. *Twenty-Five Years in the Rifle Brigade.* London: Frederick Muller Ltd., 1973.

Thackeray, William. *Vanity Fair.*

Turner, Ernest S. *Gallant Gentlemen: A Portrait of the British Officer, 1600–1956.* London: Michael Joseph, 1956.

Turner, J.D. "Army Agency." *Journal of the Society for Army Historical Research* 13 (1934): 27–37.

Uden, Grant, and Cooper, Richard. *A Dictionary of British Ships and Seamen.* New York: St Martin's Press, 1980.

Waller, John A. *A Voyage in the West Indies.* London: 1820.

Ward, S.G.P. *Wellington's Headquarters: A Study of the Administrative Problems in the Peninsula, 1809–1814.* Oxford: Oxford University Press, 1957.

Watson, J. Steven. *The Reign of George III, 1760–1815.* Oxford: Clarendon Press, 1964.

Wickes, H.L. *Regiments of Foot: A Historical Record of all the Foot Regiments of the British Army.* Reading, U.K.: Osprey Pub. Ltd., 1974.

Winter, Denis. *Death's Men. Soldiers of the Great War.* London: Penguin Books Ltd., 1985.

Wollaston, George, *Standards, Guidons and Colours of the Commonwealth Forces.* Aldershot: Gale & Polden Ltd., 1953.

Wright, Jr., J. Leitch. *Britain and the American Frontier, 1783–1815.* Athens: University of Georgia Press, 1975.

NEWSPAPERS

The London Gazette

Index

As far as possible, place names and personal names follow modern spelling. Those appearing in parentheses are Browne's.

INDEX   383

Ross and Ogilvie Agency, 7; *see also* armies,
    British
Rottenburg, Lt-Col Baron de, 355
Rowlandson, Thomas, 40
Roy, General William: *Military Antiquities
    of the Romans in North Britain* (1793), 10
Royal Americans, the, 355
Royal Engineers, *see* armies, British
Royal Naval Hotel, Bridgetown, 333
Royal Navy, 5, 38, 224; sailors' contempt
    for soldiers, 3; Copenhagen, 1807,
    36–7, 45–63 *passim*; Copenhagen, 1801,
    45, 58–9; *Chesapeake* affair, 65; Nova
    Scotia, 65–77 *passim*, 118, 121–3;
    Martinique, 85–111 *passim*; crossing the
    line ceremony, 90–1; Corunna, 129;
    Torres Vedras Lines, 131–2; San
    Sebastian, 239; Adour boat bridge, 259,
    261, 262–3; *see also* ships
Royal Welch Fusiliers, *see* regiments
Rueda (Roueda), Sp., 161, 190
rum, effects of, 117
Russia, 11, 45, 46, 131, 158, 279
Ryall, Lt-Col, 98

Saba, West Indies, 110
Sabugal, Port., 147
St Asaph, Wales, 2
St Barthélemy (Bartholomews), West
    Indies, 110
St Estavan, Sp., 233, 234
St Eustatius (Eustasia), West Indies, 110
St Helena, 279
St (San) Jean de Luz, Fr., 180, 234,
    244–61 *passim*, 268
St Jean Pied de Port, Fr., 244
St John (John's), Virgin Islands, 110
St John's, New Brunswick, 118, 119, 120,
    121
St Kitts, West Indies, 109
St Lawrence, 184
St Luce, Martinique, 100
St Lucia, West Indies, 94
St Lys, Fr., 272
St Marinha, Port., 140
St Martin, West Indies, 86, 110
St Mont, Fr., 268
St Pée, Fr., 247, 248, 249
St Pierre, Martinique, 100, 102, 108
St Pol, General, 186–7
St Sever, Fr., 266–7, 268
St Thomas, West Indies, 110

St Ubes, 146
Sainte-Croix (La Croix), Général Charles,
    134, career, 300
Saintes (Saints), the, West Indies, 109
Salamanca, 190, 197; French withdrawal
    to, 142, 148; Wellington retreats to, 190,
    191; Wellington enters (1813), 206,
    207; *also see* battles
Salices, 149
Salvaterra, Sp., 220
Samatan, Fr., 272
Sanchez, General Don Julian, 173, 179–
    80
San Cristoval Heights, Sp., 160
San Estevara, Sp., 225
San Francisco, convent of, 149
San Ildefonso, Palace of, 175–6, 184
San Miguel, 148
San (St) Sebastian, Sp., 127, 249; *see also*
    battles
Santa Cruz, West Indies, 110
Santa Maria, Sp., 185
Santa Marta (Martha), Sp., 160, 161, 164,
    167, 168
Santarem, Port., 132, 134
Santocildes, General José, 172; career,
    300
São João da Pesqueira (St Joao de
    Pesquera), Port., 155
Sauveterre, Fr., 262, 264
Saxe, Maréchal Hermann Maurice de, 10
Saxony, King of, 281
Schomburgk, Robert H., 336
Schwarzenberg (Schwartzenberg), Field
    Marshal Karl, 282, career, 301
Scotland, 40, 223
Second Armed Neutrality of the North, 45
Segovia, Sp., 175–6, 191
Seville, Sp., 143, 144, 153
Seysses, Fr., 272
Shawe, Colonel, 226
Shipley, Major Charles, 87
ships, H.M.S.:
    Banterer, 71, 74, 76
    Brunswick, 63, 64
    Cambrian, 63
    Carnation, 100
    Centaur, 64
    Columbine, 91
    Comus, 47
    Diadem, 83, 123
    Eolus, 108, 110

ARMY RECORDS SOCIETY
(FOUNDED 1984)

Members of the Society are entitled to purchase back
volumes at reduced prices.
Orders should be sent to the Hon. Treasurer, Army Records Society,
c/o Barclays Bank, 54 Lombard Street,
London EC3P 3AH.

The Society has already issued:

Vol. I:
The Military Correspondence of
Field Marshal Sir Henry Wilson 1918–1922
Edited by Dr Keith Jeffery.

Vol. II:
The Army and the
Curragh Incident, 1914
Edited by Dr Ian F.W. Beckett